Boston Mayor
Thomas Menino

Boston Mayor Thomas Menino

Lessons for Governing Post-Industrial Cities

WILBUR C. RICH

University of Massachusetts Press
AMHERST AND BOSTON

Copyright © 2023 by University of Massachusetts Press
All rights reserved
Printed in the United States of America

ISBN 978-1-62534-765-7 (paper); 766-4 (hardcover)

Designed by Sally Nichols
Set in Adobe Jenson Pro
Printed and bound by Books International, Inc.

Cover design by adam b. bohannon
Photo by Dan4th Nicholas, *Mayor Tom Menino at the Boston
Pride Parade*, 2008. CC BY 2.0, https://creativecommons.org/licenses/by/2.0/deed.en

Library of Congress Cataloging-in-Publication Data
A catalog record for this book is available from the Library of Congress.

British Library Cataloguing-in-Publication Data
A catalog record for this book is available from the British Library.

TO PROFESSOR MARTIN L. KILSON,

WHO LOVED HIS FAMILY, COUNTRY, FRIENDS, STUDENTS,

WRITING, AND A GOOD ARGUMENT

Contents

LIST OF ILLUSTRATIONS   ix
PREFACE   xi

Introduction
Contextuality and Boston Uniqueness
1

Chapter 1
On Becoming a Boston Politician
25

Chapter 2
Winning Every Four Years
49

Chapter 3
Menino, City Councilors, Policies, and the Media
76

Chapter 4
Boston's Day-to-Day and Recurrent Politics
101

Chapter 5
Who Gets Housing, When, and Where?
122

Chapter 6
Crime in the Streets and Elsewhere
152

Chapter 7
Boston's Racial Diversity Challenge
186

vii

Chapter 8
The Failure of Boston Public School Reform
219

Chapter 9
Moguls and Students in Higher Education
254

Conclusion
Drawing Lessons from the Menino Tenure
292

NOTES   305

INDEX   335

Illustrations

FIGURES

FIGURE 1. Rates and types of crime during part of Evans's tenure. 165
FIGURE 2. Overall crime rates from 1994 to 2004. 166
FIGURE 3. Crime numbers and types during the O'Toole tenure, 2004–2006. 179
FIGURE 4. Rates and types of crime during the Davis tenure, 2007–2013. 181

TABLES

TABLE 1. Voting Tallies of Brett-Menino Race by Ward. 59
TABLE 2. 1993 Results in Critical Wards. 60
TABLE 3. Race and Ethnic Breakdown in Boston. 187
TABLE 4. Types of Exempt Property Owners. 268
TABLE 5. Enrollment at Selected List of Higher Education Institutions, 2019. 272

Preface

Why write a book about Mayor Thomas Menino? Elected as the first Italian American mayor of Boston, Tom Menino sent shockwaves through the political establishment. Pundits were asking what just happened? I remember telling my students at Wellesley College that it would not happen. I was surprised that Menino won his first election as mayor of Boston and even more surprised by how he conducted himself as mayor. It was fascinating to watch the man from Hyde Park's Readville neighborhood lead Boston through the fundamental changes associated with the post-industrial economy with such aplomb. This makes the career of Tom Menino, the longest-serving Boston mayor, a compelling story to tell.

His election and mayoralty made me and other academics question what we had thought and written about Boston politics. Was he an anomaly or just a conventional politician? People who watch and write about mayors usually ask these questions: What types of political mazes did they negotiate to get to the big office at City Hall? What were the salient issues in their first and any subsequent mayoral elections? Why didn't they do X instead of Y? How did their personalities affect their governing styles? What lessons did they learn from their predecessors and other cities? Which policies did they inherit? Was there a path dependence involved with city policies? Simply put, path dependence in urban policymaking recognizes that policy actions, especially innovation, are limited by prior decisions.

We also know that cities are not free agents. They are sub-governments of their states, and local policies can be influenced, and sometimes be preempted, by federal grant-in-aid and laws. National surveys of mayors' reactions to this environment are quite telling, but it is the case study that allows the researcher to dig deeply into the backgrounds and motivations of mayors. With this approach, we can learn many otherwise hidden lessons.

Lessons Drawn from Case Studies

This book project began as a comparative case study of Mayors David Dinkins and Thomas Menino. Dinkins was the first African American mayor of New York City and Tom Menino the first Italian American mayor of Boston. When Dinkins and Menino were elected, I looked forward to how they would each handle the job and what impact their elections would have on African Americans in New York City and Italian Americans in Boston. How would these two new mayors react as the first ones of their social backgrounds to be elected to their city's highest offices and from whom so much was expected? Having lived in New York City and Wellesley (a suburb of Boston), I had done background research on both cities and thought I knew what the possibilities were. Obviously, I did not know what the future would hold and how each mayor would react to various events. I was surprised at the unfolding events and had to separate the manuscript into two sections to further delve into their administrations. The book on Dinkins was published in 2007 after he was defeated for reelection, but the manuscript on Menino took more time as he served longer. In *David Dinkins and New York City Politics*, I raised questions about racial loyalty and the policy constraints of a clubhouse politician. There were also some questions about Menino's ethnic loyalty and his mentoring by Irish American politicians.

In Thomas Menino's case, the Italian culture was a part of his identity. Professor and author George Guida argued that two narratives have dominated Italian American identity: "*Impress* is the struggle to achieve individual success in America. *Ripresa* is the reaching back to the Italian culture of the late nineteenth-century Mezzogiorno for social and spiritual fulfillment."[1] The possibilities of divided loyalties in the face of uncommon challenges made Dinkins and Menino each fascinating subjects.

One of my goals was to try to fit Menino's tenure into academic surveys, theories, and typologies. I am not naive enough to believe that mayors actually read these findings, but such interpretations play an important role in urban history. For example, in an interview with another former mayor about a subject related to his tenure in office, he quickly stated that he was too busy making the policies rather than spending time doing an analysis of them. For him, analyzing policies was the job of historians and political scientists. He believed they had the time to write about decisions after they were made. He was right in many ways, but asking mayors and aides about how a policy was made can yield insights into a mayor's decision-making process. In this book, I am trying to make a political analysis based on interviews with Mayor Menino by interviewing him and his aides and then linking these interviews with existing urban literature. Granted, interviews with Menino and his aides were not always definitive or forthcoming, but they were enlightening in unpredictable ways.

Menino was not just an interesting Boston mayor but also played a role in the history of American cities. At the turn of the twenty-first century, several cities were undergoing economic changes, and mayors learned from watching, reading, and meeting with each other. Although Menino shared policy analogies, contradictions, and disappointments with his Boston predecessors, in many ways his mayoralty was unique. This book, a contextual analysis of him and his city, attempts to explain his plans, actions, and statements.

Menino was repeatedly asked if he had higher political ambitions. Like many of his colleagues, Menino did not aspire to a higher office. He was not interested in becoming the next governor of the commonwealth of Massachusetts or President Calvin Coolidge, a former mayor of Northampton. What stood out about Menino for me was his personality, character, and ability to relate to all types of individuals. This impression was reinforced by the numerous interviews I conducted with academics, political activists, journalists, aides, and critics.

Accordingly, I have to acknowledge all the assistance I received in writing this book. I would particularly like to thank the late Thomas Menino; his assistant Howard Leibowitz and other staff members including Dot Joyce, his press secretary; David Passafaro, chief of staff (1995–1999); Elizabeth Lusk, policy advisor; Martha Pierce, education policy advisor; Linda Kowalcky, liaison to higher education; Michael G. Contompasis, chief operating officer for former Boston school superintendent Tom Payzant; Tomas Gonzalez, city liaison to the Latino community; J. Larry Mayes, chief of human services; Michael Kineavy, neighborhood services and chief of policy and planning; and Edward F. Davis, the last police commissioner under Menino, who provided insights into the mayor and his actions. I also interviewed Conny Doty, former executive director of jobs and community services; Lewis Finfer, co-director of the Massachusetts

Communities Action Network (MCAN); historian Jim Vrabel; and Donald Gillis, former Mayor Ray Flynn's director of neighborhood services. Professor Graham Wilson was Menino's co-director of Boston University's Initiative on Cities. He reviewed the last policy days of the mayor. Journalist Jonathan Keller's insight into Boston politics was very helpful. I am thankful to Rev. Eugene Rivers for reviewing his time as an activist in Boston. They were gracious in our interviews and in allowing me to construct my own analysis of them as individuals and city officials. In addition, I conducted in-person interviews with individuals who wanted to remain anonymous and utilized written correspondence, email messages, telephone interviews, recorded television interviews, and research in historic archives for the writing of this book.

I am also deeply indebted to a great team of earlier manuscript chapter readers, including Professors Marion Orr, James Jennings, Katie McDermott, Clarence Stone, Peter Dreier, and Robert Hall (who helped me with the history of Boston). Again, Professor James Jennings offered a second reading and provided more material to use in the manuscript. It was extremely helpful in understanding the internal dynamics of the Menino administration. I am also indebted to my colleagues who patiently listened as I tried to explain what I was doing and why it was taking so long. I also owe much of my postgraduate education to listening to colleagues like Professors Martin L. Kilson and Charles V. Hamilton. They were generous to give me their insights and their time. Hubert "Hubie" Jones, former dean of the School of Social Work at Boston University, provided me with one of the most comprehensive overviews of Black politics in Boston that I have ever heard. I also appreciate the time of reporters such as Adrian Walker and Brian McGrory of the *Boston Globe*. Joe Sciacca of the *Boston Herald* sent me copies of the 1997–2003 articles he wrote about Tom Menino. It is from him that readers learned about the endlessness of "Mumblennium." In January 2000, Joe Sciacca asserted, "A New Millennium—The Same Menino."[2] I appreciate the Boston journalists who wrote about the mayor. Some of them had access to the mayor and his staff and were provided inside information and opinions.

In order to write a book about Tom Menino's impact on Boston politics, one had to ask participants what they remember about off-the-record comments and specific events. Granted personal memories are fickle things. On occasion when there is almost consensus, a researcher is reassured. Memories of what events happened when and how it was interpreted at the time are especially difficult. If the political event in question is controversial, interpretations are confounded or viewed through partisan, gender, and generational lenses. In some cases, interviewees will place themselves in the middle of the events or separate themselves from the scene. In other words, people feel free to editorialize past political events. Throughout the interviews for this manuscript, I found that minorities and white actors in the city had different memories regarding life in Boston.

I also understand the positions of individuals in the Menino story who would not let me interview them. That is their right, so references to some of them were found in the public records. So far, I have done three books about mayors, and each of these mayors has written a book after leaving office. Mayors who write either autobiographies or histories of their terms provide readers with an inside look at their daily politics. Menino's *A Mayor for a New America* was extremely helpful. I decided not to read it until I had finished the first draft of this manuscript. It was important, however, to report the mayor's inner thoughts on some of the policies I documented. Menino's book was like a long second interview covering numerous policies. Obviously, all that happened during Menino's tenure was not captured in his book. I have included his personal thoughts and comments in the final manuscript. My goal is to add contextuality.

I spent the 2001 academic year with the Russell Sage Foundation Fellowship Program. This allowed me a year away from the Boston area to reflect on Boston politics with other social scientists and to consolidate the first part of this research. Obviously, the manuscript was not finished at the end of the fellowship. I am sure that I am not the only person to finish a book project twenty years late but waiting until the end of the Menino administration paid its dividends. A significant amount of archival work was required to complete this research. I would like to thank the City of Boston City Archives and Boston University's Howard Gotlieb Archival Research Center. I would also like to acknowledge Amanda Binder, the social science and history librarian at J. Murrey Askins Library at the University of North Carolina, Charlotte, for her assistance with periodicals for this research.

Finally, I would like to thank my family, who continues to support me and tease me about writing yet another book about mayors. A special thanks to Rachel, my daughter, who is now the first reader of my manuscripts. I am also especially grateful to Wellesley College for providing faculty research awards for this book, and to Brian Halley, editor of the University of Massachusetts Press, outside reviewers, and the staff for their patience and care in the production of this book.

Boston Mayor
Thomas Menino

INTRODUCTION

Contextuality and Boston Uniqueness

What most city residents grasp about local politics is that the entire process seems to be mayoral-centered. The mayor is the front person of city politics. As such, a mayor is their city's elected representative to all levels of government and sometimes the world. Throughout urban history, mayors have played a major role in shaping the character of public and city life. As the nation moves quickly into the post-industrial phase of its economic development, there has been a corresponding change in governance. American cities, most of which were developed during the industrial era, have become more difficult to lead and govern. There have been shifts in demographics, changes in available jobs, more racial/ethnic enclaving, more polarizing issues, and heightened pressure for city services delivery. Accordingly, there is a wide variety of socioeconomic and cultural issues that confront city halls. Although some of these challenges are similar, particular city responses have been dissimilar given differences in history, location, governmental structure, intergovernmental relations, demographics, economics, local interest groups, and ideas about the future. For these reasons, there is no one best way to be mayor, and there is no surefire solution for urban problems. Thus, the recruitment and performance of a mayor reflect the political context of a given city, and elections often reveal voter policy choices.

The political context of Boston is definitely very different from Chicago and for that matter Los Angeles, New York, Seattle, and so on. Indeed, the job description for Boston's mayor is also different from each of those cities.

Accordingly, classifying and evaluating mayors is a challenging process. To answer a question posed in the preface, was Mayor Thomas Menino an anomaly or just a conventional politician? Comparison with other mayors helps answer that question.

Reflecting on the diversity of mayors and their performances, John P. Kotter and Paul Lawrence's book *Mayors in Action* presents one of the most comprehensive typologies of mayoral leadership. They identified five types of mayors—ceremonial, caretaker, personality/individualist, executive, and program entrepreneur—around which they developed models of mayoral behavior.[1] They used these models to differentiate among notable 1970 mayors. Their list is descriptive, not a ranking. They made the case that all mayors were not administratively or politically alike. Mayors have different personalities, socioeconomic circumstances, expertise, political party networks, and visions. Their famous typologies are useful in understanding the style of modern mayors. I have rearranged the order of Kotter and Lawrence's mayoral types and added slight revisions where applicable.

The first type reviewed was the program entrepreneur mayor. Such mayors can also be characterized as following a "Power Broker Model." Such mayors focus on power acquisition, utility, and deal-making. Mayor Coleman Young of Detroit exemplified this model.[2] In 1974, Young, the first African American mayor of Detroit, inherited a city that was declining as an automobile-making center and experiencing high levels of economic dislocation. The combative mayor evolved from a radical labor activist into the chief salesperson/negotiator for the development of downtown Detroit. He understood the importance of making deals with the business community and how to use the land as leverage for the city's interest. To reenergize downtown shopping and the city as a tourist attraction and entertainment center, he installed a people mover in the downtown area. Young left office in early 1994, the year Menino became elected mayor of Boston.

The second model of mayors reviewed was a hybrid of the program entrepreneur and executive types. In my review of Mayor William H. Hudnut III's book *The Hudnut Years in Indianapolis, 1976–1991*, the former Indianapolis mayor was characterized as this type.[3] Hudnut led the consolidation of the city of Indianapolis with Marion County and turned this midsized city into a metropolis with a large sports center, the headquarters for the NCAA, a larger Indianapolis Zoo, and so on. The city arranged for the relocation of the Baltimore NFL team, now the Indianapolis Colts. Today, Indianapolis is considered a major sports center. The change in Indianapolis occurred not only in the skyline but also in the type of jobs available to city residents.

Entrepreneurial mayors of declining cities who seek to change the image of their cities can do so by redefining what their cities do and what they can potentially do. In chapter 3, I discuss the economic development strategy of Mayor Menino (e.g., the building of Innovation Districts). Some nationally known mayors would characterize themselves as entrepreneurial. This list includes those who built tourist attractions such as San Antonio's Henry Cisneros (San Antonio Riverwalk), Baltimore's Theodore R. McKeldin (Inner Harbor), and San Diego's Pete Wilson (downtown development). Atlanta's Maynard Jackson was instrumental in expanding the city airport. Another example is Milwaukee's longtime mayor Henry Maier. He attempted to build a downtown mall (Shops at Grand Avenue Mall) and a festival called Summerfest. These projects declined after he left office. These mayors try to bring new businesses to their cities, upgrade infrastructure, and provide new magnets for investors and amenities for new residents.

The third type seems to adhere to Kotter and Lawrence's "Public Executive and Policy Expert Model." Former New York mayor Michael Bloomberg fits this model. Chris McNickle's *Bloomberg: A Billionaire's Ambition* makes the case that Bloomberg tried to introduce several new public school reforms and build new environmental consciousness for the city, but in the final analysis, his policies did not have deep roots.[4] The mayor, a former businessman, relied heavily on data and appointing experts to his staff. He deliberately took a scientific approach to governing and introducing new ideas to the city. Norman Rice of Seattle, because of his training as a public administrator, may have considered himself an expert in policy terms. Other than these few examples, mayors rarely present themselves as policy wonks. Tom Menino did employ experts in his administration but never claimed to be a policy expert. As we shall see, Menino's self-presentation as a generalist served his housekeeping image.

David Dinkins, the first African American mayor of New York City, resembled the opposite of the previous model.[5] This style of governing could be called the "Muddling Through Model." In 1969, political scientist Charles E. Lindblom wrote a paper claiming that situations often require coping or a satisfactory strategy rather than trying to find rational solutions.[6] History is full of mayors who seem to be just time-servers and only tried to get through the week. Apparently, these mayors were attracted to the job because of its status. Dinkins spent his tenure dealing with the problems of the day. He worked hard to avoid policy mistakes, but he was defeated for reelection. After muddling through the mayor's tenure, there were few, if any, overall improvements in the city. Chicago's Michael Bilandic, Atlanta's Kasim Reed, and Los Angeles Sam Yorty come to mind as mayors who practiced this style of governing.

The fourth type of mayor fits into a "Multi-Hat Model." These strong mayors are party leaders, chief executives, and salespeople for the city. Clearly, Chicago's mayor Richard J. Daley represented this type. Daley led the local Democratic Party, the Board of Aldermen, and City Hall. He also led the city in its remaking of cultural and tourist attractions. Aside from bringing the Chicago Picasso, a sculpture by Pablo Picasso (1967), to the city and restoring McCormick Place, a convention center (1971), Daley consolidated an elaborate political submachine that allowed his regime to dominate city politics. The introduction of nonpartisan elections and federal court rulings against patronage hiring prevented subsequent Chicago mayors from amassing the type of power Daley held.

Kotter and Lawrence's fifth archetype can be called the "Formal Structural Model." These mayors are restricted by the charter construction of the office. Such mayors have limited control and jurisdiction over major city policies. The council-manager government is a classic example of this type of administrative government. In such systems, a professional city manager acts as the operations executive of the city. Mayors, whether elected by a rotation system of council members or elected separately, are not executive officials. Major cities like Austin, Texas; Phoenix, Arizona; Dallas, Texas; Las Vegas, Nevada; and Charlotte, North Carolina still use this form of municipal government. In city manager cities it is difficult for a mayor to project leadership. Yet this system remains the government of choice for these cities.

Former San Diego mayor Pete Wilson was able to overcome this limiting structure and transformed his tenure into an entrepreneurial one. There are examples of other mayors overcoming the limitations of the city-manager form of government. My research for *Transformative City* found that an innovative mayor could be effective without formal executive power.[7] Charlotte, North Carolina, is a city-manager government, but some of its mayors, such as Stanford R. Brookshire, John M. Belk, and Harvey Gantt, have proved to be effective mayors in spite of the lack of executive powers.

The sixth type of mayor is exemplified by what Kotter and Lawrence called the "Personality-Centered Model." This structure focuses on the character of the mayor and how they relate to their constituencies. Mayors with big personalities can dominate the city agenda by shifting the media coverage and political attention onto themselves. Such mayors are charismatic, creative, and entertaining. They build trust among the various constituencies. On rare occasions, such individuals can overcome the structural limitations of their positions (e.g., city charters) and achieve major changes in a city. Therefore, personalities matter, but so does determination. Some mayors enter office with almost celebrity-type personalities while others build such images while in office. A few become national figures, while others remain local phenomena. Residents admire such mayors for who they are and what they represent. If a mayor could be described as truly diffident, it would be a tag that would not be an asset to his mayoralty. Although rarely stated, many American cities want amiable mayors. History is also full of very famous mayoral personalities— New York's Fiorello LaGuardia, Milwaukee's Henry Maier, San Francisco's Dianne Feinstein and Willie Brown, Chicago's Jane Byrne, New York's Ed Koch, and Atlanta's William Hartsfield. Nonetheless, having an attractive personality does not always result in policy change.

Finally, Kotter and Lawrence characterized the "caretaker mayor" under the "Community Power Model." Following the lead of Floyd Hunter's book *Community Power Structure*, urban analysts who endorsed this model framed cities as being led by their business communities.[8] In the 1950s, in Atlanta (the so-called regional city) the local business community made most of the fundamental economic decisions, and the elected officials, including the mayor, simply legitimated and implemented those decisions. It was a pyramidal structure with the masses at the bottom of the decision cone. Under this model, there is a pyramid of interest with the economic elites at the top. When the research for this book began, some pundits thought that just like Atlanta, the Boston Vault group was the real power behind the political throne.

Although Atlanta and Boston have entirely different histories, the so-called early Brahmin domination of the Boston economy opened itself up to Boston political leadership in a way that resembles Hunter's characterization of business community power. This claim gained new currency in 1959 when Ralph Lowell and the Boston Coordinating Committee of bankers; the head of Filene's, the city's largest department store; the Liberty Mutual insurance company; and the directors of Jordan Marsh, another department store, mobilized to prevent Boston, led by Mayor John Collins, from bankruptcy. The so-called Boston Vault was organized to save the city from itself. Banks had power because they held city bonds. During that era, politicians played a lesser role in fundamental economic decisions. By the time the research for this book started, the Vault had supposedly lost some of its powers or at least had taken a low-profile role in public affairs. There had been an outbreak of corporate mergers, an unexpected rise of high-tech companies, and other changes that upended the old ways of how businesses related to Boston. Indeed, new corporate leadership had taken over the business community. More importantly, Boston had become a global city. In many ways, Boston predated the rising Sunbelt cities with their powerful business classes.

Boston's Thomas Menino becomes more intriguing because he did not fit tightly into any of Kotter and Lawrence's models. He was not a consummate power broker since he did not use his office to advance his control over the local Democratic Party or try to dominate other elected Democrat officials. Menino was an *empathic* mayor because he allowed multiple power centers to seek their own interests and assumed a more facilitating role than a commanding one. This was the opposite approach from a hard-driving mayor trying to get control of events around themself and to take credit for successes and deny failures. This is not to say that Menino was an easy mark for political actors but rather that he wanted to solve problems more than grandstand. The history of Menino's tenure saw several entrepreneurial projects initiated by the mayor, including the Boston Convention Center and Innovation Districts.

Menino would be the first to agree that he was not a policy expert, nor did he try to wear more hats than being mayor. At times he muddled through a process of policymaking. This book explains how the mayor's awkwardness and self-deprecating comments endeared him to his constituency. Indeed, he was able to use the fact that many of his peers and colleagues thought they were smarter than him to his advantage. He could seem to be guileless in interviews with the media yet acted firmly when challenged. Being seen as slightly maladroit was ironically a political resource. It encouraged him to make unpredictable choices that helped his reputation.

Historically speaking, several of Menino's predecessors had attractive personalities. Boston residents wanted to see their mayors espouse an upbeat future. In Tom Menino, they preferred someone they could relate to. Did Menino's public images match the *sui generis* nature of his real personality? Most mayors attempt to create an image—a fixer, a can-do, or a caring mayor. Journalists are critical in creating such an image. Many voters wanted to identify with Menino. Rather than assuming a posture of a commanding mayor, he employed cognitive empathy (putting himself in someone else's place in order to see their perspective) and compassionate empathy (the ability to feel other's pain and take action to help). Sometimes the mayor's story was more important than his views on policy. Americans seem to prefer an emotional connection with a mayor as well as a demonstration of leadership ability and policy competence. Once a person is elected mayor, there is a rush to get a closer look at the individual, their background, and personal preferences.

Equally important, Menino was a student of politics. He was able to draw critical lessons in public policy from his predecessors and what he heard and saw in other cities. Richard Rose, a policy analyst, defined a policy lesson as "more than a symbol invoked to sway opinion about a policy and more than a dependent variable that tells a social scientist what is to be explained. A lesson is a detailed cause-and-effect description of a set of actions that government can consider in the light of experience elsewhere, including a prospective evaluation of whether what is done elsewhere could someday become effective here."[9] Menino would ask his staff why they could not do this in Boston. He was not merely copying from other cities or blending other cities' programs into the Boston context. He was an adapter, not beholden to tradition.[10]

As we will see in a later chapter, Menino combined several elements from different funding sources and organizations to make his policies work. He had no problem borrowing ideas from other cities and giving them credit. Rose made this point: "'Copying' involves 'enacting a more or less intact program' already in effect; adaptation is similar but involves 'adjusting for contextual differences'; making a 'hybrid' consists of combining elements of programs from two different places; synthesis is combining familiar elements from programs in a number of different places to create new programs, and 'inspiration' is using programs elsewhere as an intellectual stimulus to develop a novel program."[11]

Flexibility, adaptability, and risk-taking are important attributes, but a mayor must become a student of the city's political context. What is possible in a given problem situation? When and how to speak to constituencies? What is possible in their city and its limits? How do you maneuver between the parameters of political action? To fully understand Tom Menino's approach, it is important to understand the inimitability of the city of Boston.

What Is Boston and Its Politics?

To say that the city of Boston is unique is to invite an avalanche of assenting descriptors. Ones that come to mind immediately include "the city on the hill," Olde Towne, historic, East Coast progressive, a walking city, neighborhood-centric, and an intellectual center. Defining what Boston is politically, one must compare it with other cities. Indeed, most American cities are as unique as they are different. Although Chicago and Detroit are located on the Great Lakes, they are very different cities. Los Angeles and San Francisco are located on the Pacific Ocean, yet they are different cities. Not only do these cities have different economic bases and political cultures but they also feel different when walking their streets. The same can be said of Hartford and Boston. At one point they were co-leaders as New England financial centers. Boston excelled and became a global city. The range of cities' development in terms of location, purpose, and infrastructure was not by design but rather reflects how individual cities reacted to immigration, job production, and their assets. The array of cities and their standing also reflects the nation's changing economic process. The rise of the post-industrial economy did not affect all cities equally.

In this book, we examine what makes Boston distinctive by comparing it to other cities and by showing the type of political leadership it developed. In the last decade, there has been a significant rethinking of how economics impact cities. Like most cities, Boston has its economic aspirations and limitations. Obviously, the growth of any city is linked to its political history and leadership selections. In many ways, city politicians develop their style from reading about or watching their predecessors. Boston's history is important to understanding its political context and the individual residents elected to the mayor's office. Therefore, it is essential that we outline what Boston was when Tom Menino assumed office.

In 1993, the city of Boston had a collection of weak financial assets and longstanding social problems. Ad valorem real property tax levies on land were a major source of the city's revenue stream. But unlike large cities like Houston and Los Angeles, Boston is land and space challenged. Boston has less land to tax. Also, spatial location determines the value of the land, with some space being more valuable than others. A larger challenge is the slow expansion of tax-exempt properties. Menino inherited a city with about 52 percent of its land tax exempted. For example, federal buildings, state-owned buildings, Massachusetts Bay Transportation Authority (MBTA) parking lots, and Logan Airport were tax-exempt. Of that amount, so-called famous eds and meds (i.e., higher education institutions and medical facilities) represent only 6.9 percent of these tax-exempted properties. In that respect, Boston was like most American cities in that it had to incessantly seek new sources of revenue from a shrinking tax base.

The State of the Cities, published by the U.S. Department of Housing and Urban Development, compared cities from 1993 to 1998. This report states that middle-class families were leaving central cities for the suburbs and that the rate of growth of the suburbs exceeded that of central cities. Poverty rates were unacceptable as central cities faced a spatial and skills mismatch of jobs for some of its residents. The city of Boston was not one of the cities featured in the report, but the report did cite Boston's declining crime and school drop-out rates.[12] In 1993, Boston's unemployment rate was 7.2 percent as compared to 8.3 percent statewide. The city was also hemorrhaging middle-class families to the surrounding bedroom suburbs.[13]

No one knew at the time that Tom Menino, a relentlessly optimistic politician who assumed office before mid-decade, would be in the mayor's chair at the turn of the century. When the mayor took office, Federal Reserve Bank president Richard Syron was also still bullish on the city: "We've had emotional highs and lows here. In the mid-'80s, we were going to be the Switzerland of America, the capital of money management. Then in the early '90s, we were supposed to be a bird sanctuary. Boston is still the healthiest city in New England by far."[14] Voters had elected a man from a working-class background who made no claims of a clear vision of the city's future but believed in the city's future. The remaining 1990s and the onset of the twentieth century provided illuminating lessons for the new mayor and the new Boston residents.

The economy of Boston in the twenty-first century would be very different from that of the twentieth century. The city attached itself to a fundamental conversion of its economic foundation into a completive platform for the new industries. This economic change was not just a sequential transition but one in which its nascent business leaders were unsure about the future of Boston as a host city. Perhaps claiming that they were improvising is too strong, but it is close. The politicians trusted them, and they created new jobs, attracted a new workforce, and lured similar types of businesses to locate in metro Boston. Boston and its metro area already had a critical infrastructure— higher education institutions—that would accommodate the new economic challenge. Boston became what Professor Richard Florida called a "superstar city."[15] Cities like Boston, Chicago, New York City, San Francisco, and Seattle were in the vanguard of the emerging post-industrial economy. These cities are where the "creative class," the new workforce, wanted to work and live.[16] Boston was clearly one of the archetypes of this new economy. It was a city of prestigious "eds and meds," high-tech firms, nascent startups, financial wizards, and venture capitalists. Such an agglomeration of economic actors and exchanges had an inevitable spillover into Boston's famous neighborhoods.

Some of the new workforces, unlike the professionals in the 1980s and 1990s, did not want to live in the bedroom suburbs of Brookline, Newton, Wellesley, or Weston. They wanted to live in Boston proper. Could the city cram new people into its limited empty housing? Or would these new workers coopt older spaces and neighborhoods? The answer to the first question was no; to the second question, the answer was yes. Even before the turn of the century, the so-called creative class had moved into Boston's historic Irish American enclave, the South End, and Jamaica Plain. With the turn of the twenty-first century, blue-collar enclaves like Charlestown and South Boston appeared on newcomers' radar screen. Adam Burns, a real estate developer, claimed that "South Boston has been wholly gentrified."[17] Gentrification was a byproduct of the post-industrial economy and the so-called biotechnology industry. Boston had the same housing problems that Richard Florida lamented in *The New Urban Crisis*.[18] The newfound economic status of the city of Boston would subject it to increased inequality, deepening racial segregation, and middle-class flight. The new workers threatened to overrun the prime ethnic enclaves. The stereotype of steadfast Boston ethnic neighborhoods had changed. Despite these new realities, which were often dismissed by native Bostonians, demographic and economic change had come. But to paraphrase President John F. Kennedy's inaugural address, the torch of the city neighborhoods has been passed to new generations of Bostonians.

The new light from Boston neighborhoods was in contrast to the dimmed beam of other East Coast industrial cities. Places like Baltimore and Newark were not faring well in the new economy. Granted they have a different history than Boston, but the main difference was that they did not have a Harvard or an MIT in their metro area. For these cities, the long-term future in a post-industrial world looked bleak. The telltale signs were clear. With the shutdowns of factories (e.g., Baltimore's Bethlehem Steel and a General Motors plant) came unemployment, demographic shifts, and the loss of anchor downtown retail. This increased economic dislocation. In Baltimore and Newark, the results have been widespread social pathology and disorientation, especially among poor and minority residents.

Decades ago, some mayors forecasted this future and its dire consequences. In 1971, Newark, New Jersey, mayor Kenneth Gibson was quoted as saying, "Wherever the central cities of America are going, Newark is going to get there first." This foreboding proposition caught the attention of the nation and city residents. Subsequent Newark mayors have tried to reverse this trend, but their city still seems to be on an uncertain journey. Although Newark has had several mayors since Gibson, the city exemplifies some of the same problems that it had a half-century ago.

In the same year, 1971, Boston Mayor Kevin White had to deal with some of the same economic challenges faced by Newark, but he had a niche advantage. In addition, he was in office for the next two decades. Mobile industries were moving, and Boston was in the right place at the right time with the right workforce.[19] In *City Power*, law professor Richard Schragger asserts that what matters is "historical accident, path dependence, spatial persistence: these features of economic geography suggest the geographically uneven economic development is not an aberration but rather a salient feature of economic life."[20] Unlike Newark, Boston entered the post-1970s decades in a better situation because of its history and location. It was lucky to have MIT and Harvard in the metro area. Boston had a so-called old money legacy, and deep-pocket venture capitalists spent new money. The medical researchers in the metro area also attracted the high-flying pharmaceutical industry. Accordingly, Boston was ready for the advent of the knowledge-based industry.

Again paraphrasing Gibson, wherever superstar cities were headed, Boston would get there first because it had a land space problem. A city has to have land parcels and housing for newcomers. Becoming a supercity is analogous to running the Boston Marathon. Many runners enter the race. They come with various skills and abilities. The race itself has many turns and uneven surfaces. The fittest and most talented runners have the best chance to win. In many ways, Boston should win the race. However, winning the superstar city race is not without its perils. To get there, Boston had to transform its politics, which meant overcoming its neighborhood array and land space limitations in order to accommodate newcomers. The onset of gentrification threatened to pit residents against each other. As this book suggests, however, the battle over gentrification did not become a street fight in part because Mayor Menino was able to achieve a rapprochement between newcomers and old-timers.

Size Matters

It is important to remember that the city of Boston proper is only 48.4 square miles. During Menino's tenure from 1993 to 2013, according to the U.S. Census, Boston had a 1990 population of 574,283, and by 2010 it had grown to 617,594, a 7.5 percent increase. It had more people living in the same available space. State law prevents the city from annexing the surrounding towns. The lack of elasticity with the land is a major barrier to all interest groups such as real estate and new companies. Compare that with the borough of Manhattan (New York) with its 22.8 square miles. Its multi-high-rise buildings accommodated a population of 1.6 million. In other words, if Boston wants to grow, it has to either build higher and add more vertical apartments or resettle its neighborhoods. Simply put, Boston proper has limited land space, which increased the political and financial cost of making decisions over who got to use what land space and how.

The dearth of land makes what space there is all the more important. Boston makes a large percentage of its revenues from properties. Accordingly, tax-exempted institutions become a revenue challenge. For example, in 2013, Menino's last year in office, there were in Boston forty-nine private institutions from the educational, medical, and cultural sectors identified as tax-exempted properties. The city reported, "[It] received $23.2 million in PILOT (Payment in lieu of Taxes) contributions in the fiscal year 2013, a 53.1 percent increase over what was previously paid under the prior PILOT program in the fiscal year 2011. This amount represents 82.3 percent of the $28.2 million requested PILOT amount."[21] This funding was supportive of the overall revenue stream, but it represented a small percentage of the city's annual budget. PILOT payments for higher education institutions, a controversial issue, are discussed further in chapter 8.

In the past, developers somewhat ignored Boston's land limits because of the traditional industrial job array in the city that could accommodate small, affordable single-family homes. Neighborhood patterns evolved around the locations of jobs and affinity groups. Planner Joseph D. Cutrufo observed, "Even though the 'Hub of the Universe' is technically one political entity, Boston is, as the saying goes, a city of neighborhoods—about two dozen in all— each with its own colorful history, provincial pride, and unique identity. And in many ways, Boston residents are as much defined by their neighborhoods as the city is."[22] Although this displacement of neighborhoods started during the

Menino era, it was not the center of the overall housing narrative. The pressure of the knowledge-based economy with its entirely different workforce and the demands for prime housing represent a major challenge for the city. Therefore, choices have to be made. Who is going to live in Boston and where? To remain current for all applicants, Boston has to offer a different set of amenities and living options. Ergo, land use and housing choices are critical to Boston's future.

What a city has to offer space-wise may determine its future. The housing options depend on whom it expects or wants to attract. If the city's economy is increasingly a knowledge-based one, it has to cater to higher education, finance, insurance, high-tech industries, and biomedical research workers. In many cases, jobs require college degrees. Boston gains an advantage because of the volume and quality of its higher educational institutions. Put simply, a post-industrial economy requires a highly trained workforce with different skillsets and housing preferences.

Such economies are capital, not labor, intensive, and need a certain type of work platform and provisions for after-work lifestyles. Such workers usually prefer to interact socially with people like themselves. Richard Florida's classic *The Creative Class* confirms these workers are socialized into a collective identity. These individuals are aware of who they are and what they bring to the city. They are also aware of which cities are amenable to lifestyle preferences. Few cities have the quality of educational institutions that Boston enjoys. Sociologist Henry Etzkowitz stated, "Intellectual capital is becoming as important as financial capital as the basis of future economic growth."[23]

Metro Boston, as the host community for some of the most prestigious and advanced higher education institutions in the world, is able to agglomerate more talent. This advantage would be costly, if not impossible, for rival cities to replicate. Accordingly, Boston has a high level of human capital and research talent that acts as a magnet for a highly mobile and choosy workforce. Applicants for these types of jobs go to cities with a copious amount of well-educated people. Indeed, Boston was well prepared for the new geography of jobs. As economist Enrico Moretti has suggested, American cities are increasingly defined by their residents' level of education. He called it "The Great Divergence."[24] In effect, it is a clustering or agglomeration of like-minded people with similar educational backgrounds. The city can perform this type of higher-education agglomeration and create opportunities for so-called knowledge spillover.

As a rising global city, Boston is similar to San Francisco, a small city with very expensive land space. Both coastal cities have benefited from being near some of the best universities in America. San Francisco has nearby Stanford

University and the University of California at Berkeley. Accordingly, the two cities have become magnet cities. This status has its positive and negative effects. Obviously, new businesses mean more city revenues and new residents. Because they are magnet cities, there are few ways to stop the flow of companies and workers seeking a network effect.

As magnet cities, they have arrived at a place where they may not be able to control their twenty-first-century land-use future. Without large parcels of land, they cannot attract large machinery manufacturing companies that require acres of land for production. As mayor, Tom Menino was aware of the city land situation. I discuss his protective posture toward land and space in chapter 5 and 9. Equally challenging for magnet cities like Boston is the realization of their inability to find space to house everyone who wants to live there.

Cities like Boston and San Francisco can either surrender themselves to what Florida calls the "creative class," who may demand the best living places, or they can create bounded reservations to contain the extant middle and working classes. As Florida warns in his *The New Urban Crisis*, if such cities make this latter decision, it may marginalize their poor residents and disperse settled neighborhoods. Obviously, these housing problems alerted and animated Boston leaders like Tom Menino. Older and neighborhood enclave voters saw in him a politician who would protect their turf and not sell them out. In campaigns, he repeatedly promised not to radically disrupt traditions that Bostonians cherished.

In many ways, Menino's relations with newcomers represented a "quasi-Faustian bargain." In effect, this accord was akin to exchanging the spiritual integrity of Boston neighborhood space for the job benefits of the new economy. It was "quasi" because no formal written document was signed or statement made. It was an understanding among the business elites and elected politicians. Perhaps it could be argued that only a mayor like Menino, with his background, his popularity, and the trust he acquired among residents, could have made this "deal." Trust is important in city politics. I discuss the building of this electoral bond in chapter 3. A mayor with an elite background may have had difficulties with explaining and promoting this new view of Boston's future. Boston had to adapt or lose its socioeconomic status. How did Boston get to this point? Boston's role as the New England regional city was at stake, and it had to change to keep that status.

The Growth of the Regional City

In order to understand why this change was necessary, it is important to briefly review the pre-Menino era. Boston is a small city in geographic terms, but the metro area is 4,500 square miles. It is also the largest one in New England. Before World War II, most of its so-called Yankee power elites lived on Beacon Hill in Boston. It was the city on the hill. Now that has changed. Many bankers, professionals, and developers live in Newton, Weston, and Wellesley. Still, they identify with the city of Boston.

American cities evolved along with changes in the national economy. There was always an understanding between business interests and politicians. In the nineteenth century, metro Boston grew as a regional textile and manufacturing center. By 1850, Boston Associates had established one of the nation's largest textile mills in Waltham, a suburb of Boston. With its success, Boston became the regional city and the hub of industrial New England. It was a center of garment and leather goods production. The textile capitalist class also created philanthropic organizations that reformed housing, funded schools, and established hospitals. Thirty years into the twentieth century, the city experienced the Great Depression and the end of the mills. Geography professor Cynthia Hogan wrote,

> Boston's reputation as "Hub" had fallen on hard times by 1945. The city's economic health had peaked just after World War I. By the 1930s, the outright decline had replaced slow growth. In 1929, the city fell into a 20-year depression as its manufacturing jobs moved to other regions and its middle and upper classes moved to the suburbs. Measured in constant dollars, total personal income fell by 25 percent and per capita income dropped by one-fifth in two decades from 1929 to 1950. The city's shabby physical condition was visible testimony to its economic state. Nearly one-fifth of the city's housing stock was substandard. Downtown office construction had virtually stopped in 1929. The 1950 City *General Plan* declared that almost one-fourth of the city's land area required redevelopment.[25]

In the 1960s and 1970s, Boston experienced deindustrialization and unemployment. However, Hogan noted that personal income and employment growth and new office buildings preceded the so-called 1980s Massachusetts Miracle.[26] The Massachusetts Miracle referred to the state's economic growth with a drop in unemployment from 12 percent in 1975 to less than 3 percent during most of the 1980s. For Hogan, the new Boston appeared to be independent of the state's high-tech industries. She also cited David Warsh's

1989 article, which argues that the business community was reinvesting in downtown.[27]

At the turn of twenty-first century, Boston continued to grow as a center for finance, higher education, health/biomedical, and high-tech companies. Boston grew because, like New York City, it was an Atlantic city with shipping ports, an international airport, a view of the ocean, ambiance, and a reputation of being a place to which young people wanted to locate. However, Boston's growth has not been linear. Boston had a larger population from 1920 to 1940 than it does today.

Like residents in other Atlantic cities, each generation of Bostonians has had to face ever-changing political and economic challenges. Each generation of immigrants brought new aspirations and skills. Boston is the product of dual determinants—who migrated to Boston and what businesses located themselves inside Boston proper.

Generally speaking, Boston welcomes newcomers because it is a pro-growth city. Unlike cities such as Portland, Oregon, and Seattle, Boston promotes its pro-growth reputation. In 1979, a Portland plan called Metro 2040 committed the city to smart growth. One of the slogans was "Don't Californicate Oregon." In 1990, Seattle, with the assistance of the Growth Management Act and the 2000 King County Compromise Plan, committed itself to preserving the farmland around the city and to slow growth. The so-called activists against outsiders coming to Seattle such as KBO (Keep the Bastards Out) were very active for a short time. These attitudes and measures for both cities represented a preference for a slow-growth policy. No such plans or antigrowth movements existed for Boston. It is inconceivable that Boston would have a slogan such as "Don't New York Us." Granted these smart growth sentiments grew out of a belief that a city's quality of life and environment would be compromised with more people and development. Menino was aware of these issues. In an analysis of the 2002 Metro-Future Project, developed by the Metropolitan Area Planning Commission, David Gibbs and Rob Krueger concluded,

> In Boston, the smart growth agenda appears to have been increasingly translated into a "housing action" policy. Housing provision (or the lack thereof) within the Boston city-region, is viewed as a key impediment to the city-region's economic competitiveness. Smart growth policies sought to provide two much-needed remedies for the city-region's waning competitiveness: increased housing options and housing that would appeal to younger key workers that high-tech companies were trying to attract. Smart growth has also provided ideological cover for

the administration to pursue its stated sustainability goals through the market rather than through direct state intervention.[28]

Menino's housing policies is discussed in chapter 4, but it is important to note here that his administration was lauded for some of the same city policies as smart-growth cities. Menino ventured into the controversy over climate change, and his adoption of a green agenda may have been related to listening to local climate activists and being a member of the national organizations of mayors. Indeed, Menino promoted a green agenda for Boston.

Despite having enlightened leadership, Boston's residential preferences started to change as the national economy underwent a fundamental transformation. Suburbanization started in the late 1950s, and towns like Brookline, Newton, Waltham, Weston, and Wellesley became the preferred bedroom communities for some of the city's professional class. The Boston Center Business District declined, the neighborhood demographics changed, and part of Boston could not escape looking like other Rust Belt cities.

What also strikes travelers when they visit Boston is its modest skyline compared to superstar cities like Chicago and New York. Boston has not been "Manhattanized," that is, had numerous tall buildings constructed next to each other. A month before Menino took over, *Boston Globe* reporter Martin Nolan asserted, "The successor to Mayor Flynn will not preside over the skyscraper orgy that began his two mayoral terms. In 1984, the city produced 4 million square feet of first-class office space, as lawyers, accountants, and brokers enriched the city's economy. In 1988, 3.6 million square feet were added. No major new office space is planned for this year or next. Although the commercial real estate bust is due to national economic and technological trends, those interviewed were optimistic about the long-range strength of Boston's economy."[29]

Although downtown anchor stores such as Jordan Marsh and Filenes have closed, in 1996 and 2006 respectively, the downtown retail functions survived. The downtown still attracts sightseers to its historical sites such as Old North Church and the Paul Revere House. Reporter Katherine Bowers observed in 2005, "This college town is a textbook case of the major, and sometimes paradoxical, themes roiling U.S. retailing. There is a legendary regional department store in its dying throes—big-box discounters circling, corporate consolidation, and a thriving luxury scene tied to a sizzling, if somewhat precarious, housing market."[30] What type of Boston one encounters depends on where one lives, where one goes, and for what purpose.

Different Boston for Different People

As is the case for most American cities, an individual may live within the same official geographic boundaries but experience quite different life routines and changes. Growing up in one section of Boston does not make one an authority in another part of the city. A resident of a particular neighborhood is usually familiar with the streets near them and how to get from A to B but may know little about how to get from C to D. The story of Boston was a tale of four cities: old Boston (New England Yankees), the Irish Boston (working-class white people), Yuppie Boston (middle-class researchers, creative class executives, arts/cultural entrepreneurs, health providers, and financial elites), and lastly the other Boston (minorities and low-income residents who make up the working and service classes). These groups existed as parallel universes and seldom interact. They pass each other every day. They may root for the Patriots and Bruins sports franchises, and this passing strangers' invisibility spills over into Boston politics.

Newcomers may find city politics difficult to understand. It is like a blind-folded person trying to describe a Henry Moore sculpture. An argument could be made that the newly affluent and predominately white middle class has yet to show the level of *noblesse oblige* politically as the old Yankee elites. The politics of Boston seems trivial and provincial to most of this new class. This alienation may account for the fact that most Bostonians of the creative class were not publicly engaged in the discourse about the future of the city. This is not to say that they do not support groups that advocate for and serve the lower classes. Simply put, they have yet to accept the idea that they are permanent city stakeholders.

Before Menino left office in 2013, a number of telltale demographic signs and social trends had altered the visual image of America's Athens. People who are Black, Asian, and Hispanic, who made up a tiny minority after World War II, represented over 40 percent of Boston's population. The 2010 US. Census found the non-Hispanic whites represented only 47 percent of the city population. Within this minority-majority city, there was a distinct Caribbean culture in neighborhoods like Mattapan and Roxbury. Accordingly, the future of Boston politics would have to include people who are Black, Latino, and Asian. Boston mayors before Menino had started to make more substantive alliances with the leaders of the minority communities.

The tenure of Mayors Kevin White and Raymond Flynn, who preceded

Menino, witnessed a shift of some attention to the city's growing and restless minorities. In the past, white working-class politics had been extremely ethnically oriented, almost a form of turf protection. Boston history suggests that some white residents supported the neighborhood containment of minorities. This group surprised the media and pundits with the election of Tom Menino, a "de-ethnicized" politician, as mayor. Part of Menino's challenge was to maintain the support of those residents and at the same time facilitate the political incorporation of new Black and Brown immigrants and seek places for them in the new economy. Chapter 7 discusses Menino's efforts in that regard. But even he could not stop the hemorrhaging of low-skilled jobs.

Metro Boston and Economic Development

Modern Metro Boston is one of the nation's epic centers of post-industrial society. Although General Electric was founded in 1878 there, Boston itself was never a true factory town. Most of the manufacturing took place in suburban towns like Lynn and Lowell, which had space to let. Raytheon was once located in Waltham. Retail headquarters such as TJX and Staples are located in Framingham. In 1995, economist Kieth R. Ihlanfeldt concluded, "Suburb-based companies depend heavily on central-city suppliers of corporate services, and many highly paid suburban professionals earn their livings from central-city jobs."[31] Menino would experience this trend throughout his administration.

The centering of academic institutions (e.g., Harvard and MIT, both located in Cambridge) allowed Boston to support the economy of Boston Metro and become a center of the high-tech industry. Companies on Route 128 represent the East Coast Silicon Valley. DataXie, HubSpot, and Acquia are among the nation's top-growing companies. Although some might say Boston is no match for San Francisco and Seattle, it is competitive since it has some famous venture capitalist companies—Atlas Venture, Sigma Prime, General Catalyst, and Matrix Partners. Information services includes IDG and Iron Mountain (internet services), and Civitas Solution (communications equipment). Although Boston has lost some of its one-time famous banks such as Shawmut Bank, BayBank, Bank of New England, Bank of Boston, and Fleet Bank to acquisitions and mergers, it is still a major financial center.

Boston is the home of several financial services firms such as Fidelity Investments, a mutual-fund company; Bain & Companies Advent; State Street Corporation, the nation's third-largest custody bank; Liberty Mutual

Insurance; and Longfellow Real Estates Partners. Moreover, Boston's star still shines brightest as a center of biomedical care and research. It is the host city for Massachusetts General Hospital and Brigham and Women's Hospital (now Mass General Brigham) and Beth Israel Deaconess Medical Center (now Beth Israel Lahey Health). These institutions are arguably among the best hospitals in the nation and perhaps in the world. Cambridge-Boston is also the home to several fast-growing startups. Richard Florida has called Boston a superstar city that attracts this creative class. Florida points out this has led to the segregation of the service class.[32] The plight of poor service workers is a challenge for America's Athens.

America's Athens

Boston's uniqueness and contextuality are exemplified by the critical role it plays as the center of higher education. Universities are a major cash cow for the city, providing both students and institutional spending. Of course, the city's reputation is helped by having Harvard University, the nation's oldest (established in 1636) and most prestigious university in the metropolitan area. Harvard has come a long way from training Protestant clergy. And so has MIT, established in 1861 to teach applied science and engineering. People from all over the nation and the world want to study at these two institutions as well as the other higher education centers in the city. Accordingly, the city attracts a large and famous intellectual class. Intellectuals located in the city and its suburbs have become a part of the ongoing discourse.

Boston promotes itself as the Athens of America, with over twenty-nine institutions of higher education close to the city. As the center of liberal arts education in the world, many American scholars and higher education administrators make their careers in Boston. These migrants come to Boston to enjoy the liberal and intellectual environment created by people like themselves.

A Liberal City?

For all its production of white, liberal, and progressive national politicians, some minorities do not consider Boston a truly liberal city. Some African American activists have had stories of personal discrimination. Some Black immigrants from the American South call Boston "up south." Residentially, socially, and spatially, Boston is regarded as a segregated city. In 2010, 2013, and

2017, market researcher Chadwick Martin Bailey surveyed cities and asked the question, "How welcoming is each city to people of color?" Boston came in last among African American respondents.[33]

In many instances, Boston is politically behind other large American cities. In the 1970s and 1980s, it did not elect a female or a Black mayor, as cities like Atlanta, Chicago, and Los Angeles did. During that period and into the turn of the century, women ran for mayor of Boston but were roundly defeated in the primaries. Black candidates also ran in the primaries without success. In 2021, Michelle Wu became the first Asian American woman elected mayor of Boston. Indeed, as of this writing, the Black and Brown residents whom social researcher Marilyn Johnson calls the "Metropolitan Diaspora" continue to struggle for political and status recognition at City Hall.[34] Despite Boston's progressive image and its deserved reputation of being the host to some of the nation's most prestigious literati and higher educational institutions, the city has never been and has not pretended to be an open city for minorities. This may be related to the early history of the city and how the leadership evolved. And the slow progress of generational replacement makes racial progress difficult.

Boston also has not had a strong Saul Alinsky organization like Baltimorean United in Leadership Development (BUILD) to challenge city policies. This ongoing organization was a coalition of the NAACP, churches, and social/civil organizations. Along with Greater Baltimore Committee, a business marketing organization, BUILD was able to challenge the city's school compact proposals and a range of city policies.[35] Nevertheless, Boston has been able to build a cadre of Black leaders who have challenged mayors and built an attentive constituency. The activities and personalities of Boston's civil rights and church organizations are discussed in chapter 7.

Summary

What Boston is and what it is not represents its uniqueness as America's Athens. This reputation, as we shall see, also has bred insularity and reduced attention to other cities' policy failures, successes, and experiments. The waning of manufacturing and the advent of financial capitalism changed who ran the city and how it was run. As a superstar city, Boston had to respond to economic and political challenges. Obviously, Boston had its share of political trauma and luck that defined its politics. Political events in Boston served to educate politicians like Thomas Menino as they did for his predecessors. Often city politicians are denizens of class, ethnic, and partisan bubbles. Apparently, Menino realized this and broke out of them. He may not have been aware of the total contextuality of his city politics, but he thought that he could take action to help.

This book shows in the next chapters that Menino, an Italian American, did not follow political scientist Robert Dahl's ethnic replacement sequence. Ethnic secession means that different groups replace each other once the ascendant group get a political and demographic advantage.[36] The Menino administration included many Irish American individuals and members of other demographic groups. He did not attempt to stack City Hall with only Italian Americans. Granted Menino came to the mayor's office at a different urban political time. By the 1990s, staff diversity was expected and demanded. Moreover, Menino embraced the idea of a diverse staff. In his first State of City address Menino stated, "If 100 years from now they look back at my election, I hope what they see is the beginning of a century of inclusive politics. Throughout my whole career, I have tried to be an open door to people left out of the mainstream. As mayor, I intend to continue that."[37]

In chapter 1, we locate Menino within the context of the 1950s to the 1980s. How did he become an intriguing blend of a cognitive/compassionate empathic mayor who knew how to use lessons from others? We discuss his basic and political socialization and his rise from a district councilor to the acting mayor. He surprised many when he won the 1994 mayoral election.

In chapter 2, we discuss Menino's mayoral campaigns, the issues, and his opponents. Local politicians and activists are often convinced they know what it takes to get elected mayor of Boston—what wards and voting groups are critical to getting elected. Menino's election as mayor was the political shock of the 1990s. The question was why he kept winning elections. How did he become a consummate Boston politician? We discuss how Boston's electoral politics is different from other big cities.

In chapter 3, we examine the internal relationships within the Boston government. Some policy issues are amenable to city government direct action, such as economic development and environmental policies. This chapter considers Menino's relations with the city council, political activists, interest groups, city hall staff, and the media. In the discussion of these interactions, Menino's governing style emerges.

In chapter 4, we review the recurrent politics of Boston and how Menino's political style meshed with those politics. Recurrent politics refers to the significance of sequences of elections and the variety of partisan roles mayors in big cities have to play. There were other politicians he was obligated to deal with and support. Mayors cannot separate themselves from state and federal politics and policies. Indeed, the mayor of Boston must also monitor political activities in the federal government as well as the New England region. Menino, as the titular head of the local Democratic Party, likewise had to contribute to other Democratic candidates. Other local politicians sought his endorsement and support. In addition, he had to give attention to politicians of the opposition party in the service of his role as the city's economic salesperson.

In chapter 5, we discuss the housing politics of Boston. Housing politics include reactions to rising assessments, inspections, gentrification, availability, and affordability. This level of politics directly impacts ordinary Bostonians. Race and class have always been a part of housing politics, which are at the nexus between the federal and local governments. This chapter discusses why affordable housing is the most vexing problem for the city, with its limited space and fixed neighborhoods. While the housing policies predated Menino's administration, his support for neighborhood integrity, housing for the poor, and rent control were notable.

In chapter 6, we examine Mayor Menino the crime fighter. He inherited the crime legacy and mistrust of the police from his predecessors. Menino's appointments of police commissioners and their crime-fighting strategies impacted his attempt to build a safe city. As is the case for many big cities, Menino's reputation as an effective mayor was linked to evidence of decreases in crime rates. We discuss his administration's efforts to reduce youth violence. The reduction of youth crime was newsworthy. The so-called Boston Miracle worked for a while. This chapter also examines Boston's crime statistics and the careers of Menino-appointed commissioners. To reassure residents of his commitments, he would make personal appearances at horrific crime scenes.

In view of the changes in Boston's demographics, chapter 7 discusses Menino's relationships with minorities in Boston. American mayors are often judged by how they deal with the so-called minority problem. The increased pluralization of that community can make interactions even more difficult. We introduce a typology to explain how different mayors have fared within certain parameters. We explain how Menino, with his hands-on approach, was able to achieve more respect and community trust than his predecessors achieved.

Chapter 8 analyses Menino's approach to public-school politics. In many ways, this chapter is related to the previous one as minority students have not fared as well as their white counterparts in school achievement in Boston. Accordingly, many mayors have sought to change or reform the Boston public schools. Effective public-school reform is difficult, if not impossible. Menino announced publicly that he wanted to be "an education mayor," and that he wanted to be judged by his performance.

In chapter 9, we interpret Mayor Menino's relationship with higher education institutions inside and outside the city. These institutions are among the most important economic generators for the city. We discuss issues of nonprofits, the expansion of facilities, and the role of students in the city. Presidents of these higher education institutions and their staffs usually relate to City Hall but few of them get personally involved in mayoral politics. However, the nexus of city politics and higher education does occur when leaders of the latter are seeking to change and expand their physical plants. There is also interaction in the case of public safety.

In the conclusion, we summarize the impact Thomas Menino had on Boston politics. His personality affected his governing style, but the policy challenges he faced as the city leader were new to him. He was able to do things future mayors of Boston may not be able to do. We can learn many lessons that may be valuable to other mayors of post-industrial cities. Finally, we relate how governing style has impacted Boston politics and the challenges Boston faces.

CHAPTER 1

On Becoming a Boston Politician

Thomas Michael Menino was born on December 27, 1942, in Readville, a part of the Hyde Park section of Boston, Massachusetts. These were the war years, and the nation was in the middle of the great battles that comprised World War II. The war was in its fourth year (the second of American involvement), and the nation was in mobilization and patriotic mode. American families joined in the war effort by sending their sons into the armed forces, using their ration stamps effectively, and buying defense bonds. Under the leadership of President Franklin Roosevelt, the nation was mobilized and unified. Yet old anti-ethnic and racial attitudes endured. In that patriotic moment, the nation was amenable to dual loyalty accusations for Japanese and Italian Americans. For some Italian Americans, the war years were difficult. The antics of Benito Mussolini, the Italian dictator and Axis leader, did not help the image of Italian Americans. For some of them, the postwar period was not much better.

American families learned many ethnic and racial stereotypes from post–World War II radio stations. African Americans' radio stereotypes started in the late 1920s with *Amos 'n' Andy*. The caricatures survived until the 1960s. For Italian Americans, "Life with Luigi" presented a post–World War II stereotype. These ethnic stereotypes were prevalent messages in a comedy about the plight of a newly arrived immigrant Italian, Luigi Basco, as he attempted to fit into his new country. The radio program started in 1948 and ended in 1953. What some Americans understood about Italian immigrants, they learned from listening to the show. When the show producers attempt to make the transition to television, they got backlash from the Italian American community because of the negative stereotypes. Historian Dominic L. Candeloro makes the linkage between racial and ethnic stereotypes. He concludes, "In many ways, *Life with Luigi* was to Italian Americans what *Amos 'n' Andy* was to African Americans: a comedic depiction of a subculture in which the lines between laughing *with* and laughing *at* the ethnic group were often blurred. It was also a show in which respect of the ethnic group or lack thereof lay in the mind of the beholder."[1]

During the 1950s, Readville was a predominately working-class white neighborhood. Menino grew up with two siblings, Carolyn and David. Growing up during the postwar era and being a child during President Harry Truman's Fair Deal, young Tom Menino could not have understood grownups' reactions to public discourse and radio programs. By some accounts, Menino's childhood was a somewhat unusual one for a working-class child in an Italian American family. His father, Carl, was a machinist factory foreman at Westinghouse Electric Corporation, and his mother, Susan, was a housewife. Menino described her as a "Mother Teresa to new immigrants."[2] She ran an informal settlement house for immigrants. The family had two houses. The family took in boarders, and his mother, who spoke "fluent Italian," taught them English and helped them to fill out job applications. She also helped immigrants to find social "networks."[3] Menino stated, "Eventually she extended her hand from family to strangers, and from Italians to immigrants from Greece, Ireland, and other countries."[4] Susan's humanity and concern for the less fortunate may have imprinted a norm of magnanimity on young Tom. It follows scripture: "Do nothing out of selfish ambition or vain conceit, but in humility consider others better than yourselves. Each of you should look not only to your own interests but also to the interests of others" (Philippians 2:3– 4). Tom grew up in a Catholic family, who would have embraced the meaning of this Bible passage. These ideas may have shaped his attitudes toward others, especially those who needed help. The future mayor would remain dedicated to his church, family, and community.

His father was a factory foreman and that may have added neighborhood prestige for the Menino family. Tom Menino wrote that his "father was a simple man. Worked at Westinghouse in Hyde Park, making armatures." Moreover, "My father hated politics. But he knew local politicians." Menino referred to him in his first mayoral acceptance speech: "I really wish my father was here to see this. He was a simple person who worked in a factory, but he took a lot of pride in his family."[5] Menino recalled his first political moment as when he asked Carl what it meant that John Collins had upset Johnny Powers for mayor. This was an interesting question for a politically alert teenager. Powers, the president of the Massachusetts Senate, lost the general election despite having won the Democratic Party primary over five other candidates. Yet he lost to Collins in the 1959 general election. At the time the election was considered the biggest upset in Boston mayoral politics. We don't know what Carl Menino said to his son, but we know that the upset was baffling to many observers. Murray B. Levin's *The Alienated Voter: Politics in Boston* attributed John E. Powers's defeat to voter resentment of the political elite.[6]

The 1950s were an interesting decade for Bostonians. Mayoral politics was concentrated around Irish American politicians. John B. Hynes was acting mayor because the infamous former mayor James Michael Curley went to jail for mail fraud. Once Curley got out, Hynes defeated him and served for a decade. It was Hynes who created the Boston Redevelopment Authority (BRA). It was during his tenure that the West End became the target of urban renewal. It is also noteworthy that Boston began to see its history as a tourist magnet with the development of the Freedom Trail.

Aside from tracking news of the conviction of Mayor Curley, people around the nation did not follow Boston politics. And some may not have known exactly where Boston was located. Obviously, many baseball fans knew about the rivalry between the Boston Red Sox and New York Yankees in baseball. They had possibly also read or heard on the radio about the Great Brink's Robbery. This was an attention-getter. In January 1950, armed men stole over $2 million dollars from the Brink building. (twenty-six years later a comedy movie was made about it called *The Brink's Job*). This made the nation stand up and take notice.

During the 1950s, the population of the city grew to 801,444, from 770,816, a 4 percent increase. Although it was not known at the time, this would be Boston's largest population peak. The growth sparked the need for more sophisticated planning. As noted earlier, the city began to meet its economic development challenge with the establishment of the BRA in 1957. Boston Airport became Logan International Airport, making it a transatlantic portal to the city's nascent global future. Few Bostonians were prescient to the implications of these changes, not the least of whom was a teenager in Readville. The formative years of Tom Menino included the mayoral leadership of Mayor Hynes, the ending of the Korean War by President Dwight

Eisenhower, the advent of the southern civil rights movement, the initiation of President Lyndon Johnson's War on Poverty, and the election of the first Irish American president, Brookline-born John F. Kennedy.

High School Student

In 1960, Thomas Menino graduated from St. Thomas Aquinas High School. In the 1960s, many Catholic schools had nuns as teachers. At St. Thomas Aquinas, a parochial school, young Tom had been taught the three Rs as well as the mission of the Catholic Church. Menino remembered it as a time in which nuns continually misspelled his name.[7] In his book *A Mayor for a New America*, Menino recalled,

> I'm reluctant to say much about school. Because my teeth and lips would not cooperate, I talked out of the side of my mouth, mumbling decades before I was called "Mumbles." I had trouble enunciating (a nun ordered me to mime the words because my singing was wrecking the school choir), and dreaded being called on in class. Mostly I sat in silence and fidgeted. The nuns encouraged kids who didn't need encouragement, not those who did. Me, I got the stick. One time I spilled a bottle of ink over some brand-new textbooks. A nun charged down the aisle of the desks with a stick about a yard long, backpedaled for maximum hitting power, and whaled me, "Sister, it's washable ink!" I protested, but she kept whaling.[8]

Menino's views about the nuns who taught him and about school in general are important because of their impact on him. He recalled these topics several times in interviews and in his book. As we discuss in chapter 7, Menino was quite solicitous of the plight of minority students and their school achievement.

Yet the new decade offered fresh challenges and possibilities for him and American youth. Young Americans were dancing to the "Twist" with Chubby Checker, the R&B singing star, and the future looked good. This was also the same year that the nation elected a former U.S. senator from Massachusetts as its first Irish Catholic president, John F. Kennedy. In his inaugural address, Kennedy implored the nation to "ask not what your country can do you—ask what you can do for your country." Few Americans were not enthralled by American Camelot.

After high school, the critical question for most young people, including Menino, was, What are going to do with your life? The postwar nation that he had grown up in was now a booming economy. It allowed the Menino family, like most Italian American families, to expect their children to aim for and achieve more in life than their parents' generation. In other words, he had an opportunity for class leapfrogging. This may explain why Susan and Carl Menino encouraged Tom to attend college. His father recalled, "When I'd get on him, he'd say, 'Truman didn't go to college.' He must have said it a thousand times."[9] A decision not to directly go to college meant getting a job and starting a family for individuals from the working class. Menino was so inclined to this course of life. In retrospect, Carl's advice was excellent for an aspiring Boston politician.

Aspiring Politician

For a would-be Italian American politician, there was a continual and unconscious search for role models that looked like them or had vowels at the ends of their names. During Menino's youth, two Italian American politicians had been elected governor of the commonwealth of Massachusetts. Former Democratic congressman and Yale-educated lawyer Foster Furcolo served in the Massachusetts State House from 1957 to 1961. He was followed by Republican John Volpe, a son of immigrants and businessman who served from 1961 to 1963. Volpe went on to become U.S. secretary of transportation in the Nixon administration. In 1963, Francis Bellotti was elected lieutenant governor. Bellotti also served for over a decade as Massachusetts attorney general. Italian American families had to have been proud of the elections of these men because their successes in office helped extinguish ethnic stereotypes. Overcoming ethnic slurs and gainsaying Mafia connections were ongoing challenges for aspiring Italian American politicians. Yet the Furcolo, Volpe, and Bellotti breakthroughs allowed young people like Tom Menino to dream big.

To realize those types of ambitions one needed to start at the community level and with local political actors. If Menino had such ambitions, he needed a mentor with well-built political connections. At the age of eighteen, he started his political life working for a friend of his father, Charles Patrone, who was a state representative. Patrone was born in Roslindale and considered a defender of Hyde Park. Menino recalled, "One day he asked me to hand out some fliers. That was it." For young Menino a life of political apprenticeships would follow. *Boston Globe* reporter David Nyhan stated, "No Westinghouse armature-winding for Menino."[10] Patrone represented the 17th Suffolk District, which included Hyde Park. He also had a private insurance business called Bankers

National. He served in the Massachusetts House of Representatives from 1948 to 1962 and headed the Joint Committee on Highways and Motor Vehicles. In that position, he amassed a significant amount of political power.[11] In 1962, he retired from the House, but his political connections followed him. In 1965, Patrone and other politicians were caught up in scandals and corruption investigated by the Crime Commission. The *Boston Herald* got a copy of the draft of the report, and although no names were named, it found widespread corruption ranging from misuse of campaign funds to fixing traffic tickets.[12]

Another person in young Menino's life was John Kinnaly. He was an ex-FBI agent and a Norwood selectman. Menino described him affectionately as "my second father." Menino recalled how he met Kinnaly:

> I was working on (state senator) Joe Timilty's staff.... China McFarland, a political junkie from Norwood, came in one day and said, "I want you meet this guy, Kinnaly. He used to be with the FBI. He's really sharp, and I know you'd like him." And that's how it started, a long, long time ago.... I respected him so much.... He was such a decent guy. He always seemed to find someone who had a problem, and I'd get a call: "Tommy, can we help this guy out?" . . . Today they say that's bad; you're not supposed to help anybody. But that wasn't the way it worked in John's world.[13]

So early on young Menino attached himself to successful political role models. Later Kinnaly also became Menino's "chief encourager whenever the mayor was on the receiving end of ridicule.... He'd tell me [Menino], 'Tommy, don't listen to it. People trust you, so just do what you feel is right.'"[14] There is a big difference between believing you have talent and convincing strangers you are a capable person.

A Smart Guy but No Degree

Before Menino was elected to office, he was unusual at the time for not having received a college education. The lack of a college education haunted many ambitious job seekers of Menino's age. President Lyndon Johnson's 1965 Higher Education Act was passed, in part, to encourage Americans to go to college. Supposedly, a college-educated person had demonstrated an ability to complete an assigned task and had a wider view of the world. Increasingly job recruiters sought college-educated people for new jobs. Indeed, colleges and universities were also changing to accept more students from working-class backgrounds.

In the 1970s, the College Level Education Program (CLEP) ran a television commercial showing an actor portraying Abraham Lincoln being turned down for an executive position. The employment interview scene set an agent, eating a sandwich, asking the actor playing Lincoln, "What about college?" Lincoln responds, "I have done a lot of reading and studying sort of on my own." The agent replies, "On your own. Look, Lincoln, I know you are a smart guy; you know you are a smart guy, but you ain't going anywhere without that sheepskin [college diploma] fellow. You are not exactly executive material." (A male voiceover intervenes and states, "There you are an intelligent human being but no college credit.") The agent looks at his Rolodex and asks, "Hey Lincoln, do you have a chauffeur license?" The commercial ends by encouraging students to take the CLEP examination at their local college and earn college credit.[15] One of these commercials might have resonated with Tom Menino and his peers. This was the point that Carl Menino was making when he repeatedly asked Tom to go to college: Menino's lack of a college education appeared to be a barrier to his ambitions.

Completing That Degree

After high school, Tom Menino did listen somewhat to his father and took courses at Boston College, a private Jesuit institution. But he dropped out and started working at Metropolitan Life Insurance, a mutual company. As an insurance agent, his job was to meet people, sell policies, and help clients make claims. One had to be an effective salesperson to attract and keep clients. Reportedly Menino was not fond of the job. Menino recalled, "What possessed Metropolitan Life to hire me as a salesman? Arrogance—a belief that there was no one they couldn't train to sell. Or was it that I was a big young guy with dark wavy hair who looked presentable in a suit and tie? Whatever it was, I'm grateful. Because I had met Angela, and I couldn't ask her to marry a guy with no prospects."[16] In 1963, Tom Menino married Angela Faletra. He met Faletra "as they played tennis on adjoining courts in Hyde Park one day and her errant shots kept angling his way. Their first date was that night." He commented, "She was pretty, bright, funny, and compassionate. A Roslindale girl, but you can't have everything. I've often been asked if becoming acting mayor of Boston wasn't the luckiest break of my life. No, I reply."[17] Angela Menino stated later, "We came from the same kind of backgrounds, with extended families living all around us. It wasn't like he swept me off my feet with his charm; it was more like realizing he was different from any other guy I'd known."[18] After marriage, Tom and Angela Menino lived in the Hype Park's Georgetown Estates, Section 8 public housing.[19] They had two children, Susan and Tommie Jr.

Although Menino thought that college was not for him, he received an associate's degree in business management from Chamberlayne Junior College (later Mount Ida College).[20] In 1984, twenty-four years after graduating from St. Thomas Aquinas High School and a year into his tenure on the Boston City Council, Menino enrolled in the University of Massachusetts, Boston, and four years later received a bachelor's degree in community planning from the College of Public and Community Service. Menino was told by one of his supporters, Gerard Doherty, an MIT-educated architect, that if he wanted to advance in Boston politics, he needed a college degree.[21] As a sitting city member of the City Council, he could not just drop everything and enroll full-time as a college student. UMass Boston had developed part-time, flexible courses that allowed adults to return to college and earn a bachelor's degree. Menino could keep his elected position and attend college at the same time.

Barbara Buchanan, director of urban development and field education at the university, explained the coursework. According to her, professors never failed any students. They sent students back to the books, into classrooms, and into jobs with instructions to gain more experience or insight in order to pass the courses. The program allowed adults to work at their own pace without "the burden of letter grades for scholastic work." Buchanan noted, "You don't really ever fail. If competency isn't met, the faculty will go back and ask them to dig deeper. This isn't a traditional lecture place. People make bigger the boundaries of life." His academic advisor stated that Menino was a serious student and was able to satisfy between ten and fifteen required competencies through his work as a city councilor.[22] This was a self-education curriculum that incorporated life experiences. This worked for Menino because he valued his experience and knew how to use self-learning in his career.

Menino, whose role model was Harry Truman (the first modern president without a college education), realized that having gone to a junior college was not enough. Finally getting a degree was quite an accomplishment. Menino admitted, "It is one of the best things I did in my career. It is all about how seriously you take it, what you have been able to accomplish in life, and what you got from the classroom work. It was very enlightening. I developed friendships with people who have helped me even today."[23] It may have also occurred to him that one cannot do politics in a town where higher education institutions are so central to the city's economy and not hold a college degree.

In Boston, where one attends college matters. Some people will ask that question as a part of a simple introduction. For many Bostonians, one's college alma mater signals a person's status and informs how they relate to others. People make assumptions about others based on their educational backgrounds. For example, having graduated from Harvard and MIT is often referred to as exceptional and accorded immediate respect. Menino came from a working-class neighborhood where such questions were rarely asked. People judged each other by how they behaved and what their families represented in the community. For them, Thomas Menino had learned a lot before he enrolled at UMass Boston. Attending college was commendable, but his social standing in his community was based on what he had learned in life.

Tom Menino's Overall Socialization

Getting a college degree might be a requirement for success in Boston politics but by the time Menino reached college, he already had had some basic political socialization. Who and what provided that to Menino? In general, political socialization involves all the political learning, formal and informal, about one's place in the world and what one can expect from the government. As mentioned earlier, Menino was a part of an inadvertent audience (i.e., people who unintentionally hear about the news) and was witness to major sociopolitical events. He learned things without knowing why or how he learned them. This learning process normally starts in childhood. Children are usually unaware that they are internalizing political ideas and attitudes from their parents and peers. As a result, children accept the political values of their parents. These values often define the political boundaries for children—what can be done and what is expected. There were a variety of roles a young man like Menino needed to learn. Important among these were citizenship obligations and cultural roles.

Having been raised during the postwar era, Menino received his basic socialization as a person of Italian American descent. He was made aware of his heritage, ideas from the old country, food, and customs. He was probably told stories that some Italian Americans were discriminated against in Boston. These warning messages may have been implicit or explicit. And these messages were reinforced by his peers. As he became older, he had to have appreciated his ethnic group's rivalry with the Irish Americans. Although the two groups shared European ancestry, they saw the world differently.

Although Irish and Italian immigrants arrived in the city at about the same time (1880s–1920s), they occupied different places in Boston's political and social hierarchy. Irish Americans were successful, in part, because they controlled city politics and the church. Historian Lawrence J. Luppi makes an argument that Irish Americans and Italian Americans were different because of their political aspirations. Italian Americans did not attach themselves to a political party. Luppi also claims that they did not assimilate religiously because the Catholicism they practiced was different from the Irish one.[24] This may explain why it took Italian American politicians so long to rise to the Boston mayoralty.

This may also explain why Menino's rise in Boston politics was an exception. As suggested earlier, Menino made a point of reaching out to Irish American politicians. Sociologist Mark S. Granovetter made interesting points about the strength of weak ties. Individuals who resist maintaining close ties with their primary ethnic group are more likely to have successful contacts with other groups. Granovetter called this loose coupling.[25]

In other words, if Menino, an Italian American, had been tightly coupled within his community, he would not have met many people outside his community. This is because tight coupling stresses ethnic identification and cohesion. This would have isolated him because he would have been discouraged from interacting with other groups. Put simply, if one wants to network outside one's primary social group, one needs weak ties. Granovetter believed that such ties are not generative of alienation but are "indispensable to individuals' opportunities and to their integration into the communities; strong ties, breeding local cohesion, leads to overall fragmentation."[26] For Tom Menino, weak ties with groups were the strength of his networks. It provided him with opportunities to meet as many people as possible. Lessons learned. Menino had broken the ethnic bubble. As we will examine more closely in chapter 6, Menino established an unapparelled relationship with minorities. Ergo, these loose ties worked for him. Besides, moving away from his class and ethnic moorings also exposed Menino to the professional middle class.

Menino's ability to roam among groups was unusual for individuals from his background. Roaming was important because his class position could have been inhibiting. Herbert J. Gans's classic *The Urban Villagers* (1963) found that second-generation Italian Americans living in predominately working-class neighborhoods were more working class than Italian. They retained Italian food, some habits, and religious practices but they were basically just working-class individuals. Gans came to this conclusion after conducting an ethnographic study of the impact of urban renewal on the West End.[27] Five years earlier, in 1958, many Italian Americans had been removed from this beloved enclave and many did not consider their community to be a "slum." Menino's family did not live in the West End, but the "great removal" had reverberations across all of Boston's ethnic neighborhoods.

In addition, Menino's socialization in communities outside his own was an ongoing process. Obviously, political events existed outside Boston, and awareness of the national news also shaped, albeit unconsciously, his generation. Menino was a young man during the Vietnam War and the racial turmoil of the 1960s. People his age were in the streets protesting government policies. The rise of the Black civil rights movement in the South, and the assassination of its leader Dr. Martin Luther King (a man who had studied at Boston University and had once marched for open housing in the city), must have alarmed the 1960s generation. Here again, Menino was part of an inadvertent audience. Apparently, Tom Menino learned lessons about what would be a fundamental American social change.

The civil rights movement, which the media covered, reshaped national politics and may have influenced Menino's views on race. Because the nation was also in the midst of President Johnson's War on Poverty, reacting to riots in the streets and student protests against the Vietnam War, the nation was in a fundamental transformation. As we suggest in our review of Menino's political life, there is a distinct relationship between his early predispositions and his later political action. Political learning begins early and continues through life. Obviously, Menino knew that there was a larger world than his Readville neighborhood.

Apprentice to Joseph Timilty

While many of Tom Menino's peers decided to stay clear of politics, young Tom took an apprenticeship. For centuries apprenticeships were an honored way to learn a craft. An apprentice learned from a seasoned master. It worked for medical students in residency and lawyers in clerkships. The best way to learn Boston politics was to work for and with a successful politician. Menino worked for Joseph F. Timilty, a consummate Irish American politician. This on-the-job experience did educate Menino on the nuances of running for elective office and interacting with other officeholders and exposed him to the entire city. In the 1960s, Menino was known for lolloping, a practice of holding up signs in political campaigns and making sure supporters got to polls. Coming from Hype Park, Menino was not on anyone's short-list as a future mayor of America's Athens. His real political education began when he became Joseph Timilty's administrative assistant and driver. Menino went on to play a major role in Timilty's campaigns for mayors in 1971, 1975, and 1979 against Kevin White. In 1975, the year Boston's school busing controversy exploded, Timilty lost but came as close as eight thousand votes.

Timilty was a big name in Boston Irish politics, and his grandfather had ties to the so-called Curley machine.[28] The Timilty family had been involved in Boston politics since the 1930s. Timilty's grandfather had been Boston's police commissioner. Joseph's uncle Walter was also police commissioner under James Curley and was involved in the infamous "Elk Laundry" scandal, a laundry service scheme in which police officers would solicit business for the commissioner.[29] Timilty represented the 18th Ward and served on the City Council from 1967 to 1971. He also served in the state senate from 1972 to 1985. Throughout his political career, he aspired to become mayor of Boston. He hired Menino to help him make that happen. Menino worked as the staff director of the Housing and Urban Development Committee, which was headed by Timilty.

Moreover, Timilty taught Menino how to talk to other politicians and voters: what to say, how, when, and where? Menino learned which politicians he needed to defer to and who could be safely ignored. In the process, Timilty introduced Menino to a wide range of local politicians and community leaders. Menino's weak ties allowed him to meet and make peace with Irish American politicians. He also learned another lesson from Timilty. Menino, recalling the last Timilty race for mayor, told his wife, "Timilty would lose because he had only one constituency [Irish Americans]." Menino learned his lesson about developing multiple constituencies: "You got to have multiple constituencies, from gays to preservationists."[30] *Boston Globe* reporters Matthew Brelis and Brian McGrory described Timilty: "That was his political heyday, back when he was the gruff-mannered, straight-shooting shadow leader of a city divided by race and busing. His name recognition was phenomenal. His slogan one year read: 'Joe Timilty . . . honestly.' In a city where politics is big business, he was a titan of the trade, and even now, a decade later, a generation of politicians and their consultants claim their roots in Timilty campaigns."[31]

Menino would not make his career as a single-constituency politician. Working for Timilty's mayoral campaigns allowed Menino to meet new people and develop interests beyond his district. The campaigns also taught him what not to say or do in a campaign to mobilize the entire Boston community. Menino attributed to Timilty his job at the BRA after he was fired from the insurance company for trying to start a union.[32]

The Timilty team was so impressive in the 1975 election that Jimmy Carter's presidential campaign hired Menino to work as a field organizer in Pennsylvania, Ohio, and Rhode Island. Again, this opportunity allowed Menino to travel outside Massachusetts and meet new people. When Menino lost his job at the BRA, some people believe Mayor White had Menino fired. In 1979, Menino ran Timilty's last unsuccessful campaign for mayor against White.

In *Mayor for a New America*, Menino credited Timilty for his entry into politics but publicly proclaimed Gerard Doherty, not Timilty, as his mentor. Doherty, a real estate lawyer and Charlestown state representative (1957–1964), met Menino in Timilty's 1967 campaign.[33] In 1972, Doherty was Timilty's campaign manager for the state senate race. He worked with Menino in several campaigns including two presidential ones. It was Doherty who encouraged Menino to get a college degree.[34] He also invited Menino to join the Park Street Corporation, an urban issue discussion group.[35]

Surviving the 1960s and 1970s

These two decades were eventful periods of Boston's history. The John Hancock Tower and Quincy Market were built. The city's infrastructure was changing as well as the internal social dynamics. Historian Jeanne F. Theoharis cites the 1960s and 1970s school integration struggles as the inception of the Black Power movement in Boston.[36] Aside from the busing controversy, the 1970s saw the establishment of Boston Pride and the Chinese Progressive Association. Also outside events changed minorities' attitudes in the nation and in Boston. A major racial incident occurred in 1968 with the assassination of Dr. Martin Luther King Jr. on April 4. There were riots across American cities. Richard Nixon was elected president, in part because of his anti-busing stance and his pledge to restore law and order.

The decade of the 1970s saw the decline of the civil rights movement in the South, but it caused an uptick in Black demands in northern cities to end de-facto segregated schools. In 1971, the U.S. Supreme Court held in *Swann v. Charlotte Mecklenburg* that busing used to achieve school integration was constitutional. In 1974, the Boston desegregation busing conflict started because of a ruling in *Morgan v. Hennigan.*[37] Busing schoolchildren to achieve integration would be a major problem for Boston leaders.

A former Boston School Committee member and Boston councilwomen named Louise Day Hicks created an anti-busing group called Restore Our Alienated Rights. She made national news by opposing busing. Judge Arthur Garrity ordered the busing of Black children to predominately white schools. This led to a massive protest by white parents in the Irish American stronghold of South Boston. The protest went on for several days before the National Guard had to be called out to enforce the court order.

Hicks's public anti-busing tactics left a blemish on Boston's reputation as a progressive city. Hicks also left an impression on her fellow council members. In 1967, Hicks ran for mayor and lost to Kevin White by twelve thousand votes. Her slogan was "You Know Where I Stand." Candidates use such ambiguous slogans to appeal to different voters. Harvard political scientist James Q. Wilson saw the Hicks campaign against Kevin White differently. He claimed Hicks's gender was a factor and that White announced a large tax increase and "other measures intended to help a lot of Boston Negroes [which] have earned for him, in certain neighborhoods, the unflattering nickname of 'Mayor Black.'"[38]

Hicks served in Congress from 1971 to 1973 and ran again and was defeated again by Kevin White. Hicks again served on the council from 1974 to 1978. The anti-busing leader became council president in 1976. Although the schools remained essentially segregated, the Hicks era was in decline. Perhaps unconsciously, Menino learned from Hicks's rise and fall in Boston politics. The repudiation of Hicks-type politics allowed him to break out of the ethnic and race bubble.

Breaking out of the partisan bubble is often more difficult for aspiring politicians. In 1980, Menino and Doherty abandoned President Jimmy Carter and supported Senator Edward "Teddy" Kennedy for president. Carter lost the general election to Ronald Reagan. However, choices had to be made, and supporting the hometown candidate, Kennedy, made sense. Besides endorsements are often forgotten after a general campaign.

However, staying current as aspiring politicians remained complex as the future of Boston politics was linked to the nation, which was trending toward more conservative views. Reagan, a California Republican and western conservative, was elected president with the slogans of low taxes and smaller government. His rhetorical attack on welfare entitlements was threatening to cities like Boston. Reagan curtailed the mission of federal agencies and slowed the rate of growth for welfare entitlement programs.

Into the 1980s Fracas Comes Menino

The 1980s was an interesting political decade for Boston. The city of Boston reacted to the turmoil of the 1970s by establishing the Boston Fair Housing Commission and Boston Human Rights Commission. Social attitudes were changing, and citizens accepted government enforcement of civil rights. Yet the election of conservative president Ronald Reagan disrupted the narrative of the government as a tool for helping others. Reagan repudiated President Johnson's War on Poverty and the use of government to help people. For Menino the values he learned from his parents and his political party mentors allowed him to override the new narrative.

Menino, the aspiring politician, was seeking a place in Boston, now with a population of 526,994. These numbers represented a 12 percent loss in its population since 1970. Meanwhile, in 1982 Menino's one of his mentors, State Senator Joe Timilty, successfully lobbied the state legislature to create a new Boston council district, and a District 5 including Hyde Park and Roslindale became law.

Again the lessons for Menino continued. Referring to his political partnership with Menino, Gerard Doherty recalled, "Sometimes I had to kiss him and sometimes I had to kick him. He has a great capacity for growth. He asks questions to be better. His learning process never stopped. . . . It is unfair to Tommy to call me his mentor. He shaped himself. He grew himself.[39] After Timilty got the state legislature to create the new District 5, Menino saw his opportunity.

After reading that the announced candidates did not care about the neighborhoods, Menino saw his campaign theme. In 1983, Menino, the man from Readville, entered the Democratic primary with five other candidates—William G. Broderick, Constance L. Brown, Richard E. Kenney, Robert MacGregor, and George L. Richmond. Interestingly, most of the other candidates spoke about law-and-order issues. Menino did not stress this issue and described himself as the most active in the community. In the primary, he received more than 11,000 votes, twice as many as the rest of the field. Kenney, a Hyde Park resident, received 3,174 votes. After a recount, Kenney led the other three candidates by 52 votes, qualifying him for the runoff against Menino.

Kenney had been a Boston police officer and now owned a security firm. During the campaign, he promised to donate $30,000 of his $32,000 salary to a district advisory committee.[40] Menino was endorsed by the *Boston Globe* and *Boston Herald* and won the runoff by 75 percent of the vote. Kenney stated that Menino had "an unbelievable organization," and Joseph Timilty that it "did me in."[41] The reality was Menino was a better campaigner and had a network of supporters.

Tom Menino, Officeholder

As the councilor from Hyde Park, Menino was concerned with community issues, zoning, and overall ordinance-making. Each district councilor had a defined district and a political base. Menino rose up through the ranks of the City Council and learn from his new colleagues. This allowed him to meet people from neighborhoods across the city. For a man who had always been staff to other politicians, a role change would be challenging. There were lessons to be learned outside the Hyde Park bubble.

The 1980s may have offered a defining political education for Menino. Reconciling Reaganism with Boston's progressive agenda was not necessary as the city kept its commitments to liberal policies. Reaganism swept the nation's airwaves and had a profound impact on local politicians. By 1984, Menino had been a councilor for a year. Reagan was a popular president in many Boston neighborhoods.

In 1984, Raymond Flynn was elected mayor of Boston. The same year, Ronald Reagan was reelected president. The late 1980s also brought more national attention to Massachusetts and Boston when former governor Michael Dukakis became the 1988 Democratic Party nominee for president of the United States. Dukakis was the first Greek American to be a major national political party presidential nominee. He ran against Reagan's vice president, George H. W. Bush, and lost.

For young politicians like Tom Menino, every year was a learning one. In 1989, a white resident in the Mission Hill neighborhood of Boston named Charles Stuart murdered his pregnant wife and accused a Black assailant. This accusation was believed by many, including the Boston Police Department. They searched the Black community in Mission Hill looking for the assailant. They found a Black suspect but the plot was uncovered, and Stuart was revealed as the murderer and arrested. Stuart subsequently committed suicide by jumping off the Tobin Bridge in Chelsea. The distrust between the department and the minority community was further fractured with a 1989 stop-and-frisk campaign to address a gang problem. Overall, the incident represented a shameful drama that demonstrated the shocking race relations in the city and emphasized the city's reputation for racism.

These events provided yet another education for Councilor Menino. He did not directly participate in these events, but he had to explain them to his district constituency. Reporter David Nyhan described Menino's time on the Council just before he took the acting mayor job: "If he is not a symphony conductor of a politician, he'll settle for being a master mechanic. As the City Council's Ways and Means chair, then as president, he had his hands on all the paper. In the Land of Lilliput that is the City Council, he was a giant standing tall, a steady, sober centrist with a grip on reality and the city's needs, the tent pole that held up that crazy Little Apple Circus of a big top. Now incumbency is his hold card."[42]

Watching and learning would become a preoccupation for Menino. He watched as a Dorchester-born Irish politician, William Bulger, became president of the Massachusetts State Senate and one of the most powerful men in state politics. As we discuss in chapter 4, Bulger was critical to Menino's battle for a Boston Convention Center. As described in chapter 7, Menino supported charter schools and school choice. Generally speaking, the 1980s were not good years for American cities. But the overall economy was good, or at least good enough to elect George H. W. Bush as president.

Ten Years to Learn City Politics

As the councilor from Hyde Park, Menino had to establish a solid council career. He nurtured a reputation as a pro-neighborhood advocate, which along with his relatability made him popular. Menino was careful to build both an electoral career and an internal council career. He had to climb up the ranks in the City Council, and with Mayor Ray Flynn's assistance, Menino was appointed chair of the Ways and Means Committee. As such, he gained a reputation as a "vigilant watchdog of the city budget." The position allowed him to understand how the fiscal structure of the city worked. He also served on the new Committee on Tourists and Tourism. Menino claims that Ways and Means was his education: "You got to know the Budget work. You control the budget; you can control the government. I had fun at Ways and Means."[43] As chair, he learned a lot about expenditures, revenues, and taxes. The chairs of this committee were also lobbied by interest groups. Ed Capasso, a reporter who reviewed Menino's record in the committee, thought it was modest. He described Menino as a "journeyman."[44] His colleagues felt otherwise and elected him council president in 1993.

In the council, Menino was considered a loyal point man for Flynn, not a rival. As chair of the Ways and Means Committee, he disagreed with Flynn on budget issues. He also disagreed with Flynn's views on tenant rights. In 1984, Flynn ran on a tenants' rights and rent control platform. Professor and activist Peter Drier stated, "We couldn't get him [Menino] to support us [Mayor Flynn] on rent control and tenant rights. On the council, he didn't swing. His constituencies were homeowners. Menino was more of a centrist than conservative."[45]

As an interesting side note, in 1992 Menino toyed with the idea of running for Congress, a seat once held by Brian Donnelly, but the Eleventh District was redistricted out of existence. Again, Mayor Flynn supported Menino's career in his bid for city council presidency. In 1992, *Boston Globe*'s Alan Lupo sized up the Hype Park councilor as a man who knew where he came from. Menino told him, "I still have the commitment. The way their lives go, my life goes. I just feel I have to be there. They elected me. If I'm able to help people through the bureaucracy, that's the best part of the job." Lupo concluded that "Menino has a reputation as one of the best pols for constituent services, whether it's the barrier-breaking he or his aides do for somebody who's just plain confused or brokering various interests to keep the Patriot Paper Corp. in business."[46] His colleagues took notes and made the man from Readville president of the Boston City Council.

Becoming Council President

The fight for the council presidency began as early as 1992 because Council President Christopher Iannella had died and there was speculation that Mayor Flynn would take a job in Washington. Despite having Flynn's support, Menino was considered a compromise candidate. Many believed that longtime councilors James E. Byrne of Dorchester or David Scondras would get the job. Menino summarized the politics. "The 'progressive-versus-conservative' labeling confused what was really going on. 'What's a progressive? I'm more liberal than most of the progressives.' . . . As I saw it, ideology wasn't driving progressives. Political ambition was. Four of Maura's six wanted to be mayor. They assumed I did, too. (It was a safe assumption.) They knew the next council president might vault to acting mayor. And they did not want me to be the one."[47]

However, the contest came down to two people. In 1993, Menino beat Maura Hennigan Casey by a seven-to-six vote on the first ballot. If she had won, Casey would have been the first woman mayor of Boston. It was a close vote with Tony Clayton, a Black councilor, emerging as the swing vote for Menino.

Although the press tried to characterize the contest as a battle between the establishment and the liberals, it was not. Menino and Casey cast quite similar votes on the council. In the internal contest, Menino simply outflanked her. In such a context, promises needed to be made, and colleagues needed to be flattered. Menino was considered safe and simply one of the boys. He claims that no deals were made: "I just needed seven votes."[48] The majority of fellow politicians liked him and voted for him. After winning the presidency of the council, he quickly moved to distance himself from Flynn. He said, "I'm not the mayor's's man."[49]

Menino rewarded his supporters with key committee appointments. He named Brian McLaughlin to the Committee on Housing and Albert O'Neil to the Committee on Public Safety. At that point, people became aware of the possibility that, per the city charter, Menino would become acting mayor if Flynn took a job in the Clinton administration. This speculation ignited yet another round of political maneuvering among potential mayoral candidates.

The visibility of the council presidency afforded a high degree of name recognition. The job of the president of the council is also a powerful position in that it controls committee appointments and presides over council meetings. Thus, it elevated Menino to a citywide constituency.

The Council President Becomes Acting Mayor

Mayor Flynn had campaigned with Bill Clinton in swing states like Ohio and Pennsylvania to help him shore up ethnic white swing voters, particularly Catholics. In March, Flynn was interviewed by President Clinton for a position in the new government.[50] Flynn was known for working for progressive issues, promoting housing reform, advocating for people who are homeless, supporting unions, and challenging banks over racist redlining. Peter Dreier, one of his former aides, stated, "Flynn's profound sense of social justice was rooted in his Catholicism—exemplified by St. Francis, Dorothy Day, and his idol, Pope Leo XIII, the workers' Pope—and his outrage at the privileges and indifference of the rich and big business."[51] Flynn hoped to be named labor secretary or secretary of Housing and Urban Development (HUD), but he accepted Clinton's offer to appoint him ambassador to the Vatican. Clinton appointed Harvard professor Robert Reich as labor secretary and Henry Cisneros, the first Latino mayor of San Antonino, as HUD secretary.

Menino had to wait 122 days before he became acting mayor but he was now in the catbird seat. In early March 1993, Menino recalled that Flynn summoned him to his office: "Go out and get some new suits; you're going to be acting mayor."[52] On July 12, he formally became acting mayor. In a way, Menino's ascendency was like that of former Mayor Daniel A. Whelton. In 1905, Whelton, chair of the Boston Board of Aldermen, became acting mayor after the death of Mayor Patrick Collins. Whelton became the first native-born Irish American to become a Boston mayor.

Menino quickly discovered that working at City Hall is like being on alert at a firehouse. Mayors act like firefighters who spend time putting out fires. Extinguishing the fire can be enervating and revealing. As a new mayor, Menino encountered a work environment, unlike anything he experienced as a city councilor. It was not lost on anyone that Menino still had to win the November election. Winning a citywide election for an executive position is different from winning a council district election and a council presidency contest among his council colleagues. First, mayoral elections can be difficult for first-time candidates because they have to raise money, compete in primaries, interact with party leaders, and visit all parts of the city. Menino had an advantage because he had been a part of Timilty's three mayoral campaigns and had learned from their failures. He was also a better networker than his mentors and teachers.

Four months later, Tom Menino was elected on his own terms. His ascendency to the city's top political office represented the first mayor not of Irish descent since Malcolm Nichols in 1929. Naturally, Italian Americans throughout the city saw his ascendency in symbolic and ethnic terms. One resident stated, "Now people will realize that Italians are not Mafia, but workers." Another stated "It's about time an Italian came out. It's wonderful."[53] Menino made little of his ancestry and presented himself as a candidate of a new electoral coalition. And Menino was the first to deny that his election represented an "ethno-racial transition."[54] Such a coalition replaced the previous ethnic or racial coalitions. Menino's election was not a victory for Italian Americans as an ethnic group but rather a win for him, his views, and new electoral coalitions. Menino described his feelings during the transition. The win would be one of the greatest moments of his life:

> I was in charge. I had to act quickly. I did. I said no to the teacher contract. It was exciting. My god, it is all on my shoulder. I had to trust some people. I went from a staff of three to 18,000 employees. I had to gain the confidence of the workers. Some of the people were working for the opposition. My job is to help people. I have to make people feel comfortable. I had to focus on the quality of life. I had to make people stay in the neighborhoods.[55]

Menino was smart enough to know that celebration of him as the first Italian American mayor would only last so long. His new constituency expected him to get the job done. Some pundits and journalists thought that Menino would be a caretaker as acting mayor and would only last until the next election.[56] Reporter David Nyhan thought that Menino was a man only interested in simple city housekeeping duties: "Not the littlest thing to like about Menino is his penchant for the little things. Like clean streets. Menino relishes neat pavements and tidy curbs the way Kevin White prized luxurious libraries and Ray Flynn preferred basketball courts. Say hello to Mayor Menino, Pothole Buster. Do not be surprised to see the no-longer-acting may-ah cruising the Freedom Trail at dawn, on litter patrol. It starts from the ground up with this guy."[57]

The image that Nyhan captured was of a non-threatening, hard-working officeholder. Soon after taking the acting mayor job, Menino started to define himself and his goals. Few expected him to articulate a new vision for Boston or to make the needed administrative changes in city government. They were wrong. Three days in office, Menino terminated the practice of using one underwriting firm for the city's debt. Flynn's contributor Mark Ferber of Lazard Frères & Co. had held the city bond business, and now Menino opened it to other firms.[58]

Menino also merged the Boston Redevelopment Authority (BRA) and the Economic Development and Industrial Corporation. Menino had once worked at the BRA and described his job as moving small businesses out of the way of the federal highway slicing through Boston. He claimed that his vision of government was born out of the experience of watching what happened to that community. He recalled, "My job was to move small businesses out of the way of a federal highway slicing through Boston. Protest Politics stopped the highway, but not before bulldozers had scraped all the signs of life off once-thriving commercial arteries from Roxbury to Charlestown. The 'Inner Belt' was the dying gasp of Boston's 'urban removal' era. My vision of government was born then. It was the opposite of everything happening around me. Government should be about helping people, not destroying their way of life, which is how merchants in its path saw the federal bulldozer."[59]

Defining government as helping people was consistent with the Democratic Party ideology and Menino's perceptive/compassionate empathic values. Fighting for neighborhood integrity for the powerless was the essence of populism. Menino would agree with Professor Herbert J. Gans's notion of a "user-oriented paradigm [that] focuses on urban residents as actors shaping their cities rather than as passive victims of 'impersonal forces.'"[60] The plight of powerless citizens would influence Menino throughout his political life. This does not mean that Menino governed with a precise ideology. Jim Vrabel, the author of *A People's History of the New Boston*, concluded that "Menino had little in the way of vision or ideology. He was a cautious man. He wanted to *be* mayor. He wanted to *stay* mayor and he didn't risk change. His was an ideology-free administration."[61]

Perhaps the boldest decision by the acting mayor was his strong support for a new convention center, discussed in chapter 4. But it was clear that Menino wanted to be judged by the good housekeeping—keeping the city running and providing constituency services. His new constituencies were homeowners in West Roxbury, South Boston, Hyde Park, and so on. He wanted to keep the streets clean and safe. In effect, he had lower expectations, and the public was judging him on those terms. This posture worked. After Menino was elected mayor of Boston, a 1994 opinion poll found that he had an approval rating of 78 percent.[62]

Summary

Thomas Menino's political socialization by his parents and peers plus Joseph Timilty's mentoring made him into the politician he became. Growing up in a town that was regarded as an Irish stronghold, he was able to gain the respect of local Irish American politicians and managed to be in the right place at the right time. If Menino had followed Timilty's mayoral electoral strategy straightforwardly, he would have found himself in an ethnic tunnel that might have compromised his efforts to get elected citywide. He also witnessed

Louise Day Hick's anti-busing tactics and saw this politician mount a campaign around a popular but shortsighted issue and burn herself out. Menino did not want to be on the wrong side of history. He watched closely and apparently took notes on the Kevin White and Ray Flynn administrations. He knew firsthand why his mentor Joseph Timilty had lost his race for mayor.

This chapter begins the discussion of why Menino became a politician. Early on in his life, he concluded that working-class people like his family and his peers were not given a fair shake, and he used this view to outline criticisms and develop strategies for change. His brief stint at the BRA and what happened to Boston's Inner Belt reinforced these views. For him, working-class people (including minorities) were denied basic economic mobility opportunities and the solicitous consultations accorded other Bostonians. This history affected Menino's knowledge of politics and his notion that a mayor could be a change agent. His public decisions were mediated by his childhood and peer socialization. He would always be an Italian American from Hyde Park. Becoming a public figure or a celebrity opens one up to jokes and put-downs. He would be called "mumbles" and speaking "mumbonics." Using a successful politician as a pinata is a staple of American journalism. If the politician reacts, they can be called "thin-skinned." Yet becoming mayor was unlikely to change his basic personality. This is why it is important to understand the linkage between Menino's socialization and his intuition, negotiation style, and decision-making process.

As we see in the next chapter, Menino spent his days as the acting mayor of Boston saying and doing the right thing. He avoided career-ending gaffes. The interregnum between his becoming the acting mayor and his being elected allowed him to confirm his authenticity and trustworthiness. Establishing trustworthiness by a politician is a way to establish a bond between politicians and their constituencies. Character defines one's personality and exposes what one has learned ethically. This is why the study of Menino's character is so important for understanding who he was. This is why his former press secretary Dot Joyce stated, "The mayor's character was above reproach. He worked fiercely to protect the city in the only way he knew how. He worked from 6:00 a.m. to 11:00 p.m. crisscrossing the city and meeting people. He understood the neighborhoods block by block. They called him an 'urban mechanic.' But he worked hard to build the trust of the city in order to make policy changes. The strategy he employed was brilliant. Everything worked at the basic level. The streets were clean. Taxes were as low as possible."[63]

As mayor, Menino was allowed to show his real character. Abraham Lincoln said, "Character is like a tree and reputation like a shadow. The shadow is what we think of it; the tree is the real thing."[64] To understand Menino, one must understand why his basic socialization mattered. He grew up in an intact family and with the help of his mentors became an alert and altruistic mayor. As George Guida stated, such individuals seek *ripresa*, a search for social and spiritual fulfillment. Menino was also a church-going man. At his funeral at Most Precious Blood Church in Hyde Park, a priest held up Menino's prayer book and said that "he read his prayer book every single Sunday."[65] In the following chapters, we show how Menino's character made him an attractive candidate for elective office and a man who was so admired.

CHAPTER 2

Winning Every Four Years

The old saying is, "If you want to win a mayor's race in a big city, all you have to do is to keep repeating the two refrains—jobs, jobs, jobs, and housing, housing, housing." However, getting elected mayor of a city is more complicated than just repeating the two trinities. Presenting oneself as a problem-solver and civic representative requires talent and an ability to read and appeal to voters. Mayoral contests are often described as retail politics on steroids. Candidates have to go where the voters are and convince them that they alone can make life better. In effect, candidates have to build an electoral constituency. Indeed, they must speak to several constituencies—homeowners, renters, shop owners, city workers, and political activists. All are looking for cues in a candidate's speeches. There are also registered voters who show up at the polls and non-registered residents. How do candidates get registered voters to vote and get non-registered individuals to register? In the academic field of voting behavior, municipal elections have not received the attention given to congressional and presidential elections. It is interesting to discover that few local academic scholars claim to be experts on Boston voting behavior. Perhaps this gap in research is because municipal elections are truly what Tip O'Neill meant about politics in general: "All politics are local." Usually, mayoral elections are held in off- or odd years, that is, against the federal election cycle. Municipal elections usually do not involve a large amount of money, and the ads created for candidates are not as sophisticated as in campaigns for federal offices. City elections are notorious for low voter turnout. Absent a scandal or outright incompetence, incumbent mayors usually win reelections. More importantly, many cities have adopted nonpartisan election systems, which have resulted in intra-party contests among personalities within the same party. This situation has led some cities to adopt term limits to prevent a single individual from dominating the city's politics.

In the classic *The American Voter* (1960), Angus Campbell and colleagues found that American voters were habitual and predictable. Their voting patterns and political attitudes were reflections of their socioeconomic backgrounds. Voters grew up either as Democrats or Republicans. They voted for the party of their parents unless some cross-pressure caused them to switch parties or candidates. Although the book is sixty-three years old, subsequent voting behavior research has yet to refute their findings. However, municipal elections are not mini versions of national elections. So, the voting profiles of the three electorates—local, state, and federal—can be somewhat different. The campaign issues in city elections are usually local, but candidates do mix their promises with a critique of local, state, and federal policies. Local politicians that grow up in the city and went to a local high school or college have an advantage over newcomers. One can be born in a different city, but candidates have to establish residency and become permanent residents. Voters want to think that they know the candidate.[1]

In 1971, political scientist Howard D. Hamilton found that the "composition of the de facto municipal electorate is far less representative of the populace than is that of the presidential electorate."[2] Many people who vote in presidential elections don't bother to do so in municipal elections. Subsequent studies of municipal elections suggest the same patterns of low turnout in municipal elections. Do voters feel that national issues are more relevant to their life chances than local ones? What has changed since Campbell and colleagues' classic study is the declining significance of party identification, nonpartisan electors, and party organizations, and the increasing significance of media and money in campaigns. These early analyses have been replicated and modernized by later political scientists. Party dealignment and the rise of independent voters have changed the context of post-1990 city elections and the political strategies of candidates. City elections, especially in Boston, are contests between the same party members. The Republican Party is more active across the state than in the city. Within both parties, self-starters and mavericks are not uncommon.

In this chapter, we review the five mayoral elections of Tom Menino. He won these elections despite an incredible and rapid change in the Boston electorate. He had a series of attractive opponents, but they were not competitive until his last race. We identify how Menino created an electoral coalition of diverse members and how he kept it together. Over Menino's twenty-year tenure, the issues in Boston changed, therefore his opponents had to reformulate issues against him.

In Boston elections, voters select mayoral candidates based on popularity, social background, and leadership ability. Name recognition is critical. Building name recognition requires ambitious politicians to do or say something salient and newsworthy. Being well-connected, experienced, and famous is not enough. One must be considered trustworthy and constituency-oriented. Also, the issues are usually local ones. Property taxes, crime, neighborhood integrity, economic development, and school improvements are the most common campaign issues. The choice voters make is often determined by who makes the best case. Candidate A is better than candidate B because they promise to keep the streets clean, stop crime, and bring jobs to the city. Voters tend to reelect incumbents if they believe they are doing a good job or the best job under the circumstances. In Boston mayoral elections, the advantage goes to the incumbent because they can act on issues, raise more money than their opponents, and get the most media coverage. Mayors like Tom Menino tend to grow on voters. A prudent mayor tries to avoid disruptive controversies, scandals, and intergroup conflicts. In doing so, a mayor can disarm local politicians and make themself unbeatable.

Tom Menino, the Candidate

Generally speaking, most citizens rarely get a chance to interact with a mayoral candidate directly. However, those who do—such as journalists, fellow city politicians, and community and corporate leaders—are afforded a look that enables them to size up the person, their skills, and their shortcomings. In Boston, City Council members have often imagined themselves as the next mayor of the city. It is from this small circle of people a challenger to the sitting mayor is usually born. Membership in the council is not without its perks and privileges, but it lacks the political power and visibility of the mayor. So, when Menino ascended to the mayoralty, many of his former City Council colleagues became convinced that they were more qualified and better suited to lead the city. Furthermore, in some pundits' opinion, Menino's tenure as acting mayor was essentially uneventful. Many of his friends on the council decided to challenge their former colleague from Hyde Park.

Anytime a mayoral candidate has the prefix "acting or interim" before their title, they become the target of would-be mayoral candidates. Potential candidates assumed that Menino got the job because he had Flynn's support and the votes from the City Council. Many of them did not believe Menino had supporters in other parts of Boston. They thought he would be vulnerable in the upcoming primary. Most of his opponents discounted his organizing ability in presidential campaigns and his campaign work for Joseph Timilty. For them, Menino had proven he was a council vote-getter, a nice guy, but not the type of guy the voters wanted to represent the city. Coupled with the fact that Menino had never run an at-large citywide campaign, many city politicians were convinced they could beat him. They thought that whatever Menino was selling in Hyde Park could not be sold citywide. Besides, Menino was considered a poor campaigner, and the media made fun of his speech impediment. Bostonians supposedly expected a certain verbal sophistication that Menino lacked. But Menino presented himself as a neighborhood candidate. As his opponent, Councilor David Scondras, described him, "Tom tends to be careful about undertaking innovation. He tends to want to make sure it will work before he tries to do it. Therefore, you are liable to get decisions that are relatively risk-free. That is exactly what you want out of a caretaker."[3] Such statements were designed to lend support to the media framing of Menino.

Media Framing of the Acting Mayor

When it became evident that Menino was going to be a player in Boston politics and history, the media began to frame the man from Hyde Park to make him amenable to the inadvertent readers or listeners as well as to the attentive public. They had a choice to package his story and his political rise in either positive or negative terms. Otherwise, how could they explain candidate Menino as a choice? The process started by referencing his awkward speaking style. Menino was considered inarticulate. Brian McGrory, a *Boston Globe* reporter, stated, "At first blush, few would make the argument that Menino cuts an impressive figure. His tongue is often tied, his voice is guttural and his attempts at humor sometimes veer to the awkward. The only apparent benefit of hours of speech lessons is that now when he talks of zoning ordinances and business incentives, he gesticulates like a Shakespearean actor."[4] *Boston Herald* reporter Marjorie Howard opined after Menino was elected,

> We may have grown fond of the way Mumbles Menino drops entire syllables and mangles his sentences. But would his words be deciphered in D.C.? Would his speech sound like sputtering in Spokane?

> Image makers and speech consultants say Menino's local campaign strategists correctly chose not to polish the rough image or clean up the mayor's mumbling. Voters, they rightly figured, would view the malapropisms and lost syllables as the characteristics of someone they feel comfortable with; someone, perhaps, from their own neighborhood.
>
> But now that Tom Menino is officially the mayor (or mayah) of what portends to be a world-class city, consultants say he should learn to speak properly.[5]

In other words, the mayor is not like journalists and educated people, but he is a caring person, and his election demonstrates that anyone can ascend to the city's highest elected office. This comment was also an attempt to make sense of the 1993 campaign and why a sophisticated city like Boston would elect such a person. In Boston society, glibness and locution have their place. The ability to speak in paragraphs and reference oneself with memorable quotes is prized in some circles. Menino had none of that *suave in da boner*. The *Boston Herald* called Menino "Tongue-Tied Tom."[6] Would young Bostonian vote for a man cut from a working-class cloth? Could Menino compete for voters outside of Hyde Park? Would the rising Yuppie class vote for a guy who had trouble pronouncing simple words? These questions were intriguing to pundits as they waited for the pending September 1993 eight-candidate primary.

Bostonians Go to the Voting Booth

The pre-election narrative about Menino being a simple "housekeeping mayor" and the need for a more articulate and vision-discerning individual was not enough to defeat him. Reporters began challenging Menino's credentials for the job. What was his vision for the future of Boston? A *Boston Herald* reporter reviewed a WBUR pre-election interview with Menino. When asked by two reporters, Menino dismissed the concept of vision. Then he turned the tables on the reporters: "What do you mean by vision?" Menino asked. "You tell me." There was silence." The reporter, Monica Collins, concluded, "Tom Menino is right. A vision of the shining city on the hill doesn't amount to a hill of beans if the streetlight outside your house doesn't work. No city shines when the bulbs burn out. . . . Surprisingly, it was the one issue raised to which the mayoral candidate responded absolutely forcefully, even articulately. . . . Menino defiantly said he didn't have a vision. Certainly, he had ideas for making the city better, but he didn't have an overall, overreaching scheme."[7]

Perhaps Menino should have repeated the alleged aphorism of Yogi Berra: "It's tough to make predictions, especially about the future." Menino wanted an economically stable city, and he sold himself politically to voters as a caring, meticulous, down-to-earth candidate who respected everyone regardless of districts, neighborhoods, and social background. His opponents needed to develop a narrative that Boston would be better off without him. Accordingly, they needed to develop an appropriate appeal for the various demographics of the major city neighborhoods. A speech in South Boston had to promise the same things as one in Roxbury but somehow had to be stated differently. In the latter, a presentation must be done neutrally and not evoke racism, provincialism, or class preference.

In order to understand where these different 1993 voters were located, I decided to select eight wards for observation. They were selected because of their demographic makeup and at the suggestion of local longtime politicians and activists. The first four were North Dorchester, Ward 14; North Dorchester and parts of Mattapan and Roxbury (so-called Black Dorchester); Dorchester Ward 15, which covers the Meeting Hall and Adams Street area; and Dorchester Ward 17, which includes Codman Square and Lower Mills. Having over 80 percent of nonwhite residents, these wards were considered minority ones. The predominately white wards included West Roxbury (including Roslindale), which had over 80 percent white residents. Tom Menino's home ward, Hyde Park, had 72 percent white residents, but it was considered a mixed ward. This was also true for Charlestown, with over 70 percent white residents. South Boston, which includes East and West Broadway and Broadway Station, with its 90 percent white residents, was considered the major haven for Irish Americans.

For a candidate to win the primary, they had to make substantial inroads into Dorchester, West Roxbury, and South Boston. Since Boston had nonpartisan elections, the top two vote-getters in the primary would be allowed into the runoff. Nonpartisan elections, once thought to be good government reform, had morphed into a system of large numbers of Democratic candidates competing with each other, leaving Republican candidates with no forum and spot on the ballot. The year 1993 was going to be the test of Menino, the acting mayor's policies and popularity.

Mayoral Primary, 1993

The beginning of the 1990s would be challenging. By 1990, Boston's population had grown to 574,263, a modest increase of 2 percent. These could be new voters, and the candidates had to introduce themselves to these new residents. Acting Mayor Tom Menino initially faced eight opponents in the 1993 nonpartisan primary, some of whom were City Council members and had nearly as much name recognition as Menino himself. Pundits did not know it then, but this was the critical election in the Menino era. Bostonians wanted to see what they had in the acting mayor. The campaign allowed the voters to evaluate Menino against his opponents. Menino's personality was so different from his predecessors. He was not flamboyant but steady and likable. Menino came across to voters as an empathic person.

The local media organized a series of debates to have the candidates talk about city problems. Some were televised live and followed by reporters asking questions. The question topics included the budget, taxes, crime, schools, and economic development. In the debate, some of the candidates, particularly the more articulate ones, sounded more informed than Menino. But having served as acting mayor, Menino had a record from a few months of service. In the debates, many of his opponents came across as just being critics of Menino rather than being able to present an alternate way of managing the city. Menino came across as doing the best he could, given his temporary status and the unfinished business of Boston.

Although many of Menino's opponents had endorsements from other politicians, none of them had campaigned across the city. Former mayor Ray Flynn, now ambassador to the Vatican, supported Francis Mickey Roache, a boyhood friend and his police commissioner, in the primary. Yet Roache, who was once thought to be a rising star in city politics, had had an embattled tenure as commissioner. He failed to distinguish himself in that job and had not made much of an impression on Boston voters. The same could be said of Norfolk County sheriff Robert C. Rufo. If this primary had been a law-and-order election, Rufo and Roache could have been able to use their credential as crime fighters to shift the political discourse from other issues to the turmoil in the street. Rufo opened his campaign by announcing that he would give Roche "a failing grade in terms of his ability to manage the Boston Police Department."[8] Rufo believed the contest was between Roache and himself. Dismissing Menino proved to be Rufo's undoing.

City Councilor-at-Large Rosaria Salerno, having run citywide three times, supposedly had more citywide support. Salerno was thought by many pundits to have the best chance to beat the Menino. A former Benedictine nun, she had made several controversial statements about Catholic church leader Cardinal Bernard Law. Called Sister Mary Sunshine, she was regarded by pundits as the most serious female mayoral candidate since Louise Hicks. She received a dispensation from the Vatican in 1980 to leave the church, but she had continued to do much of the work she did as a nun.

Salerno asserted, "Tom Menino has been generously rewarded by the real estate speculators for his loyalty. . . . The residents of Boston's neighborhoods, however, should ask whose interests their unelected acting mayor will ultimately protect."[9] In an early poll, Salerno was running even with Menino, 21 and 23 percent, respectively.[10] However, she could not raise enough money to be competitive. What worked for her in the council elections did not work in the mayoral one. Political scientists Arnold Fleischmann and Lana Stein found that "money was not an important predictor of outcomes in city council elections, which may not be surprising given small districts, where 'shoe leather' campaigns are possible. However, the degree to which money gravitated toward powerful citywide offices and safe candidates suggests that the power relationship between contributors and candidates may be reciprocal: not only might contributors exert power, but groups may be afraid not to give to powerful officials."[11]

James Brett, a state legislator from the Suffolk district, was also thought to be a true comer in Irish American politics. In the state senate, he was known for his advocacy for handicapped citizens. He had also fought for a ban on assault weapons. Dianne Wilkerson, one of the most powerful Black politicians in the state, endorsed Brett. His wife had worked for William Bulger, the powerful state senate leader, and Brett had endorsements from several unions. He supposedly had the Irish American political machine behind him as well.

Bruce C. Bolling, a Black city councilor, was long considered to have a chance to become the first successful African American candidate for mayor. His family had been identified with Boston politics for a generation. His father, Royal Bolling Sr., was a state senator. Bruce Bolling, the first African American City Council president, had built a reputation in the council as a moderate. Unlike the mayoral candidacy of Mel King, a Black political activist, Bolling was presented as a deracialized candidate like David Dinkins in New York and Norman Rice of Seattle. However, the Bolling candidacy was undermined by various political conflicts within the Black community. His primary campaign was hampered by the decision by Wilkerson to endorse Brett. Councilor Anthony Clayton, the man who cast the deciding vote for Menino to become City Council president, also endorsed Menino for mayor. Despite an endorsement by the *Boston Globe*, Bolling finished with just 6 percent of the vote in the primary.[12]

The primary contest was mainly fought at community forums with 97,234 members of the public voting. Brett came in second to Menino with 25,052, or 27.9 percent of the vote. Menino led the primary with 30,060, or 30.9 percent of the vote. Roache got only 3 percent. This was less than Lydon (3.2%). Robert Rufo ended up with 22,517, or 23 percent of the vote. Bruce Bolling got 5.8 percent. Moriarty received fewer than 1,000 votes (0.89%), and Salerno finished with 19,605, or 20 percent. The general election was next, and Menino would face James Brett.

In her concession speech, Rosaria Salerno asserted, "We are disappointed because we waged a campaign against politics as usual and politics as usual prevailed."[13] Later, she and Bolling endorsed Menino. The *Boston Globe* editorial board endorsed Menino for the general election, stating, "He is better prepared by experience and temperament to make the drastic changes needed to ensure that vital services, such as public education, are maintained despite fiscal constraints. . . . Tom Menino is not a flashy candidate and is not likely to be a flashy mayor. But he understands the city and represents its solid values."[14]

Menino versus Brett

The runoff between Brett, a man from Savin Hill, and Menino, a man from Readville, was supposed to be high political drama. The *Boston Globe* ran a picture of a large crowd of Brett's supporters marching down West Broadway in South Boston.[15] The race was framed as a contest between an inarticulate accidental mayor against an eloquent speaker and the so-called establishment candidate (backed by the powerful state senator William Bulger). Again, for some this race was supposed to be a defining political moment in Boston's history. However, it was a contest between two insiders. In a late October poll, 70 percent stated that they approved of Menino's performance as acting mayor.[16] In this poll, Brett ran well among minorities and high-income Bostonians. Yet he was also losing among Irish Americans.

After the runoff election, Menino appointed Tomas Gonzalez as his aide. Gonzalez recalled,

> When I first met Menino [in 1993], I was interviewing to be the Hispanic liaison. He said, "Your people [Puerto Ricans] cause me a lot of headaches." A flashback, during his mayoral campaign the Cuban community supported Menino while the majority of the Puerto Rican community supported Jim Brett, a Dorchester state representative. Although, the Puerto Ricans comprised the largest share of the Latino vote—80 to 90 percent of the Latino community—their efforts couldn't propel Brett to be the mayor. There was also an organization called "Communities of Color" led by Darry Smith and Brooke Woodson. They were a part of the first Menino campaign and every campaign since.[17]

In the general election, there were some daunting issues before the city, but the media decided to concentrate on both the personalities of the two men and Irish American domination of Boston politics. Ironically, Menino ran a nonethnic race. He reported that his pollster, Tubby Harrison, told him "to be tough on crime" and that law and order were the top issues.[18] The *New York Times* thought that it was "grim times and dwindling hopes," as most of the nation's city mayoral races were focusing on crime. The paper reported that Menino and Brett had competing plans for combating crime. Brett pledged to add four hundred new police officers and pay them with federal money and new taxes. Menino countered with a pledge to add one hundred new officers every year of his term. He also wanted to merge the three police departments, Boston Police Department, Boston Housing Authority Police, and the school police.[19] The problem with the law-and-order issue for a candidate like Menino was that it had the potential of alienating growing minority communities. Menino refused to take Harrison's advice and concentrated on neighborhood issues instead.

As a former council member, Menino understood why Bostonians, especially small homeowners, were concerned about their future in Boston. They wanted better city services and to feel safe. Most of all, they wanted someone who cared about the neighborhoods. After the primary, Rosaria Salerno was one of the first to endorse Menino. She asserted, "I have decided to endorse Tom Menino because I believe that he is the candidate who is most committed to fundamental change. The other candidate may use the rhetoric of bold change, but his voting record has been in support of the status quo at the State House."[20] Bruce Bolling also endorsed Menino. Menino's theme of taking care of neighborhoods proved to be a winning one. He defeated Brett 64.4 to 35.6 percent, a landslide victory. Table 1 shows voting by wards.

Table 1. Voting Tallies of Brett-Menino Race by Ward

WARD	MENINO	BRETT
1	5,598	1,551
2	2,630	1,972
3	4,035	1,300
4	2,563	739
5	4,104	1,336
6	2,701	3,062
7	2,620	3,634
8	792	256
9	1,638	513
10	1,785	818
11	2,218	776
12	2,088	579
13	1,331	2,556
14	2,388	657
15	921	862
16	2,520	5,123
17	2,349	1,706
18	11,162	3,353
19	4,618	1,706
20	9,647	5,353
21	2,647	1,094
22	4,006	2,187
TOTAL	74,361	41,133

Note: Other candidates received 13 votes.
Source: Boston Department of Elections, 1993, 80.

For the Menino campaign, certain ward voters were critical to establishing his base. First instituted in his initial campaign, these wards remained consistent throughout his electoral career. Table 2 shows voter turnout percentages in critical wards and the margins by which Menino won in a 1993 neighborhood breakdown.

60   CHAPTER 2

Table 2. 1993 Results in Critical Wards

WARDS	PERCENTAGE OF VOTES CAST	WINNING MARGIN FOR MENINO
Dorchester 14	78.4	56.8
Dorchester 15	51.6	3.31
Dorchester 17	56.8	13.3
Hyde Park	77.7	99.9
West Roxbury	64.5	29.0
Charlestown	57.1	14.3
South Boston	46.8	-6.2
Roxbury	78.2	56.6

Source: Boston Department of Elections, 1993

Menino got 74,361 votes (64.5%) to Brett's 41,133 (35.5%). With the exception of South Boston, the Irish American stronghold, Menino defeated Brett in other critical neighborhoods. These results would prove to be an important election as many of the pundits' predictions were proved false. It was a shock to the political establishment, the Democratic Party, self-declared political analysts, and the local media. Was this a deviating election or was it a realignment of ethnic and racial groups? Menino was not the most articulate politician in the city. He did not promise to redistribute the wealth of the city. How could this happen in the Athens of America and to its reputation of being the incubator for the nation's most prominent progressive politicians?

This election was a surprising landslide victory. It proved that Boston did not want a caretaker and, more importantly, Menino agreed: "I am now your mayor.... The city can't afford to have a caretaker. Over the next several weeks and months, there are a lot of decisions to be made. You have to move the city forward. You can't be a caretaker for four or five months. We can't let the city float for the next several months. This is Boston; this isn't one person's empire." Menino further stated, "I rejected those voices that said, 'Tom, sit back and be a caretaker.' We went to work shaking the cobwebs out of City Hall. We began to change Boston. Tonight we made clear our bottom line. The status quo must go.'"[21]

In the same article, Menino repeated his mantra, "I'm no fancy talker."[22] It worked. Menino was able to defeat some of the city's best-known politicians because he read voters' policy preferences and expectations. However, it was the way he did it (winning the key ethnic and minority wards) that was so impressive. Menino has achieved something that his mentor Joseph Timilty had failed three times to accomplish. However, Menino's election was also not about the rise of Italian Americans as some reporters wanted to frame it nor was it what political scientist Robert A. Dahl called "the new men." These were ascending politicians that succeeded the descending ethnic election officials.[23] Indeed, Thomas Menino would be a de-ethnicized "new" man. He had tipped his hat to the Irish American politicians and greeted and listened to well-known leaders in the Black community. Also, as acting mayor, he had attended several events with Black organizations, something that Menino's opponents did not do and that paid dividends in winning over minority voters.

After the election, *Boston Globe* reporter Peter Canellos claimed that Menino remained impervious to embarrassment and his mind was fixed on results. Canellos noted that when debate panelists questioned Menino's intelligence and ability, the acting mayor brushed off the insults. Menino recalled spending two hours with a CEO to attract business to Boston. He stated, "I've always had to work twice as hard as anyone else" to get ahead, "but it's been worth it. I've always felt you have to build a solid foundation to get anywhere. That's what I did over the past 10 years. I built a foundation."[24]

Wisely, Menino spent the next four years consolidating his popularity. He did the small things—housekeeping tasks—and no serious controversies stuck to him. In many ways, he reminded urban historians of Baltimore mayor William Donald Schaefer (1971–1981), who spent his attention on the street problems. Schaefer rode around the city looking for uncollected garbage and ordered that it be collected immediately. Like Menino, Schaefer appointed African Americans to important city offices. Schaefer was called "America's Best Mayor."[25] Menino also received honors from his colleagues. Regardless, despite staff turnover and notable political events, Menino kept his eye on the prize.

In 1996, *Boston Globe* reporter Patricia Smith, who was considered one of the most influential columnists at the paper, wrote,

> Thomas Menino touts the neighborhoods, becomes part of them, pounds the pavements, and lends his ear, looking silly and solemn and donning the gear, talking the talk, being there. His conversation always steers back to that place that is most comfortable for him, that place with a million accents and shades of skin, that place where people cry and work and fight and make love and raise children and that is the city that is many cities, and he works to make all those cities his. Mention Mattapan or Southie or Blue Hill Ave. and he has stories to tell, stories with real people inside. Indeed, there are concepts beyond his grasp. He

mispronounces, misunderstands, and still seems ill at ease in a world of tight collars, backroom deals, and burnished wingtips. But the closer he gets to real people, the better he looks. This isn't a love letter. Mayor Menino may screw up royally sometime soon; after all, he is a politician, and this is Boston. But the end of a year is traditionally a time to count blessings. And this city could do a lot worse than a guy spending his Christmas Eve bringing a little Christmas goofiness to the 'hood, zooming an unfamiliar appliance toward the head of a nervously laughing constituent. Citizen Tom, keep strolling, keep listening, keep insisting on the melting pot. Your being everywhere, real in the midst of this, is incredibly cool.[26]

This quotation captured and defined the image Menino was attempting to achieve. Near the end of his first full term, no major politicians would challenge him in the primary. Running unopposed denoted a recognition of Menino's political skills. Meanwhile, Menino oversaw the merger of Boston City Hospital and Boston University Medical Center. The new, private Boston Medical Center would provide more healthcare for the city's poor residents.

Running Unopposed, 1997

The conventional wisdom has been that Menino's strategy of taking care of the neighborhoods, dialoguing with minority leaders, replacing school superintendents, de-ethnicizing Boston politics, and inviting economic development was successful. Tom Menino was so popular in the second elected term that he had no primary challengers. His inclusive leadership style had worked. For a man who was not a good public speaker, the next challenge was to address the maligned Boston school system. As is discussed in chapter 8, the successful 1996 fight for an appointed school board demonstrated Menino's electoral invincibility. It was a dress rehearsal for the 1997 mayoral election. Aside from a high approval rating, Menino had garnered massive business support for keeping an appointed Boston School Committee. Menino was also adept at including minority leaders in his electoral coalition. There was simply no room for his opponents to grow a campaign.

He had made peace with most of the city's interest groups and community leaders. The mayor had attended prayer services in Black churches. Community leaders could call him directly, and he would respond to their complaints and suggestions. Reverend Eugene Rivers, a community organizer and highly visible African American pastor of the Azusa Christian Community, endorsed his reelection: "I think Menino deserves a second term for two reasons: He's done an excellent job building bridges and he's got an agenda for education which I think needs to be aggressively supported."[27]

None of the City Council members dared to challenge Menino after what happened to James Brett. This was unique in modern Boston history. One would have expected some of the 1993 challengers to try again but they did not. Why not? The short answer was that Menino's leadership style had grown on voters. Even with no serious opponents in 1997, Menino ran a sophisticated reelection campaign. According to Abraham, this was done "to draw enough voters to the polls to give him a convincing stamp of approval."[28] He was not interested in using the position of mayor as a steppingstone to a higher position like his predecessor, Ray Flynn. Although Menino was elected president of the U.S. Conference of Mayors, he was content with being the mayor of Boston. He once stated, "I'm satisfied with being mayor. This is the best job in America. One minute you're sitting with a bank president, the next you're with a bunch of kids in a classroom. Being with the people, that's my oxygen."[29] He had few critics and had not presented himself as an ethnic politician or a partisan. Irish American politicians, as well as other groups, were allowed to keep their space in city politics.

The long answer is that there was a sea change in Boston politics. The so-called Boston Miracle, in which there was a 63 percent reduction in youth crime, discussed in chapter 5, had lasted two years and four months. No teenagers were shot and killed during this period. There was also an exponential growth of the minority population. In chapter 6 we discuss how these groups fragmented themselves along the lines of their families' origins. City voters were exhausted from the Flynn years and wanted a less ambitious mayor. More importantly, Menino depoliticized city politics by stressing housekeeping over ideology and group conflict. This was a clever strategy that emphasized discerning the perspective of others, recognizing self-appointed spokespersons, and finally smothering competition among competing interests. However, even such a clever strategy can wear thin. Four years later, there emerged new mayoral candidates from the City Council.

The 2001 Election

In March 2001, the *Boston Herald* found that 74 percent of respondents thought Menino should run for a third term.[30] The polls pitted him against several potential candidates—Francis Roache, Peggy Davis-Mullen, Maura Hennigan,

Speaker Tom Finneran, and Suffolk County district attorney Ralph Martin. None of them got over 16 percent support. Althea Garrison, a Black former state representative and so-called perennial candidate for the City Council, also ran.

According to that 2001 poll, Davis-Mullen got only 11 percent in that poll, but she decided to run against the mayor. A South Boston native who had moved to West Roxbury and a former member of the Boston School Committee, she emerged as Menino's major opponent. She was a city councilor at large and argued that the mayor lacked the vision Boston deserved. A former head of the council's Education Committee, she had developed a reputation as an activist and advocate of neighborhood schools. On the council, she was one of the mayor's most verbal critics. She attempted to present herself as the candidate of the have-nots. However, the *Boston Globe* discovered that she had not filed income taxes for 1998 and 1999. This revelation undermined her candidacy.

In the April poll, the *Boston Globe* found that Davis-Mullen would likely lose 63 to 17 percent if the election were held then.[31] The *Boston Herald* did a poll that found that the mayor had an 85 percent favorable rating. Davis-Mullen only had a 42 percent favorable rating.[32] Her campaign had few resources and no major endorsements. Her fundraising was in the thousands while Menino raised over $1 million. Journalist Jon Keller described her campaign as "running on empty."[33] She was trying hard but didn't catch on. Her campaign was doomed to fail.

During the campaign, Davis-Mullen's aides and campaign staff began to quit before the election, as she had no money to pay them. Sensing a weak opponent, Menino decided to agree to one debate. During the debate, Davis-Mullen, who was the more articulate of the two, attacked the mayor's record and put him on the defensive.[34] Otherwise, the campaign was uneventful, and the incident was never again discussed.

The 2001 campaign was also overshadowed by the 9/11 terrorist attacks in New York City. Boston city residents were concerned some of the terrorists had actually lived in Boston before the attack and had come from Logan Airport. Although this event did not happen in Boston, the city reacted with an intensification of security measures. Like most major cities, Boston prepared for additional potential attacks at its airport, buildings, and streets. Once such an event occurs there are always perceived and real threats to all city residents.

New York mayor Rudy Giuliani and President George W. Bush made a point of projecting images of being strong men in this time of crisis. It became even more difficult for a woman with no experience managing a crisis and little political support to make a case to replace Menino. And Menino said all the right things during and after the crisis. In a WBUR radio interview, he later reflected on that day:

> As mayor, I had to keep my upper lip, I had to be strong, I had to show the public that I was in control. That weekend it was so strange in the city, nobody was out and I walked most of the city that day, just so people [could] see that I was walking around. I went to three or four restaurants just to be seen because people were staying home, they weren't leaving their homes, they were afraid to leave their homes.
>
> It was very difficult, but that was my job. I had to stand up and try to reassure the public that we were in control, we never lost control of the city, but you have inner feelings, you have feelings for people, you knew a couple of those folks. One of the kids on the plane was a hockey line mate of my son's.
>
> You know, you get off your public piece and then you go in your back room—two different pieces, two different pieces of you. Because you go in your back room and you just sit there and you pray and you wonder, would we be the next place that was going to be attacked? And you did that for about five, six, seven, eight minutes, then you have to go back out and face the questions of folks and I have to make sure that they know what's going on.[35]

Many Bostonians were concerned and frightened. They needed to be reassured. The *Boston Globe* endorsed Menino's reelection bid: "He deserves good marks for improving neighborhood business districts, spearheading crime reduction strategies, and pressing continuously for reforms in public education. The Globe endorses his bid for reelection."[36] Menino got 31,715 votes (73%) in the primary against Davis-Mullen's 9,958 (23%). Althea Garrison got only 1,552 (3.5%). In the general election, Menino got 68,011 votes (76%) while Davis-Mullen got only 21,393 votes (24%).[37] The election was an overwhelming vote of confidence for the mayor. Menino was strong in critical wards and neighborhoods. He would again meet new challenges in the city and tackle the recurrent politics of the state and federal government. At the end of the third term, he decided to run again.

The 2005 Election

Tom Menino's decision to run for a fourth term was mildly controversial. Kevin White had served four terms. Menino was still popular, in good health, and loved the job. In the 2005 primary, Maura A. Hennigan challenged Menino.

Hennigan, a longtime City Council member, had lost to Menino in the 1993 election for council leadership. If she had beaten Menino in that election, she would have been the first female mayor of the city. Hennigan took the unprecedented step of mortgaging her home in Jamaica Plain to fund her campaign. The subtext of her campaign was that Menino had been in office too long and had lost touch with the people. A newspaper poll, which had 66 percent of people supporting the mayor, also indicated that Menino had low marks for services and safety. In the same poll, 28 percent did not know Hennigan.[38] She claimed that she would do a better job than Menino on issues of economic development and managing city problems. She raised questions about Boston University's proposal to build a level 4 bio-lab in the South End. She also attempted to link Menino to the death of Emerson College student Victoria Snelgrove, who was killed by a police pepper pellet gun during a celebration of the Boston Red Sox winning the American League Championship in 2004.

Hennigan proved to be a good speaker and held her own in a televised debate, but she could not make the case to replace Menino. The media was polite but not enthusiastic about her. She also had no noteworthy endorsements from leading city politicians, but she did get an endorsement from the Black Political Task Force. However, the African American–owned *Bay State Banner* endorsed Menino. The paper cited the merger of the Boston hospitals, neighborhood development, and the school superintendent's Efficacy Project. It stated, "While she is a very likable person, Maura Hennigan has not been able to amass a significant record even though she was first elected councilor-at-large in 1981. On the other hand, after 12 years in office, Tom Menino has been able to prove himself to be one of Boston's outstanding mayors in recent history."[39]

During the last seven days of the campaign, Menino received support from a recorded phone message to voters from former president Bill Clinton: "I am asking you to vote Tuesday for my friend, Mayor Tom Menino, perhaps the best big-city mayor in America."[40] A Suffolk University poll found that 58 percent of likely Boston voters planned to vote for Menino and only 28 percent for Hennigan. Fourteen percent were undecided. The mayor's personal popularity was 71 percent favorable and 20 percent unfavorable. David Paleologos, director of the Suffolk University poll, stated, "Mayor Menino's numbers are clearly off the charts." The same poll found a total of 66 percent of likely Boston voters gave Menino an "excellent/good" rating, while just 33 percent indicated "fair" or "poor."[41]

Four days later, Menino got 64,001 votes (68%) of the vote to Hennigan's 30,468 (32%). Again, the mayor was able to prevail in the critical wards he needed to win. But he had served for a long time and people began speculating about whether he would try for another term. In 2006, Menino joined New York mayor Michael Bloomberg in his fight against illegal guns. Menino was co-chair of the Mayors Against Illegal Guns Coalition. In 2007, fifty-two mayors joined the two mayors. Menino stated, "Illegal guns are a national problem that demands a national response. We are only as strong as each of our members."[42] This was not a risky position to take for a mayor who led a liberal city. Gun control was part of the progressive narrative. Massachusetts has strict gun control laws but that does not stop guns coming in from other states.

A year earlier, in 2006, the mayor had proposed selling City Hall and building a new one on the south waterfront. He also supported building a thousand-foot tower called Trans National Place on a city-owned parking garage. None of these projects were ever started, but this did not deter him. Menino liked his job, and the voters liked him. Recurrent election issues were the declining supply of affordable housing and the fear of Bostonians that their homes were headed for higher property taxes. Also, gentrification was an unspoken issue after the Flynn administration. Factors that promoted gentrification were the increased cost and time for commuting to suburbs like Newton, Waltham, Weston, and Wellesley, not to mention the growth of double-income households and the rising assessment of housing. According to a 2006 CNN survey, Boston had some of the nation's highest-priced housing $1,275,000, though it was behind San Francisco ($1,363,750).[43] Yet his last challenger would be the toughest of all for a variety of reasons. These factors, among others, made the upcoming 2009 election interesting.

2009: Menino versus Michael Flaherty

The decision to run for a fifth term was unprecedented in Boston's political history. No mayor had done so, and it was a risky enterprise even for an ever-popular mayor. A clever opponent could make the argument that Menino had served too long and fresh ideas were necessary. If Menino had lost the race, the defeat could have affected his legacy.

The 2009 primary race began with three candidates besides Menino: Michael Flaherty, Kevin McCrea, and Sam Yoon. The latter was the first Asian American elected to the City Council. In the primary, Menino got 41,026 votes

(51%) to Flaherty's 19,459 (24%). Sam Yoon received 17,179 votes (21%), and Kevin McCrea 3,340 (4%).

Flaherty had been elected to the City Council in 1994 as an at-large councilor. He was a very popular politician, winning the highest vote totals in 2003, 2005, and 2007. He had a good record and had raised $600,000 for the campaign. In the runoff Sam Yoon endorsed Flaherty, and Flaherty announced that Yoon would be his deputy mayor.[44]

The big issues were the future of the Boston Redevelopment Authority, term limits, and a scandal known as "email-gate." This last was a claim that Menino's aide Michael Kineavy had routinely deleted emails from City Hall computers. Why? Was there corruption at the BRA? This became an issue in the campaign. Email-gate also included suggestions that Menino was deleting rather than archiving emails. Flaherty tried to make an issue of it but failed.[45]

Popular Massachusetts attorney general Martha Coakley initially refused to investigate Flaherty's claims of possible corruption. In 2010, she cleared Kineavy of criminal wrongdoing. "He [Kineavy] acknowledged that he routinely, every day, would do what he called double-delete his e-mails. He did not do it randomly. He did not do it for particular files. It was his practice," Coakley said. "Employees at City Hall were led to believe their records would be retained on a back-up system."[46]

This was considered a big deal at the time because Coakley was a candidate for the U.S. Senate and had Menino's support against Scott Brown, the Republican candidate. In 2009, her hesitancy to investigate may have hurt her candidacy.[47]

The mayor's reputation was unfazed by the so-called scandal. Just like his previous campaigns, Menino raised more money and had many volunteers During the election, the mayor formalized his constituency service with a Constituency Response Team. The team included the police, public service department, transportation, neighborhood services, parks, recreation, and so on.

In the general election, Menino won 63,123 votes (57%) to Flaherty's 46,768 (42%). This was the tightest margin of any of Menino's mayoral elections.[48] Beating the admired Flaherty was further evidence that Menino had a solid base of voters, and he continued to be an extremely popular mayor.

The Forever Popular Mayor

Why was Menino so popular? What made him unbeatable in Boston's mayoral politics? Was it his reading of neighborhood angst? Was it his nurturing of minority leaders and making them feel a part of the decision-making in Boston? Was it his housekeeping skills that endeared him to Boston voters? Was it his triumph over an Irish American candidate in the 1993 election that convinced Bostonians the era of ethnic politics had ended? After eight years in office, Journalist Rob Gurwitt called Menino a "Main Street Maestro." The secret of Menino's success was his attention to neighborhood development. Gurwitt summarized the situation after two terms.

> Over his eight years in office, Menino has doted on the little things that make city neighborhoods attractive to the point where critics have derided him as little more than an urban "mechanic," and the Boston Globe calls him "a mayor straight out of the Middle Ages." Through Menino's neighborhood "Main Street" program, Boston has spent money on the mundane work of facade and design improvements, recruiting shop owners, and reinforcing those already there. It has worked hard to help supermarkets open—no small achievement, to anyone who has spent time in an urban core in the past two decades—while making sure that the location of the large stores doesn't threaten small merchants nearby. The city has spent money cleaning up parks, refurbishing schools, and reorienting police to focus on neighborhood safety.[49]

Gurwitt admitted that this strategy had not made Menino a statewide or national figure. But he was successful. By everyone's description, Menino was a modest man with much to be modest about. The Boston Globe summarized his assets: "[He] brings into the office an old school style of political pragmatism, a notable lack of oratorical flair, and a finely honed sense of the everyday problem of city neighborhoods."[50] Mike Barnicle, the famous and outspoken columnist for the Boston Globe, called Menino an "urban mechanic." He saw Menino as "the first mayor in 50 years to have working knowledge of each city department and many of the people employed in them. . . . There is a bit of Richie Daley, mayor of Chicago, in Tom Menino of Hyde Park. Both are more skilled in execution than elocution and prefer running a town to running off at the mouth."[51] The comparison with Chicago's Richard M. Daley, with his highly developed political machine and his strong control of the local Democratic Party, was puzzling. Menino never had that type of control. Why not compare him with New York's Mayor Abraham Beame? Beame came to the office after working for years around City Hall as city controller and knew everybody. However, this experience didn't help Beame much during the start of the fiscal crisis of 1975. As we will see in later chapters, the longer Menino served, the more experience he gained and the more he was able to somewhat bridge the gap between his generation and young Bostonians.

Aside from being asked to be so many things to so many people, one of the banes of serving as mayor is the incessant and inevitable comparisons with predecessors and counterparts in other cities. Some political pundits continued to focus on the personality differences among Menino, White, and Flynn. Granted Menino lacked the charisma and speaking ability of his predecessors, but these repeated characterizations of him may have been a journalist's recourse rather than insight into how he governed the city. Bostonians thought he was honest. They liked the man. He was a "what you see is what you get" type of guy. While serving as acting mayor, Menino brought a new sense of reliable housekeeper ethics to the office. His actions were administratively correct but not newsworthy material. Journalist John Power's portrait of Menino contrasted the differences among the three mayors: "Kevin White was the city-builder, gazing out of his fifth-floor window at cloud-topped towers. Ray Flynn was the racial healer, jogging through the neighborhoods in search of social and economic justice. Tom Menino is the urban mechanic, cruising the streets with his fix-it list, wanting to know why the grass hasn't been mowed at Garvey Playground."[52]

In city politics, mayoral comparisons between former mayors and a sitting one are quite common. Menino learned from watching his predecessors, but his socialization and instincts were different. Donald Gillis, a chronicler of the Flynn administration, agreed with Power:

> Ray Flynn was a new kind of mayor who championed redistributive politics. He wanted to create jobs and affordable housing as a redistribution and racial equality strategy. He fought hard to exact contributions in the form of linkage and community benefits from the development community. Tom Menino was a product of the growth machine–oriented strategy. He took care of his friends and was similar to Kevin White in many respects. However, White was more elitist than Menino, who focused on the downtown. Menino was an instinctive politician who sought to consolidate power and at the same time be ever present in the city neighborhoods. He missed a singular opportunity in the Seaport to create an inclusive neighborhood in favor of the growth imperative which had led to major commercial and luxury housing development to the exclusion of the average Bostonian.[53]

After first being elected, Menino maintained a low profile in state and national politics. Except for supporting Ted Kennedy's reelection to the U.S. Senate and endorsing Kennedy against President Carter, Menino said little about other presidents or Washington's relationship with cities. He preferred to be seen as a school policy activist, crime-stopper, and pothole fixer. One of his innovations was what he called "strike teams." Heads of departments and their deputies were assigned to these teams, which were the eyes and ears of the mayor. They reported and fixed broken streetlights, found parking spaces for horses, and gave directions to tourists.

The mayor wanted to be seen as directly and personally involved. Reporting unfixed parking meters and visiting victims of crime helped him to create and consolidate this image. His personal involvement in crime fighting did draw much media attention. In the summer of 1996, there was a major incident of gang violence with a drive-by shooting. The mayor went on television vowing to apprehend the people who did the shooting. He was photographed talking to the victim at his home in Dorchester. The media coverage was one of a caring mayor, precisely the image he sought. He asserted, "We want to show in the communities that we care. Crime is at a 20-year low, and we can't let 30 or 40 kids prevent residents from feeling the trend toward increasing public safety in our neighborhoods that our statistics show."[54] Crime fighting got the mayor on the front page, but the real test of his leadership would be determined by the choices he made in economic development. Bostonians wanted safe and clean streets, but they wanted city jobs hemorrhaging to stop. Once elected on his own terms, Menino reversed Flynn's reduction of city employees and increased the workforce by 5.7 percent. The city's total rose to 20,588 employees including 609 in the Education Department.[55]

This is not to say that Menino completely avoided socially controversial issues. Like other big-city mayors, Menino marched in pride parades. In the summer of 2012, he went on record against allowing Chick-Fil-A to open any restaurants in Boston. This fast-food chain considered itself a Christian company that closed on Sunday and had opposed same-sex marriage. He received a lot of support from the LGBTQ community, but some free-speech advocates disagreed with him. Some Black leaders sent him an open letter supporting him in his fight against the restaurant chain, but their letter also took the opportunity to complain about the slow process of employing Black contractors and the promotion of Black police officers.[56] The mayor won that struggle. It was not until 2018 that the restaurant chain opened its first store in Boston, five years after Menino left office.

Summary

Tom Menino became the consummate Boston politician that few people predicted. His elections represent several illogicalities in Boston politics. As early as 1991, Alan Lupo mentioned the idea of Menino becoming the first Italian American mayor of Boston. Lupo observed, "No Italian has ever been mayor of Boston, large pockets of Italian residents notwithstanding. Both Gabriel Piemonte, the late city councilor, and Chris Iannella, the ailing council president, ran serious campaigns for mayor but could not break the Irish lock on the office. The common wisdom was that Menino could not win in such a field and that the others have citywide constituencies and were better on camera. Menino smiles and says, 'I'm not the charismatic candidate. I'm the working candidate.'"[57] With such self-effacing comments, Menino received the support of voters every time he ran for mayor of Boston.

How could such a candidate be elected and reelected in one of the nation's most progressive cities? Did Menino's several elections represent the end of the so-called Irish machine? Some people joked that pigs would fly when an Italian American became mayor of Boston. Pigs did not fly but there were some overreactions. In 2004, Jennifer Peter, an AP reporter, asserted that "Italians not Irish rule Boston."[58] However, Menino's goal was not to establish an Italian ascendency but rather to open politics to all.

What accounted for the turnout and winning? The political science literature is somewhat explanatory. Boston municipal elections are off-year elections, that is, stand-alone elections. According to research by Zoltan L. Hajnal and Paul G. Lewis, off-year elections generate low turnout, and on-cycle national elections increase turnout.[59] Their research was done with California cities, but an argument can be made that only the truly interested and motivated vote in Boston municipal elections. In the 2005 and 2009 mayoral elections, turnout was just 36 and 31 percent of registered voters, respectively. Boston's registered voter turnout for the 2008 and 2012 presidential elections was 62 and 66 percent, respectively.[60]

During his short interregnum as acting mayor, Menino followed Flynn's strategy of multiethnic appointments. Tomas Gonzalez, Menino's aide, confirmed the mayor's attempt to involve him in all aspect of his campaign. He stated, "Politically Menino let me participate in every campaign I wanted to get involved with. The opportunity was there. I got to do and learn whatever

I wanted to do. City Hall was a campus, and once hired Menino welcomed you to campus. It was an amazing learning experience, especially for someone like me who really wanted to learn all there was to learn. From 2002 to 2007, I participated in almost every single special election held in Boston. I learned about the numbers, targets, polling, new software systems, robocalls, branding exercises, etc."[61]

Menino's elections also conformed to political scientist Curtis Wood's research. Voters tend to be more interested and will turn out in strong form mayoral cities or what he called political cities.[62] According to political scientists Daniel J. Hopkins and Lindsay M. Pettingill, retrospective voting (i.e., voting based on evaluations of an elected official's last four years in office) accounts for voters' support for incumbent mayors. They note that crime rates or rising property values do not hurt an incumbent mayor's chances of reelection. In addition, they suggest that the media has played a critical role in retrospective voting.[63]

In simple terms, Menino was a popular politician because of his personality and his ability to reach out to the rest of Boston's neighborhoods. Voters thought that they were well served. They felt that he was accountable and expected to be disciplined.[64] There was no eruption of corruption during his terms. In the minds of some voters, Menino's administration was an open one. The media's attempt to make fun of the mayor's enunciations backfired on them and endeared him to voters. Moreover, his personality and actions enabled him to outwit the seasoned city politicians, glib city newspaper columnists, and local politicians who harbored national ambitions.

Menino was a product of a small homeowning community. He understood the fear of rising assessments and gentrification because he lived in a working-class neighborhood. He never let his neighbors or his city constituency forget that. These neighborhoods wanted the mayor to stop condo developers, expanding universities, and Yuppies who were willing to pay more for a house than it was worth. More importantly, Boston voters wanted a mayor who would try to repair the infrastructure and keep the city clean. The average homeowner or neighborhood-oriented voter wanted a doer rather than a talker. It seems that Menino knew this as he entered the 1993 race. Accordingly, he had to be highly visible and stressed neighborhood preservation.

Paradoxically, previous Boston mayors did not occupy the center of community life in Boston. There was a notable difference between mayors who were elected before and those after the school segregation busing crisis of the mid-1970s. Working-class white Bostonians lost that fight and along with it their reliance on the mayor to save the city's old white traditions. Ironically, Menino's election had an undertone of the old days in Boston politics, but voting expectations had changed. Menino, with his endorsement of neighborhood schools, neighborhood-oriented policy agendas, and the selection of white superintendents of schools, was reminiscent of the old days in Boston. He was alert enough to realize that Boston was changing and his high profile as an ethnically and racially inclusive mayor somehow coexisted with old Boston politics.

In addition, Menino never took issue with the existing political arrangements, and no one expected him to do so. The Boston electorate was told that Menino was a good housekeeper and that is what they wanted. The fact that he was somewhat inarticulate in a city where glibness is considered an artform did not matter. Menino continued to enjoy a high approval rating after assuming the office of acting mayor of Boston. Yet he seldom drew down heavily on this enormous political capital. According to historian and activist Jim Vrabel, "It is hard to lose an election for reelection for Boston mayor. Menino was popular with people who did not need anything from him. He was always out there [i.e., in neighborhoods]. People loved it. He was one of them. They keep voting for him."[65]

Mayor Menino did not support unpopular ideas, causes, or individuals and always seemed to find a positive position on issues and avoid conflicts. Political scientist Barbara Ferman's conclusion about Menino's predecessor Kevin White applies to Menino. She concluded that "the executive's ability to be a shrinking violet—that is, to avoid taking on unpleasant or unprofitable responsibilities—is facilitated when institutional mechanisms for integrating all citizens into the political system are absent or not working."[66] Like his predecessors, Menino faced little if any institutional challenges to his acquisition and use of power. The City Council remained weak, and the mayor appointed the Boston School Committee and superintendents. Finally, there was no viable opposition political party (i.e., Republicans) demanding accountability.

Did the election and reelection of Thomas Menino and his subsequent policies provide a lull in city politics? In 2008, *Boston Globe* reporter John C. Drake evaluated ten years of Menino's promises to business leaders in his annual State of the City addresses and before the Boston Municipal Research Bureau. In 1997, his Boston 400 Plan was characterized as "the boldest thing to happen in this city in a long, long time."[67] Led by the BRA, it was an ambitious plan that included results of meetings with community leaders and development partners to create a plan for Boston's 400th anniversary (2030). Drake also credited Menino with expanding afterschool programming and selling the Berkeley Street police headquarters to fund affordable housing. Menino also established neighborhood response teams.

The 2001 reelection of Menino did not mean that the city of Boston was set politically for the second decade of the twenty-first century. As we will see in the next chapters, his legacy continued to be challenged by recurrent (ordinary, day-to-day) politics, an uncertain economy, and turnovers in the national administration. Menino's response to these policy challenges was to engage with housing needs, crime outbreaks, public school reforms, minority grievances, and higher education expansion.

CHAPTER 3

Menino, City Councilors, Policies, and the Media

In many American large cities like Boston, there is an attempt to imitate a federal analogy, the executive (mayor) against the legislature (council). Theoretically, the mayor and council are supposed to check and balance each other. In such mayor-council governments, there is a single executive elected by the voters and a separately elected legislative council. The mayor conducts day-to-day management of the city, implements government policies, appoints department heads, and represents the city. The mayor has veto power over the council legislation, ordinances, rules, and resolutions. Mayors also have more control over the budget. To override a mayoral veto, a two-thirds council majority is necessary. Accordingly, the reality is that the most visible and powerful figure in city government is the mayor. Yet the council can and does play a critical role in city politics. The interaction between the mayor and the council is sometimes fascinating. This is the case for Boston's City Council.

The elected Boston City Council's thirteen members represent nine separate districts and four members at large. Research on city councils suggests that district members are usually more partisan and diverse. Members serve a two-year term with no term limits. Aside from formulating and approving ordinances, overseeing city agencies, holding hearings, and making budget decisions, the council also makes land-use decisions. The last of these is critical to Boston because it has limited numbers of parcels for development. The other important role is asking the state to draw new districts after each federal census.

Members of the Council Play Different Internal and External Roles

In the 1990s, council districts had neighborhood reputations. District 1 was composed of Charlestown, East Boston, and the North End. The last neighborhood was an enclave of Italian Americans. District 2 included Downtown, South Boston, and the South End. District 3 was Dorchester, a racially mixed neighborhood including African Americans. District 4 included Mattapan, part of Dorchester, part of Roslindale, and Jamaica Plain. The last of these was a mixed area with a large progressive population. District 5 was the old Menino district, which included Hyde Park, District 6 covered South Boston, an Irish American enclave, and District 7 covered Roxbury. District 8 included a variety of residents of the Back Bay, Beacon Hill, the Fenway-Kenmore neighborhood, Mission Hill, and the West End. District 9 included Allston and Brighton. Each district had unique internal dynamics. Residents identified with these communities.

Because four at-large council members are citywide elected, these at-large councilors supposedly have a citywide orientation as opposed to their narrowly district-elected colleagues. The benefit of running at large is that it provides an opportunity to build a citywide constituency. This can be useful if one decides to run for higher office.

Boston has a tradition of electing the mayor from the City Council. Tom Menino, who represented Hyde Park and Roslindale, was a man of the council. He made his early career there and he developed friendships with individuals outside Hyde Park there. Few thought he would leave it and become the mayor of Boston. Menino's colleagues elected him president of the council. Elected every year, the council president decides committee assignments. The president also serves as the acting mayor when the mayor is out of town. In his term as president, Menino gained a reputation as a man who could act outside his district. Menino had served as a district member and was chair of the Ways and Means Committee. He had personally gotten to know everyone on the council, and they knew him. According to political scientist Sidney Verba, such small groups have their own internal dynamics sometimes unknown to the public.[1] Menino was a man of the council and respected its role. He learned a lot about city politics while serving on the council.

As we shall see, members were not reluctant to offer opinions on a variety of public policy issues ranging from the Big Dig (the Central Artery/Tunnel Project) to Boston exam school reform. Members of the Boston City Council are not averse to challenging the sitting mayor. Elected mayors who have never served on the City Council are often unaware of the internal power.

Service on the Boston City Council is a full-time position but the members' salaries are half of the mayor's. Accordingly, the council determines its salary and that of the mayor. As we saw in chapter 2, after Menino became acting mayor, many of his colleagues did not see him as an electable mayor. Several colleagues challenged him then and continued to challenge him throughout his tenure.

When Menino served on the council, he protected its institutional prerogatives. When he became mayor, he protected Boston's strong mayoralty. In some initiatives, he shared the stage with the councilors, and with others he did not. School reform was one of the issues that drew opposition from sitting council members, a subject discussed in chapter 8.

Indeed, it is relatively easy for councilors to achieve citywide visibility as the mayor's opponents because of the city's nonpartisan elections and the lack of a political machine. Former Chicago mayor Richard J. Daley was a commanding or shutdown mayor because of his control over the city's Democratic Party. Menino could never achieve this type of power. He could not control what councilors said or how they voted. Besides, he had no desire to dominate the Democratic Party narrative. Indeed, the media meticulously covered the councilors' disagreements with Menino. Disagreeing with the mayor is a way to educate the public about the issues. Nevertheless, no one claimed that Mayor Menino had neglected the neighborhoods in his revitalization schemes. If anything, his critics claimed he spent too much time on "nuts and bolts" and not enough time providing a new vision for Boston. Menino also wanted to move the Boston City Hall, a building known for its Brutalist aesthetic, to the South Boston Seaport district. Despite his encouragement of the idea, no change was made.

There always seem to be recurrent council district drawing issues. Redistricting occurs after every U.S. Census. Although elections are nonpartisan, district seats are critical to Boston Democrats. Democrats are strong in Boston but not so much statewide. In Boston, a new seat can be a steppingstone to local politics. Whatever rivalries, missteps, and disagreements occurred during Menino's tenure, the media would be the first to write about it. As every mayor discovers the media is omnipresent and must be attended to.

The Boston Media and City Hall

As was the case for other mayors chronicled by academics, the media coverage of the mayor was critical to the story of a mayor. For voters, local politicians, journalists, academics, and community activists, a mayor's glowing actions can be the beacon of a city's political life. Some mayors provide more illumination of city politics than others. During Menino's tenure, the way media covered City Hall changed. It was not just the normal competition of print and broadcast media. Twenty-first-century journalism underwent a profound transformation. Print media experienced declining subscriptions. Like other cities with two daily newspapers, the Boston print media spent their time fighting off financial collapse. In 1982, Rupert Murdoch, the billionaire Fox news publisher, tried to save the *Boston Herald*, the city tabloid, but had to sell it after acquiring the Fox television station. Digital First Media now owns the tabloid. In 1993, the *New York Times* bought the *Boston Globe* for $1.1 billion. In Menino's last year in office (2013), John W. Henry, an investor and owner of the Boston Red Sox, bought the *Globe* for $70 million. The *Globe* had lost 94 percent of its value, as newspapers in general have lost subscribers and advertisers to cable TV and the internet.

Yet the Boston media, both print and broadcast, continued to play a critical role in reporting the news and evaluating the performance of elected officials. They wrote down Menino's statements and his ruminations and kept the recordings. In a note to this research, Writer-reporter Joe Sciacca once noted, "In one case, I even turned my column over to him for a say!"[2] Journalists and commentators were quite aware of their influence on the city's readers, viewers, and listeners. Hence, individual journalists and commentators wielded tremendous influence on the political class. For example, if the media decided to focus on a particular member of the City Council, the coverage could make that person a rising political personality.

Local journalists can laud politicians as well as second-guess them. They collect rumors and background information on political candidates, office-holders, and their staff. As singer Louis Armstrong once said, he had a hundred dollars more than he intended to spend. Local journalists have rumors that they don't intend to use, so they bank them. They sometimes exchange them for alerts (leaks) that enable them to create attention-grabbing stories. Print media can also float alternatives to solving problems. More importantly, politicians like Menino paid attention to journalists, especially print media, and responded to them. This proximity and access accentuated the role of the media as the watchdog for the public. Ironically, the media coverage often compounded the social problems of Boston. Professor Peter Dreier summarized the situation:

> Major news media coverage of cities reinforces an overwhelmingly negative and misleading view of urban America. The images from the nightly news, newsweeklies, and on the pages of our daily newspapers are an unrelenting story of social pathology—mounting crime, gangs, drug wars, racial tension, homelessness, teenage pregnancy, AIDS, inadequate schools, and slum housing. Moreover, this perspective on our cities is compounded by misleading news coverage of government efforts to address these problems. Government programs are typically covered as well-intentioned but misguided, plagued by mismanagement, inefficiency, and, in some cases, corruption. There is very little news coverage of collective efforts by unions, community organizations, and other grassroots groups to address problems. Only when such efforts include drama, conflict, and/or violence do the major media typically pay attention.[3]

Boston reporters and journalists would respond to Dreier's claims by arguing that they are obligated to reveal the backstories and provide the public with information about their local government, warts and all. They solicit comments from relevant interest groups. As the city's watchdogs, they sometimes simultaneously positively framed Menino's career and acted as his critics. Journalists believed that their products are read and viewed by a discerning public. Interestingly, journalists also recognize their roles as nurturers of politicians.

In the 1990s, Boston was a city with over half a million residents and two major newspapers, the *Boston Globe* and *Boston Herald*. Many Bostonians also read the *Metro*, which published weekdays. There were thirteen weekly and fifteen neighborhood papers including the *Bay State Banner*, an African American newspaper. *Boston Magazine* followed and commented on Boston politics. Boston was also a city that listened to talk radio. Broadcast media included stars such as John Kelly at TV Channel 56, talk radio host David Brudnoy (WBZ), and Howie Carr (WRKO). Newspaper writers such as Mike Barnicle, Brian McGrory, Alan Lupo, David Nylan, Patricia Smith, Joan Vennochi, and Adrian Walker worked for the *Boston Globe*. Ed Cafasso, Joe Sciacca, and Wayne Woodlief were writers for the *Boston Herald*. In addition, there was Yawu Miller of the *Bay State Banner*, a critical voice for that community.

Radio talk show hosts Howie Carr and David Brudnoy played a critical role in the political narrative in the city. The Brudnoy show covered a range of

MENINO, CITY COUNCILORS, POLICIES, AND THE MEDIA   81

political issues with acerbic wit and nonpartisanship. (When Brudnoy died in 2004, Mayor Menino declared January 5 as David Brudnoy Day.) The Howie Carr Show commented incessantly on Boston mayors and city politics from a conservative perspective. Boston residents would often ask one another if they had heard what these two individuals had said about the mayor. Some Bostonians carefully monitored newspaper columnists and broadcast political commentaries.

As we will see, some of these journalists were not above playing up Menino's Italian American background, his mumbling problems, or the faux pas and mistakes of his aides. This made for interesting radio and newspaper commentaries. Reporters soon dropped the issue of Menino's Italian American ethnicity. However, Menino's rhetoric and actions prevented the media from framing some crime incidents as racial ones. Although Menino wrapped himself in the flag of the caring and sensitive mayor, reporters reported little, if anything, about the social and economic forces that drove his decisions. The editors of the *Globe* and *Herald* were apparently satisfied with the image of the mayor their journalists had carefully nurtured.

Noticeably, modern mayors operate in an arena of multimedia outlets. They often cajole, manipulate, and criticize the press. Menino did have his share of frustrations with journalists and newspaper coverage, and he was sensitive to national coverage. He also learned from the media and sometimes responded to its critiques.

When *Bicycling Magazine* ranked Boston one of the nation's worst biking cities for seven years, Menino responded in 2007 by appointing Nicole Freedman, a former Olympic cyclist, as what he called a "bike czar." The city created 120 miles of cycling paths.[4] The mayor wanted to be able to say, "The car is no longer the king in Boston." This was part of his role as an empathic mayor, making things happen and also being alert to coverage by any national media.

Menino had to govern in an environment of 24/7 cable coverage and rising social media competition. At the same time, Menino's ascendancy to the mayoralty came at a time when the local print media had deemphasized its coverage of City Hall and broadcast media lessened its day-to-day coverage. Fewer beat reporters were ensconced on the City Hall's third floor. Menino was not a publicity hound and did not want to be the center of media attention. Reporter Joe Sciacca of the *Boston Herald* might have been right when he said, "Menino would be happy if he never was in the papers."[5] Neighborhood papers covered Menino. Otherwise, Menino would go for days without much coverage in the dailies. Jon

82   CHAPTER 3

Keller agrees, noting, "He [Menino] is an unexciting copy. This [his first term] was not a controversial time. We don't have enough loud mayoral critics like Al Sharpton in Boston. There is also the availability of other colorful characters such as Governor [William] Weld and Speaker [Thomas] Finneran."[6]

Menino's First-Term Staffing

Tom Menino began his administration with the appointment of a forty-one-member transition team headed by John White. White had been an economic advisor to former 1992 presidential candidate Ross Perot. He was also a former Kodak executive and had held the directorship of the Center for Business and Government at Harvard University's Kennedy School of Government. Alyce Lee, chair of the Codman Square Community Development Corp, became the vice-chair of the group. The transition team produced a 340-page report that reviewed the challenges facing the city and recommended a cabinet form of government. This reorganization of the office of the mayor's proposal would eliminate having over forty department heads reporting directly to the mayor. This resulted in limiting the independence of some departments. Howard Leibowitz, Menino's spokesperson, stated that "what you had, at times, was three or four different voices, each giving you their particular agency's take on development."[7]

Menino accepted the cabinet's reorganization recommendation and asserted, "I am creating a strong form of Cabinet government with each Cabinet position for the primary function of city government."[8] Recruiting people to serve in the cabinet and help Menino run the government was challenging because talented people from the outside do not normally seek permanent careers in government. They are likely to become frustrated by the slow pace of city departments. Talented people use the government to gain visibility and expertise. As we shall see below, high turnover was the norm. Nonetheless, the advantage of such people is that they are smart and creative and can bring new ideas to the government.

Menino's cabinet structure was to oversee and control the traditional line departments, such as fire, police, and sanitation. Menino's appointment of Alyce Lee, an African American and a Wellesley College graduate, as his chief of staff. This appointment was generally hailed. He appointed Marisa Lago to head the BRA, which is one of the most powerful agencies in city government. Lago had been a counselor to the New York City Redevelopment Department, and she was one of the few "nationals" appointed to the mayor's staff. Lago left to take a job at the Securities and Exchange Commission. When the women left their positions, the Boston media did not raise the issue of gender balance.

Howard Leibowitz, his liaison for intergovernmental relations, explained the difference between the Boston and New York appointments. In Boston, there are nonpartisan elections: "In New York, there are Democrats and Republicans. In New York, the new mayor defeats an incumbent. There is a more confrontational relationship. The new guy wants his people. In Boston, no incumbent mayor has been defeated in fifty years. They don't run against each other. There are people who worked for White and Flynn. It is not an adversary relation. The head of the Public Works Department Joe Casazza worked for White, Flynn, and Menino because he is good."[9]

Interestingly, there were many holdovers from the Flynn era. Surprisingly, keeping those people enhanced Mayor Menino's image. In effect, if he had brought in a new group of department heads, that would have been a story of ethnic or generational replacement. Instead, he appointed new people to his immediate staff but did not disrupt the bureaucracy during the transition. Leibowitz, his director of intergovernmental relations, estimated that 20 percent of the forty-five department heads, including himself, also served under Ray Flynn. Overlapping staff members between the two administrations was not uncommon. Although Menino had a public reputation for being an empathic person, he ran a tight ship at City Hall. Conny Doty, a longtime agency administrator, described Menino's interactions with staff:

> He was a demanding boss, but in a way that made you want to put in the extra effort to get something tangible done for Boston residents. Rather than stewing about something if he wasn't happy the Mayor would let you know. People understood where they stood with him. His staff understood that the city of Boston and its communities were uppermost in all his planning decisions. He was careful not to overpromise. And he used the word "partnership" in every department meeting. And ended each meeting for twenty years reminding us that "the most important call you take today will be from someone in our neighborhoods who needs your help."[10]

Tomas Gonzalez, his Latino liaison agreed: "Menino did not like people [staff] who came to him with problems without solutions. He wanted people who could think through problems and provide real tangible solutions based on their experience, proximity to the situation, and what you knew about what the mayor valued. What's up? What's going on? These were not salutations. These were legitimate questions, and you'd better have answers."[11]

Many of Menino's appointees decided to leave before the end of his administration. In the case of Lago, the *Herald* explained her leaving by asserting

Lago was an unknown and had been working in New York City when Menino picked her to take over the high-profile BRA. Lago never fitted into the Boston political milieu, and the media picked up on her shortcomings. The story also suggested that people in the Menino administration wanted Lago to leave and that she had said Menino lacked respect for her.[12] The subtext was that she was an outsider who was out of the loop, quoting sources as stating they were undermining her for months After Lago's departure, Menino brought the once semi-independent BRA under his control.

Openness and Change

In his inaugural speech, Menino pledged an open administration, one to which all types of individuals could serve and to which all residents would have access. This was an important statement for the minority community as many African Americans had felt left out of the previous administration. He stated, "To Boston's African-American community, I want to say, I regret that as much as you do. And because of it, I promise during my time as mayor to be especially responsive to your concerns. What I'm trying to do is be more inclusive. The key is working together to solve problems."[13]

Menino's remarks about openness were an attempt to differentiate himself from the previous administration. His administration would be housekeeping-oriented but would be open to innovation and change. Again, the mayor was appealing to his constituency and audience. He would support the neighborhood organizations but wanted them to understand that changes would be made. An example of this came with a controversial attempt to forge a coalition with the expanding Longwood Medical and Academic Area (LMA). The Longwood area included twenty-four so-called meds, that is, medical schools and hospitals. Harvard Medical School, as well as other facilities in Longwood, were located adjacent to the Fenway and Mission Hill communities. The 213 acres also included parts of the town of Brookline. The complex was very successful in getting services and research funds. Professor Malo Andre Hutson noted,

> On any given day, more than 43,000 employees and approximately 19,200 students come into the LMA, although only a third of LMA employees are Boston residents. Federal research grants awarded to LMA institutions have grown precipitously since the early 1990s. Between 1991 and 2005, the National Institute of Health (NIH) awards

more than doubled for the LMA institutions from $302 million to $927 million. In 2008 (most recent available data), the total revenue for the Medical Academic and Scientific Community Organization (MASCO), a nonprofit member organization for LMA institutions, was $6.2 billion. In terms of land use, the LMA had developed 18.1 million square feet as of June 2010.[14]

Jamaica Plain community leaders also wanted more services for poor communities. The Jamaica Plain Neighborhood Development Corporation (JPNDC) organized a private-public partnership that wanted to provide healthcare jobs for local disadvantaged residents. The JPNDC established the "Bridge to the Future Program." Menino, along with the BRA and other municipal agencies, developed the SkillWorks workforce development initiative (Longwood Medical Area Master Plan).[15] This project was an example of how Menino worked simultaneously with institutions and community leaders. The negotiations were high-profile and allowed the mayor to demonstrate his brand of mayoral leadership.

Mayoral leadership is a political managing process that is partly a matter of performance and partly the ability to arrive at a working understanding with constituencies. This requires both the mayor and their constituencies to overcome their biases and pursue a consensual understanding of their situations. Menino attended the Bridge to the Future ceremony, putting the city imprimatur on the project. It was important that the mayor convey inclusiveness and total regard for all constituents. Conversely, constituents must be willing to interact with the mayor in a relatively constructive manner. If this is done, then the appeal to the audience will be easier.

Mayoral Governing

The political context is the background music of any mayoral administration. And managing groups is the essence of mayoral leadership. Urban academic literature documents how difficult this task can be. Political science professor Robert A. Dahl's *Who Governs?* applied the pluralist theory to the study of the evolution of New Haven, Connecticut, politics.[16] His work showed that each issue attracted a separate set of interest groups that rarely overlapped. The interest groups concerned with economic issues were not the same ones that cared about school politics. Accordingly, policymaking was a decentralized and fragmented process. Therefore, governing was a process of addressing conflicts that grew out of the narrow interest of divergent groups. Successful negotiations with one interest group do not lead to success with others. For example, making peace with the Boston's Teacher Union did not help Menino win public support for the Boston Convention Center over the New England Patriot's Metroplex proposal. There are a variety of interest groups such as housing, health, banking, retail, universities, and so on. These interest groups rarely encroach on each others' domains.

Political scientists Wallace S. Sayre and Herbert Kaufman's *Governing New York City* found a similar pluralistic, decentralized, and fragmented policy-making process in New York. Their work concentrated on mayoral interactions with the bureaucracy. Although the mayor of the city appointed the head of city agencies, the mayor was by no means the sole authority on department matters. In chapter 5 we discuss Menino's relationships with the Police and School Departments. Besides, there were a plethora of groups vying for a role in department decision-making, not the least of which were the public employee unions. Sayre and Kaufman felt that this competition among interest groups made for more acceptable public policy.[17]

Bryan D. Jones and Lynn W. Bachelor in *The Sustaining Hand* introduced the notion of sectors of interest. They found a variety of interest groups in Detroit, each operated separately and for its own interest. Maintaining and controlling one's sector became the primary preoccupation of group leaders. However, there were occasions when the interests of all sectors overlapped. On these occasions, groups would meet and engage in "peak bargaining." Jones and Bachelor understood bargaining is necessary to resolve conflicts. These insights are all applicable to Boston.[18]

What are the important interest groups in American city politics? My research in two cities discovered that the relative power of these groups was not the same in every city.[19] Public employee unions were major players in New York City and Detroit but did not wield that type of power in Boston. Although there were both ad-hoc and permanent groups in these cities, group leaders did not behave in the same ways. In Boston, ad-hoc groups developed around a particular crisis and had short shelf-lives, such as the Boston megaplex coalition, a proposed facility discussed in the next chapter. Over a long period of time, leaders of such interest groups had difficulty developing and sustaining public support. The permanent groups had paid staff that settled into organizational roles. In other words, such groups had institutionalized their relationship with the city bureaucracy. Although higher education institutions and high-tech companies did not have full-time staff advocacy groups, they did have an enormous impact on Boston politics given their strategic positions.

Apparently, Menino understood that having a good relationship with the various interest groups was critical to the governing process. Governing is formulating, advocating, and implementing policies. Mayors must also be able to interpret the constituency feedback from ongoing policies. For Menino, orchestrating and maintaining the reputation of policies was part of the job. As soon as the mayor tried to build policy on a foundation of perceived consensus, he encountered environmental constraints. Some of these constraints were fiscal and others were legal. Analogous to governing is trying to sew buttons onto gelatin without destroying it.

Some mayors only appear to be in control and end up with a positive outcome. Mayors are said to have "it" when they have charisma and espouse new ideas. Voters value such mayors. For a long time, Boston voters considered Mayor Ray Flynn as someone who had "it." After repeated racial incidents, however, some concluded he had lost "it." They elected Menino because they thought he would be a conciliator. Menino, by downplaying his leadership style, insulated himself from this type of test that other mayors set for themselves. More importantly, the critical interest groups were more inclined to acquiesce to his low-key approach.

Economic Development Plans

An inevitable correlate of national economic cycles is their impact on local economic development. As Richard Schragger's *City Power* argues, a city economy is a process. Schragger asserts that "historical accident, path dependence and spatial persistence: These features of economic geography suggest that geographically uneven economic development is not an aberration but rather a salient feature of economic life."[20] So it has been with recurrent politics of Boston's economy. Although Schragger is not a policy determinist, Boston's economic development seems biased toward the creative class.

Boston is blessed with the location of first-class educational institutions that were in the right place at the right time, that is, at the onset of the post-industrial economy. These industries needed the talented workers these institutions had trained. In addition, many such institutions were research centers, which were so crucial to the success of these new industries. More importantly, such industries aspired to locate in cities with similar industries. With a location in Boston, these industries could recruit experienced employees and give workers more employment choices. Additionally, the concentration of producers triggered dependent businesses in Boston.

Unlike his counterparts in other cities, Menino had the new economic geography working for him. He had a location advantage and sought federal economic development funds. The Boston neighborhoods expected to get funds to develop local community enterprises. These had little to do with the overall Boston advantage in the post-industrial economy. There was still poverty and job development problems in several Boston neighborhoods. The Clinton Empowerment Zones program, which combined tax credits with obligatory training for inner-city residents, seemed to be a good fit for these communities.

Empowerment zones (EZ) were an attempt to provide tax incentives for companies to invest and locate in inner-city communities. EZs also focused on job training and neighborhoods. Accordingly, cities had to build a compelling proposal for the funds. In 2001, Boston applied for $94 million. The Boston steering committee included over a hundred residents, academics, and business leaders. Under the proposal, the catchment area included 12 percent of the city's land. The empowerment area included Mattapan, the South End, South Boston, Chinatown, Downtown, and Roxbury. The purpose of the grant was to reduce poverty rates in those neighborhoods. The proposal stated,

> The poverty rate of the Zone is twice that of the City (36% versus 19%). The unemployment rate is twice that of the City (16% versus 8%) and three times that of the country (5.5%). Over the last ten years, this poverty rate has risen by 2.1% while poverty in the City has declined by 1.5%. But these are just numbers. Their true significance is that deepening poverty only divides a city. If these trends in poverty continue, it will become a city of rich and poor.[21]

The proposal had the backing of the commonwealth of Massachusetts, and the planning credibility was enhanced by the financial commitment of local banks, which committed $35 million in flexible capital terms for the Boston EZ. The state-designated Boston as an "Economic Target Area," that is, an economically distressed area, and committed over $10 million to the EZ. Despite having widespread support and being well-designed, the proposal did not make the cut. Boston failed to get the grant, though the city received a different $25 million federal grant. Boston lost out to cities such as Atlanta, Chicago, Baltimore, Detroit, and New York.[22]

Mayor Menino, Senator John Kerry, Representative J. Joseph Moakley, Joseph D. Feaster Jr., chair of the Boston Zoning Board of Appeal, and others tried to spin the loss to no avail. The chairman of Menino's steering committee stated, "These dollars are going to help us enhance the city's economic future."[23]

The commonwealth continued to support state EZs. Political scientist James Jennings analyzed the state EZs between 1999 and 2009. He concluded that the EZ helped to build collaborative strategies among organizations. He stated,

> The Boston EZ did not reduce the level of poverty or reduce significantly the unemployment levels of residents. But this 10-year initiative was successful along several dimensions. First, it did generate a level of economic robustness that had not previously been associated with some of Boston's poorest areas. The EZ also provided direct support and capacity-building resources to smaller, local, and neighborhood-based businesses. This sector is too easily overlooked in favor of economic development initiatives favoring big businesses and corporations. Rather than utilizing only tax strategies, the EZ leadership and staff believed that local businesses represent a critical arena for stimulating economic growth and generating employment opportunities within a community.[24]

In effect, Boston's attempt to change the fortune of low-income communities with EZs had failed. This failure was consistent with a 2011 article that evaluated the city's economic elite.[25] It was also a failure of lobbying. Julia A. Payson's studies of city lobbying found that "affluent communities with more local resources available to them receive substantially higher returns to lobbying than their revenue-poor counterparts, despite enjoying a local revenue advantage."[26] Boston should have been able to get the EZ grant. Journalist Margaret Pantridge lamented a "power failure" in the city leadership. She stated that for the first time in thirty years, no CEO wanted to chair the Boston Vault, the historic power brokers of the city. In her interview with civic leaders, they saw the city as "adrift" and "unsure of itself." Businesspeople told her, "Boston needs a new Dick Hill."[27] Hill, the chair of the Bank of Boston during the Governor Michael Dukakis era, took the lead in persuading the governor to cut the budget and raise taxes. There is no indication that Terrence Murray, then CEO of Fleet Financial Group, was interested in assuming such a role. Besides, there had been an erosion of the power of bankers as mergers had reduced their numbers. Boston's redevelopment strategy of the 1990s was only partially successful. What would be the big projects that would take the city into the year 2000? Initially, Boston was part of the overall downturn in the fortunes of New England. Massachusetts was the hardest hit in the region, losing 11.5 percent of its jobs between the end of 1988 and the summer of 1992.[28] Since 1988, the city had lost 69,000 jobs. In 1993, only 11,600 new jobs were created. That same year, unemployment stood at 5.3 percent, low by the standards of other central cities.[29] The city continued to lose middle-class residents to suburban communities.

Seeking a Cornucopia of Blue-Collar Jobs

The politics of Boston competed with a seemingly endless succession of economic setbacks and surprises. It was an old city that managed to keep enough of its New England traditions and yet attracted hordes of newcomers every decade. Many of these newcomers were minorities. Most did not come to attend some of the finest universities and colleges in the world and to work at leading research and development centers, biomedical facilities, or in the financial industry. Yet, they came to live and sought opportunities. They might have heard about life in the American Athens but wanted other jobs.

Former Mayor Kevin White, who became a professor at Boston College, compared Boston to Rome as a city of "moderation." He stated that "in Boston, there's no, 'there there,' economically downtown, so there's no center of economic power to deal with, no one big enough institutionally or personally to reaggregate it."[30] Others would disagree with that assessment, but it was interesting coming from the former mayor.

Still, Boston retained its facade as the flagship city for the Brahmin class while simultaneously celebrating its history as a place where Irish Americans achieved ultimate sociopolitical participation. Kevin White's successor, Ray Flynn, inherited a city with changing city economy. Professors Zebulon Milesfshy and Tomas Gonzalez cited Peter Dreier's observations:

> The Flynn administration had been given a mandate by the voter to 'share the prosperity' of Boston's downtown economic boom. . . . He [Dreier] goes on to say, What the Flynn administration inherited was a city of contrasts. By 1984, Boston's economy was well along to shifting from a manufacturing base to a service-based economy, spurring the development of downtown buildings, university and medical research centers, and high-technology industries. This economic boom created new problems and compounded some old ones. Neighborhoods near downtown or close to universities and hospitals were becoming gentrified, pricing working-class and moderate-income residents out of the market. . . . Lower-income neighborhoods faced redlining and disinvestment; the

minority unemployment rate was twice that of the city at large; and many of the jobs held by Boston residents were in the low-paying portion of the new service-oriented economy.[31]

Yet the "other Boston" included economically distressed enclaves that looked very much like their counterparts in Chicago, New York, and San Francisco. The emergence of new high-end and high-income workers in these cities created a rampant gentrification trend. The jobs of these workers allowed them to delegate household and other menial chores to low-wage workers. Following the insights of sociologist Saskia Sassen's *Global City* thesis, Professor William I. Robinson described how this "outrageous" situation created a need for low-wage service workers while making their struggles more difficult:

> Yet, high-income gentrification, and the valorization dynamic that pushes prices upward to the purchasing power of the upper strata rest on a vast supply of low wage workers. The concentration of high-income workers in major cities has facilitated rapid residential and commercial gentrification, which in turn has created a need for legions of low-wage service workers—residential building attendants, restaurant workers, preparers of specialty and gourmet foods, dog walkers, errant [*sic*] runners, apartment cleaners, childcare providers, and so on. The fact that many of these jobs are "off the books" has meant the rapid expansion of the informal economy. The low-paying, dead end jobs are tied to four types of activities: (1) producer services themselves (e.g., clerical, janitorial); (2) servicing the affluent lifestyles of the high-paid professional workers; (3) services internal to new low wage communities; (4) downgraded manufacturing jobs now competitive with Third World offshore production centers.[32]

In effect, the new job market has made socioeconomic mobility more difficult. It has created a cadre of low-wage earners in the "other Boston." Increasingly, the incorporation of the other Bostonians has slowed down. Political activists and community leaders spoke out against racial containment and lack of upward mobile opportunity. They did not use fancy sociological terms like "downward social mobility," but they had a sense that something was happening to the Boston job market. They were not able to attain the same types of jobs their parents held. A household now took two wage earners. They sometimes saw new immigrants as competitors for jobs and housing. There was rising discontent that manifested itself in a series of crises in civil society. In the decade before Mayor Menino, Boston mayors did not handle these crises well. The question for the 1990s was how to fashion a politics that would cope with the social problems of the other Boston? One of the first challenges came with youth crime in minority communities.

Finding jobs for young people had been a recurrent theme in the minority community. Most local politicians and community activists rushed to assert a position on this issue. Mayor Menino set a goal each year of his administration to find employment for ten thousand Boston teens each summer. The most effective recruiter for private-sector paid internships for Boston teens was Menino, as through his efforts three thousand teens were hired each summer at hospitals, banks, retail, insurance companies, and other businesses large and small. Additionally, using federal, state, and foundation-coordinated funds, over seven thousand additional Boston teens worked at a variety of community service positions helping at day camps, museums, and recreation programs as well as the well-known Mural Crew whose work is seen throughout the city to this day. The Mayor's Mural Crew covered the neighborhood graffiti with painting by high school students.[33]

Mayor Menino saw employment as a critical piece of economic development. He required that large-scale development projects include the city's workforce development agency—the Office of Jobs and Community Services (JCS)—as part of the negotiating process for community benefits. JCS was moved under the aegis of the city's quasi-governmental agency the Economic Development Industrial Corp at the end of Mayor Flynn's term, which in turn was partnered with the BRA, thus providing more options to holistically connect development and institutional expansion with Boston residents and employment opportunities. Conny Doty, the JCS executive director described the program.

> Youth Options Unlimited [YOU-Boston] was one of the programs directed toward high-risk or proven-risk youth and managed under JCS. At the end of a five-year empowerment zone grant from the Department of Labor, a new, more focused direction was undertaken by that staff. YOU-Boston provided three essential services: case management, alternative education, and supported work opportunities to the court- and/ or gang-involved youth. Serving over three hundred young people per year, the staff worked closely with community organizations including clergy, the Department of Youth Services, a variety of education providers, and law enforcement.[34]

According to Doty, "Menino has totally supported it. He raised an additional $1 million for the program at a critical moment and supported a variety of governmental and foundation grants to continue its operation."[35] These programs played a critical role in preventing youth crime.

Remember that before Menino became mayor, social scientists thought the city's economic outlook was not encouraging. In H. V. Savitch and John Clayton Thomas's edited volume *Big City Politics in Transition*, Phillip Clay characterized Boston's economy as an incomplete transformation.[36] Menino entered office with three big development plans in progress. The first of these was the so-called Big Dig, the Central Artery Tunnel, 7.5 miles of highway located on the Eastside near Downtown. It was a $10 billion project replacing the old Boston Central Artery and providing a new tunnel to Logan Airport. It extended the Mass Pike (I-90) to Logan. The city promoted the plan as an economic development strategy for the city's Eastside. There was planning for replacing the city sports stadiums and the Hynes Convention Center.

Developing a new convention center was essential to attracting national meetings. In March 1995, the BRA approved the private development of the vacant Sears building in the Fenway neighborhood. This $110 million private commercial development was the largest of its kind during the Menino administration. To be more competitive for convention visitors with cities like Chicago and Miami, Boston needed a larger convention facility. Menino understood that competing with these cities required a first-rate convention center. However, private-sector leaders, sports franchise owners, and state legislative leaders preferred a large multiuse facility that included a convention capacity. This became a dispute about how to fix the downtown retail losses.

Fixing Downtown

In yesteryears, the axiom was, "as goes American manufacturing, so goes cities." Today it is the service industry that leads cities. The obvious question remains as to whether Boston's central business district occupies more space than it deserves and is in more economic trouble than it is worth. The maintenance cost for downtown retail may be the unspoken bane of the city's existence. For years Filene was the anchor department store for downtown Boston. It provided the same anchor role as Detroit's Hudson and Chicago's Marshall Fields. In August 2007, the BRA approved development at the Old Filene's department store site. Menino fast-tracked the project. The funding collapsed, and it left a hole in the ground for five years. Vornado Realty Trust had planned a $700 million mixed-use development called One Franklin in the parcel.[37]

In 2008, some of the buildings were demolished but other properties were left standing. A *Wall Street Journal* article reported that in a lecture at Columbia

University, Steven Roth, head of Vornado, revealed that he used delays so that the price would go up and then he could get more help from the city. In 2010, Menino send a letter threatening Roth with the use of eminent domain to take over the vacant lot. The March 8 letter quoted Menino as saying, "Blight kills jobs by destroying an area's appeal to businesses and consumers. Inflicting pain on people, businesses, and communities to inflate the return to your enormously profitable company is reprehensible." The *Wall Street Journal* noted, "The tactic is often viewed as a bane to small, private owners and a boon to cities and developers. But in this case, Boston is threatening to use the process to force a developer to build—and being hailed by the public for it."[38]

According to the *Wall Street Journal*, Menino said that Roth had apologized to him. Menino said, "I'm a professional. I accept [Roth's] apology, and I want to move forward [but] I have a fiduciary responsibility. I'm not going to let developers hold the city hostage as they have for almost two years now."[39] This response helped the mayor's image among local supporters like Rosemarie Sansone, president of the Downtown Crossing Business Association. In February 2012, another developer named Millennium Partners took over the project.

Neighborhoods and Magnet Zones

In 1997, Menino told reporter Joe Sciacca, "I'm not dynamic. People underestimate me. We're doing a vision. Developing lower Washington Street, that's a vision. A new convention center, that's a vision."[40] In 2001, Menino created a "back streets" program to encourage job and light industrial development in Boston neighborhoods. In 2008, Menino and the BRA decided to rezone Hyde Park, the mayor's home neighborhood. They established an eleven-member advisory group through a nominating process. They held twenty community planning meetings and created the Hyde Park Strategic Neighborhood Plan. According to Professor Lisa M. Hemmerle, the BRA introduced the community to a "new" face. This included a Sky Zone (a trampoline gym), Dancing Deer Cookies, My Grandma's Coffee Cakes, Fire Fly (a custom bicycle manufacturer), and several "green" manufacturers."[41] Residents who live near these businesses are likely to support these new entities.

In 2010, Menino proposed that one thousand acres on the South Boston Waterfront become what he called an "Innovation District." The mayor wanted the destination to be a location that fostered entrepreneurship and provided space for startups. Given the area's history, trying to designate parts of South

Boston (the Seaport District) and Fort Point as an Innovation District was a surprise. The area was once a manufacturing and freight hub. However, it is located close to Downtown, the airport, and two major interstate highways. This prime location made it a perfect place to develop.

In 2011, planner Joseph D. Cutrufo quoted Richard McGuiness, a BRA official, on the South Boston waterfront: "It's been pretty left dormant since the 1960s. Even though it's just a 10- or 15-minute walk from downtown, its highest and best use for several decades has been surface parking. You have to unlock that potential with public investment. The city and the commonwealth enhanced the area's infrastructure with the creation of the Silver Line; the extension of I-90 through South Boston and under the harbor to the airport; and the depression of the Central Artery expressway. Those investments add value to the neighborhoods and help them realize its potential."[42]

Babson College, a business institution based in Wellesley, was innovative in agreeing to offer an MBA at Boston's Innovation District on Summer Street. Menino commented on the institution, "An outstanding program for entrepreneurship is coming to an outstanding cluster for innovative businesses. Babson and Boston are a great match. Colleges and universities are engines for talent and new businesses, and we know Babson will help fuel Boston's growth."[43] In another interview, Menino made the neighborhood connection: "Nobody creates jobs like entrepreneurs, and nobody creates entrepreneurs like Babson. . . . The inclusion of a top-tier academic institution here in the Innovation District is a key part of the supportive infrastructure we are building and providing to the people and businesses in this neighborhood. Babson's expertise and partnership undoubtedly will help us fuel even more connectivity and growth across this district."[44] By the end of Menino's tenure in 2013, over two hundred companies had moved and expanded into the district. In Menino's book *A Mayor for a New America*, he explained the rationale for the district: "Why Boston? location, location, location. The Innovation District is just four subway stops away from MIT and Harvard and the Kendall Square biotechnological center billed (for now) as 'the densest square mile of innovation on the planet.'" Menino cited a *Governing* magazine article that called his commitment to the Innovation District "perhaps the biggest gamble of my career. . . . The gamble is paying off. Growth on the waterfront has surged."[45] Obviously, many things have happened since Phillip Clay's 1991 chapter in the *Big City Politics in Transition* book.

As the Menino-led governing regime prepared for the last half of the 1990s and the first decade of the twenty-first century, Boston found itself in a transition crisis. The Massachusetts congressional delegation had lost power in Washington. The Republican-controlled Congress and presidency seemed committed to making massive cuts in entitlements. The cost of real estate in Boston made it a poor location choice for medium-sized corporations. The high-tech and biotech companies were tax productive but not labor-intensive. Boston's leadership in the high-tech industry continued to compete with California's Silicon Valley and the Research Triangle in North Carolina. Boston's largest financial institutions underwent tremendous change while Menino was in office. They were in a period of mergers and buyouts. The Bank of Boston merged with the Society for Saving and bought many local banks. Fleet Financial Group was brought out by Shawmut Bank. This made Fleet an $81 billion bank, the ninth largest in the nation. But it eventually merged with Bank of America.

The success of a Menino-led economic development project depended on his relationship with the economic elites in the city. The leaders of the "new Boston" were not rushing to share the spotlight with him. Yet, the job of an entrepreneurial mayor is to convince divergent interest groups to work together. In Boston, there were several economic elites. Todd Swanstrom has divided economic elites into two types, mobile and immobile.[46] The immobile interest stays inside the metro Boston area, whereas the mobile elites can move their investments anyplace. Local elites such as banking, utilities, and real estate interests are closely linked to the city and tended to be more intensely involved in local development and politics. They are represented by organizations such as the Greater Boston Chamber of Commerce, Associated Industries of Massachusetts, Massachusetts Business Roundtable, and Massachusetts High Technology Council.

The latter group, the high-tech and research corporate elites of Boston, considered themselves international players and mobile. Although their headquarters were located on Route 128, much of their business operations and sales were outside the city. These corporate headquarters considered themselves a part of the suburbs. Others, like Vertex, a pharmaceutical company, and Battery Venture, a financial investment company, were lured into Boston proper. Margaret Pantridge believes that they used Boston for recreation but ignored the problems of the inner city. According to her, these new elites were more interested in state tax policies than city problems.[47] They also wanted to live in an environmentally conscious city.

Beantown as Greentown

The partner of economic development is the maintenance of an environmentally safe city. As early as 2008, Boston was lauded by *Popular Science* magazine as the third greenest city in America behind Portland, Oregon, and San Francisco. Aside from establishing a Climate Action Advisory Plan, Menino's goals were to increase recycling of all material by 10 percent by 2012, plant 100,000 trees by 2020, commit to solar/green roofs, require 11.7 percent of power to come from renewable sources, and require all new construction to obtain a Leadership in Energy and Environment Design (LEED) certification. Menino asserted, "We've already made Boston a leader on climate change issues and this acknowledgment only inspires us further to be number 1 when it comes to being green.... Beantown truly is Greentown. Being green helps us build a better city and improve our economy at the same time. The success of Boston depends on us making the City greener."[48]

Mayor Menino became a strong supporter of the environmental movement. In his 2007 climate action plan, he launched a fifteen-point plan to reduce gases by 2012 and signed an executive order to reduce carbon dioxide emissions, methane, nitrous oxide, and other greenhouse gases from four hundred buildings and two thousand vehicles in Boston.[49] In 2011, Menino got the city to support the use of solar technologies. Building owners got reduced permit fees in they agreed to go solar. Menino stated, "Boston has consistently been ranked among the nation's top green cities and the passing of this ordinance proves once again that our City is committed to forward-thinking and innovative environmental policy. Now, Boston developers will find it easier to adopt new solar technologies, while further reducing energy costs and providing long-term benefits to the environment and our local economy."[50] This allowed Boston to have the lowest solar permit fee in the nation.

The Boston City Council also supported the mayor when it passed article 37, an amendment to the Boston Zoning Code. The amendment required new construction to be designed and built to meet the U.S. Green Building Council's LEED certification. The BRA was tasked with implementing the change. This sustainability project, which included green building standards, was a tough policy that called for more efficient energy use.[51] A seven-year study by Sandy Beauregard and colleagues raised questions about the impact of article 37. They concluded that "article 37 sends a message to the development community that City officials care about green building, but it seems to allow them to address the concern by simply paying lip service to sustainability initiatives."[52] Although there were strong environmental groups in Boston, they were not strong enough to inhibit economic growth. Many of the leaders of these groups thought that the new economy and environmental consciousness could coexist. History suggests that urban change is replete with uncertainties.

Coping with Change

Pre–World War I cities like Boston took out a mortgage to host the industries of the nation and are now coping with a new economy. Boston built low-cost housing, created public schools, and designed infrastructure to be industry friendly. When the plants closed, it had a ripple effect on housing, families, services, and retail businesses.[53] Even before the 2008 downturns, there were omnibus signs of deindustrialization and economic dislocation. City leaders discovered that they had little control over economic dislocation, tax-base decline, and rising maintenance costs.

A prudent mayor needs to have the acumen to cope with change within the city and the metro area. There is both planned and unplanned change. Planned change is a deliberate disaggregating process. In this case, the state of Massachusetts and Boston government officials actively decided what types of economic development they wanted to subsidize and support. In doing so, they decided what types of residential neighborhood they wanted to protect. Yet Boston's mayor would not say, "Let the North End and South Boston disappear," or that they were going to close A or B street down and make way for economic expansion.

Coping requires the city to publicly announce that it is closing parts of the cities and that it has no alternative housing or opportunities for the affected residents. Just as urban renewal gained a reputation as "Negro Removal" in some cities (in Boston, it was West End removal), such planned redevelopment can be the removal of the poor, uneducated, and unskilled. The poor are the most vulnerable, and they draw the least sympathy from more affluent residents. A planned redevelopment would attempt to preserve high-value infrastructure and locations. Obviously, these decisions are biased toward residents who are still productive and those who can afford to occupy space in the city. It is not axiomatic that the poor always lose space. There is some off-putting by the silence of political leaders regarding their plight. Professor J. T. Metzer observed,

The ownership of homes, rental property, and other real estate is the principal source of individual wealth in the United States and is used to pursue social mobility and middle-class status. The neighborhood life-cycle theory and triage planning have undermined this system by accommodating the discriminatory consequences of racial infiltration and the trends of urban housing abandonment. This has accelerated disinvestment in low-income and minority neighborhoods, exacerbating disparities in wealth, the wasteful consumption and desertion of urban land, and outward suburban sprawl.[54]

The role of city planning is to develop a strategy to improve the city and keep or develop a positive city image. Retaining environmental achievements is trying. Political leaders seek to avoid reputations of converting a working-class neighborhood into a middle-class professional enclave. Nevertheless, beginning with the turn of the twenty-first century, Boston was in the midst of relatively unnoticed gentrification. Can Boston remain blue-collar-job competitive? Changing a labor-friendly city like Boston into a "right-to-work" city is unlikely. Changing a neighborhood-based city into a transient, upscale one is more likely. The creative class is a part of the new service economy, and they are often high-wage earners and make aggressive demands on the housing market.

Summary

Tom Menino's interactions with his former colleagues on the City Council were sometimes adversarial and at other times a pure bargaining endeavor. He had served and understood what their districts expected of them. District representatives had to reference most issues to the welfare of their own districts, whereas the at-large members had more leeway and could be potential supporters. The economic issues were critical to the entire city of Boston. The mayor needed support for the EZ proposal and the Innovation District proposal.

An aspect of recurrent politics is the challenge of the national economy and its impact on Boston. Governors and mayors are theoretically supposed to work together to keep jobs in the city, solicit new industry to come to the Bay State, and do whatever is necessary to keep companies in the state. Menino got along with Massachusetts governors regardless of their political parties. Menino learned to avoid stepping on their toes when dancing for change but also to swing away from them when necessary. This was similarly true for his former colleagues on the City Council.

Nevertheless, no one claimed that Mayor Menino had neglected the neighborhoods in his revitalization schemes. If anything, his critics claimed he spent too much time on "nuts and bolts" and not enough time providing a new vision for Boston.

Tom Menino was in office for twenty years. With the help of state politicians and his own personal connections with investors and developers, he was able to determine the political and economic agenda for the city. Although the mayor's leadership of the Boston governing regime has not been under constant attack for concentrating its resources downtown at the expense of local neighborhoods, the longer the mayor stayed in office the more his personal popularity kept his opponents at bay. Council members, journalists, and activists did criticize him. Mayor Menino responded to such criticisms with, "I am doing the best I can."

CHAPTER 4

Boston's Day-to-Day and Recurrent Politics

Perhaps the best way to understand Boston politics is to identify what the city is not. Conventional wisdom would suggest that a city like Boston would have created a political structure consummate with its superstar status. Despite being an old city and near the top of the growth curve of economic change, Boston did not develop a political infrastructure like other American cities. In *The City on the Hill*, political scientist Thomas K. Ogorzalek asserts that cities with strong party systems such as political machines had cohesive congressional delegations that allowed them to coordinate with mayors and local elected officials to achieve what he called "institutions of horizontal integration" to continue the "Long New Deal."[1] Boston never developed a longstanding and entrenched political machine like New York's Tammany Hall, the Daley Machine in Chicago, the Pendergast Machine in Kansas City, or the Crump Machine in Memphis. The political context of the city of Boston did not allow an individual mayor to attain Daley-like political power.

Professor Patricia A. Kirkland analyzed 3,500 mayoral candidates for 259 cities over 50 years. She found that one-third of the candidates were business owners and executives.[2] This was not the case for Boston. Famous white male candidates for mayor such as James Michael Curley, Kevin White, and Thomas Menino were not former business owners or executives. These politicians ran on ethnicity, social issues, and personalities. They were attempting to establish a citywide political order. Yet Boston's residents have had a high demand for federal public goods and entitlements. The struggle over the distribution of those goods has created a conflict between white and minority communities. It is true that demands of redistributive policies has resulted in federal urban-oriented actions, but the cohesion of Boston's congressional delegation was not as strong as those in machine-dominated cities. In chapter 6 we discuss the rise in organized Boston's racial protests. Mayors Kevin White, Ray Flynn, and Tom Menino were obligated to keep the peace. Moreover, the faces of minority politicians in other cities might have looked the same and their demands sounded the same, but their histories were different. Boston did not have the Chicago history of Irish political machines (Kelly-Nash Machine), nor did James Michael Curley, apparently the model for Edwin O'Connor's *The Last Hurrah*, have the same Depression-era reputation as New York's Fiorello H. La Guardia.[3] Journalists occasionally reference what they believe was a Boston Irish Machine, but the reach of the machine was limited to local politics. Political scientist Steve Erie suggested the so-called Curley machine was never consummated to the point he could overcome the opposition of the state governors and President Franklin Roosevelt's decision to deny him federal patronage.[4] Besides the so-called machine had no sub-bosses or elaborate infrastructure. Equally important, Boston never had complex organizations among nonwhite groups. For example, the Bolling family, an African American Boston dynasty, was not as powerful as the Ford family in Memphis. The Ford family's political rise started with the Ed "Boss" Crump machine in the early twentieth century (1910–1950). Ford family members were elected to state and county politics. The Ford dynasty ended with Harold Ford Sr. though Harold Jr. was elected to the U.S. Congress.

Since Boston did not have a highly developed political machine system, the city never had strong mayoral control of a local political party. Opposing Boston's mayors was not a political career-ending blunder. Yet Jim Vrabel's *A People's History of the New Boston* concluded,

> Menino proved to be a hybrid of his recent predecessors. Like Flynn, he spent much of his time in the city's neighborhoods. Like White, he involved himself intimately in downtown development and put together a formidable political machine. In Menino's case, it was once described by Paul McMorrow as running on "loyalty and fear." Like Collins, he was an autocrat, and an even thinner-skinned one at that. Like Hynes, he had no ambition for higher office.
>
> But unlike all of the city's recent mayors, Menino never tired of the job—nor did he bring anything resembling a new vision to the new Boston."[5]

In his own book, Menino stated that "fear is power. I owed it to my city to keep fear alive."[6] Yet Menino's organization or power never matched that of the infamous Chicago political machine with its ward- and precinct-based infrastructure. None of the Boston mayors had a political machine. Otherwise, it might have survived their tenure and still been in place. Dorchester and Mattapan, Boston's minority enclaves, never developed a precinct-level Black leadership that compared with Chicago's Southside and Westside submachine bosses. Boston Black politicians ran against racial exclusion from city offices and were not a part of a political machine. If Boston had had an ongoing political machine, it would have been closer to a liberal city because the minority community would have had a stronger political infrastructure.

Obligatory Recurrent Politics

Even without a phantom of a political machine, some pundits are fond of saying politics ain't bean bag in Bean Town. There is much at stake in day-to-day Boston politics. Every day is different. Winning every time is necessary but not sufficient to master the recurrent politics (i.e., expected political reciprocities, campaigning for party members, reacting to interest groups and political activists) in the city, region, and nation. Therefore, recurrent politics is defined as the continuous intersection of politics at the various levels of government that connect elected officials and policy. Accordingly, in order to understand Menino, it is important to define the context of being mayor of Boston and how that relates to other politicians, staff, and people who want change. The mayor is obligated to be involved with continuous or recurrent politics. Endorsements of other politicians were a part of Menino's party leadership role. For example, in 2012 Menino endorsed Elizabeth Warren, a Harvard Law School professor, for the U.S. Senate against Republican senator Scott Brown. Although Warren was a passionate progressive, she was an outsider. Menino claimed that the endorsement took a long time because he did not know her. The mayor appeared with her in Boston's Roslindale neighborhood and stated, "I got to know Elizabeth Warren, and now Elizabeth Warren's got my vote, she's got my help."[7] This was a critical endorsement as his predecessor, Ray Flynn, had endorsed Brown. Warren won the election.

Recurrent politics also refers to the interactional politics with others in a higher office—that is, vertical relations—and with others in elected office on the same level—horizontal relations. These interactions often feel endless and relentless. There are scheduled off-year elections and presidential elections. There are also unexpected special elections when a vacancy occurs. Candidates may range from presidents to city councilors. There are unexpected upsets and surefire reconfirmation elections.

To stay on top of this flow of events, a prudent mayor has to prepare for all types of elections. Therefore, Menino could not ignore the official inter-regnums of elections. This is because politicians at the local, state, and federal levels are involved in making policies that affect the mayor's job. Accordingly, it is important to interact early and often with these political actors. Being members of the same political party is helpful, but this is often not enough. There needs to be something as simple as a common interest that keeps politicians united. Politicians at all levels of government must maintain some level of communication. Mayors who ignore recurrent politics do so at their peril.

Tom Menino inherited many of these recurrent political challenges, but some were new to him. First, he had to operate in a vertical federalism context that involves federal and state policies. He also had to deal horizontally with local politicians and with local interest groups with disparate preferences. He arrived at City Hall at a time of nationalization of local politics.[8] He was after all a politician in a sea of other politicians. No American mayor can avoid party politics, interest group challenges, and economic shifts. This job description defines the recurrent politics of being mayor.

Playing in Different Political Arenas

Being an elected official puts someone into a select club—a club that allows members to meet other elected officials at different levels of government, glad-hand strangers, receive requests to speak, and be the guest of honor at public events. For these politicians, city politics is a quest for power, status, and sometimes money. For some, it is a matter of playing amateur social worker. Still others simply love the game of politics. Loving the game also attracts staff. This was the case for Menino's former chief of staff and longtime associate David Passafaro. He took a huge pay cut and had to move back into the city to work for Menino because of residency laws. He had served as chief of staff for the City Council and chair of Menino's campaign committee before serving as Menino's chief of staff from 1995 to 1999. Passafaro said that after he left that office, people asked him if he still worked for the mayor: "I said I still work for him, but I don't get paid anymore. It was a labor of love; I enjoyed doing it. It was interesting and fun."[9] For elected politicians and their staff, public service was enjoyable. They could identify with the challenges of individuals in the office. This may explain why politicians sometimes regard nonelected political actors as interlopes, hustlers, amateurs, publicity seekers, or even trouble-makers. Newly elected members are neophytes and have to prove themselves. When newly elected officials enter the political arena, their motives and ambitions are questioned. Any elected official who is seen as only interested in staying in office, consolidating power, and making money is ironically regarded as reliable. If someone seeks to change the world, they are viewed with suspi-cion. Menino was not seeking to change the world. He convinced his fellow politicians that he simply wanted to make Boston a better place to live. To be successful and be a trusted mayor, Menino had to present himself as only interested in the overall welfare of all residents.

Again, a prudent city politician like Thomas Menino had to stay current with these various actors at different levels of government. Boston politics intersect at the neighborhood, district, congressional, state, and federal levels. Often policymakers at every level of government see problems differently. Howard Leibowitz, who was Menino's director of intergovernmental rela-tions, played a critical role in initiating and maintaining these relationships. He maintained relations with officials at the three levels of government. Menino enjoyed this this type of contact. Staffer Connor Doty recalled that "he [Menino] really enjoyed fellow mayors. If something was working in another city, he asked, 'Why aren't we doing that?' He was very popular among small city mayors. He accepted calls from them and returned their calls."[10] Urban partisanship matters in the short term (getting elected) but in the long term (dealing with political policy), it may not.

To keep Boston from being overlooked, Menino had to be open to a vari-ety of relationships. Accordingly, he had to create working relationships with many elected in-state and out-of-state officials. Local politicians know they cannot solve housing or transportation problems without outside assistance. Neither can city politicians deal with issues without paying attention to orga-nized interest groups and city gadflies. Failure to solicit outside assistance at a policy junction can result in a series of mistakes, delays, and frustrations. Because Menino spent a long political apprenticeship before he was elected mayor, he understood the recurrent nature of politics.

Although Menino was better prepared than some of his predecessors to deal with the various competitive interest groups, there was still much to be learned. The 1960s, 1970s, and 1980s had exposed Boston and Menino to protests (e.g., the busing controversy of the 1970s and the Mandela Separatist Movement in the late 1980s—a referendum to separate some Black neighborhoods from the city of Boston).[11] The social fabric of the city was not torn asunder by such events. But it became clear that to govern successfully in the future, one needed to be inclusive.

In the late 1970s, political scientist Douglas T. Yates Jr. offered a devastating indictment of cities and declared them to be ungovernable. In his *The Ungovernable City*, city mayors are portrayed as powerless to control protests by unions, social activists, and minorities. Using New York City as his example, Yates argued cities were doomed to mindless "street fighting pluralism." This type of pluralism "is political free for all, a pattern of unstructured, multi-lateral conflict in which many different combatants fight continuously with each other in a very great number of permutations and combinations."[12] Indeed, Boston had its share of managing dueling neighborhood organizations, teacher groups, police unions, housing advocate groups, and activist clergy. These groups predated Menino's rise to the mayoralty. When he assumed the mayoralty, they tested him.

Menino had an effective political apprenticeship, and his time on the City Council provided him with yet another learning experience. But like his predecessors, he inherited a new set of problems. Between 1988 and 1992, the city lost 75,000 jobs. There was also a $30 million revenue gap.[13] New Mayor Menino was expected to take ownership of these problems.

Former mayor Ray Flynn left many unsolved problems. One was the plight of the Boston City Hospital (BCH). BCH served poor and low-income residents, but it was also "a drag on the city budget."[14] There was a need for a merger to help offset some of the cost. The plan was to merge BCH with Boston University (BU) Medical Center Hospital. In the *Boston Globe*, Loretta McLaughlin noted, "While it is true that neither BCH nor BU Medical Center Hospital can survive alone, they do not need to merge to stay alive. . . . BU Medical Center Hospital is not hampered by any of the legal baggage that hobbles BCH. To the contrary, it is a free agent."[15] Menino believed that the only way for these two hospitals to survive was to merge. Menino saw the partnership created between Massachusetts General and Brigham and Women's Hospitals (Partners), and that created a perception in the city that if you didn't find a partner to create synergies, your hospital would be left out. Beth Israel Hospital merged with New England Deaconess Hospital, so in many ways, size did matter.[16]

McLaughlin's article was written to warn the City Council not to play politics with the proposed merger. After the failure of President Bill Clinton's 1993 healthcare proposal in Congress, there was a new revolution in the healthcare industry. McLaughlin continued, "And it is this revolution that is driving the BCH-BU Medical Center merger far more than the local politics of Mayor Thomas M. Menino or the parochial interests of the hospitals' executives, Elaine Ullian and Tom Traylor." McLaughlin also noted that both sides were "fortunate to have Menino."[17]

Menino appointed his chief of staff David Passafaro to lead the city team in the negotiations. The task was to merge a private nonprofit corporation with a public hospital. The latter was fully unionized. Passafaro worked with Dorchester's Maureen Feeney, chair of the City Council Government Operation Committee. Passafaro stated that he was in lockstep with Feeney and met with her every day. The Home Rule petition (i.e., asking the state legislature for permission on certain municipal actions) had to run through her committee.[18] Menino appeared before council and stated, "The hospitals that resist change, that fail to remain competitive, that are not open to new ideas, simply will not be in operation at the start of the 21st century. Let's protect our hospitals from that horrible fate. The people who need our hospitals deserve better than that." Elaine Ullian, president of the BU hospital, also appeared before the council and claimed that consolidation of the two institutions would "free up savings to build a fiscally sound health care system with a unique public health mission." She stated, "Doesn't it make sense to direct money to support programs that diagnose and treat heart disease when we have communities in Boston with 50 percent higher rates of heart disease, rather than run two billing departments 100 yards apart from each other."[19] In an article in *Modern Health Care*, Clark W. Bell noted that Menino and Ullian had worked together when he served as a councilor. She ran Boston Faulkner Hospital in Menino's district. Bell claimed, "The mayor helped grease Ullian's 1994 appointment as president and CEO of BU Medical Center, knowing full well they would attempt to merge it with the adjacent Boston City."[20]

The merger between the two hospitals was consummated after it was approved by the City Council and the state legislature. It entailed a $500 million deal that included solving the union issues, campus linkages, and a new governing structure. Menino appointed a planning commission to be headed by former State Senator Patricia McGovern. The commission recommended a new governing structure with a thirty-member board with staggered elections.

The new not-for-profit facility had 633 beds serving the indigent population and with a new slogan, "Exceptional care without exception." The merger was an example of Menino's ability to work with the medical community.

The hospital merger was an example of solving significant constituency problems while under the intense review of an attentive audience. Menino received congratulations from a wide audience. But there was much to be learned about pleasing that audience.

Constituencies and Audiences

Menino may not have read political scientist James Q. Wilson's article in *Public Interest* in which Wilson makes a distinction between a mayor's constituency and audience.[21] Obviously, a mayor's constituency includes residents, voters, and nonvoters. It is noteworthily, that Political scientist Martha Wagner Weinberg's 1980s explanation for former Kevin White's political survival held for Menino too:

> This is not merely to say that White is a good politician. It is also to acknowledge a crucial personal skill that the mayor of Boston must possess to be able to govern and to be reelected, for Boston is a heterogeneous city, a city of neighborhoods and tightly knit ethnic groups. Political followings have historically been personal followings and have lasted only as long as individuals have been able to hold them together. Though a majority of voters registered in Boston are nominally Democrats, the Democratic party in Massachusetts is so badly fragmented that the party has meant little as a stimulus to organizing voters, especially in nonpartisan city elections. No single organized group or economic organization dominates Boston politics. The business community does not speak with a single voice on political issues. Unions, though organized, have not been monolithic on political issues nor have they dominated the political landscape. In short, the politics of Boston has always been coalitional politics, but coalitional politics whose stability has depended on the talents and skills of the individual politicians rather than on the strength of ongoing loyalties or organizations.[22]

As noted in chapter 2, Menino was quite solicitous to his electoral coalition. He knew what to say and to whom. His wider audience was a different challenge for him. They had to get to know him. A good speech and visit would help but they wanted to know more. And he needed them to meet the needs of his constituencies.

Wilson recognized that the mayor's audience—the state legislature, the business community, and foundations—also have political power and require attention: "The audience also controls much of the free resources that a mayor needs so urgently, given his pinched tax base, the rising demand for services, and the shortage of able people to staff city hall."[23] Foundations can award cities with prizes that can bring them national recognition and attract industries and people looking for a place to locate. Menino's audience included his constituency, state legislatures, media, the business community, higher education institutions, and foundations. For the mayor, there were three types of foundations. The most important might be the Boston Foundation, which was founded in 1915 and has had an ongoing investment in the city. The second type was the national foundations such as the National Science Foundation, Ford Foundation, Verizon, and the W. K. Kellogg Foundation. The third type was local and national family foundations (e.g., Carnegie and Annenberg). City Hall had to keep up with their policy interests and what they were funding (e.g., public schools and the environment). If partisan politicians provide hard advice for a mayor, foundations proffer soft promptings. They can walk into a mayor's office and say, "If you do X, we will make a grant to either cover the cost or match your budget allocation." Ergo, foundations do shape a city agenda by offering to fund mayoral projects, even ones that are openly political.[24] This happened several times during the Menino administration.

The business community likewise influences city policies. This influence can range from advisory to preemptive power. Few mayors have been successful in ignoring the business community's interests or nurturing an antibusiness reputation. Organizations such as the Chamber of Commerce provide advice and a forum for mayors. Menino addressed the influence on the business community. He stated, "For years, the city government has acted as an opponent of business rather than an ally. The city government acted as a gatekeeper to slow business down rather than a responsible partner to find ways to help businesses grow. No more."[25] Menino was signaling to the business community that his administration would be "business-friendly." He promised to cut new venture approval times in half. He discovered that each member of the audience expected a signal.

In many ways, the media is the most intense audience. Besides the local media (the *Boston Globe*, the *Boston Herald*, *Bay State Banner*, and *Boston Magazine*) and the broadcast radio and television stations, there have been occasions when the national media pokes around in Boston politics.

Finally, there are the commonwealth of Massachusetts's elected leaders. As we discuss in the following chapters, the state legislature has preemptive powers. The legislature meets in Boston, and its members often consider themselves experts on Boston's social problems. Members are not usually averse to offering opinions about what should be done in the city.

In each case, Mayor Menino learned that both the audience and constituencies often wanted different policies and needed to be treated differently. His time as a councilor taught him how to treat constituencies, including voters and nonvoting residents, local retail businesses, and community advocacy groups. Like many city politicians, Menino often stayed within a safe constituency bubble. In many ways, this strategy was a safe position, but it was also limiting. It could result in rewarding people who supported you and ignoring others. As a leading community advocate Lew Finfer discovered,

> Menino liked some people more than they may have deserved. Menino disliked some people more than they deserved. He really wanted to be in control so if a person was supportive of him or did not show signs of disagreeing, he/she might be seen as a good guy/gal by Menino, whether or not they deserved that in the context of the work they were doing. Similarly, someone could oppose anything Menino did or not be appreciative enough and would be exiled in Menino's mind as someone to ever work with whether or not he/she deserved that based on what they were trying to do on issues in their job and organization.[26]

But this wider audience was an entirely new challenge. Wider audiences are most diverse and want different things. They might take collective references as personal. They are also more likely to rate a mayor's performance based on what they viewed in their policy interests rather than the person themself. Menino would learn more about the power of the audience after he became the elected mayor.

As a new mayor, it was critical that Menino understood the needs of this larger audience and surrounded himself with a good staff who could act as informal liaisons to these groups. In his campaign, Menino had promised his staff would be inclusive and diverse. This promise was exemplified in Menino's selection of a transition team. The transition team included minorities, urban experts, outsiders, and insiders, and was designed to impress both his constituencies and audiences.

The Mayor and National Domestic Politics

Mayors of big cities like Boston cannot avoid presidential politics or ignore national domestic policies. National politics are a true recurrent process. Mayors are an attentive audience for presidential domestic policies regardless of political party. Aside from their aides for intergovernmental relations, mayors depend on their state's congressional delegation. The congressional delegation must alert the mayor to changes in policies and alert them about opportunities in the federal grant-in-aid trough. Thomas Ogorzalek's *The City on the Hill* makes this point.

All presidential candidates claim that they will improve the lives of the American people. They will create jobs, make sound economic decisions, and increase public safety. However, there are ideological differences between the two national political parties and the implementation of domestic policies. When Menino became mayor, Bill Clinton, a fellow Democrat, was president. Clinton had run for president as a member of the moderate Democratic Leadership Council. His domestic policy was characterized by one writer as a "small change."[27] Some critics claimed that Clinton's urban policy was a stealthy one. He made changes that helped cities but did not call them urban policies. Clinton was able to increase the earned income tax credit and funding for the Head Start program. He also enacted empowerment zones. Clinton was able to obtain more money for the homeless and funds for food stamps. All of these policy expansions had a positive impact on cities like Boston. On the other hand, Clinton also signed a major change in welfare policies with the Welfare Reform and Personal Responsibility Act of 1996, which altered how long recipients could remain on the program. He also signed a crime bill that allowed funding for more street police officers. The Clinton presidency ended with an impeachment (acquitted by the U.S. Senate) and the subsequent election of Republican George W. Bush. Nonetheless, mayors must work with both political parties.

The 2004 National Democratic Convention

In 2004, the Democratic National Committee selected Boston's Fleet Center for its convention. This required a lot of local planning and financing. Menino and Senator Edward Kennedy were great friends and worked together on financing the convention. To avoid a conflict of interest, they divided the types of donors and contributors they would solicit. Kennedy worked with local types and Menino worked with federal ones. The city raised $50 million from locals and another $50 million from the federal government for security. Menino appointed David Passafaro as president of the Host Committee. Passafaro recalled, "The mayor and I went down to Philadelphia to be briefed by Mayor Ed Rendell. Philadelphia hosted the 2000 Republican Convention. Rendell told us 'Don't pay for stuff unless you have the money. He said that he had to go back to local vendors and ask them to accept 50 cents on the dollar. They ran out of money.' We took Rendell's advice, and we ended up with a surplus of $9 million. We dispersed it to the nonprofits, vendors, museums, and USS *Constitution* ship, the Freedom Trail, and other institutions in the hospitality and tourism industries."[28]

A convention requires a lot of security planning from federal, state, and local agencies. It also required a massive planning operation directed by Mayor Menino. Menino stated, "Thousands of people had devoted eighteen months of planning to the convention."[29] National conventions are by nature disruptive. But for many, this was a special convention since one of their own was being nominated.

Menino delivered the welcoming speech. The July convention nominated Massachusetts U.S. senator John Kerry for president and John Edwards of North Carolina for vice president. At first glance, it looked like a competitive ticket, but after a series of errors were made, the ticket went down to defeat. One of the most memorable moments was the keynote speech by Barack Obama, a junior African American senator from Illinois, who would be elected president in four years.

Long before Senator Kerry and Massachusetts governor Mitt Romney ran for president, Menino got involved in national party convention location competitions and lobbied for them for several years. As early as 2002, journalist Joe Sciacca warned others not to doubt that Menino would get the Democratic National Convention prize. The title of his column read, "Don't Be fooled by Mr. Mayor's Simple Demeanor."[30] He predicted that Menino would get the job done.

In 2008, Barack Obama, the first African American president, was elected. Democrat Obama came to office in the middle of the so-called Great Recession. His first months in office were dedicated to rescuing the nation from a serious financial crisis. Congress passed several bills to stimulate the economy. Examples were the America Recovery and Reinvestment Act of 2009 and the Job Creation Act of 2010. Generally speaking, Obama's domestic policy followed Clinton's strategy by not labeling new entitlements as urban-specific policies. His biggest welfare impact was the passage of the Affordable Care Act, which provided healthcare for many Americans including poor Bostonians. In 2009, President Obama also made available $5 billion in grants to cities to improve their low-performing schools. Menino reacted by endorsing district-run charter schools. This reform is discussed in chapter 8.

Interestingly, Menino was the only mayor in the nation who served with an American African governor (Deval Patrick) and an African American president (Barack Obama). These two men represented a change in racial attitudes in the nation. In 2012, former governor Mitt Romney lost to Obama. Throughout those years, the challenges that came across Menino's desk were difficult and sometimes mangled. The economic development issue was the most difficult.

Some Boston mayors have attempted to address economic problems by climbing Beacon Hill to the State House. The maxim that as Boston goes, so goes the state of Massachusetts, is probably true. Boston's financial district remains one of the most successful in the country. After the turn of the twenty-first century, Boston grew as a tourist center. First-class hotels changed the skyline of the city, but there was still a need for a large convention center to be competitive for larger conventions. The question was what should be the priority for Boston, a convention center or a megaplex (a multipurpose stadium and convention facility)? This became one of the most visible struggles among Menino, state leaders, and some of the state's economic elite.

Convention or Megaplex

In many American cities, there had been a discernible shift to creating tourism jobs downtown since the manufacturing jobs were disappearing. However, Boston has a limited amount of land space in Boston proper. To increase the city's profile in the entertainment business, Menino thought that a larger convention center, not a megaplex, would best serve the city's interests. As early as 1994, Menino had indicated that he recognized the need for an upgrade of Fenway Park, but he did not want the Red Sox baseball team and the Patriots football teams to share a stadium. He stated, "Everyone loves Fenway Park, and we also recognize it to be one of the most revered plots of real estate in the city. . . . But the sagging economics of the stadium require the city to investigate alternatives . . . and a baseball team will make this whole [Megaplex] plan work."[31]

Robert Kraft, the new owner of the Patriots, revived the idea of a megaplex with the football team being a part of it. At first, Menino wanted to get both projects done separately. Menino asserted, "We should seize this opportunity and get both things done at once."[32] The Krafts saw the projects in zero-sum terms, however, and Menino took a stand for the convention center. David Passafaro, Menino's chief of staff, recalled, "The Krafts wanted to locate a stadium on the waterfront. In the fall of 1998, the mayor and I went to the Bank of Boston and met with Chad Gifford, president of the bank, and Robert and Jonathan Kraft. It was 7:00 in the morning. They had a demonstration room [outlining the structure of the project]. The mayor said, 'the timing is not really right.'"[33]

The following year was an election year for the mayor, and traffic was an issue. The Krafts had proposed a one-way-in, one-way-out configuration for the tunnels leading to northbound traffic from the waterfront. NFL games customarily played on Sunday at 1:00 p.m., which meant that the one way out could be around 4 p.m., part of the Sunday rush hour to and from Logan Airport. The Krafts were upset with the mayor. Governor Bill Weld said to the mayor, "Let me take a shot at it. You stay out of the way." Weld and his administration conducted neighborhood meetings to judge the feedback in South Boston and were roundly criticized.[34] When the community meetings didn't go well, the Krafts and Governor Weld quietly let the idea die.

After the mayor made his convention preference publicly, Weld supported an alternative megaplex site in Roxbury. Menino supported a stand-alone convention center that would be partially financed by a one-dollar user hotel fee. In addition, the center would be financed with over $400 million of public funds.[35] The mayor and governor had to agree on the funding if the state was to be the senior partner in this development.

The proposed building of the megaplex—the combined sports and convention center—put the Menino administration and Governor Weld at odds. In August, the mayor took a firm stand against a domed stadium for football in Boston. Menino asserted, "Everyone agrees we need a convention center. What's holding it up is how to finance the stadium piece. We don't need a new football stadium right away, but we do need convention center business and jobs. So, let's do what's doable and what's needed today."[36] A new park for the Red Sox was a different matter. The Boston Red Sox held a critical part of the city's history. Eighty-one home games were played there whereas the New England Patriots only played eight home games. Besides, if Boston wanted to get into the large convention business, it had to move beyond the small Hynes Convention Center.

Conversely, having a professional football team identified a city as a major player in professional sports. Like other large cities that acted as host cities for

NFL teams, the mayor knew that a new stadium would involve serious funding. Not only do football facilities have short shelf-lives, but NFL team owners demand first-class stadiums. NFL teams have the leverage of threatening to leave if the stadium is out of date. Boston would be no exception. This may explain why Robert Kraft proposed a plan to combine an entertainment center with a new domed stadium for the Patriots in Boston. Menino rejected the idea. The BRA conducted a study of the proposal but suggested a free-standing convention center instead.

Nevertheless, the state legislature called a megaplex summit and established a Megaplex Commission. To control the site of the megaplex, the mayor needed to build his own coalition. The BRA opposed locating the stadium in Boston. But the recommendation of planners was not enough. State Senate president William Bulger supported the convention center. Representative Byron Rushing, a rising Black politician, opposed the idea but several state officials supported the proposed megaplex. This resulted in a political standoff.

The results were a free for all with the governor and state legislators supporting a domed stadium in Boston and Menino and his supporter opposing it. Football fans were told they could lose the Patriots if the deal was not made. There were rumors of moving the team to Hartford, Connecticut. This would mean a long drive for fans, and the city would lose prestige.

Menino was attacked for not being forceful enough. He was accused of being a "small-time mayor." The mayor responded, "I don't want to lose the Patriots, but that's not going to make the decision on whether it's a first-class or second-class city." The otherwise empathic mayor continued, "I hate to see them go, and I'll do everything I can to keep them here, but it is not the be-all and end-all of everything."[37] The fight for the megaplex involved many heavy hitters in state and local politics.[38] At the time of an earlier study of the megaplex, the research was unaware of what was happening behind closed doors. In his book *A Mayor for a New America*, Menino remarked that Governor Weld had gotten the idea from a visit to the Toronto SkyDome. He wanted to build the "WeldDome." For Menino, this "dream" matched with that of the former owner of the Patriots football team, James B. Orthwein.[39] Menino took the occasion in his book to spike the football.

Political scientist Alan DiGaetano concluded that the failure of the megaplex was evidence of the declining influence of the pro-growth coalition. He stated, "Indeed, the often contentious politics of the Megaplex development illustrates that Boston's political and economic leaders failed to construct a pro-growth regime that exercised preemptive power."[40] The controversy that started in 1994 and went on for five years was finally solved with the help of NFL commissioner Paul Tagliabue. In the end, Robert Kraft built a stadium in Foxboro, Massachusetts. The Patriots went on to win several Super Bowls.

The settlement of the megaplex project did not stop the debate about a new Fenway Park deal. Professor Richard M. Perlmutter stated that Menino was "solidly behind a new ballpark in the Fenway neighborhood." He claimed the mayor needed to "placate" John Kelly, president of the Boston City Council. Some people believed that the new park should be located in South Boston, but Kelly and his constituency did not want it. The problem was a lack of space and lack of citizen support. Perlmutter cited a "ballpark summit" in 2000 called by Governor Paul Cellucci and Mayor Menino. As a result of the summit, the legislative leaders were able to enact chapter 208, entitled "City of Boston Infrastructure Improvements for the Fenway Area." The new law provided $100 million of state funds for "essential infrastructure improvements" within a "ballpark development area." Specific reference was made to streetscape and transit improvements, bridges, underpasses, and pedestrian walkways.[41] The construction funds would be raised by issuing general obligation bonds.

The deal would have allowed the city to issue bonds for up to $140 million for land acquisition, site cleanup, and a three-thousand-car parking garage. The project involved the city's using its eminent domain powers to acquire private land. The new $352 million park would be built by a private fund. Journalist Stacey Higginbotham outlined the debt cost strategy in the deal: "To cover Boston's debt service costs, the agreement allocates $12.1 million from an array of sources, largely related to activities at or around the stadium. The city would receive the following revenues: .25% of the convention and hotel tax, a $5 parking surcharge for each of the 9,000 spaces near the ballpark on game day, a ticket surcharge, a 15% tax on luxury boxes, and an increased tax on sales within the park."[42]

Problems arose about who would pay the cost of highly contaminated soil from the privately owned land. Who would pay for cost overruns became the issue. Supporters of the new park began to question the project. Organizations like Save Fenway Park and the Fenway Community Development Corporation opted for the renovation of Fenway Park. The deal was further complicated by the Florida Marlins owner John Henry's decision to sell his team to the Montreal Expos owner and then buy the Boston Red Sox. This increased the uncertainty of the park deal. The deal began to look like a Rube Goldberg machine, and it fell apart quickly.

Perlmutter reported that Menino along with others rejected the idea of an alternative location for a new Fenway Park and changes in the funding formula. The collapse of the Fenway Park and megaplex deals demonstrated how the mayor emerged as the center of negotiations. Menino was able to create an alternative economic development coalition and lead it.

Making a New Mayor-Centered Coalition

Again, framing the economic agenda is the essence of a modern mayoralty. In this task, most city mayors have rivals. Since Boston is the state's capital city, the State House provided rivalries between the mayor and the state's politicians. Menino's nonthreatening and conciliatory personality allowed his citywide political base to neutralize most of the competition. Beating up on Mr. Nice Guy was not good politics. However, continued cooperation between political leaders and business leaders was needed if a convention center was to be built.

The development of a Menino-led urban economic regime took years. All the parties had to learn to adapt to the working styles of the new leadership. Establishing a good working relationship tends to support what political scientist Clarence Stone calls "social production."[43] This type of economic elite–politician cooperation was needed if Boston was to move ahead. Over the years, Menino was open to creating such a coalition. The question was whether members of the coalition could continue to work together when they faced disagreements over development.

Throughout his tenure, Menino remained popular copy among reporters. They focused on his style and statements, and less on his ability to create and build working coalitions. Menino's loose coalition of liberal reformers, corporate leaders, and the new Black political leadership stayed together. Menino openly encouraged the business elite to deal with him directly. Boston journalists believed the business community had never connected with Ray Flynn.

Journalists admired the fact that Flynn kept a "lid on the city" but they did not like his style or lack of consultation with them.[44] Menino, on the other hand, made clear that he intended to seek their advice. Soon after taking office as acting mayor, Menino repeatedly stated that he was not using the office as a stepping-stone. He stated, "I have no ambitions for higher office. You can either be mayor or campaign for something else, but you can't do both real well."[45] Menino stated over and over again that he had no higher political ambitions.

Menino discovered this when he decided to take a grassroots approach to plan for the enterprise zone application. Yet he seemed just as committed to mediating conflicts among the neighborhoods as was his famous predecessor, Ray Flynn. The pro-convention coalition was composed of a different set of actors with different political strengths. Menino had the support of downtown leaders, and he won the fight against the megaplex.

Remember, Menino was a man who was obsessed with being judged on his own terms. He was quick to provide an explanation for his actions and to downgrade unrealistic public expectations. On a weekly television talk show, *Keller at Large*, Menino defended his approach by referencing his personal involvement in the choice of Boston's school superintendents and allowed that his greatest achievement by 1995 had been the merger of Boston City Hospital with Boston University Medical Center Hospital.[46] He admitted that he had not created as many jobs as he had promised, but he was trying hard. At that point, it remained to be seen whether trying hard in a transition period would be good enough.

Menino's neighborhood strategy, backed by the real estate industry, construction unions, banks, and downtown merchants, was aimed at creating a new and more diverse city economy. Early on, Menino had indicated that he also wanted to develop a large parcel of land on which the former Boston State Hospital currently resided. On Kelley's show, he rejected the proposals offered by small investors. He stated that he was interested in a more comprehensive plan. He wanted to attract major financial services businesses. The development of existing city properties was crucial to the mayor's economic development strategy.

One uncertainty was the future direction of the federal government. Federal politicians of both parties were calling for an end to big government. Even President Clinton had made such a statement in his State of the Union address. Congress wanted state and local governments to have more flexibility and responsibility, but local politicians saw this as a smoke screen for less federal funds. Without federal money, Boston, like other cities, would not make all the infrastructure and economic changes it needed to position itself for the twenty-first century. Tom Menino was just one actor in this drama. Other politicians had different roles to play.

Other Government Actors

The other aspect of recurrent politics is the challenge of the Massachusetts economy and its impact on Boston. Governors and mayors are theoretically supposed to work together to keep jobs in the city, solicit new industry to come to the Bay State, and do whatever is necessary to keep companies in the state. As is the case for most states, the relations between the State House, the governor, and the mayor of its largest city can be complicated.

Boston City Hall is located only a few blocks from the state capital on Beacon Hill. Thus, the mayor is always competing with state politicians for public attention. Boston has always suffered from an embarrassment of riches when it comes to politicians. Over the years it has been blessed with several clever, flamboyant, talented, and powerful politicians. Since World War II, Massachusetts has had two Speakers of the House (John McCormack and Thomas O'Neill), a president (John F. Kennedy), and three presidential candidates (Michael Dukakis, John Kerry, and Mitt Romney).

The state was also the birthplace of the Kennedy dynasty. Senator Ted Kennedy was a liberal leader of the U.S. Senate. Although Kennedy's dynastic power had diminished greatly when Republicans took over the U.S. Senate, Kennedy remained a senior member of the Senate until the end of his life. Senator John Kerry also assumed a high profile through his reelection in 1996. Despite the challenge for his senate seat by Governor William Weld, Kerry was an effective representative for Massachusetts and was later nominated for the nation's highest office and became President Obama's secretary of state.

In 1995, Senator William Bulger, president of the State Senate and one of the most powerful politicians in the state, left the government and accepted the presidency of the University of Massachusetts. This represented a major change in state politics as new politicians filled the void. In Boston, state politics is local politics.

Besides these veteran officeholders, there was a whole cadre of relatively young politicians with ambitions. Congressman Joe Kennedy, State Treasurer Joe Malone, and Attorney General Scott Harshberger were examples. None of these politicians saw Menino as a threat to their political careers. This made it easy for them to help the city and for the mayor to solicit their assistance. Although the mayor managed to represent himself as a threat to no one, there was still more conflict than consensus in Boston's transitional politics.

Finally, politicians are criticized once they decide to leave office. Reporters Jason Schwartz and Rachel Slade asked who got rich under Menino. Slade criticized the choices by the BRA and the high salaries of its employees. Reporter Jannelle Nanos identified Menino's two friends John Fish and John Fallon, who owned construction companies and got billion-dollar projects.

She also mentioned Anthony Pangaro, a former BRA employee who likewise received lucrative contracts:

> Anthony Pangaro was a BRA alum who cashed in when Menino took over. After years as a civil servant, he joined New York–based Millennium Partners and shepherded the company through the process of building the $500 million Ritz-Carlton towers, then built the $160 million One Charles Street condo building on Beacon Hill. Grateful that the developer risked building luxury condominiums in the former Combat Zone, Menino—through the BRA—awarded Millennium the rights to build $220 million in luxury condos on Hayward Place, a deal that raised questions about the bidding process. Then, in 2012, Pangaro and Millennium took over a $700 million project connected to Filene's, which suddenly got one hundred feet taller (and thus more profitable), and [was] being considered for major property-tax breaks by the BRA.[47]

This article suggested that any attempt to place a halo on Menino was problematic. Menino's reputation for having thin skin grew out of what he thought was a media hit job. Menino would defend himself when journalists attempted to link him to favoritism. Few politicians enjoy being criticized by the media. However, deal-making and doing favors with politicians and others are essential parts of being a mayor.

Summary

Normal recurrent politics and economic challenges cannot be avoided. A president's positions on urban issues matter. For mayors, federal officials meddled and preempted city initiatives. Menino had to deal with a variety of politicians. For some, politics is a way to serve, make a living, and earn a reputation. Politicians usually enjoy campaigning because it connects them with other members of the fraternity of politicians. Tom Menino apparently enjoyed it and stood on the same platform with presidential candidates and presidents. Big-city mayors like Menino were expected to be involved with party candidates and nominees for offices ranging from council districts to presidential campaigns. Supporting the candidacy of at-large councilors can be tricky in that it helps them develop stronger citywide images. They can potentially challenge a mayor. In 2011, Michael Flaherty came closer than any other of Menino's mayoral opponents. Supporting the party nominees for the State House, U.S. Senate, governors, and representatives was relatively easy. Yet Menino was expected to go all out for candidates, and when he didn't he was criticized.

Menino served under three Republican governors. Menino got along with governors regardless of party. David Passafaro recalled, "The Mayor liked having Republican governors. They were not competing with him. He had a strong position and organization as a leader of the Democratic Party in the state. He had a great friendship with Bill Weld. Two days after Menino was sworn in as acting mayor, Governor Weld walked the six blocks from Beacon Hill, came to City Hall, and asked to see the mayor. He is my mayor. He reached out to him. Menino thought it was one of the most impressive acts of political kindnesses done to him."[48]

Weld was conservative on tax issues, but he was considered a social liberal on many other topics. Like many Massachusetts governors, Weld had higher political ambition. In retrospect, his tenure was about achieving national visibility. However, he did disagree with Menino on the megaplex issue. The point is that the two did not have much of a rivalry. As NFL owner Robert Kraft discovered, Menino was more focused on Boston than on a regional image.

Menino won the battle over the megaplex proposal, but the looming and continuing theme of Boston housing politics posed a different challenge.

CHAPTER 5

Who Gets Housing, When, and Where?

> Few things intersect with and influence as many aspects of life as housing does: it is far more than shelter from the elements. As a home, housing is the primary setting for family and domestic life, a place of refuge and relaxation from the routines of work and school, and private space. It is also loaded with symbolic value, as a marker of status and an expression of style. Housing is also valued for its location, for the access it provides to schools, parks, transportation, and shopping; and for the opportunity to live in the neighborhood of one's choice. Housing is also a major asset for homeowners, the widespread form of personal wealth.
>
> —Alex Schwartz, *Housing Policy in the United States*

Housing options in Boston, like most American cities, mean different things to different people. A house, be it large or small, made up of one or two stories, can be a simple dwelling to shelter a primary family. Other types of houses may include extended families. The universal meaning of housing is to allow individuals to live together under the same roof. This is the definition of a home. It is more than a set of bedrooms and a cooking area. A house is a place where residents establish a stake in the community. Tom Menino's socialization included internalizing these values. To say that Menino was a neighborhood-centered mayor is an understatement. He grew up in a multigenerational home with grandparents who lived on the first floor, while he and his parents resided on the second floor. After he bought his first home, he lived in the same house for all of his life, including during his tenure as mayor. Much of his identity was formed by owning his family house and living in his neighborhood. For the future mayor, his house was a way to become and remain a part of an affinity community. Over the years, he acquired the resources to move but he felt comfortable at 192 Chesterfield Street, Hyde Park. It was a personal choice and a statement about who he was. It would be his ambition to create homes for others and maintain the status of Boston's middle-class homeowners.

Housing researchers David P. Varady and Jeffrey A. Raffel's *Selling Cities* asserted, "The vitality of American cities depends in part on their ability to retain and attract the middle class."[1] Home-buying decisions are complicated. Cities must provide incentives for residents to buy and sell. Boston mayors, city councils, and real-estate agents have to be alert to what potential house buyers seek. The quality of schools and the safety of the neighborhood's reputation matter. Each decade presents new challenges, but the basics remain. Neighborhood niches are critical to buying decisions.

In a book written before Menino became mayor, *Boston Politics: The Creativity of Power*, philosopher Tilo Schabert wrote,

> Cities are telling the story of politics, and politicians are caring about cities. The good politician knows that the story cities tell is his own, the politician's story. They constitute the most enduring record of his craft: politics transposed into space. Politicians therefore also like to be architects. City architects pursue politics as spatial politics and thus through its essence. In constructing the city, they construct the polis. In shaping urban space, they shape political space. In being architects of the city, they are the architects of society....
>
> Architecture is a social construction. The politician as architect constructs society. And society constructs itself, through the innumerable architectural decisions and acts which its members make and perform every day. People continually participate in the architectural construction of society, simply by doing what they do in everyday life: by renting an apartment or by buying a house; by moving from the old neighborhoods in the inner city to the suburbs or by moving back to the city; by using the automobile or public transport on the daily trips between the dwelling and the workplace; by spending evenings in movie houses, theaters, concert halls, restaurants or by staying mostly at home with the family, the hifi or the video set; by patronizing the small shops in the neighborhood rather than the department stores in the shopping mall; by filling the streets of the city on weekends with their voices and bustle, or by fleeing every Friday night from the city to the country.[2]

In many ways, Tom Menino understood these dynamics. He reshaped Boston politics with his housing policy. Simply put, dwellings mean different things to different people. Owning a house allows families to accumulate wealth, but many are not capable of acquiring a mortgage and buying a house. They will be lifelong renters. This does not mean renters will be disinterested in the impact of housing politics on their neighborhoods.[3] For others, real estate represents an investment income. They become landlords and real-estate speculators. As we shall see, these individuals organized associations to protect their interests. Hence, they interacted with the City Council, the mayor's office, and even the state of Massachusetts.

Some Americans live in the same house their entire life while others have a more extended housing career. They move up, around, upsize, and downsize. In effect, they can exercise their housing mobility. A city is expected to protect the homeowning class. Sadly, some Americans find themselves homeless. They have no options. A mayor is expected to protect them as well as residents who have humble dwellings, provide safety for the neighborhoods, create affordable housing for upward mobility, do something about those who are homeless, and support rent control. Herein lies housing politics.

Boston's housing politics can be understood as reacting to these disparate demands for living space, class preferences, and site locations. Obviously, the changing economy and its effects on housing choices and neighborhoods, population density, and patterns affect what City Hall can do. A growing city like Boston must build infrastructure to support new industries and create housing stock for new workers. Leaving housing to the marketplace has never worked as a strategy. The city needs its most valuable workers to live in Boston proper for a variety of reasons. Aside from tax income, the city hopes these new workers will become authentic stakeholders.

Housing in Boston has been a mix of traditional units in old neighborhoods juxtaposed with a variety of modern housing choices. The single-family detached home was the standard, but other types of units are now a part of the newly built environment. Some condos with their glass exteriors can match buildings in any skyline. There are also new tenant apartments created for transient renters. This new, diverse architecture is at variance with Boston's image of historic Beacon Hill, the Irish American enclaves of South Boston, and the Black enclaves of Roxbury. More importantly, changes in housing types are an attempt to cater to the various groups of people who wish to live in Boston.

This chapter examines the housing politics of Boston. Who lives where and why? What are the housing careers of residents? What is the relationship between neighborhoods and citywide housing politics? Boston housing politics can be divided into old and new politics. Decisions that were made in the old housing politics will impact new housing politics. And some aspects of new housing politics can trace their policy to the path dependency (i.e., the history) of Boston's old housing policy. In other words, an incredible amount of housing history and policies took place before Menino took office and had a mayor's influence on his policy options.

The Old Politics of Boston Housing

Before the twentieth century, there was what may be called an old Boston period of housing politics and policies. The main issue was what type of housing needed to be built and where. The housing boom was a reaction to the influx of new immigrants. The early demand did not match the supply. New residents shared existing housing stock with other immigrants. Many of them stayed in tenements. Tenements were sets of rooms within a block of apartments. They were crowded, unhealthy, and unsightly. Between the years 1815 and 1860, over 5 million European immigrants came to the United States. Many of them settled in Boston. For some of them, these tenement dwellings were better than the old country. Back then the city government was not dedicated to housing development.

In nineteenth-century Boston, mayors were aware of the impact of poorly constructed and maintained tenements on the health and safety of the immigrant community, but the prevailing attitude was that housing was strictly a matter of private property that precluded city government intervention. There were no housing departments or funds to build new housing.

The so-called good government groups sounded the alarm on low-quality housing and asserted the problem was a moral issue. Aside from the unhealthy conditions, these units were a breeding ground for social pathology. Hence, the lives of children were at stake. As a result, philanthropic organizations led Boston's tenement reform. One of them was the Boston Committee on the Expediency of Providing Better Tenements to the Poor. It was organized in 1846 and worked to protest the Irish working class. The group wanted to provide drainage, ventilation, fire escapes, and places for garbage. These reforms were made more urgent with rising waves of Irish immigration. Professor Cynthia Zaitzevsky stated,

> Before the mid-nineteenth century, Boston had been relatively free from overcrowding and extreme poverty. It had even escaped the great cholera epidemic that spread from Europe in 1832 to almost every large city in

the United States. The situation changed suddenly in the mid-1840s, due largely to the Irish potato famine of 1845–1850. By 1855 more than 50,000 Irish immigrants, most of them impoverished, had settled in Boston—only slightly less than the entire number of residents, mostly native-born, in 1825 (59,277). Before the fillings of the South End and Back Bay and the annexations of adjoining towns, all of which occurred in the third quarter of the century, the city was ill-equipped to handle such an abrupt surge in population. There was no build-absorbing an earlier group founded in 1827 as the Labourer's Friend; and another organization, the Metropolitan Association for Improving the Dwellings of the Industrious Classes, had been established in 1841. The first was primarily a benevolent society and the second a commercially based group, but one with philanthropic goals and a limited rate of profit.[4]

Early Boston mayors like Josiah Quincy Jr. may have been aware of the effects of unhealthy tenements on immigrants but the city did not have the authority and resources to do much about the situation. In 1846, *The Report of the Boston Committee on the Expediency of Providing Better Tenements for the Poor* found squalid conditions in the tenements and considered them a peril to general health and morality. Some tenements did not have proper ventilation. Reformers were also appalled that the poor paid high rents for these dwellings.[5] Tenements were the only housing available for the Irish American working class. Another philanthropic organization, the Boston Cooperative Building Company, attempted to provide sanitary and attractive dwellings for the poor.[6]

Robert Treat Paine, a lawyer, outlined the political struggle to pass tenement laws in Boston. New York and London had such model laws, but Boston never attained that level of government action. The notion that poor tenants needed the government to make changes failed to catch on during the nineteenth century. The advent of the twentieth century saw governments at all levels getting involved in the housing policy arena. In 1902, Paine reflected optimistically,

> On the whole, the outlook is full of hope. Vigilance and vigorous action are demanded of all municipal authorities. Public interest is aroused. The action of other cities in Great Britain as well as in New York and other American cities warns Boston not to fall behind in this movement, which will surely give to us and our children a healthier city for the homes of the plain people, with its plague spots extirpated, and an increasing proportion of the population living out in suburban homes in this city of unsurpassed suburban beauty.[7]

With the assistance of muckraking journalists, city halls across the nation were forced to take more interest in the tenement situation. Funding was the main problem, but landlord organizations remained a strong lobbying group against government intervention. The "roaring twenties" created an economy that promoted the notion of homeownership. Americans were able to make a lot of money and buy things. It was the apex of the American Dream. Of course, the Great Depression temporarily disrupted the efforts of federal and city governments to promote homeownership. But during the Depression, the federal government still promoted homeownership because it viewed owning as a mechanism to create jobs and wealth for a nascent lower middle class.

Higher Governments, Regulations, Preemptions, and Grants

The federal government got into the housing business with the U.S. Shipping Act of 1917. This authorized housing for workers at American ports. This policy only lasted for two years but in 1932, Congress created twelve federal home loan agencies. These banks were designed to prevent homeowners from defaulting on mortgages. Yet in 1934, Catherine Bauer's *Modern Housing* argued building homes for the poor in isolation from the social fabric of the neighborhoods along with administration from a top-down government would be politically unpopular. She wanted nonprofits and cooperatives to create large-scale housing programs, divorced from commercial interests and designed for families.[8]

Elected president in 1932, Franklin Roosevelt took office in 1933. In reaction to the Great Depression, he started the New Deal. In 1936, the Federal Housing Administration (FHA) was established to promote homeownership by guaranteeing mortgages to risky borrowers. It also provided lender confidence to make loans. Two years later, the National Mortgage Association (commonly called Fannie Mae) created a secondary market to secure loans for lenders so that they could reinvest into more lending. By reducing the risk of home mortgages, federal housing policy also helped stabilize the banking industry. Although opposed by the U.S. Chamber of Commerce, the National Board of Realtors, and the Banking Association, Congress in 1937 passed the U.S. Housing Act. It provided loans to assist cities in slum clearance. It also contained funds to build low-income rental housing. The U.S. Housing Authority was designed to make long-term loans to local housing and the authorities. This established the principle that local communities would decide for themselves whether to build and develop public housing. Historian Kenneth T. Jackson's *Crabgrass Frontier* concluded that public housing segregated the races, concentrated the poor in the inner city, and created the suburb as a haven from the problems of race and poverty.[9]

After World War II, Congress passed the Housing Act of 1949, promoting urban renewal. It authorized local public authorities to select sites and declare them blighted, then use eminent domain to buy the land or try to attract developers. Cities like Boston used the authority of urban renewal to redevelop the West End. The urban renewal of the West End changed the composition of the city.

The postwar period was an era of economic prosperity, and the Housing Act of 1954 expanded the FHA's ability to guarantee loans to rehab urban renewal areas. Ira Katznelson, a scholar of the New Deal, suggests that the FHA consolidated a rising white middle class but had a lending bias against Black people.[10] The act also provided a grant to increase urban planning.

In 1966, Congress passed the Omnibus Housing Act of 1966. This so-called Model Cities Program was designed to provide 80 percent of the money for funding programs to take a more holistic approach to housing. The program supported education job opportunities and new housing projects. Boston was scheduled to receive $7.7 million between 1969 and 1970. But then President Richard Nixon cut the funds. Mayor Kevin White reacted: "Cutting back this downplays the Model Cities program and thereby establishes a dangerous precedent, because this program, unlike poverty programs, is the direct responsibility of big-city mayors."[11] For mayors, the planning for model cities was incorporated into their budgets.

Another change for public housing came with the Brooke Amendments of 1969, introduced by Massachusetts's first African American U.S. senator, Edward Brooke, a Republican, who tied housing rents to 25 percent of a tenant's income. This was regarded as the first benchmark to measure housing affordability. The percentage was later raised to 30 percent of the tenant's income. Ironically, this requirement did not help the financial problems of public housing.

Federal housing policies kept coming. In 1974, the Community Development Act created the Section 8 program, which provided a system of rent supplements for low-income Americans. The Housing Assistance Plan was designed to make housing planning a local activity. The Department of Housing and Urban Development (HUD) had to assist local planning by collecting data. In short, the federal government was heavily invested in local housing and financing. It

WHO GETS HOUSING, WHEN, AND WHERE? 129

did so to create a society with more housing opportunities and to promote a national housing industry. Professor David Donnison observed,

> In the housing field, as in every field of social policy, these days, politicians and opinion leaders on every side generally adopt an egalitarian standpoint. They want—or say they want—to create a more equal society by improving opportunities and raising the standards of the worst housed. Their approach is more than a passing fad. They are coming to recognize that in a rich country with few fundamental scarcities, the problems which they and the nation's public services are supposed to resolve—bad or overcrowded housing, poverty, poor educational standards, and so on—are, in large part, the visible evidence of an unequal society and the fate of its least fortunate members. Thus, little progress can be made toward a solution unless that society gives these people a more equal share of the things which luckier citizens already enjoy.[12]

City housing policies have always been linked to social welfare issues. This was the case for cities like Boston. However, a critical difference between Boston and other supercities is the political use of public housing. With the exception of Columbia Point, a housing project razed in 1988, Boston did not build acres of high-rise public housing. There was no equivalent to Chicago's Cabrini-Green or St. Louis's Pruitt-Igoe complexes. As referenced in chapter 4, political theorist Tilo Schabert suggested that cities tell stories about politics. In the 1980s, I outlined the differences in the role of public housing in city politics and compared Chicago with New York. The Chicago political machine used public housing to contain and organize Black poor and new immigrants in support of City Hall. Few of the residents were able to move out of these apartments or achieve upward mobility through housing. However, New York City developed its public housing differently. It provided housing for the poor as well as the working and lower middle classes. This explained, in part, why New York residents were able to organize tenant organizations and fight for better facilities and services.[13]

City governments tried to solve housing inequality by building more and better public housing, imposing rent control on rental housing, and creating affordable housing programs. Such activities had their origins in the old politics of housing. The old politics of housing were successful in convincing the working class that homeownership was part of the American Dream and worthy of heavy personal investment. People believed they could become legitimate stakeholders in their cities. Having a place of one's own and paying a mortgage was better than paying rent. And taxpayers could deduct the interest on those loans from their federal taxes.

The federal government wanted to protect banks from mortgage defaults. Affluent people could receive a bargain when purchasing a house. They could buy bigger homes and get tax deductions like other homeowners. This arrangement worked until the advent of suburban living. Neighborhoods became crowded, and schools became more diverse. The Highway Defense Act of 1956 allowed some homeowners to live further from their workplaces and acquire more living spaces, lawns, and trees. It allowed middle-class white people to escape ethnic enclaves that were becoming less attractive because of integrated schools and crime. With changes in housing preferences, the city now had to compete for middle-class residents. This marked the onset of the new housing politics of Boston.

The New Politics of Boston Housing

Although many national and Boston housing policies were made before Menino became mayor, he ended up in the middle of the new politics of Boston housing. The central premise of new housing politics was the question of how to keep middle-class homeowners secure, attract new ones, and contain/preserve ethnic and racial enclaves within city boundaries, while at the same time keeping property taxes low. This was a near-impossible challenge. High property taxes continued until the 1980's Proposition 2½. Led by the antitax group Citizens for Limited Taxation, the initiative petition won a statewide referendum. The vote was 988,839 to 1,438,768 in favor, or 56 percent of the vote. Subsequently, the Massachusetts legislature passed a 1982 law that placed a ceiling on property taxes raised by Boston. It stated that property taxes shall not exceed 2.5 percent of the assessed of the taxable property. This included residential real property, commercial property, industrial real property, and business-owned personal properties. Cities and towns with taxes above the limit had to cut taxes by 15 percent a year. Those below were limited to an annual tax growth of 2.5 percent. The new law also allowed citizens to override the law if their communities needed to do so. Indeed, overrides of the proposition have occurred frequently. Of the over 4,000 proposed, over 1,700 have passed.[14] In 1990, *Boston Globe* reporter David Warsh asserted, "When Proposition 2½ went to a vote in 1980, establishment figures railed against it like a well-rehearsed choir. When it passed, politicians and pundits predicted dire things. Instead, Massachusetts entered a period of a prolonged boom that made an adjustment to lower property taxes relatively painless."[15]

WHO GETS HOUSING, WHEN, AND WHERE? 131

Nevertheless, the proposition made new housing politics more complicated. Housing and taxes became the central topic in Menino's 1993 campaign for mayor. His service on the council's Ways and Means Committee helped him to understand the role taxes played in city affairs. The critical question for many taxpayers was whether taxes would drive them out of their homes. Keeping one's house involved a lot of variables: job security, taxes, unexpected demographic shifts, and differing public safety. A house that a Boston family had inherited from grandparents, who paid less than $50,000, might be worth $350,000 according to new assessments in the early 1990s. Higher taxes followed changes in assessments. Neighborhoods where every family looked the same declined. Children could no longer find the same type of work in Boston. If the neighborhoods believed their humble dwellings were at stake, they might organize and get caught up in housing politics. Menino understood this angst. In his book *A Mayor for a New America*, Menino acknowledged it:

> "Prosperity brings its own challengers . . . and none is more acute than the region's severe housing crisis," noted a Boston Foundation study. Only New York and San Francisco have higher rents than Boston: $2.1 million is the median price of a single-family residence on Beacon Hill, in the Back Bay, and the South End, the city's skid row as recently as the 60s.
> The average household income in Boston is $49,000. But in 2012–13 a couple earning $75,000 could afford only 5 percent of houses sold in Charlestown, 7 percent in South Boston, and 15 percent in Jamaica Plain. In 2005 the Economic Policy Institute found Greater Boston "the most expensive place to live in the country." It hasn't got any cheaper since.[16]

The new politics of housing has consistently been on the urban agenda but so-called housing deals, incessant competition, and conflicts over land use were not always covered by the local news. Menino had been active in local housing policies since his days as a city councilor. When he was elected mayor, he did not have an empty drawing board. Menino inherited the housing policies of Ray Flynn. In 1992, HUD started the Urban Revitalization Demonstration (HOPE VI program). It was designed to create a national action plan to eliminate severely distressed public housing. The model for the program was Boston's Columbia Point Housing Project. The project when built in 1954 had 1,500 but now housed only 300 families and was in serious disrepair. The Flynn administration decided to turn rehabilitation of the project over to Corcoran-Mullins-Jennison, a private developer. In 1990, the rebuilt units became mixed-income housing, and the name was changed to Harbor Point

Apartments. After Menino became mayor, the housing crisis became more severe. Location, supply, and demand increasingly dictated choices for the new mayor. Menino also had to deal with continuing federal housing policies.

In 1998, Congress passed a law reauthorizing the HOPE VI program. The law was designed to help low-income families (families with income no greater than 50 percent of the median) and also to allow frail elderly people to continue to live independently. The rental vouchers covered 40 percent of the cost with the city paying 50 percent and the individual 10 percent. One purpose was to prevent elderly people from being prematurely placed in nursing homes. Roxbury, a major minority community, was also very dependent on subsidized housing. Joseph D. Cutrufo, the program manager for the Cultural Organization of Lowell, concluded in 2011,

> Today, about half of all of the housing in Roxbury is subsidized—by the city or a local community development corporation, or through Chapter 40B, the Massachusetts affordable housing statute. The number of affordable units is expected to drop in 2012, however, when many subsidy contracts will expire, dramatically changing the housing landscape. Other factors that could eventually drive up housing costs are the recent decline in the number of multifamily housing units (with a nearly threefold increase in condominium conversions) and an influx of artists, often considered an indicator of a gentrifying neighborhood. . . . Changes like these are often seen as welcome signs that a neighborhood is "turning around." In Roxbury, however, residents are fighting to keep their neighborhoods affordable with the guidance of a strong set of community organizations and leaders.[17]

Section 8 only addressed part of the growing housing crisis. Apparently, Menino anticipated the looming affordable housing situation. After taking office, he asserted, "We're facing a crisis. We have to come up with a game plan, or you're going to see a lot of poor people forced out on the streets."[18] In March 1997, Menino declared a "Housing Week." He offered new housing initiatives: "Our message is that the city is trying to do what it can to address the need for more affordable homes in Boston."[19] In 2000, Menino announced "Leading the Way," a three-year plan to increase affordable housing. Its agenda called for the production of 7,500 new housing units by 2003.[20] The plan received notice from the media.

Journalist Sarah Barmak of the *Toronto Star* lauded the mayor and stated that "he made the uncommon move of spending $33 million in city funds, rather than relying only on state and federal dollars."[21] Menino's aggressive policy supported a new politics of housing. In 2003, the *Boston Globe* declared his housing policy a success. It conceded that a mayor has limited control of the cost of labor, building materials, and mortgage but an effective effort can still be made. The editorial stated,

> But Menino gambled in October 2000 when he declared that his administration would stimulate the production of 7,500 units, including 2,100 homes affordable to low- and moderate-income families. A preliminary city report cites permits for 7,728 homes during the past three years, including 2,238 low-income units. Roughly 80 percent of the total number of permitted units are complete or under construction. That figure drops to 68 percent for the affordable units. . . . Most mayors limit their housing budgets to funds received from the state and the federal government. Not Menino. He committed $33 million in city funds to close the gap between construction costs and what modest earners can reasonably afford.[22]

What is interesting about the new politics of housing was the obligation of the mayor to balance the needs of ordinary residents with those of rising postindustrial corporate elites, universities, and foundations. Unlike their predecessors, these workers wanted to be in close proximity to their workplace. They did not want to fight traffic but they also did not want to send their children to local public schools. Some elites understood the mayor's dilemma. In addition, higher education institutions coveted the land space around them. Colleges and universities worked with City Hall to co-manage the housing changes. Harvard University donated $20 million to a low-interest loan program to be administered by housing nonprofits. It also supported housing efforts that made the host communities more attractive to potential employees. By 2004, Menino had offered a new plan to build 10,000 more housing units within four years.[23] In 2013, Menino announced a program called Housing Boston 2020, with plans to build 30,000 new units, 5,000 of which would be affordable, deed-restricted housing. At a cost of $16.5 billion, Menino projected this work would produce 100,000 new jobs by 2020. The proposal was to build housing for "a highly educated workforce between the ages of twenty and thirty-four, as well as seniors, empty nesters, and downtown families."[24] To make this happen, there was a 2014 referendum on the Community Preservation Act to get the authority to add a 1 percent surcharge on real-estate tax bills. This money would be used to build more affordable housing.

This plan came near the end of Menino's tenure, and it conformed to Boston housing politics. The policy had class tiers with three levels. Menino admitted as much: "We don't want to be a city of the rich and poor. We want to make sure the working-class people have a place to live."[25] This sounded simple and fair enough but implementing this policy was difficult.

The first level created space for upscale housing. This housing was reserved for the affluent economic elite. Developers are willing to pay for the land for such housing. High-income buyers are generally not willing to live among the poor. The city's leadership attempted to piggyback on such preferences by charging them fees to build affordable housing in other areas.

The second level was to maintain existing ethnic enclaves. These enclaves were reserved for those who wanted to live in such communities. For example, some Irish Americans wanted to live in South Boston among their friends and neighbors. Politicians like Menino tried to reassure these residents that they would be protected from gentrification, but the record was mixed. The housing market in those communities was quite amenable to new buyers.

A third level was made up of public housing. It was designed as starter housing for poor, low-income families. Unfortunately, many poor newcomers to Boston's public housing were never able to leave public housing. They became permanent residents in the Boston Housing Authority facilities.

Boston Housing Authority

Established in 1935, the Boston Housing Authority (BHA) was the eighth-largest city housing agency in the nation. Most housing in Boston was constructed before World War II. Between 1938 and 1942, public housing opened in Orchard Park in Roxbury and Mission Main in Roxbury/Mission Hill. These units were basic settlement homes for Black people moving from southern rural communities. These new workers were employed in manual labor jobs and in the emerging service sectors. These simple units were built like dormitories. They often looked the same.

After World War II, the BHA developed a reputation as an inefficient organization. In 1975, the agency was put under a court decree. Four years later it was put into court receivership. In 1986, Ray Flynn racially integrated public housing. According to Donald Gillis, "Flynn put it on the front burner. When the neighborhood reacted, he decided to call them out. When he ran for reelection, he won in every ward except South Boston. Menino would never do that." In 1990, the BHA was returned to mayoral control. When Menino entered office, the BHA was adjusting to its relationship with City Hall. Gillis characterized Menino as more of a "manager of public housing."[26]

As of 2014, the BHA managed seventy developments across thirteen Boston neighborhoods. Public housing in Mattapan became one of the centers of African American life. Public housing has residential and citizenship requirements. Since some members of the Latino community were undocumented individuals, they could not qualify to live in these units. Despite efforts to integrate housing, there was still an affinity for certain types of neighbors. Many residents chose to live near people like themselves.

Reforming public housing seems to have been a permanent part of the city housing agenda. British prime minister Margaret Thatcher passed the Housing Act of 1980. This law allowed residents to buy their public housing units. At the time, it was considered the ultimate and final reform of public housing. Some thought the British system could work in America. In 1998, MIT professor Lawrence J. Vale interviewed 293 residents to determine their views about buying their apartment homes. He found the idea got a mixed review from tenants:

> That said, these interviews provide less than a ringing endorsement for reviving plans to sell off public housing to its residents, at least in large apartment complexes like the ones in Boston. Still, since half of the respondents indicated a willingness to own their public housing apartment, the idea clearly cannot be dismissed out of hand because of a lack of resident interest. The central problem of homeownership in public housing remains the one already identified by previous studies: The financial and employment status of many of the residents who claim to be most interested in homeownership cannot sustain it. Moreover, given the absence of overwhelming interest in ownership at any one development, any plan to accommodate the wishes of those who want to buy in would be burdened by the problem of what to do with those who resisted such a change.[27]

The idea of tenants' buying units also did not get much support nationally. In 1994, HUD started the Moving to Opportunity for Fair Housing Demonstration Program (MTO). This was a lottery that offered poor families vouchers to move out of public housing. They would be able to afford private apartments. Many housing advocates thought that this would be a solution for people who wanted to get out of public housing. Few thought that moving would have political implications for voters. Political scientist Claudine Gay found that MTO reduced voter turnouts. People who moved away lost their social ties as they strived for economic mobility. Social ties were connected to political participation.[28] Aside from losing social ties, for many of these residents the emerging threat was gentrification. Gentrification became a threat to all Bostonians.

Affordable housing would also be a continuing challenge for most Bostonians. The low-range housing rates were below the $100,000 assessment and located in lower-middle-class neighborhoods. Such housing was subject to the swinging of the economic pendulum. Rent control has been suggested as a possible housing solution. Some economists, however, believe it introduces inefficiencies into the housing market.[29] Yet the scheme continues to be a part of the politics of housing. Another controversial aspect of housing politics is city zoning policies. Zoning was one of the tactics used to control land use and space. Although racial exclusionary zoning was illegal, overall zoning could be a highly effective planning tool.

Boston and Zoning Politics

In general, Boston used zoning policies to determine the locations of businesses, housing, and green spaces. Zoning was supposed to promote commerce, ensure livability, and make strategic land use. In the past, exclusionary zoning had been used to inhibit the mobility of low-income families. It had also been used to stop unwanted development and to keep property values up. Developers and neighborhood associations were organized to protect their investments. As such, zoning became a controversial part of new housing politics.

The U.S. Supreme Court was thrust into zoning issues as early as 1926 with its ruling that zoning laws were constitutional in *Village of Euclid v. Amber Realty Company*. In effect, cities had the authority to determine the location of housing. In 1948, the U.S. Supreme Court in *Shelly v. Kramer* outlawed restrictive covenants. This prevented the practice of residents' agreeing not to sell homes to Black people. In 1968, Congress passed the Fair Housing Act. In 1971, the U.S. Supreme Court ruled in *Kennedy Park Homes v. City of Lackawanna* that cities could not zone Black people out of neighborhoods.

In 1977, in the *Village of Arlington Heights v. Metropolitan Housing Development Corp*, the Supreme Court held that proof of racially discriminatory intent is required in the claim that race is a motivating factor in a land-zoning decision. This decision had the effect of proving race discrimination claims in exclusionary zoning difficult. Cities could prohibit the construction of multifamily homes and create area limits and green spaces. However, cities could not use zoning to exclude people of color. This ruling was thought to be a major breakthrough in the struggle for fair housing. The 1968 Fair Housing

Act, which was one of the last civil rights policies of the Lyndon Johnson administration, was also expected to promote fair housing. Promoting fair housing gets to the core of housing discrimination and de facto school segregation. Keeping Black residents out of white neighborhoods has a long history in Boston. Steering Black house hunters away from all-white neighborhoods and other form of intimidation, such as making it difficult to get a mortgage, were some of the tactics used to perpetuate housing segregation.

The commonwealth of Massachusetts reacted to local zoning policies by passing an inclusionary approach to zoning. The 1969 act was called an "Anti-Snob Zone" law because it invalidated laws that interfered with building low- and moderate-income housing. Donald Gillis believed that Menino "belatedly issued an executive inclusionary zoning." He claimed that Menino promoted luxury housing development downtown without requiring affordable housing concessions. Reporters also alleged that developers contributed to Menino's campaign committee. Menino responded, "Donations did not determine my decisions."[30] In 2008, Jonathan Witten called the state action "reckless, hopeless flawed and corrupt."[31]

More than any other policy, housing policies define the quality of life in Boston. This policy has to stay current with the changes in the housing preferences of the residents, thus the development of even newer housing politics.

A New, New Housing Politics?

As the city of Boston entered the twenty-first century, its housing and neighborhoods were beginning to reflect changes in residential preferences. The housing market was transforming faster than lawmakers could respond. Interestingly, American workers were even more nomadic than ever and moved in and out of superstar cities. Boston, like other eastern U.S. cities, has always had its share of transnationals and domestic immigrants.

The overall demographics of Boston had changed as more nonwhite faces were visible. One was just as likely to hear a Caribbean accent in Dorchester and an old fashion Boston one in the North End and South Boston. Some residents of Boston retained a unique ascent. The bright side of Boston's cultural separateness spun superficial solidarity and on the dark side it perpetuated provincialism. One aspect of this provincialism was Boston's refusal to fully assimilate outsiders. In some parts of Boston, it could take generations for new families to be accepted. It did not matter whether newcomers came from neighboring New England states or another part of the country or whether outsiders were rich or poor. But becoming one of the good old folks took time.

In Boston, old families mattered. Networks mattered. Accents mattered. Family history mattered. Ethnicity and whiteness mattered. Neighborhoods matter. New families had to serve a quasi-probation before they were regarded as insiders. African Americans and Latino immigrants were particularly viewed with apprehension.

Before the turn of the twenty-first century, newcomers of all types had to be re-socialized into Boston traditions and neighborhood norms. One of those norms was the racial hierarchy. Anglo-Saxons, regardless of income, were thought to be better than any "ethnic," regardless of education and income. On the one hand, white and Black residents were separated in all things social and economically, but on the other hand they shared a common city government.

The white society imposed a rigid socioeconomic separation that forced Black people to create separate churches, retail facilities, and community organizations. Although they worked in the same spaces, the two races lived isolated lives. This parallel universe worked for several decades at the expense of Black people. Menino had to directly confront these issues.

White people, especially in the twentieth century, controlled the overall economy and politics. Some Black people accepted this subordinate political role and stayed within the social boundaries. Others resisted it and fought for open housing and neighborhoods. For them, housing integrating was the key to safety, good schools, and social recognition.

Housing and Race

All city housing patterns are testimonies to the housing arrangements exemplified by these segregation legacies. In nineteenth-century Boston, different races were thrown together in a mix of housing. This worked in part because there were few people of color. In 1940, Black residents represented only 3.1 percent of the population and by the time Menino took office in the 1990s, they were 23.8 percent.[32]

As stated, the process of financing homeowners was accelerated in the 1930s by the federal government's promotion of mortgages. The FHA's policies blatantly discriminated against Black citizens.[33] White and Black people did not interact with each other, and some still do not. The city government traditionally underserved Black neighborhoods. What residential overlap that existed

WHO GETS HOUSING, WHEN, AND WHERE? 139

was torn asunder with the school busing controversies of the 1970s. Suddenly Black and White residents became more conscious of place and race. Economist Robert Schafer provided Boston data and reviewed the earlier research of housing economist Ann Schnare, concluding,

> Our research indicates that blacks experience substantial neighborhood markups in both the ghetto and in the transition area to increase their housing consumption. On the other hand, we have also observed a willingness of whites to pay more for otherwise identical housing located further from black residence areas. Blacks, however, nearly always pay more than whites for the same bundle of housing attributes at the same location. These findings support all three theories of racial discrimination. The dual housing market, a strong white preference for segregation, and pure racial price discrimination are all operative in the Boston urbanized area. Schnare's simplistic view of the housing market masked these important price differentials by assuming that the bundle attribute prices were constant across races and neighborhoods. Policies to counteract the historical pattern of racial segregation must be cognizant of all three forces to be successful.[34]

In the 1980s, John Yinger analyzed a survey called the "fair housing audit," studying six neighborhoods in the city: Back Bay/Beacon Hill, Central, South End, Dorchester, Hyde Park/Roslindale, and Jamaica Plain. The survey confirmed that there was an extremely high level of discrimination. Black auditors were invited to inspect 36 percent fewer apartments than white auditors. Although discrimination varied with neighborhoods, Yinger believed that housing agents catered to the racial prejudices of white customers.[35]

The housing discrimination patterns began before Menino took office and continued while he was mayor despite his efforts to stop it. There were court cases, newspaper studies, academic findings, and premature victory statements, yet housing discrimination persists. Some landlords resist tenants who use assistance and vouchers. There is also mortgage lending discrimination.[36] Of all form of racial discrimination, housing discrimination may be the Gordian knot. As Judith D. Feins and Rachel G. Bratt pointed out during the Menino administration, this behavior is in contrast to Boston's liberal image.

> The Boston audit underscores a major paradox confronting the city. Boston enjoys an image of liberal enlightenment while providing its black citizens unequal housing opportunities. The city today is an ironic mixture of urban renaissance and racial and class tensions. While these contradictions may be more readily observable in Boston than in other

cities, it is still important to recall the statistics presented earlier on disparities between blacks and whites. Discrimination is not a local Boston problem alone; it is a national issue. Discrimination in housing has been outlawed by the federal government, but it is clear that the problem must also be addressed at the local level.[37]

The result of this racial segregation was that Black and white Bostonians were ignorant of each other. Even their hometown trademark accents were different. Many white people were surprised when middle-class Black professionals seemingly wanted to "encroach on their turf." Court-ordered busing provided some white middle-class families with a cover to move out to an outskirt town like Newton or Waltham. White flight in housing patterns transformed city politics. First, there was white flight, then later came a new influx of immigrants. As new, more educated immigrants came to the city, the housing policy has informally shifted to accommodate high-tech industries and open the market to the highest bidders. Some white neighborhoods fought zip code invasions and forced racial integration of neighborhoods.

Black home-seekers rarely challenged these white exclusive neighborhoods. A real-estate agency routinely steered Black newcomers to Black neighborhood, a "place where they would be comfortable." In Boston, steering occurred but it was buttressed with a strong class component. Like their northern and western city counterparts, racial separation in Boston housing was transacted in part by enlightened real-estate agencies. Newcomers were steered toward neighborhoods with people that looked like them. Simply put, realtors did not show middle-class minority professionals the most expensive properties in the most exclusive neighborhoods.

The cost of housing also served to keep races and classes apart. Of course, this was also true for highly educated Black and Latino professionals recruited by leading financial, higher education, and corporate interests. Some metro Boston companies took steps to make sure their professional employees were shown the more desirable neighborhoods even if they were actually located in suburbs such as Newton, Wellesley, and Weston. Despite Boston's reputation as a progressive city, incoming, noncorporate, Black middle-class families were reportedly steered away from white neighborhoods.

By steering newcomers to certain neighborhoods, they kept races and classes apart. Public housing and schools were placed close to where people of color lived. This practice maintained exclusivity and kept housing costs inflated.

Real-estate commissions are determined by the cost of housing. This was an incentive to carefully locate classes of buyers in the same neighborhoods. Race and class steering remained an acceptable part of selling homes. Despite court cases outlawing race discrimination in housing, the patterns of separate neighborhoods persisted.

For years site selection and zoning politics have not only kept Black people out but also isolated social classes from each other. In certain neighborhoods, it was difficult to purchase lots for multifamily homes or lots were restricted in size. An alert mayor must be aware of these practices but changing them proved difficult.

Housing provided the race and class separation template. In chapter 7, we discuss how the social isolation of minorities affected student enrollment and the quality of the public school systems in Boston. Where one lived mattered because it determined school zones and where one's children were assigned. Poor schools could affect a child's life chances in the long run. Few parents wanted to send their children to poor-performing schools. However, in Boston, ethnic groups tended to prefer life in affinity enclaves, like South Boston or Dorchester. Sometimes individuals seek out people who look like them, speak like them and behave like them. They look for kindred souls with whom they can identify. These enclaves can be based on social class, race, religion, or ethnicity.

By contrast, housing location played a different role for white people who aspired for visibility and social mobility. Families who wanted to be identified as upwardly mobile moved into neighborhoods that signified success. For them, it was an investment or a form of self-advertising. Other families just seemed to end up in communities that replicated their parents' neighborhoods. Mark Abrahamson's *Urban Enclaves* takes a broader view of the use of the term. He asserts that "enclaves typically grow by serving as magnets that attract other people who share the same significant quality as the pioneers." Enclaving is also a function of segregation: "People in enclaves are also kept in their places by the actions of others that set them apart."[38]

This might have been true for homeowners, and it was also true for renters. Their lives were impacted by rising rents. Granted renters had a flat-rate deduction on their state taxes, but this was not enough. They began to ask the City Council and the mayor to do something about it. Menino, as a neighborhood councilor and as mayor, was acutely aware of the so-called tenant class and promised to do something about the rent crisis.

Menino and the Great Rent Control Debate

The great challenge for superstar cities like Boston is how to create and maintain livable housing for poor and senior citizens. Boston is a classic case of the lack of affordable housing in a rising housing market. Richard Florida's book *The New Urban Crisis* highlights affordable housing as one of the chief challenges to American cities.[39] Florida's work heralds the rise of a creative class that would change what a city does and how it allocates living spaces. Theoretically, it is possible for Boston to become a place where only the elite can afford to live. The issue becomes whether this possibility is good for society or the culture of the city.

Cities like Boston have experienced increasing income inequality and even more housing segregation. As stated in earlier chapters, there are limits to geographic space in Boston. The pressure on the city has been relieved by having bedroom suburbs like Newton within commuter rail distance. However, the new creative class may prefer living downtown and closer to its center. High-income members of the creative class are not only a threat to the poor neighborhoods but most of the current residents. This rise in the cost of housing and rent is a threat to the middle class as well as the poor who have lived in the city for generations.

In the 1980s, Boston politicians did not focus so much on the rising cost of single-family homes. They lamented the forces of change in the housing marketplace. Meanwhile, the assessors continued to raise the appreciated values of Boston homes once considered working-class dwellings. However, politicians seemed to be more amenable to doing something about rising rents. Renters, like homeowners, organize and vote.

How could the city help the tenant class financially in the homes and apartments? Rent control was one suggested policy solution. In a rent-control city, limits are placed on rental costs. This means regulating what landlords and property owners can charge based on the tenant's income. In cities like New York, San Francisco, and Boston's close neighbor Cambridge, Massachusetts, the city government could limit what a landlord could charge for renting a house or apartment. In some cases, landlords could not raise rents while the tenant lived on the property.

The argument for rent control has been that a city's government must defend the interest of low-income families, seniors, and those on fixed incomes. The justification was to keep Boston as a multicultural and multiracial city. For rent-control advocates, the emergence of Boston as an all-wealthy and white enclave would rob it of its diversity and be morally incorrect.

However, most housing economists found problems with rent control.[40] They believe that housing properties should respond to the law of supply and demand. They claim that rent control leads to neglect or abandonment of properties. Some property owners do not make enough income to cover the maintenance and upkeep costs. As a result, properties fall into disrepair. Tenant organizations have taken to the courts to protect the interest of renters. Property owners have also organized to protect their interests. For them, there was a looming threat of a renter revolt and subsequent income loss. Both groups got themselves involved in the Boston City Council and mayoral primaries. Their spokespeople also had access to the media.

In 1994, a group of Massachusetts landlords and property owners was able to gather seventy thousand signatures to put the issue of rent control on the statewide ballot. At the time one city and one town in the state (Cambridge and Brookline) had rent control. Anti-rent-control advocates, primarily landlords, made the argument that rent control was hurting the property-tax base in those cities, and that the rest of the state was making up the revenue difference created by rent control in those cities. Such an appeal was aimed at towns and cities like Framingham, Springfield, and Worcester.

During the election rent-control advocates appealed to the public to save living spaces for the poor and the elderly. The landlord initiative was won by a narrow electoral majority, 51 to 49 percent.[41] Although there was now no limit on rent that landlords could charge, median rents in some places did not increase for five years.

In 1999, Derrick Z. Jackson wrote an editorial for the *Providence Journal-Bulletin* in which he argued that Massachusetts governor Paul Cellucci had appointed himself the chief landlord after he promised the Rental Housing Association that he would veto any rent-control legislation. Cellucci asserted, "I will not waive the rules of the competitive free market. The free market got us into this situation, and it will be the free market that gets us out of it." Jackson thought that many people would leave Boston and "wave goodbye."[42]

Jackson concluded, "So it is time for Cellucci to stop saying things like 'a hot economy comes at a price,' as if it is perfectly acceptable that the price is being paid by families who pay so much in rent that they could never afford the down payment for a house. It is time for the leeches to stop talking about the infusion of wealthy high-tekkies and think about the housing choices those tekkies are going to make when they start pushing around innocent tykes."[43]

The debate on rent control kept reappearing on Boston's agenda. In 2002, Menino proposed a new rent-control plan that allowed tenants to challenge a rent hike before a city-appointed board. The proposal would have allowed landlords the option of an annual rent increase if they did not exceed 10 percent of the tenant's income. The proposal would have rewarded landlords who charged below-market prices. Landlords had to prove increases in operating expenses or pressing capital improvements. Menino's proposal failed. Two years later, the issue was again back before the council. This time the council again rejected the proposal. Menino reacted, "I was frustrated by the vote. They continually say to me we have to do more housing for working people. I had a pretty reasonable proposal on the docket and a majority of the council did not see fit to support it. They're not hearing from the same people I'm hearing from. They must be in a different neighborhood than I'm in."[44] Kathy Brown, the coordinator of the Boston Tenant Coalition, which led the fight, stated, "This is a critical tool that the council just gave up that could help tens of thousands of households."[45]

Having lost the rent control battle, Menino continued the fight for affordable housing.

The Politics of Affordable Housing

The politics of affordable housing in Boston is a recurrent issue. Without affordable housing, the city could lose its lower-middle- and middle-class residents. Hence, affordable housing remains the Achilles' heel of central cities. If politicians cannot keep housing costs down, there will be a decline in the sense of neighborhood. If residents lose interest in their housing, then the city cannot prevent blight or gentrification. There is also a need to keep residents in the central city to support the retail functions of a central business district.

Endorsing affordable housing can be a win-win strategy for politicians because it has little political risk. It is what politicians call a "mom and apple pie issue." No politician wants to be seen as against affordable housing. However, such units are a real issue for many city dwellers. City residents with marginal incomes see such housing as an opportunity to buy. Yuppies and gentrifiers want places to live in the city. The working poor hope that the city will create more buying and renting opportunities. For reformers, the idea of mixed-income housing represents a way to bring the city together. It is touted as an alternative to much-maligned, high-rise public housing developments.

In 1998, the *Wall Street Journal* characterized Mayor Menino as "Playing Robin Hood in the development world." Menino had an affordable housing plan that would have expanded the fifteen-year linkage program established by Mayor Kevin White. Under the White plan, developers were asked to contribute $5 per square foot on the development of over 100,000 square feet into an affordable-housing fund. The *Wall Street Journal* reported the city had collected $47 million by that time. These funds were used to build 4,000 houses and apartments. Menino then wanted to take 10 percent of the funds to build luxury condos in the North End. He intervened to insist on a 10 percent set aside, money reserved for a special purpose. Without it, it would be difficult to attract professional workers. He asked, "Why don't we do this on the seaport?" and stated, "I told the BRA to make it happen."[46]

In 2000, a ballot question asked Boston voters to hike property taxes to pay for affordable housing, open space, and historical preservation. It would have attached a 2 percent surcharge on property tax, sparing the first $100,000 in home value. Businesses would pay 80 percent more of the $14 million generated every year under a Community Preservation Act (CPA) tax. The state would match the CPA tax, giving Boston $28 million for affordable housing. The question lost by ten thousand votes.[47]

Menino continued his quest for affordable housing throughout his administration. Creating reasonable-cost housing units was a key factor for effective multiracial and class-neutral living spaces in an urban community. An ideal urban community for some people is one that is both multiracial and mixed-income. This embraces Henri Lefebvre's idea of the poor's "right to the city."[48] Accordingly, all income groups have a right to public spaces. Are the poor allowed to live in diverse neighborhoods and enjoy participatory space? In most American communities there is an affordability gap between housing costs and household income.

The reality is that a family's income dictates the amount of living space, the location, and the type of neighborhood where someone lives. Schools, retail shops, and other amenities are a part of the housing calculation. State and local governments have low-cost housing programs, but they cannot fully close the gap. In most cities like Boston, there is a politics of affordable housing. "Affordable housing" is code for preserving economic diversity in cities. If

Homelessness in Boston

One of the most vexing problems in the new finance-based economy is the economic dislocation it produces. The rise of homeless Americans reflects the excessive ups and downs of the economy, drug abuse, the closing of state mental hospitals, and changes in the political culture. In a post-industrial society, the primary family has triumphed over the extended one. People are more inclined to expect the government to care for the destitute. Americans seem to be able to tolerate more visible and public misery among strangers. These individuals and families simply have no place to live and manage by living on the streets and in shelters. In the 2000 census, one out of one hundred Americans had used homeless shelters. Many of the people who are homeless shun shelter life and live permanently on the streets. Given the difficulties of making actual counts of homelessness, city officials arrived at population estimates. In Boston, the census found there were 5,906 homeless adults and children.[49] More and more individuals with mental and drug problems are pushed into homelessness. There are homeless kids staying overnight at a friend's house or engaging in "couch surfing."

Some scholars disagree about the causes of homelessness. Some blame rising home prices and the decline of affordable housing, while others see the problem as a byproduct of the reduction and often elimination of custodian care facilities for the mentally ill. Other scholars see the rise as the result of growing disaffiliation and detachment of individuals from society.[50] Americans are losing those familial and neighborhood bonds. Still, another view is that homelessness is the result of the decline of collective responsibility and a growing tolerance of the suffering of others. In 1997, Brendan O'Flaherty's *Making Room: The Economics of Homelessness* concluded that income inequality was the main cause of contemporary homelessness. O'Flaherty believed that modern-day homelessness could be traced to a shrinking middle class.[51] Boston city politicians, like their counterparts elsewhere, were sensitive to the problem but perplexed about ways to prevent homelessness. Whatever its cause, Menino had a growing problem on his hands.

In 1994, a Boston survey of the homeless found a 10.2 percent rise over the 1993 total (4,809 people). There were 5,229 homeless men, women, and children.

Children's rates increased by the largest margin, up by 13.2 percent. Menino responded, "We're here not just to identify the problems of homelessness, but to begin a new partnership with shelter providers, homeless advocates, and the business community to find solutions to the problems of homelessness. Every night, Boston has a place for every homeless person to stay. . . . But that's just a place to stay. Where we should be going is beyond just shelter."[52]

Local housing policy operated under federal laws. In 1998, Congress passed the Quality Housing and Work Responsibility Act to change the housing situation for low-income Americans. This may have inadvertently driven many former public housing residents into homelessness.[53] What the city did not need was more homeless people on the street.

In Boston, the homeless population is not always seen or noticed. There exists the ubiquitous disheveled men and grocery cart pushers, but most homeless people are not so obvious. One could pass a homeless person in the street without knowing it. In 1980, Professor Martha R. Burt noted that the majority of homeless individuals were single men.[54] Currently, the homeless include more women and children.

At first glance, it seems that solving this problem would be intuitive (e.g., building more affordable housing and single-resident room units). A closer look suggests that it is not that simple. Moreover, the new economy has exacerbated the problem of homelessness. These individuals do not fit well in a post-industrial economy. Not only are these individuals homeless but they are also politically powerless. Homeless people do not have addresses; they often don't protest and do not vote. They depend on the kindness of strangers, shelter operators, and charities. Increasingly, the sheer number of homeless individuals has overwhelmed this system of volunteers.

Unaffiliated and unprotected people are the ignominy of modernity. Cities have always had their share of vagrants, beggars, and derelicts. Except in the winter, Boston's homeless population often looked like their counterparts in other regions. Downtown congregations of homeless people are not uncommon in many American cities. Of course, individuals who are homeless in Boston have to endure harsh winters. They want to stay in Boston, and they have a right to do so. Yet living out in the elements is a dangerous and unhealthy existence. During the winter, people who are homeless cannot just move to the Sunbelt. Many such people are attached to Boston and have learned to survive on the streets. However, these individuals may encroach on tourism spaces and affect the overall marketing of the city.

148   CHAPTER 5

The mayor's office, civic volunteers, and churches often work to get these individuals into shelters. For them, these unkempt and visible individuals represent an eyesore for visitors and tourists. In 2006, Menino announced the Boston Homelessness Prevention Clearinghouse. The city of Boston matched a $1 million grant from the Paul and Phyllis Fireman Charitable Foundation program that provided emergency funds for those who are homeless. Menino remarked, "We all know that the most humane and cost-effective way to end homelessness is to prevent it from happening in the first place. As part of my housing strategy, I issued a call to action to do more to end homelessness before it ever begins. The Paul and Phyllis Fireman Charitable Foundation responded, and we are building a homelessness prevention network to assist in the most timely and targeted manner possible. Keeping low-income tenants across our city housed is a top priority."[55] In 2009, Menino opened the first city-operated center (Weintraub Day Center at Woods Mullen Shelter) for chronically homeless residents in Roxbury.

In 2011, the Massachusetts Housing and Shelter Alliance (MHSA) awarded Menino a Public Innovation Award. MHSA reported that the number of critically homeless—that is, people homeless for more than a year, or four times in three years—dropped from 962 people to 725. The number of homeless dropped from 3,944 to 2,747. Since 2005, this represented a 30 percent reduction in homelessness and a 25 percent reduction in chronic homelessness. In a press release, Lynda Downie, president and CEO of Pine Street Inn, a network of homeless shelters, stated, "The Mayor has been a leader in ending homelessness and you can see the results of his work in these numbers." Joe Finn, president of the MHSA, also praised the mayor, saying, "Under Mayor Menino, Boston has been a national, innovative leader in developing programs that work to move homeless individuals [into permanent housing]."[56]

Homelessness and affordable housing are more visible than the real threat of the lack of space in Boston proper. Simply put, the land on which all classes reside has become more valuable, limited, and coveted. The availability of housing responds to cycles and changes in the economy.

Housing and the New Economy

The new economy of the late 1990s and early 2000s paid some workers very well, giving them enough money to pay more for home and land space in Boston. Families could create wealth by buying homes. However, in cities with higher priced housing markets, housing is controlled and operated by highly organized private interests. Hence, as the market changes, so does the cost of housing. The other element is the increasing number of affluent retirees and second-home buyers in the market. People started to invest in homes they could barely afford.

The 2008 Great Recession was caused, in part, by housing financing schemes developed by hedge funds and banks. In late 2000, there was a nationwide glut of housing and few buyers. The demand for subprime mortgages allowed people with weak credit records and modest incomes to get loans. The entire scheme was financed by mortgage companies, the insurance industry, and rating agencies—thousands of subprime lenders. The edifice built on credit default swaps unraveled and caused a banking crisis. In 2008, the nation experienced a rapid downturn in the housing market.

Housing prices fell quickly. For the nonprofessional, subprime mortgages lured them into bigger and more expensive homes. This situation became a source of many foreclosures all over the nation. Minority homeowners were especially affected. Americans everywhere were living in homes that were not worth their mortgages. What looked like a surefire investment turned out to be a disaster. It took the federal government to dig the housing industry out of the ditch. Congress passed the Housing and Economic Recovery Act of 2008. Among other things, it provided $300 billion in mortgage relief for 400,000 homeowners. It made mortgages more transparent, but it did stop the decline of affordable housing. Mayors across the country were relatively powerless.

Yet the lessons of the Great Recession were not well learned. As Richard Florida points out, some workers have more money and influence than others. The new housing economy worked in their favor. Housing cost, race, and gentrification have been the essence of Boston housing politics. Property taxes have been the main source of funding for the city. As the city gentrified, it not only lost diversity but also increased its housing assessments. Houses that cost resident grandparents $30,000 were now worth over $300,000. Grandchildren could not afford to pay the taxes and were forced to sell and move outside the city. They sold their properties in South Boston, for instance, and moved to Revere. Proposition 2½ from the 1980s had been an attempt to slow down this growth, but the twenty-first-century leaders did not anticipate the strong demand for housing space.

Summary

Historian Lawrence J. Vale's classic *From the Puritans to the Projects: Public Housing and Public Neighbors* outlines how the nation's poor have received aid and are also located to the margins of the city.[57] Early Boston mayors had no authority to prevent the segregation of the poor. Most modern mayors have a larger role in housing politics. Yet there are still problems. How can a mayor create and maintain good housing stock for all? How can one keep housing costs reasonable at times when the city needs more revenue for its operations? Obviously, there are many actors other than the mayor. Thomas Menino discovered that in his crusade for rent control. As we discussed earlier, historically low mortgage rates fed new locations in the western and eastern coastal American cities. Boston had a limited amount of geographical land making it difficult for the mayor to maneuver around housing politics. Menino also learned the lesson that the state legislature can and will preempt the city's actions on housing. More importantly, mayors cannot stop market forces, nor can they determine who can afford to live within the city proper. Tenants and housing groups have a right to organize and advocate, but the forces against rent control are often better organized and funded. Yet Menino remained a housing warrior throughout his tenure.

Affordable housing is the highest priority for most mayors of large cities. Defining what "affordable" means and where to locate it is complicated. There are limits to what a city can do to landlords and property owners. In 1994, Massachusetts abolished rent control but Menino continued to support some form of it. Tenant organizations attempted to put it back on the agenda. Some rental units have been rehabbed and converted into condominiums.

Affordable housing is a good talking point for Boston politicians, but many questions remain. Under Menino, more than six thousand new affordable housing units were built.[58] Affordable housing in a post-industrial economy may be an oxymoron. What is affordable housing and where to locate it? It is better than first-rate public housing? How can senior citizens be protected from gentrification? How can longtime Boston ethnic enclaves keep their character? Or should they? How can the influx of the "creative class" be accommodated? Should we rethink exclusionary zoning? Using Massachusetts data, Political scientists Katherine Levine Einstein, David M. Glick, and Maxwell Palmer in *Neighborhood Defenders* found that policies like open hearing laws, which are designed to increase citizen participation in the politics of land use, have resulted in unintended consequences such as an increase in the numbers of privileged homeowners who oppose housing projects in their communities.[59]

Mayor Menino historically wanted to maintain a diverse resident population. This was difficult because the poor had fewer housing choices and had little voice in Boston's overall housing politics. One of the ubiquitous signs of cities like Boston is the widespread building of townhouses, condos, rental apartments, and what is called infill construction. In addition, there needed to be a serious attempt to maintain historical downtown living areas. The history of housing in Boston has not been able to escape its past. The ghost of urban renewal's impact on the West End, as described in chapter 1, is still there for housing planners to see. Historian Thomas O'Connor studied the urban renewal changes in Boston and concluded,

> The story of twentieth-century Boston is, in actuality, a tale of two cities—literally "two Bostons." During the first half of the century, Boston had been divided by two major social and religious groups that had constituted its hostile warring factions. One Boston, the central area, was the traditional preserve of the Protestant, Anglo-Saxon, Yankee Brahmin population that occupied the Victorian residences of Beacon Hill and the Back Bay. The other Boston was made up of the more recent communities of the Irish and the Germans, the Italians and the Jews, the African-Americans and the Puerto Ricans, and all the other races and nationalities that had come into the city in the nineteenth and twentieth centuries and settled in the waterfront wards and the surrounding neighborhoods.[60]

Although urban renewal took place during the 1960s, the decision made by Mayor John Collins and later by Kevin White and Ray Flynn impacted Menino's housing politics. Affordable housing and race are an even bigger conundrum. Although President Lyndon Johnson signed a law outlawing housing discrimination in the twentieth century, it persisted during the Menino administration and afterward. Since the creation of HUD, the agency has done several things to create housing for the poor (e.g., offering Section 8 vouchers), and it has supported local public housing authorities' attempts to rid public housing of drug offenders.

CHAPTER 6

Crime in the Streets and Elsewhere

Throughout the history of Boston, preventing and reacting to crime was supposed to be the number one priority for City Hall. Like most major 1990s cities, the city of Boston expanded its police department and added technology. The department apprehended more criminals apprehended and increased incarceration. Yet trends of increasing murders, assaults, rape, and robberies punctuate that history. Crime fighting is an endless enterprise. Bostonians expect to live in a secure environment with safe streets and homes. They elect mayors to ensure that this is the case. A fragile city cannot protect its residents. Creating safe spaces requires the government to pass laws and assign police officers to enforce them. All city officials have some responsibility for this effort, but the mayor is expected to lead this fight against crime. This solemn obligation adds legitimacy to the administration at City Hall. The crime-fighting leadership style of the mayor is critical to residents' sense of security.

Some city mayors are office-centric, allowing professionals to manage crime. They espouse law and order but make crime-solving announcements from their offices. They are photographed in their offices condemning the crime, and they stay in their offices most of the day. Other mayors consider themselves street-level crime fighters. They stress safety and assist crime-fighting professionals by being physically present. They seek the opportunity to ride along in patrol cars and be seen at crime scenes talking to officers and victims.

General Crime Fighting in Boston

When Thomas Menino took office, the nation was undergoing a sea change in attitudes about punishment for violent crime. This was exemplified by the Violent Crime Control and Law Enforcement Act of 1994. Democratic president Bill Clinton and twenty-six of the thirty-eight members of the Congressional Black Caucus supported it. This law ensnared more citizens into the criminal justice system and expanded correctional facilities. Yet this draconian act contained some controls for semiautomatic weapons and a provision to protect victims of domestic violence. This launched a shift in what the state of Massachusetts and the city of Boston did about crime.

The federal government can make laws, offer grants, and denounce crime but enforcement is primarily a local matter. Generally speaking, Boston's crime fighting has been different from that of a city like Los Angeles. Because the mayor of Boston selects the police commissioner, no individual could amass the power of Los Angeles police chief Daryl Gates (1978–1992). Gates was selected by the civil service system and was effectively not under the supervision of the mayor. Gates emerged as an aggressive, race-baiting chief running the department by his own instincts. Yet he was innovative with the founding of SWAT (Special Weapons and Tactics). This reprobate behavior could not have administratively happened in Boston, and while the city has had several strong police commissioners, the mayor has always been in charge. Unlike Philadelphia, Boston has never elected a former police commissioner comparable to Police Chief Frank Rizzo (1972–1980), an aggressive law-and-order advocate as mayor.

Mayor Menino was never a tough law-and-order braggart. This was especially true regarding youth crime. Unlike cities like Los Angeles and Chicago, Boston has never had violent and institutionalized street youth gangs. Boston's youth gangs have been different from their counterparts in those cities. The threat from such gangs became a national concern during the Clinton administration. The president tried to assist city gang control programs. To the surprise of journalists, Boston was selected as the city to test the effort. *Chicago Tribune* reporter Andrew Martin wondered why Clinton selected Boston, not Chicago, to launch his national campaign against gangs and youth violence. This was a strange choice since Chicago had the notorious Vice Lords, the Gangster Disciples, and the Latin Kings. These gangs were among the nation's most dangerous and violent ones. Boston had the Intervale Posse and Orchard Park Trailblazers, but these gangs were not comparable to their Chicago counterparts. Martin quoted Walter Miller, a Boston gang expert, as saying, "I was astounded they used (Boston). We don't have a gang problem that begins to approach Chicago and Los Angeles."[1]

Martin was correct that these two cities had different youth violence problems. Each youth gang has its reasons for existence (drugs or to expand operational territory). Chicago mayors and police departments were aware of street gangs. Even today drive-by shootings represent a safety problem for the residents of the city's Southside and Westside. In mayoral campaigns, Chicago voters asked candidates to address the gang problem. For decades, the summers in the city could be deadly. This is not to say that Boston did not have an infamous drive-by shooting. In 1992, there was a shooting in Morning Star Baptist Church. This was one of the reasons the Black clergy established the Boston TenPoint Coalition, an anti–youth violence organization.

Tom Menino presented himself as a street-level mayor in his campaigns and actions. He was comfortable in the streets. Most Bostonians saw him giving news conferences on the street, standing at a crime scene, and visiting the relatives of crime victims. In addition, he spent the early part of his mayoralty riding around the city's neighbors looking for broken lights, uncollected trash, and things that need to be fixed. For some he was the quintessential empath, that is, having the ability to understand the anxiety of others and feel the pain of victims. Crime fighting was a part of his image. When he expressed outrage and sympathy at a crime scene, people believed him. Few people discerned hidden meanings in his public statements. What Menino said was what he meant. He was working and not trying to impress the media or make a name for himself. In that sense, the mayor was an uncomplicated person.

The policies of the mayor were usually reflected in his posture toward street crime, choices for leadership of the police department, and reaction to white-collar crime. Accordingly, Menino had to make a policy choice: adhere to traditional, strict law-and-order policing—dispassionately enforcing the law—or promoting a better police-community relations approach, that is, treating crime as a social problem and asking citizens to help enforce the law. Either way, the mayor was expected to assume a sentinel position.

Menino as Boston's Sentinel

Mayors are supposed to be sentinels watching out for and protecting the residents in what Norton E. Long called the "unwalled city," that is, places in which

CRIME IN THE STREETS AND ELSEWHERE   155

people can come and go without permission.[2] Menino understood this when he first ran for mayor. As discussed in chapter 2, he outlined his position on crime. During his tenure voters were incessantly reminded of his sentinel role. He would accompany police officers and go directly to a crime scene. Yet he never campaigned as a tough law-and-order candidate. Rather, he ran on a theme of protecting neighborhoods. The implicit message was that safe neighborhoods make safe streets. If a neighborhood had solidarity, residents would look out for each, assist the police, and build what social scientists called "social trust."[3] Social trust alone cannot prevent a crime, but when the crime occurs, it can help to restore unity. Some Boston neighbors are not closely knit groups of families. Criminals select loosely organized neighborhoods because residents tend to be less concerned about each other. In white, working-class neighborhoods like the one in which Menino was born, this sort of neighborhood-centered reasoning made sense. But he had to understand the ethos of all Boston neighborhoods, especially the ones that had high crime rates.

In minority communities such as Roxbury, Mattapan, and Dorchester, crime prevention was difficult. These communities were more likely to have a constant stream of new immigrants, unemployed males, and parolees. As is the case for some poor communities, released criminals were attracted to them. Many of these individuals were products of broken homes. It was a complicated matter that was not amenable to initiative solutions. Assigning more police officers to these areas was necessary, but it did not always work. Besides, these communities sometimes had an awkward relationship with the police. Nonetheless, these residents wanted safe streets, like their counterparts in white enclaves. Menino won the votes of these communities as he promised more police officers and more openness to City Hall. These residents heard the promise, but they also knew that crime was a part of city life.

Crime as a Part of City Life

No candidate has successfully run for the mayor's office without a pledge to be a crime fighter. Boston is like all modern American cities in that it is relatively open to crime. Living in cities exposes residents to street crimes perpetrated by strangers. These crimes are not limited to muggings, pickpocketing, and shoplifting. Murder, rapes, burglaries, assaults, and car thefts can take place at any time in some neighborhoods. Street crimes are not exactly random. They happen in some neighborhoods and public places more than in others. Some crimes are never reported or receive media coverage. Some neighborhoods had a reputation for being crime-ridden, and few are shocked at these incidents.

Even less shocking for residents are the incidents of white-collar crime. These involve bribery, insurance fraud, embezzlement, forgery, and racketeering among public and private individuals. When politicians are involved, the local media often covers the arrests and trials. Otherwise, this type of crime involving nonpoliticians happens every day, and the ordinary citizen may not be aware of or directly affected by it. Indeed, the history of Boston politics includes many famous politicians who had their careers ended after getting caught in the web of bribery and kickbacks. For example, in 1947 Mayor James Michael Curley was sent to jail for bribery. More recently, in 2011 State Representative Diane Wilkerson and Councilor Chuck Turner, two of Boston's leading African American politicians, were also sent to jail for bribery. These convictions may confirm political cynicism among some citizens, but the real fear was street crime.

The most shocking of street crimes are those defined as horrific, that is, a crime with multiple deaths or severe property damage. These crimes do happen, but they are relatively rare. Nevertheless, throughout its history, Boston has had its share of horrific crime and violence. There are also recurrent incidents of what may be defined as common criminality. The media sometimes accord only passing reference to property crime, murder, armed robberies, aggravated assaults, and rapes. Some of these events become a part of the folklore of the city. Boston, like many cities, had its mob icon (James "Whitey" Bulger), but the main narrative has been about street crime and the relative safety of particular neighborhoods.

Bostonians are vulnerable to national and regional economic cycles. During times of economic downturn, crime may increase. Also, Boston is by no means a fortress city. Anyone can enter and leave the city at any time and without requiring permission. The city has no way of knowing that a crime is being planned or committed. The Boston Police Department was designed to enforce state and federal laws and the ordinances of the city. But this does not mean it can prevent or solve every crime.

Boston, like most of its urban counterparts, has a history of poverty and unemployment, racial tensions, and drugs. There are local individuals that the police departments define as "regular" criminals and others as deranged/stressed individuals. Violent crime is part of the fabric of urban life. For centuries there has been a debate about the causes of crime. Some try to link criminality to economic conditions such as unemployment and social disadvantages. This may be an oversimplification of this causal relationship. The origins of criminality have multiple sources.

The only thing that is common about crime in American cities is that street criminals are similar in terms of background, modus operandi, and fate. Obviously, there are differences between regular and horrific crimes. The latter attracts media attention and may require the mayor to comment. Mayor Menino had to make comforting and reassuring statements to grieving and victim families on numerical occasions. All city leaders have endeavored to assuage fears of crime and to temper residents' reactions to crime and violence. Unfortunately, the media often links street crime to disadvantaged minorities. The local TV evening news incessantly makes this point, and this narrative has its consequences. Part of the job of mayors like Menino has been to disabuse the public of this stereotype and assist neighborhoods that seek to improve safety and assist law enforcement officers.

Which Sides Are You On, Menino?

When Tom Menino was serving as acting mayor in 1993 and during his campaign for an elective term, crime was a major topic. In the early 1990s, there was a national trend toward electing law-and-order mayors. Since most big-city mayors were white, the subtext of these campaigns was race and crime. Such candidates often stoked the fear of street crime to mobilize their voters. Mayors who ran on a liberal platform were thought to be easy on criminals.

In 1995, during an extensive interview, Menino was asked a direct question regarding race and crime as to whether "racial change in the city by itself is leading to increased fear of crime." Menino answered,

> Yeah. Not actual crime, but fear of crime. Because when you get to know those people they become part of the mainstream. How do I say this? You get in an old neighborhood in the city and some people move in who don't look like you. The reaction is "Oh-oh, there's our neighborhood because they're going to bring in crime." But no one's actually looking at the situation. They have the same hopes and dreams; a steady job, to be able to educate their kids and have their kids have a future.[4]

This type of testimonial defined Menino's attitude toward the linkage of race and crime. It suggests that he had not internalized stereotypes about Black people common among working-class whites. Reading it also suggests that he took a liberal position that fear of crime was not the same as actual crimes. Menino acknowledged that newcomers who don't look like or talk like the other members of the neighborhood might share law-abiding and safe neighborhood aspirational goals as old-timers. The mayor and sometimes city councilors supported the narrative that Boston was a safe city and that specific crime incidents were anomalies.

As is the case in most cities, some Bostonians were more likely to be at risk for victimization than others. Street crime was more likely to occur in an inner city within poor neighborhoods. If one lived in the inner city, one was at risk for a crime at night. Such incidents were less likely to occur in affluent neighborhoods. Although there might be fewer police officers in upper-class communities, criminals often avoided these neighborhoods. Obviously, crime did not happen only in minority and poor communities. Violent street crime had a different origin than domestic crime or white-collar crime. As we discussed in regard to Menino's first mayoral election, candidates debated over who would increase the number of police officers the most. The assumption was that a surge of police officers effectively reduced crime and increased arrests. For the two general election candidates, this narrative was necessary to convince voter they would keep the city safe.

A new mayor will discover that crime rates are cyclical. Often the causes of crime defy rational explanation. The overall quality of life, high employment, and the number of police officers assigned to a given community may not matter in crime prevention and arrest. A famous Kansas City study of policing (1971–1973) found that patrol levels did not affect crime levels or residents' sense of security. This came as a shock to city police departments and generated a debate about the saliency of more police presence.[5]

Among the most disconcerting crime statistics are increased rates of homicides. Homicide rates are usually a key indicator of deep social pathology and despair. Homicides among youth gangs may also indicate a war on drug turfs. In any case, no city wants the title of "murder city." Random killings create a sense of anomie. Yet there is little the police can do to prevent homicides. Police react to them. They usually arrest someone for the crime, but this is not a deterrence. This type of crime only makes media coverage if it is deemed horrific or if there is a racial element—such as Black-on-white crime or vice versa.

What do crime statistics tell us about the success of a mayor as a crime fighter? Two years after Menino was first elected, there was a drop in crime. Homicides fell 13 percent, to a total of eighty-five citywide, while most other

CRIME IN THE STREETS AND ELSEWHERE 159

crimes fell by 5 percent or less. Among the areas that recorded the sharpest decreases in crime were Allston-Brighton, where crime fell 17 percent; Dorchester, with a 10 percent decrease; and Roxbury, where crime fell 8 percent. Menino claimed that the drop in crime was the result of community policing and the increase in the number of police officers. There may have been other factors that generated these decreases, but Menino was politically committed to community policing. These rates confirmed his views about law enforcement. Menino stated, "These groups have come together and have fought to take their streets back from the dangerous and criminal-minded. We have formed a lasting partnership that has worked and will continue to work in the future."[6] Like his predecessors, Menino wanted to build a safe city.

Building the Safe City

A safe city can make for a higher quality of life. A safe city has to be defined as more than a lack of street crime. It is realized when residents indicate a relative lack of fear of using the streets and public spaces. It happens when residents feel safe to go out during the day and at night. In a safe city, the criminal element cannot impose an informal curfew at night on residents and impede entry into certain neighborhoods. Some families buy homes in certain neighborhoods because of their reputations for safety. Indeed, real-estate agents tout the expected appreciation values of homes in safe communities.

In 2001, a Gallup poll found that Americans felt safer than they had in thirty years. Again, safe was defined differently by different cities and residents. In 2004, the *Boston Globe* did a telephone survey of four hundred respondents and found that "more than half of Bostonians surveyed said they believed the city is less safe than it was a year ago, and they were dissatisfied with city government's crime-fighting efforts after a spate of fatal shootings and stabbings this summer, a Boston Globe poll concluded last week."[7]

Nothing stirs fear more than the media characterization of crime-ridden streets. As was suggested earlier, the reputation of a neighborhood and indeed a city is related to its crime rate. Mayoral elections can turn on who appears to be the best guardian of the neighborhood and properties. For example, New York City mayor Rudy Giuliani (1994–2001) and Philadelphia mayor Frank Rizzo (1972–1976) were elected on law-and-order platforms. Giuliani and Menino were elected in the same year but not for the same reasons. Both cities had their iconic crimes, including the 1986 Queens mob attack on Black men and in 1993 Colin Ferguson, an African American man, shooting white people on a New York City commuter train. In Boston, there was the 1989 Charles Stuart murder hoax and the 1992 teenager shooting and stabbing at Morning Star Baptist Church.

Political scientist Norton Long's book *The Unwalled City* describes a city in which there is no natural or human-made barrier between outsiders and insiders or between the criminal and the law-abiding. Police officers are expected to establish a "thin blue line" and maintain law and order. If they fail, residents blame the mayor for an increase in crime and the lack of effective policing. Accordingly, Menino felt obligated to assume a high profile in stopping crime and to appoint the right people to carry out this function. This meant selecting the right person to lead the police department.

The public may not know individual law enforcement officers by name, but the police commissioner is the face of the department. Hence, a newly elected mayor must get this appointment right. Menino was expected to create a national search committee, consult with leaders from the Boston Police Patrolman's Association, and listen to community leaders. However, the final choice was the mayor's. The choice came down to appointing a person from the local law enforcement community or a candidate with a national reputation for crime fighting and experience in managing large police departments. Selecting an outsider would have suggested that Menino did not feel the local candidates were competent or independent enough to make changes in the department. His predecessor, Ray Flynn, decided to hire forty-five-year-old William Bratton, a Dorchester native and head of the New York City Transit Police, after his friend Mickey Roache proved ineffective. During Bratton's time in New York he had become one of the leading advocates for community policing. He thought that it was "the best hope for improving race relations in the city."[8] Massachusetts Minority Law Enforcement Officers, an organization of nonwhite law enforcement officers, endorsed his plan.[9] However, the appointment of Bratton alienated some police officers and had little impact on the crime rate. Obviously, Flynn's struggle with these appointments was an education for Menino.

The Appointment of Police Commissioners

All candidates for the mayoralty promise to reduce crime and make the city safer. Once elected, a mayor like Menino would select a commissioner and articulate a crime reduction plan. Then the police department, from the so-called top

CRIME IN THE STREETS AND ELSEWHERE *161*

brass down to police officers on the beat, is expected to implement the plan. The leadership of the police force is critical to what has been called the "regime legitimation process."[10] In other words, validating a mayor's crime-fighting reputation is an important function of the police department.

A mayor's crime-fighting policies are also revealed in the selection of the top police leadership. The policies of the top leadership are designed to validate the mayor's policies. Social scientists Harrell R. Rodgers and George Taylor found a racial component in attitudes toward the police. There were differences in attitudes between Black and white respondents. The selection of police leadership was a cue to the city's commitment to fairness in law enforcement.[11] Accordingly, the police leader alerted residents of various races as to how police would behave and how crime would be fought. In effect, promises made in the mayoral campaign would be implemented. In the 1970s, sociologist Richard L. Block's research suggested that "citizen support for the police is constructed out of good and respectful policework. The negative effect of fear of the police on the support for the police was far stronger than the positive effect of fear of crime."[12]

In a classic study of childhood, political scientists David Easton and Jack Dennis found that the behavior of police officers played a critical role in "children's acceptance of external authority and officers remain important in the understanding authority of the state." In other words, acceptance of authority figures is related to one's socialization. If one grows up with a negative view of police officers, their attitudes will probably remain so unless something happens to change those views.[13] A kid growing up in South Boston would probably have a different attitude toward the police than one growing up in Roxbury or Dorchester. This is important because the leadership of the department can change public attitudes.

Commissioners are political appointees, but they are expected to have experience as regular police officers. Although they usually wear a suit and tie, most climbed up through the rank to the top of the force. Their ascendency is based on performance and merit. In most big-city police departments, there are still uniformed chiefs and superintendents.

In modern history, big-city police commissioners were usually recruited from the existing force. There are also examples of cities (e.g., Los Angeles) that recruited outsiders with national reputations. Outside commissioners usually are recruited from other departments and other cities. Customarily, a person who is recruited from inside the department is hailed by fellow officers.

They know the department members and understand the street culture. And importantly, such commissioners respect fellow officers and the ethos of the thin blue line. Presumably, outsiders have to learn the city, department culture, and crime hot spots. For most street officers, a good commissioner is defined as one that insulates the department from external politics and keeps discipline problems within the department. Increasingly, police officers who wish to ascend to the commissioner rank need to obtain college credentials.

Commissioners manage the day-to-day activities of the department. The research of political scientist James Q. Wilson found that police behavior varied in different cities. Large city officers were more likely to follow a traditional law-and-order approach to crime. In smaller communities, they played a less rigid role and acted as watch persons and social problem-solvers.[14] It follows that mayors would select commissioners who agreed with their own views on crime fighting.

Commissioners are the public face of the department and expected to address the media when there is a major crime event or when there is a need to discipline rogue officers. They are also members of the mayor's cabinet. Each of Menino's commissioners had a crime incident that defined their tenure.

Thomas Menino's Choices

When Tom Menino first took office as acting mayor in 1993, he inherited William Bratton, who was a Ray Flynn appointee. Bratton was an advocate of community policing and decided to return to New York City to become police commissioner there. His Boston tenure (1993–1994) was controversial because the crime rates were extremely high at that time. The increase in the crime rate built anxiety among residents. As acting mayor and a mayoral candidate, Menino would have had difficulty removing Bratton, a Dorchester native, given his high-profile image. Compared to former Boston police commissioner Mickey Roache (1985–1993), Bratton was a clear improvement in leadership. Under Roache's tenure, Boston established the notorious City Wide Anti-Crime Unit, which mishandled the Stuart murder and established the city's stop-and-frisk policy. This policy permitted police officers to stop individuals who looked suspicious and search them for weapons. As in many large cities, minority young males were most likely to be stopped and searched.[15] Such tactics often lead to resentment toward the police and increased fear of Black men. The Stuart investigation, which involved arresting an innocent Black man, was characterized as the police "bungling basics." Even the *Boston Globe* questioned Roache's leadership.[16]

Menino needed to appoint his own person to make his safety regime credible and embrace his crime enforcement strategies. Menino said, "It is an opportunity for me to have a commissioner who reflects my goals."[17]

In 1993, there were several high-profile murders, prompting the *Boston Herald* to describe the city as "Gripped by Violence."[18] During Menino's campaign against James Brett, he promised to add one hundred new officers to the department. He added forty-five as acting mayor and sixty-five after the election. Menino also promised to consolidate the Boston Police Department with Boston Housing Authority and school police officers. Later, when Bratton accepted the commissionership of the New York City department, the *Herald* ran a picture of a ticket saying "Now Playing: Top Cop: The Search Is On. Starring Tom Menino." The headline read, "Broadway Bill a Tough Act to Follow."[19] Menino's first attempt to put his stamp on the city police department was to appoint Paul Evan as commissioner.

The Paul Evans Era (1994–2004)

The purpose of having his own person in the job was to legitimate Menino's safety regime. After being elected mayor, Menino appointed Paul Evans, a forty-four-year-old decorated Vietnam Marine Corps veteran, twenty-four-year veteran of the Boston Police Department, and a resident of South Boston, or "Southie," as his police commissioner. Evans was selected after a "national search." He made his career by moving up in the ranks. Menino's choice was an attempt to maintain the police traditions of Boston with a community involvement twist. Sworn in on February 14, 1994, Evans was a safe choice. Furthermore, his appointment was consistent with Menino's low-profile leadership style and image.

This appointment went against the advice of Patrick Murphy, former New York commissioner Patrick Murphy stated in December 1993 to the *Boston Herald*, "One of the worse flaws of American policing is inbreeding and insularity. It is very narrow-minded to feel that all the wisdom is within your own agency. It is a tough job, and you need the best, not just some who grew up in your neighborhood."[20]

Nevertheless, the Evans appointment contained three basic symbolic messages. First, insiders could effectively manage the department. Evans was born and raised in South Boston, had moved up the ranks, and was respected by his fellow officers. Evans's predecessor William Bratton was called "a charismatic publicity hound," and Evans's low-key style reassured department members.[21] Second, the appointment reflected the mayor's confidence in rank-and-file police officers. Third, it signaled that the era of the flamboyant mayor and the glamor cop was over. Menino preferred low-key professionals overseeing his law enforcement policies.

Old ethnic ties in the police department mattered. Indeed, Evans did not launch any fundamental changes in operations. Although he was accused of once characterizing neighborhood policing as a "bunch of crap," he denied ever making such a statement to then-commissioner Mickey Roache. Evans publicly took the position that he took his leadership cues from the mayor. Accordingly, he became an advocate of neighborhood or community involvement in police work. He told recruits, "What will be expected of you? You will be expected to be a good listener—to meet with community groups and listen to them—and work actively to solve their problems, problems that lead to fear in our neighborhoods. You will be called on to arrest young people. But you will also be called upon to work with them and to make a difference in their neighborhoods."[22]

As an advocate of neighborhood policing, Evan incrementally reshaped the police department's reactive strategy into a proactive one. This tactic was aimed at getting police officers closer to city residents and preventing crime. More officers were walking the beat and there was less use of car patrolling. In addition, the new police commissioner saw his role as a problem solver and conciliator. Evans decentralized the police department into ten smaller districts. This was greeted with enthusiasm within the department because the district leaders, the potential captains, were to be chosen by civil service examinations.

However, Evans resisted the establishment of a civilian review board. Such boards had become a rallying cry after an incident of police misbehavior. Under such proposals, these citizen committees would have the authority to investigate police behavior and make personnel suggestions to the commissioners. Alternatively, and in the spirit of Menino's community-oriented politics, Evans introduced what he called "strategic planning teams" consisting of police officers, church leaders, and merchants. This idea worked for a while as the community saw the teams as a way to achieve better police-community relations. Menino supported Evans's community approach and stated that Evans was "my best appointment."[23]

The *Economist* magazine compared Evans's approach to his predecessor, William Bratton:

> What makes Boston's crime-fighting different is the willingness of the police to work with other organizations and community groups. "We are always looking at who we can collaborate with," says Mr. Evans. Among the Boston force's partners are the local US attorney, probation

officers (who have started evening home visits and have raised the rate of compliance with probation terms from 30 percent to 70 percent), local employers, and the TenPoint Coalition, a group of black clergy. The Boston Police Department has backed its cooperative talk with cash, awarding substantial grants to help nonprofit organizations.

The Boston model has worked to the greatest effect in tackling the teenage gangs responsible for a sharp rise in drug-related killings in the early 1990s. Meetings between police, probation officers, and clergymen identified the main people involved; these offenders were then told that the Police Department would use all its legal powers against them unless the killings stopped, a message that was reinforced by the probation officers and the clergy.... This policy, a big part of which was reducing the number of guns in circulation, helped to lower gun murders of under twenty-four year olds from 51 in 1990 to only 16 last year.[24]

The magazine quoted Reverend Jeffrey Brown, a cofounder of the Boston TenPoint Coalition: "We told them we'd rather see them in jail than conduct their funerals."[25] Many of these deaths were related to war over drug turfs. Commissioner Evans, by working with the TenPoint Coalition and other community groups, was able to achieve the so-called Boston Miracle. In 2002, the city reached a thirty-year low in violent crime. And there was also a lessening of police-Black community conflicts. Figure 1 shows the decline of noteworthy crime incidents during the early part of Evans's tenure.

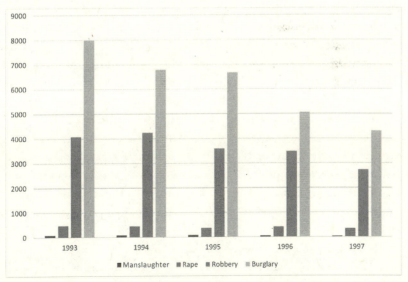

FIGURE 1. Rates and types of crime during part of Evans's tenure. Source: FBI Uniform Crime Statistics, 1993–1997

Figure 2 shows the overall crime rates from 1994 to 2004.

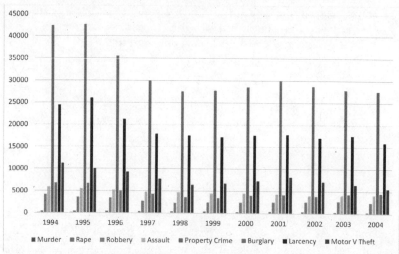

FIGURE 2. Overall crime rates from 1994 to 2004. Source: FBI Uniform Crime Statistics, 1994–2004

This second chart shows a reduction in crime in every category, but the trend is not without an uptick in incidents. In 2001, the community policing approach attracted a lot of national attention. The mayor of New York stood rigidly on one side of the crime-fighting stage and the mayor of Boston at the other end. Although Rudolph William Giuliani and Thomas Michael Menino were of Italian American descent, they were recruited into different political parties and the contrasts in personalities and political ideologies were tellingly distinct. They were in the mayor's office at the same time. Both Boston's Menino and New York City's Giuliani wanted to reduce crime in their cities. However, they used different approaches. The former embraced community policing while the latter adopted more traditional law-and-order tactics. In his farewell speech, Giuliani took a shot at Boston because its approach had received equal attention as New York's. The *New York Times* reported that the Boston model had succeeded in other cities. Giuliani took the occasion to defend the broken window theory, which supported arresting offenders for small crimes in order to deter them from committing more crimes. It also involved the deployment of officers in high-crime areas. These deployments were based on Comostat data, a daily crime statistical system that created

CRIME IN THE STREETS AND ELSEWHERE   *167*

maps for all city police precincts and reported the information to police head-quarters. Menino's former chief of human services J. Larry Mayes recalled, "He [Giuliani] was pissed about [the] *New York Times*'s coverage of the two approaches." He compared over time the Boston crime rates with New York: "This doesn't have to do with baseball, it has to do with policing."[26]

In Giuliani farewell address, he asserted,

> In the eyes of many police chiefs and criminologists, San Diego and Boston have become the national models of policing. And while New York's accomplishments are also studied and admired, there's a sense of sadness that a great opportunity has been squandered....
>
> That kind of annoyed me when it was written but I waited.... Crime goes down in New York, but it goes down all over the country and it really isn't about policing, it isn't about our theories, our ideas, our policies or our approach or our management.[27]

The debate about police tactics continued but none of these tactics had the local impact of the invasion of Accelyne Williams's home by the Evans-led Boston Police Department in 1994. This was perhaps the defining incident for the first year of Menino's crime-fighting reputation and the Evans era. People told several versions of who did what, why, and when.

The Reverend Accelyne Williams Incident

On March 25, 1994, a police SWAT team, wearing bulletproof shields and armed with a no-knock warrant, broke into the Dorchester home of Reverend Accelyne William, a retired minister. They rammed the door and handcuffed him. According to one newspaper report, "When the announced team—armed with shotguns and semiautomatic sidearms and wearing masks and helmets—battered down Williams' apartment door, he fled in horror to the bedroom."[28] They had the wrong address in an apparent drug raid. Two officers struggled with the elderly man until he started to vomit. Williams, a seventy-five-year-old man, suffered a heart attack and died.

This could have been an explosive situation. The SWAT team had the wrong address in a surprise drug raid. No drugs or weapons were found in Williams's apartment. The entire situation could have lent itself to a variety of interpretations including acts of police brutality, negligence, or racism. Mayor Menino recalled that he got a call from the police commissioner at about 2:30

a.m. saying, "We just killed someone, a Black minister. We did make a mistake. It was based on bad information. They got their information from a person from another county. They thought the first floor was on the second floor."[29]

The *Boston Herald* reported the news on the front page, but it was not a banner headline. The headline for that issue belonged to the Boston College Eagles basketball team, who had beaten a famous Indiana team. The headline read, "Minister Dies as Cops Raid Wrong Apartment." The article also quoted Police Commissioner Evans as saying, "Everything was done right, except it was the wrong apartment."[30] The wearing of masks was designed to psychologically freeze people where they stand.

Two days later, the *Herald* reported that the police thought Reverend Williams was a lookout for the armed Jamaican Posse, a drug gang. Deputy Superintendent Pervis Ryan, head of the Drug Control Unit, told reporters that the informant said the second floor but he meant the third floor.[31] Explanations and regrets were not enough. Many in the Black community were angry. Now it was time for conciliation. Mayor Menino and Police Commissioner Evans attended the funeral services at the Dorchester Temple Baptist Church.

Menino had been just elected, and his connections with the Black community were not fully consolidated. A single incident managed incorrectly could have damaged his mayoralty. The incident remained forever in the mind of the mayor. Years later, sociologist Donald A. Gillis asked then-former mayor Menino if there were any specific racial incidents he recalled during his tenure as mayor: Menino chose the 1994 William incident. Menino stated,

> Just a couple of times, like when we raided the wrong apartment with the minister. [Police Commissioner] Paul Evans calls me up, it's a Friday afternoon, and he asks me, "what kind of a day you are having." I told him, "I'm having a great day. I'm ready for the weekend." He says, "after I talk to you mayor you are going to have a shitty day." So he explained to me what happened. He says, "What do we do?" I say, "Be honest about it. Let's tell people exactly what happened." I told him to get on the phone and call all the so-called black leaders. I'll make some phone calls. I went to the NAACP dinner that night; I explained it and apologized for it. If you look at the incident, what saved us is that we apologized. Nobody ever apologized for mistakes like that before. We were sensitive to the issue. I never really had a bad racial thing when I was a mayor, not really, no.[32]

CRIME IN THE STREETS AND ELSEWHERE *169*

The Media Coverage

The Boston television reporter Jon Keller contended that the situation was diffused because Menino "instinctively did the right thing. He admitted an error. He had to own up to it. He knew it would infuriate the community. In a blue-collar community, when you screwed up and fess up to it [the explanation is accepted]. In contrast to Mayor Flynn, he didn't try to hush up the incident."[33]

The Williams incident could have been framed as an example of overzealous and racist police officers. For example, the headline could have focused on white cops in plainclothes attacking an unarmed seventy-five-year-old Black minister who they thought was a lookout for a drug gang. In the debate about the incident, several Black leaders supported the framework Menino gave to the situation.[34] Nonetheless, the NAACP president initially called for an independent investigation, though he later withdrew his request. Minister Don Mohammed of the Nation of Islam stated, "I cannot criticize them at this point, and I certainly hope that they do apologize to the family."[35] Boston City Councilor Charles Yancey, an African American, called the incident a mistake. Highlighting the ambiguity of the situation was essential during the days following the event. It must have been clear that alternative framing was likely.

This incident might also have been seen as an example of a mayor spending too much time checking damaged streetlights and not enough time working on the city's race relations or keeping tabs on the police. It wasn't. The police insisted that they had followed procedures. The press reported the statement but never questioned it or asked Black leaders to comment on it. Everyone seemed to be involved in quelling reactions to this tragedy.

The Post-Williams Reaction

Paul Evans tried to suspend Lieutenant Stanley Philbin, the supervisor of the raid, but instead Philbin chose to retire. His suspension was later overturned by the state civil service commission. Evans called the state ruling a "mockery of the disciplinary process in police departments."[36]

Reporter Leonard Greene wrote an article that began, "One of the first things we must do regarding the death of Rev. Accelyne Williams is to stop comparing its investigation to the probe of Carol Stuart's murder. The two deaths have virtually nothing in common." In the same article, State Representative Byron

Rushing, a Black leader, declared, "We don't have Ray Flynn, who did not know how to say, I'm sorry."[37] In effect, Rushing was supporting Mayor Menino's apology. The press and leaders of the Black community decided not to deviate from the narrative that the mayor and the police department were innocent. Menino reported that he had reached out to the people: "That night I went to the Urban League. I had several private meetings. I spoke to a couple of elected officials. I had credibility built up in the community."[38]

Menino established a close relationship with Black community ministers. Menino could talk to all the ministers and had an ongoing relationship with them. Menino and his wife, Angela, along with Evans attended services led by Reverend Bruce Wall at Dorchester Temple Baptist Church two days after the event. Television cameras were not allowed but the mayor stated after the service, "We wanted to be out in the community and putting the healing process in place. A mistake was made, and we're going to heal those mistakes." The mayor also supported Evans's apology. Menino said Evans had reassured him: "He [Evans] pledged when he was wrong, he will admit it. That's a sign of a true leader."[39]

Some people in the Black community gave Menino and Evans the benefit of the doubt. Menino was a new mayor and had spent time building trust in the Black community. Although not spoken about at the time, there were many other more important racial inequality policies to contest. There was a small protest, but the protest leaders did not ask anything from the city. According to Alyce Lee, Menino's chief of staff, "The incident was not seen as an onslaught against the Black community."[40]

The Williams incident simply became a "house was erroneously invaded" story. The fact that the occupant was an elderly Black man who could hardly be confused with a member of the Jamaican Posse drug gang didn't matter. Yet, few people were prepared to say the police deliberately chose the wrong house. In the media's initial coverage of the aftermath of the incident, no grassroots Black leaders were interviewed nor did eager editorial writers jump to support Police Commissioner Paul Evans. Some police officers were suspended only to be reinstated by an arbitrator. Evans objected to the arbitrator's ruling, and the situation was quietly dropped.

On May 18, 1995, two hundred community members organized a forum to protest the death of Reverend Williams. The *Herald* pointed out that after a year, the protest about Williams was too late. This protest exposed the fact that Black leaders could not mount an oppositional discourse to the media

CRIME IN THE STREETS AND ELSEWHERE 171

discourse regarding the Williams incident. If only two hundred people showed up, the mayor was safe. A *Boston Globe* reporter asked, "Where would we be in this country, particularly black people, if black folks in Montgomery, Ala., waited a whole year before they organized and demonstrated on behalf of Rosa Parks?"[41] *Herald* reporter Leonard Greene suggested that Black leaders lost an opportunity to "strike while the iron was hot."[42]

Black leaders not only lost the window of opportunity to make a protest but they were powerless, and the media discourse shifted from police brutality to compensation for Williams's widow. The issue became how much would she get from the city. Initially, the mayor offered $600,000 to settle. Black *Boston Globe* columnist Derrick Jackson took the occasion to criticize the mayor's spending in his office. He called Menino "Mayor Scrooge."[43] The mayor's staff response was to quickly move away from the proposed lowball settlement. When a settlement was finally made, the press almost triumphantly reported that Williams was paid a million dollars for wrongful death.[44]

Another blemish on Evans's tenure was the mistaken beating of one of his own Black police officers. On January 25, 1995, a decorated Black detective was beaten by other Boston police officers. Michael Cox was chasing a suspect and was attacked by fellow officers. *Boston Globe* reporters characterized members of the department as "a double wall of silence: a tight inner circle of officers protecting themselves with false stories surrounded by the department's broader effects to keep details of the horrific incident from public scrutiny."[45] Some police officers also offered a so-called ice patch theory that Cox lost his balance on the ice and fell. None of this was true. The city and department did not handle the situation well and wanted to make a low-ball settlement of $300,000 to Cox. The *Boston Globe's* Brian McGrory characterized the Cox controversial situation as such: "The quiet rustling coming from the city government is the sound of Mayor Thomas Menino and Commissioner Paul Evans seeking cover from the controversy, protecting themselves at the expense for the city.... Menino told a gathering of Globe editors and reporters that the Cox case 'was an occasion we'll never be proud of. It's not a happy, a good day, for the Boston Police Department.'"[46] Evans's reaction was to initiate the use of signals and safety measures so that officers could identify plainclothes officers.

Another controversial event during the Evans period was the McLaughlin murder. On September 25, 1995, Paul McLaughlin, an assistant attorney general, was murdered in West Roxbury by someone described as a young Black male. Some thought that the murder was a reaction to his prosecuting of gang members. It turned out to be a random attack without any political implications. Nevertheless, it exemplified a pattern of youth violence that was unacceptable.

Operation Ceasefire

Gang and youth gun violence predated Menino's election as mayor. It was a problem that Menino inherited from the Flynn administration. Members of the Black community became alarmed and began organizing. In 1992, Black activists led by Reverend Eugene Rivers and his colleagues started the TenPoint Coalition. This group of forty churches became a regular critic of the Boston Police Department. The coalition organized a forum with teenagers. These forums explained why street crimes were increasing and why they had youth and racial components. They created a new committee to monitor and cooperate with the department. Professors Christopher Winship and Jenny Berrien reported,

> The creation of the Ten-Point Coalition marked the official beginning of Boston's African-American religious community's organized involvement in the youth-violence epidemic. As of 1992, relations between African-American community leaders and Boston's law-enforcement agencies were still strained. Rivers was constantly "in the face" of Boston law enforcement and viewed as a "cop basher" in police circles. He established a constant presence in the troubled neighborhoods of Dorchester and was in contact with the same kids as the Anti-Gang Violence Unit [AGVU]. Rivers' aggressive advocacy for local youth, in and out of the courts, led to many confrontations with the AGVU. But this initial antagonism was eventually replaced by cooperation. A number of events, along with the new, improved policing approach, spurred the turnaround.[47]

The same year, a group of ministers and law enforcement officers established the "Police Practices Coalition." This coalition gave awards, called Police Youth Leadership Awards, to officers they considered good cops. When a new commissioner takes over the department, they often create new programs that identify their approaches to crime reduction.

Police Commissioner Evans organized a fight against gun violence. In 1994, Operation Scrap Iron attempted to catch Boston gun smugglers. They used a tactic called "area warrant sweeps" in what were thought to be dangerous neighborhoods, notably public housing. In 1995, the Boston Police Department organized the Boston Gun Project, also known as Operation Ceasefire. It was an interagency program among the Boston Police Department, the Boston school police, and the Suffolk County district attorney. This three-year effort also included federal participation with the Alcohol, Tobacco, and Firearms

Bureau. The Gun Project was designed to interrupt the supply side by going after suppliers of illicit firearms. The project also wanted to identify high-risk individuals. According to Winship and Berrien, "These individuals, 1,300 in all, representing less than 1 percent of their age group city-wide, were responsible for at least 60 percent of the city's homicides."[48]

The more success stories Operation Ceasefire generated, the more analysis it received. In 1996, David Kennedy, a Northeastern University professor, suggested crime reduction was the result of Operation Ceasefire, which was designed to go directly into the community and speak to the people who were committing these crimes. Menino joined a coalition of law enforcement officers, federal and local, to stop gun violence in the city. This group went into minority communities and spoke to leaders and known gang members and troublemakers. They told them the killing had to stop, and the law would be strictly enforced. Indeed, violent crime did go down for two years. This program got national attention and was called the Boston Miracle. This was a two-year, four-month-long interregnum in which no teenagers were shot or killed. This record received a lot of media coverage for the city. It unofficially ended when Eric Paulding was shot and killed on December 11, 1997. Several lessons were learned. Among them was that miracles can be disrupted and are evanescent.

In 1997, Boston announced that it had its lowest crime rate in twenty-nine years. Burglaries and vehicle thefts were at the lowest rate in thirty-three years. Homicides involving firearms dropped from twenty-six in 1996 to eight in 1997. Some of these statistics can be explained by the decline in the population of individuals aged thirteen to twenty-four, because that age group is more likely to commit crimes. Nevertheless, Menino jumped on these positive statistics, calling for lower insurance rates for Bostonians. Nothing came of his appeal, but the mayor was able to state that he tried to get insurance rates down for Boston. It was a great use of mayoral symbolism and image-making.

The so-called Boston Miracle gained Paul Evans a national and international reputation. Evans resigned as Boston police commissioner and took a job in a British police unit. The *Guardian* of London was curious about the new recruit and decided to do a story about Evans's Boston career. There were two questions: How did the Boston Miracle work and was it still working? The story quoted Paul Alves, a Cape Verdean American who worked with Boston youth gangs, about the plight of the Boston Miracle. "At the moment, right now, it's real iffy. . . . The kids that were maybe just getting into fistfights, they're picking up guns. It's teetering towards getting hot again, maybe getting back towards where it was 10 or 12 years ago."[49]

In effect, it had worked for a time, but now it was losing its efficacy. The end of the Boston Miracle was telling but inevitable. Professors Anthony Braga, David Hureau, and Christopher Winship wrote,

> To observers in the public management field, the unraveling of the so-called "Boston Miracle" may not be surprising. It is challenging to sustain effective collaborations over time. No one institution by itself can mount a meaningful response to complex youth violence problems. Institutions need to coordinate and combine their efforts in ways that could magnify their separate effects. There are strong reasons for relying on collaborations that span the boundaries that divide criminal justice agencies from one another, criminal justice agencies from human service agencies, and criminal justice agencies from the community. Such collaborations are necessary to legitimize, fund, equip, and operate complex strategies.[50]

Nevertheless, *Boston Globe* reporter Kevin Cullen concluded that Evans's handling of two major racial incidents—the Paul McLaughlin murder and the Accelyne Williams case—was that "Evans may be the right man at the right time for the job."[51] Yet six years into the Menino mayoralty, Ralph Saunders, who studied Boston's community policing, concluded, "Community policing can be seen, therefore, as an effort by the BPD [Boston Police Department] to get the most out of the resources it has available. Similarly, the rhetoric of community policing can be critiqued as an attempt by the BPD to make the department appear to be doing more than it really is—more, even, than it possibly can do." For Saunders, the idea of community police was supposed to be a "podium" for citizens to express their needs, but it was the police who "are doing most of the talking."[52] Mayor Menino was also talking to people in the neighborhoods and decided to take some initiatives.

Menino's Initiatives

Menino's public safety program was not limited to street crime. He was also concerned with rising domestic violence. In October 1997, he issued an executive order on domestic violence. It stated that any mayoral appointee named in a restraining order or charged with or arrested for domestic violence would be required to attend mandatory counseling at the City Employment Assistance Program. Such individuals would be immediately put on administrative leave. If found guilty, employees would be dismissed.[53]

Another program aimed at youth was a fight against selling mature (M)-rated video games to underage children. J. Larry Mayes recalled,

CRIME IN THE STREETS AND ELSEWHERE 175

The program was started by the Campaign for Commercial-Free Childhood led by Susan Linn, director of media for the Baker Center at Harvard. Ms. Linn was asked to give a video presentation at the Crime Council. She showed a video that was targeted toward 12 years old boys. It contained a scene in which "a John" beat up a woman after a sexual transaction. Menino was appalled and proceeded to jump up and left the room. Menino thought it was wrong to sell these videos to young people and he was willing to do something about it. He did not care if he would get into trouble with the free speech people in [the] American Civil Liberties Union [ACLU].[54]

Menino also supported a bill in the state legislature that called for labeling violent video games as pornography. Mayes said that he told the media, "Children aged seventeen and under should not be sold this stuff. They [the gaming industry] are not getting [games] into the hands of nine- and ten-year-olds. Is it going to be an uphill battle? Sure. But it absolutely a battle that the mayor feels he should take on."[55]

Menino took on the battle with the video game industry. Mayes recalled, "We needed to have proof that twelve-year-olds were buying these games. We decided to use a sting operation. We sent twelve-year-olds into video stores to buy M-rated videos." The stores were not supposed to sell M-rated videos to customers under age eighteen, [but] they did. . . . Store clerks and others were not ID-ing these kids." Menino knew that he would get pushback from the ACLU, Federal Communications Commission (FCC), and the Entertainment Software Association, an umbrella group for video game makers that was powerful and had its own media and reporters. Mayes recalled, "They sent me two thousand emails a day!" Menino also pushed back against the Massachusetts Bay Transit Authority (MBTA) receiving advertising dollars from the video industry. Reporter Jonathan Elias of channel 7, an ABC affiliate, ran a story about and showed that the FCC was negligent in allowing the selling of these games to underage youth. This helped expose the practice of selling illegal videos to underage kids.[56]

Moving against domestic violence among mayoral appointees, restricting violent video games, and encouraging citizen cooperation with police officers were critical to improving the quality of life in the neighborhoods. Menino also wanted to hear from the police, but he recognized that community policing could be subverted if citizens were not talking to police officers. Menino looked for a way to make this happen. He decided to have a monthly meeting with the police leadership. He asked Mayes and Merita Hopkins, his chief of staff, to create a forum for that discussion. It was first called the Public Safety Task Force (later changed to the Crime Council). One of the programs they recommended was the so-called stop snitching program. After horrific crimes, sometimes involving youths, some people would not cooperate with the police. Mayes described the "program to provide information to the people as more of [a] philosophy. The purpose was to get young people to cooperate with the police in identifying criminals." Simply put, individuals would refuse to say anything about what they had seen or heard. In the minority community, it might have been a part of an unwritten community code that no one should ever tell the police anything. If you did, you were a snitch. For the youth, "It was considered a badge of honor not to cooperate with the police. Stores were selling T-shirts saying, 'No Snitching.' Folks would show up in court with T-shirts with 'Stop Snitching.' They would leave 'No Snitching' leaflets on the front porch."[57] It was critical that Menino change that attitude, otherwise his community policing program could not work. The police needed the trust of community residents.

These initiatives raised Menino's crime-fighting profile in the neighborhoods. Menino was not willing to leave policing to the professionals. He also knew that crime prevention required a holistic approach. During the transition between police commissioners, he further educated himself in the dynamics of crime prevention and community response. The job of crime fighting was not only a stressful job for the police commissioner but also for the mayor.

To do the public safety job effectively, he needed a new police commissioner who understood what he was trying to do in the city and with whom he could work. For his second commissioner, Menino took the opportunity to appoint the first woman to be Boston police commissioner.

The Kathleen O'Toole Era (2004–2006)

Mayor Menino decided to go in a different direction for his new police commissioner. In February 2004, Kathleen O'Toole became the first female department leader in Boston's history. Although the nation's first female police chief was Portland, Oregon's Penny Harrington, O'Toole's appointment attracted a lot of national attention. However, her appointment continued in the Irish police officer tradition. The *Christian Science Monitor* wrote,

> Growing up in Marblehead, Mass., a tiny maritime town north of Boston, O'Toole gave little indication through her college years that she would

someday go into police work. It was during a summer when she was looking for part-time work, and a friend persuaded her to take the police exam, that she first had an inkling to carry a badge. "My mother nearly fell off her chair when I told her what I was going to do," says O'Toole. She spent some of her first years working on the city's subway as a decoy for would-be purse-snatchers. It was a duty, according to her sister, Mary, that she found exhilarating.[58]

O'Toole went to Boston College and had a law degree from the New England School of Law. She became a police officer and held the rank of lieutenant colonel in the Massachusetts State Police. She served there from 1992 to 1994. More importantly, she had also served as secretary of the executive office of public safety in Governor William Weld's administration. Also, she had been a part of the search committee that recruited Evans.

In 2005, O'Toole announced command staff changes in the department. She promoted new officers to her staff. Charles Horsley of the Boston Police command staff was promoted to superintendent and Bruce Holloway to deputy superintendent. She also restructured Operation Neighborhood Shield, a program that included state and federal law enforcement officers to fight crime in high-crime areas. More police officers were assigned to certain areas of Roxbury and Dorchester. These changes sent signals to all officers under her command. She planned to do things differently than Evans, hence the new leadership. Commissioner O'Toole supported the broken window theory of crime prevention. This approach was a departure from the Evans approach. For her, it was one element of a balanced crime-reduction policy. She also called herself a disciple of George Kelling, a Rutgers University criminologist and one of the originators of the broken window theory of law enforcement.

Indeed, O'Toole held talks with Kelling about doing consulting work with the department, though that never happened. O'Toole said, "We're not going to abandon our broken windows strategy. It's worked for us all along, and it will continue to work for us."[59] A 2005 Suffolk University poll found that O'Toole received a 53 percent "excellent/good" rating and a 38 percent "fair/poor" rating.[60] The poll may have captured her personal approval, not the respondent's understanding of her law enforcement philosophy. Moreover, crime did increase and appeared to be escalating. During the summer of 2006, Menino accepted and then decided against Governor Mitt Romney's offer to use state police in fighting crime.[61] Perhaps the defining event in O'Toole's tenure was her management of the police killing of Victoria Snelgrove.

Death at Fenway Park

As previously stated, police commissioners provide leadership for uniformed officers and speak to the media. In that capacity, the commissioner is expected to manage big crowd events. The 2004 American League Conference championship series between the Boston Red Sox and New York Yankees qualified as a big event. The Boston Red Sox defeated the New York Yankees and during the celebration, an Emerson College student journalist, Victoria Snelgrove, was shot with a pepper spray projectile that hit her in the eye and passed into her brain. The crowds prevented the first responders from getting her proper medical attention and she died.

Fans were outraged. O'Toole condemned the act and reacted by demoting Superintendent James Claiborne and suspending two superior officers involved in the incident. However, the pressure mounted on Mayor Menino to do more. He decided to put O'Toole on paid leave. The county district attorney, Daniel F. Conley, decided not to prosecute the identified police officers. The Snelgrove incident turned out to be a major political trauma event, and the city made a wrongful death settlement of $5.1 million.[62] The company that made the spray gun, FN Herstal, quietly settled with the Snelgrove family, who asked for $10 million.[63]

During the O'Toole years, there were also several corruption scandals. Federal authorities arrested three officers involved in drug trafficking and one officer involved in a sex scandal.[64] The corruption of Boston police officers was not new, but it was particularly embarrassing to the city's first law-and-order female commissioner.

Although the appointment of O'Toole was seen as a breakthrough, the purpose of a commissioner is to represent the administration and implement the mayor's safety regime. After O'Toole resigned, *Boston Globe* reporter Joan Vennochi lamented her resignation and asserted,

> O'Toole was not his first choice when he appointed her in February 2004. Initially, the mayor basked in the praise he received for naming Boston's first female police commissioner. However, Menino did little to empower her and much to marginalize her. He ignored her plea for more police officers to take on the rising violence on some Boston streets. Increasingly, he micromanaged the Police Department from the fifth floor of Boston City Hall. Clearly, Menino lost faith in O'Toole, if, indeed, he ever had it. A natural tension always exists between the

political and police worlds. It is exacerbated in times like these, money is tight, violence is escalating in mostly minority neighborhoods, and the affected community is desperate for answers and help. Some who witnessed the dynamic between this mayor and this police commissioner see another chapter in a now-familiar story: Menino being Menino, especially when challenged by an intelligent, independent personality.[65]

The metric for evaluating any police commissioner is the number of crime incidents. O'Toole only had three years to prove her expertise. Figure 3 shows the crime numbers and types during O'Toole's time.

During her three-year tenure, the number of murders remained below 75 per year, and the number of rapes never rose above 275. Compared to her predecessor, Paul Evans, Commissioner O'Toole's tenure was about the same despite her adopting a different law enforcement philosophy.

As we suggested personality and chemistry with aides mattered with Menino. Like her predecessor Paul Evans, O'Toole resigned to take a police job as chief inspector in Dublin, Ireland. Her resignation allowed Menino to appoint his third police commissioner. Again, he went to a local police department for a new commissioner. This time the new man was Lowell superintendent Edward F. Davis.

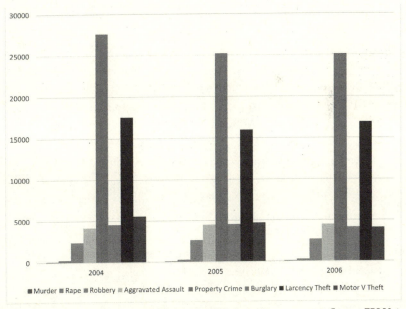

FIGURE 3. Crime numbers and types during the O'Toole tenure, 2004–2006. Source: FBI Uniform Crime Statistics, 2004–2006

Edward F. Davis (2006–2013)

Edward F. Davis III had grown up in Lowell, Massachusetts, a suburb of Boston, where his father was a police officer. Joining the force was part of the family business. He attended New Hampshire College (now Southern New Hampshire University) and received his master of science degree at Anna Maria College in Paxton, Massachusetts. Davis started his career in the Lowell Police Department and became its youngest uniformed officer to become a superintendent at age thirty-seven.[66] He established a regional reputation as a police officer and administrator.

On December 5, 2006, Davis became commissioner of the Boston Police Department. He was a police officer's police officer. He knew members of the department and thought the "department was full of courageous members." His salary as the commissioner was $167,000 per year, $7,000 more than that for O'Toole. He described Mayor Menino's views on crime fighting: "The mayor was focused on community policing. He was constantly in the community talking to people. He would bring me with him. He thought that it was a wise idea in order to raise arrest rates, you need to work with the community to prevent crime. His refrain was: We need a plan. We need to be thoughtful about how to prevent crime. We need new approaches."[67]

In many ways, the Davis appointment represented Menino's and Evans's approach to crime fighting. The new police commissioner was sworn in at the Mildred Avenue Middle School in Mattapan. Selecting this location was designed to give a signal that Davis was committed to community policing. This act impressed Darnell Williams, president of the Urban League of Eastern Massachusetts. He thought that the Davis appointment sent a "different message," praising his commitment to community policing.[68]

Another change was Menino's approach to the civilian review of police street behavior. Ray Flynn had asked attorney James D. St. Clair to review the police department. The report of the Boston Police Department Management Review Committee was released in 1992. It called for the creation of a Community Appeal Board to review investigations by Internal Affairs and more management training. Fifteen years later, in 2007, Menino finally established a three-member Community Ombudsman Oversight to review civilian complaints, but it did not include subpoena power.[69]

Before Davis became commissioner, there had been a reduction of force, that is, mandated cutbacks of officers in the department. Davis stated, "We were very active in looking for funding support."[70] In 2009, Boston received an $11.8 million grant from the U.S. Department of Justice, a grant under the American Recovery and Reinvestment Act. The money allowed the department to add fifty officers. Thomas Nee, president of the Boston Police Patrolman's Association, and Boston's congressional delegation worked to obtain the grant. Mayor Menino stated,

> Today is a great day for public safety in Boston. I am grateful for all of the work done by President Nee of the Boston Police Patrolman's Association and our partners in Washington for helping us secure this competitive grant money. This award is a terrific example of Boston's strong commitment to public safety. This funding will keep officers on the streets of our neighborhoods and continue our progress in community policing. I am proud of the work done by the Boston Police Department in reducing crime across our city, and this funding will allow us to continue these effective strategies.[71]

Davis said, "It is precisely what we need during this difficult fiscal time to stave off workplace reduction. This initiative will assist us in maintaining the level of public safety service that Boston residents and visitors have become accustomed to."[72] Avoiding a reduction in force was important to working police officers but it did not have an impact on crime reduction rates when compared with his predecessors. Yet Davis claimed that during his tenure there was a 5 percent reduction in crime. The number of arrests went down.[73] Figure 4 shows the crime incidents during the Davis tenure.

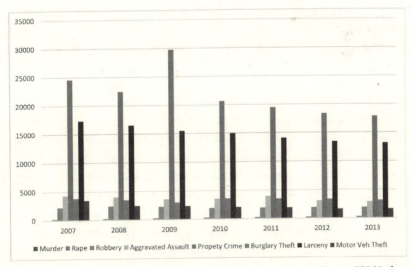

FIGURE 4. Rates and types of crime during the Davis tenure, 2007–2013. Source: FBI Uniform Crime Statistics, 2007–2013

There was some reduction near the end of Davis's tenure. Remarkably, there was no large increase in crime categories during the Great Recession. Reporter O'Ryan Johnson pointed out that police experts think that "most of the city's homicide victims end up dead due to gang beef over petty slights that spiral out of control and explode into violence the next time the two sides meet."[74] Davis reported several incidents of homicides: "This was horrific for the families. I had to go to every scene. There was an active shooter at the Massachusetts Eye and Ear Clinic. A prisoner had overpowered a security guard. We had to deal with the situation."[75] Davis also recounted several hostage situations during his tenure. During that time, there were occasional fan disruptions and violence after local professional sports franchises won national sports companionships. The police department had to be on high alert to manage large crowds. The Boston Red Sox won the World Series in 2007, the second time since 2004. The New England Patriots won the NFL Super Bowl during 2002, 2004, and 2005 but not during Davis's tenure as police commissioner. The Boston Celtics won the NBA title in 2008. In 2010, the Boston Bruins won the NHL Stanley Cup. The Boston Police Department successfully managed these celebrations, but they did not expect and were unprepared for the 2013 Boston Marathon Bombing. This would be the defining event of Davis's tenure.

The Boston Marathon Bombing

Big-city racing marathons have become an annual event in many cities around the world. Few have the prestige of the Boston Marathon, which is held on Patriot's Day, a Massachusetts holiday commemorating the Battles of Lexington and Concord. The Boston Marathon, which began in 1897, is an annual international event that attracts thirty thousand runners from all over the world and a half-million spectators. Runners range in terms of talent, age, gender, and physical capacity. The race begins in the western suburb of Hopkinson and follows a designated route around Boston to culminate on Boylston Street in downtown Boston. It is common for Bostonians to celebrate professional sports events, but the marathon is the biggest sporting event in Boston. It is also a huge money-making enterprise for the city. Throughout its history, the famous race has had its controversies and incidents. These were minor in comparison with the 2013 bombing. For the ordinary Bostonian, an act of terrorism like the Boston Marathon seemed to come out of the blue. For the city, this event had no warning.

CRIME IN THE STREETS AND ELSEWHERE *183*

On April 15, 2013, two perpetrators, Tamerlan Tsarnaev and his brother Dzhokhar, American terrorists of Chechen descent, planted bombs in pressure cookers two hundred yards apart and blew up the spectators attending the venerated Boston Marathon. The explosions happened downtown near the end of the race. Three people were killed, and 246 others were injured. Spectators fled the scene and bags were left all over the route. Rumors spread that there were other bombs. Transportation was stopped, and the crime scene included fifteen blocks around the incident. Uniformed state and local law enforcement officers were all over the city. The FBI also joined the investigation.

Commissioner Davis spoke to the media:

> On behalf of Mayor Menino, I would like to offer my sympathies to the victims and the families of this horrendous event. This cowardly act will not be taken in stride. We will turn every rock over to find the people who are responsible for this. We're working very closely with my partner Rick DesLauriers, the Boston Police Department is on the scene and has been there since this incident happened.
>
> There's been a horrendous loss of life; at least three people have died in this event, but this—the number of injuries and the people injured is an unfolding issue right now.[76]

The event shocked the nation and the world. Three days after the attack, the FBI released photos of the two suspects, still at large. The brothers kidnapped a man and killed MIT police officer Sean Collier. Another officer was wounded by a hand grenade. Tamerlan was eventually shot numerous times by the police and run over by his brother, which ultimately killed him. Dzhokhar was captured in Watertown, a suburb of the city.

The Boston Marathon will never be the same, and security has been expanded. The slogan "Boston Strong" became a way to honor survivors and assert solidarity for the city. Runners returned to the marathon in the following years. On September 22, 2013, Commissioner Davis announced his resignation. His twelve years were the longest for a modern-day commissioner.

Summary

Political scientist Elaine B. Sharp conducted a study of cities with high-profile new economy–style post-industrial cities and found that police in such cities practiced enhanced order maintenance in which police are expected to suppress any of signs of disorder.[77] Mayor Menino's crime-fighting record is a matter of debate. He certainly placed a priority on safe streets and neighborhoods. These strategies were not considered overwhelming. He endorsed community policing and appointed commissioners who shared his views, although O'Toole was an exception. The Black community praised the mayor for advocating community policing. In 2006, the Boston Police Department launched a variety of crime-stopping programs. These included Operation Rolling Thunder and Operation Home Safe. The former was a show of force with officers on foot, in cars, on bicycles, and on horseback. The latter was a program that claimed the first line of defense against youth gangs and criminal was the family. These programs were not very successful. In an anonymous letter to the *Boston Globe* editorial page, a writer summarized Menino's tenure:

> Police, by and large, keep a watchful eye on the city. A bigger challenge during the Menino years has been the age-old question in law enforcement circles: "Who watches the watchers?" Evans was driven to distraction in the 1990s when his efforts to discipline rogue officers were overturned by Civil Service or labor arbitrators. The low point came in 1995 when Michael Cox, a black undercover officer, was mistaken for a murder suspect by fellow officers, and badly beaten and abandoned. His fellow officers then erected a "blue wall of silence" around the incident.[78]

The writer went on to say,

> Menino has been too generous with the city's public safety unions. Police officers, for example, enjoy the Quinn Bill, which boosts the salaries of many officers for earning marginal criminal justice degrees. And Menino, for no good reason, supports a paid detail policy that drives up road construction costs by paying officers for jobs that could be done as well and less expensively by civilian flaggers. Still, Menino and city residents can walk away feeling like they get something in the deal—a department that takes its share of responsibility for the city's crime rate and works diligently at both prevention and apprehension.[79]

Menino did not respond to this anonymous writer. It was just one person's opinion. Obviously, crime fighting involved more than just putting more officers on the streets. Crime fighting is an issue most voters can understand and relate to. Accordingly, the recruitment of police commissioners was critical to the construction of Menino as an alert crime sentinel, a caring and neighborhood-oriented mayor. The selection of insiders as police commissioners was telling. Menino respected the attitude of police officers and was prepared to oblige them with one of their own as long as they supported his community policing policies.

CRIME IN THE STREETS AND ELSEWHERE   185

Ed Davis's long tenure was testimony to his relationship with the force, the public, and the mayor. He just happened to be in the office at the time of the 2013 Boston Marathon bombing.

Having the right person in the commissioner's chair is a necessary but not sufficient strategy to consolidate a mayor's safety regime. The crime rate is random and cyclical. It does not always respond to economic downturns. Yes, crime fighting is eye-catching for the public because the local television media uses it as a lead topic for the evening news. Moreover, the organizational culture of the police department continues to dominate the beliefs of uniformed officers. Once a mayor leaves office or a commissioner resigns, the members usually return to their old ways of policing the streets. This may explain Ralph Saunder's conclusions.

In summary, community policing is an illusion that serves to legitimate the police without fundamentally changing the way police do their job. Therefore, community policing serves an ideological function—in the pejorative sense—in that it masks relations of power and serves primarily as a means by which police are able to implement and maintain their power. But community policing is not merely rhetorical. Attached to its rhetoric are concrete practices that expand the capacity of police to observe subjects and that attempt to bind police and some city residents within a partnership. Without those practices—without the work of community service officers and the elaboration of a network of crime watchers, without the walking beats and the Safe Neighborhood Initiative—the illusion of community policing would lack the power to convince its audience. Thus, ideological illusions such as community policing are produced and reproduced in rhetorical and actual forms that are complementary initiatives.[80]

CHAPTER 7

Boston's Racial Diversity Challenge

Cities are places where people of different phenotypes, races, skin colors, and cultural backgrounds come together to live, work, and engage with each other. Since the beginning of the republic, Boston has been a magnet for all types of immigrants—people from Europe, Asian, Africa, and Latin America. They come to the "Cradle of Liberty," Boston, to improve their life chances. Many early migrants came to the city for low-skill jobs but in the twentieth and twenty-first centuries, they came to work in the expanding service economy. Boston's history illustrates that in both centuries ethnic and racial groups competed for jobs, housing, elected government offices, and social recognition. Herein lies the potential for racial and ethnic conflict. In such conflicts, there are winners and losers. In addition, this type of conflict is never without negative publicity and consequences. In some ways, the city's history is punctuated by these conflicts. Boston mayors often find themselves at the center of these conflicts, though obviously not all racial and ethnic conflicts are mayoral centered.

The job description for a mayor may not include a formal obligation to address racial conflict but it is one of its unspoken roles. A mayor should model how these disparate groups live and work together peacefully. Mayors, whether they acknowledge it or not, set the tone for city residents' attitudes toward immigrants and toward racial/ethnic issues. For most white Bostonians, these issues may or not be a part of their everyday lives. However, for most nonwhite Bostonians these issues are omnipresent and manifest themselves in the job market, public schools, street encounters with law enforcement officers, and housing searches. Many residents often believe it is the mayor's responsibility to deal with these issues. Concerning resolving minority issues, American mayors like Menino had structural and resource limitations. The structural limits involved a lack of jurisdiction over all jobs, welfare, and education policies. The resource limits included a lack of funds directly targeted to limit racial inequality.

Yet some nonwhite citizens believe that mayors are more powerful than they indeed are. Obviously, in campaign speeches, mayoral candidates have asserted a commitment to equal treatment for all citizens. The reality is that it is difficult to overcome generations of discrimination from City Hall. Nevertheless, mayors try to fulfill these promises in a variety of ways. Some mayors will hire diverse members for their inner staff and promote affirmative action policies in municipal departments. Others create a cadre of nonwhite leaders who act as unofficial advisors. Still other mayors, in their role as chief city consoler, can condemn violence in particular communities and provide solace for families who are victims of this type of violence. A few mayors will establish race relations committees to study ways in which the city can improve race relations. Nevertheless, these actions alone will not necessarily improve race relations within these communities and in the city in general. A diligent mayor who wants to improve race relations should try to delve deeper than the official count of nonwhites in the city. There is often pluralism within counted groups. Table 3 shows race and ethnic breakdowns in Boston across several decades.

Table 3. Race and Ethnic Breakdown in Boston

RACE/ETHNICITY	2020	2010	2000	1990
Non-Hispanic Whites	44.7%	47.0%	54.5%	59.0%
Blacks	22.0%	24.4%	25.3%	23.8%
Hispanics or Latinos (of any race)	19.5%	17.5%	14.4%	10.8%
Asians	9.7%	8.9%	7.5%	5.3%
Two or more races	3.2%	3.9%	——	——
Native Americans	0.2%	0.4%	0.4%	0.3%

Source: U.S. Census

This chapter discusses Tom Menino's responses to his minority constituencies, their demands, and some of the intragroup conflicts within communities. When Menino left office in 2014, the city's demographics had begun to change. He embraced heartily the administrative outreach tactics outlined above. Yet in Boston, as in other cities, managing the plight of minority constituencies could be overwhelming. White mayors like Boston's Ray Flynn and Tom Menino had different strategies for dealing with nonwhite communities. Some of the differences in style were related to the ways they governed. Other differences were related to the political periods in which they governed. In both Flynn's and Menino's cases, they discovered the limits of their powers. Yet both mayors spent time trying to convince minority communities and the public at large that they were attempting to build and maintain a city where equal treatment would be available to all. So, given these commitments, what should be the most important questions? Are these challenges amenable to City Hall action? What are the political costs and benefits of mayoral action? Can City Hall make fundamental changes without compromising the political support of the overall community? Writers Brian Wright O'Connor and Peter C. Roby stated,

> The brutalist concrete of Boston City Hall cannot convey the degree of power concentrated within those walls. Boston's mayor is able to set funding levels without major City Council or School Committee meddling. The mayor retains significant local control over development, schools, hiring municipal employees, contracting, and grant-making. The mayor deals with a large delegation on Beacon Hill and has played a uniquely significant role in the state's political life. While no person of color has been able to reach that fifth-floor office, the seat has remained the envy of aspiring black politicians who passed through city hall during the *Banner* years.[1]

Minority citizens demanding better schools, jobs, and housing was not just limited to the African American community. When Menino took office, African American communities represented 23.8 percent of the city population. As demographics changed and other minority populations increased exponentially, priorities changed. According to the 2020 U.S. Census, Latinos are now 19.5 percent of the population and Asian Americans are 9.7 percent. These groups shared mayoral attention and required place-based strategies, that is, approaches based on residential patterns. Some of the residential locations of minorities changed during Menino's tenure. Accordingly reaching them required a place-based strategy.

For each of these ethnic groups, their issues may have seemed unique to themselves and their enclaves. Although different minority enclaves may have pockets of inequality, they cannot be treated the same way. Political scientist

James Jennings believes that the way to approach the problem of spatial inequality is to adopt a place-based strategy. In his research, using geographic information systems and community indicators to map out distressed neighborhoods, he found that "the Asian-descent population is more dispersed than that of Blacks and Latinos. But pockets of Asian-American residents are still found in the areas with higher neighborhood distress scores." For him, "Neighborhood distress is defined as, a situation reflecting concentrated social and economic conditions which point toward lower living standards for residents, and where such conditions can raise organizational demands on local and small and service-delivery nonprofits."[2] Jennings agrees with Professors Peter Dreier, John Mollenkopf, and Todd Swanstrom that place matters.[3] Equally important in the fight to overcome inequality and economic disadvantage is the leadership provided by a committed mayor. Strong leadership is essential. Many cities have the advantage of having a strong mayoral form of government, but it is the character and personality of the mayor that makes the difference.

The Advantage of a Strong Mayor

Boston has a strong mayor form of government called the mayor-council government. Under this system, the mayor is the chief executive officer of the city, and the council serves as a legislative body. This type of government has fewer structural limits over the mayoral control of city departments. Yet mayors are not totally free of structural and fiscal limits or encroachment by the state government. In Massachusetts, a mayor needs council approval for policy initiatives, support for budget making, and changes in local laws. Legally the state can overrule, preempt, and limit a city's action on any policy issue. This has happened in areas of education, taxes, and housing policies.

Furthermore, all mayors are restrained by the policy tunnels that were dug by their predecessors. A policy tunnel is defined by shaping solutions in such a way that it is expensive and difficult to take policy in a different direction. In other words, predecessors can start new projects, as we saw in Ray Flynn's housing policy, with its financial commitments and promises that would cause a spillover into his successor's terms. In many ways, this was an example of a policy tunnel.

This legacy was also certainly true for the mayor when managing race relations. It is not just a matter of governing style. Political time and the quality of opposition also matter. History suggests that, on the subject of minority relations policies, strong mayors can be divided into four types. Mayors, regardless of race and gender, have adopted one of the approaches discussed below. Personality, politics, and ambition play a role in style adoption.

The first type of leadership style may be called a *using* mayor. Using is not meant to be a pejorative adjective. Such mayors attempt to use racial incidents and conflicts as an opportunity to advance their careers, either to get reelected or attract national attention. Also, some of these mayors are ambitious and legacy-sensitive. They seize the opportunity to make minority betterment statements that are quoted by the local media and historians. This may have its place, but rhetoric may not result in problem-solving. Mayors who adopt this tactic understand that whatever action they take or say may overwhelm the incident and the media will spin it into a story about the mayor and how they handled the situation.

The second type is a *deterring* mayor. Such mayors see racial incidents as an opportunity to delay or put off managing the situation. This can be done by changing the subject or allowing time for the media to change the lead headlines. They will concede that an incident happened but there are more important subjects on City Hall's agenda. Such mayors are willing to create blue-ribbon commissions or committees on race relations, made up of concerned citizens with the goal of hearing all sides and allowing them to let off steam. However, city departments are usually not told to do anything or to change procedures. Such mayors are not above engaging in dramaturgy. Dramaturgy is staging dramatic acts to demonstrate concern without making change. For example, after several incidents of violence in public housing, former Chicago mayor Jane Byrne stayed overnight in the infamous Cabrini Green public housing. It got a lot of publicity but there was not much overall change in the Chicago Public Housing Authority to develop safe operations for its residents.

The third type is an *impeding* mayor. These mayors deliberately try to slow down, stop, or discredit claims of inequality and mistreatment lodged by minorities. These mayors make it difficult, if not impossible, for minorities to move out of their enclaves, enter predominately white public schools, and question alleged abusive behavior by law enforcement officers. These types of mayors were quite common in the South prior to the civil rights movement. The Jim Crow era would openly inhibit the rights of Black residents. Mayors in the North also engaged in this type of impeding behavior but most did so in more subtle ways. Some like former mayor of Philadelphia Frank Rizzo and New York City mayor Rudy Giuliani presented themselves as law-and-order mayors. Racial profiling was common. In modern times such mayors can show disrespect for minority communities by appointing as their chief liaison for minority relations a staff member with no credibility in minority communities. Former New York mayor Ed Koch used this tactic by appointing Haskell Ward to run the city poverty programs.[4] He also appointed former representative Herman Badillo as deputy mayor without defined duties. Former Chicago mayor Rahm Emanuel appointed Barbara Byrd Bennett as CEO of the Chicago Board of Education. She was an outsider without a distinguished record in other cities. While the minority community continued to complain about the appointment, nothing much got done.

Finally, there is the *solicitous, compassionate, and empathic* mayor. These mayors are facilitators of minority aspirations and allow minority spokespeople to gain high visibility and speak for their minority groups. Such mayors take the position that minority grievances are legitimate and that their leaders have good intentions. More importantly, such mayors seek out minority spokespeople to help deal with the problems that confront the minority community. Granting respect to these sometimes-self-appointed people, the mayor gains credibility in the minority communities. Indeed, the mayor can appropriate the language of such a spokesperson and endorse the activities of the organizations (e.g., in Boston, the TenPoint Coalition) they represent. The result is a perceived easing of racial tensions and a collective effort to address the grievances of minorities. It is important that such mayors be seen as decent people with good intentions. The personality of the mayor is critical, and Menino was archetypal of such a mayor.

Empathic Mayors and Minority Betterment

Mayors who aspired to be accepted as supportive leaders for minorities are not exempted from criticism and conflicts with minority leaders. One can be a liberal on minority issues but not quite understand the nuances of activist rhetoric and why some members of minority groups never complain. To thrust oneself into an ongoing conflict with such poise and with few long-term associations or contacts in a minority community reflects a high degree of sureness. Simply put, Tom Menino defied his working-class socialization. One anonymous interviewee stated that "race was never an issue for him." Another stated that Menino was "blind to differences."[5] Cities led by such mayors see fewer violent incidents with a racial framing. Sometimes minority leaders help them define a Black/white incident as nonracial. Under such mayors, minority enclaves often remain relatively stable, and optimism is rampant. Minority voters are inclined to believe they have a friend at City Hall and that the mayor will listen to their leaders.

Menino nurtured this image and included minority leaders in formal and informal meetings. In racial crises, he solicited and respected their input. And in turn, the mayor referred media reporters to these leaders for comments about minority issues. Seeing and hearing the mayor's statements was critical. Equally critical was the changing image of Black activists and political leaders. By the 1990s, television began to play a larger role in defining the image of African Americans in general and Black Bostonians specifically. Public television programs like WGBH's *Say Brother*, an interview/panel show, provided a platform for debates on minority issues.[6] Writer Devorah Heitner concluded, "As *Say Brother* reflected black Boston to itself, and to the region, the program represented new cultural practices to reify and disseminate them; it provided a forum where African Americans who had been wronged could find an arbiter more open to their concerns than courts or police. . . . By attempting to teach audiences how to live 'according to new principles of Blackness,' *Say Brother* aimed not to pacify its audience but to electrify it."[7]

Again, the Menino administration benefited from having such programs that allowed the Black community to educate Bostonians. Granted public television mainly attracted a white liberal audience. The *Say Brother* program, in which Black activists, celebrities, and politicians were interviewed, became a must-see hour for the minority community. In some ways watching a television program might have been a more effective educating tool than reading a book about race relations. Menino and his staff wanted to know more about minority aspirations, and they reached out to traditional minority leaders as well as ordinary Bostonians. Feedback from minority constituencies served to educate Tom Menino.

The Education of an Empathic Mayor

In chapter 1, we discussed Tom Menino's political socialization. Menino's edification on race brings to mind the famous Oliver Wendell Holmes quote, "Man's mind, once stretched by a new idea, never regains its original dimensions."[8] People from his background usually did not get the opportunity to interact with minorities or come into close contact with people outside their neighborhoods. For them, minorities were not invisible but rather outside of their daily lives. Some of Menino's fellow Hyde Park residents might have been oblivious to the racial turmoil of the 1960s. But politics in Boston's Black community kept churning, and newspapers kept reporting events.

Since the 1950s, Black leaders and activists had been getting their names in newspapers, but they held no elected office. Mel King, a community activist, called this the "service stage."[9] In this stage Black institutions operated with City Hall patronage. The "organizing stage" described community organizing during the civil rights movement. The last stage was "institution building" in which Black leaders openly sought political power.[10] Electing minority members to political offices was seen as a way to get inside the decision-making centers like the Boston School Committee (BSC), City Council, and state legislature to make a difference. Activists were organizing and running for office. King ran for the BSC three times and lost. At that time, he was perhaps the most famous Black activist in Boston. But others were seeking to hold citywide offices. When John D. O'Bryant, a Black person, was elected to the BSC in 1977, it was considered a political breakthrough.

Menino entered Boston politics in 1968, a year after the nation experienced yet another major racial breaking point. Several major figures were assassinated. Boston had a long history of racial conflicts and school desegregation resistance. Yet two years earlier, an ambitious African American Republican politician named Edward Brooke was elected as the U.S. Senator from Massachusetts. He served two terms and was the first Black Republican senator since Reconstruction. This took place in the middle of the civil rights movement in the South and after the signing of the 1965 Voting Right Act.

Again, these events shaped young Tom Menino's views of minority aspirations. The racial tensions in the 1960s escalated. In February 1965, Malcolm X, a Muslim minister and civil rights advocate, was assassinated. In April 1965, Martin Luther King Jr., a Nobel Prize winner who had lived in Boston as a graduate student and received his Ph.D. at Boston University, returned to lead a march from Roxbury to the Boston Common in protest of school segregation. Boston's Reverend Michael Hayes and Hasan Sharif were instrumental in getting Dr. King to come back to Boston.[11] Coming after his rise to the top of the leadership of the southern Black civil rights movement, Martin Luther King's return and protest march had to be quite an embarrassment to the city's progressive reputation. The city of Boston's shortcomings made the front pages of national newspapers. Three years later, King was assassinated in

Memphis. The nation had several urban riots after the assassination but not in Boston.

Some pundits attributed this exception to then-mayor Kevin White. He is remembered in part for asking singer James Brown, an extremely popular R&B performer, to continue with his planned concert at the Boston Garden. Allowing this event to go on was supposed to calm things down among Black Bostonians. Brown performed and asked for calm. The concert didn't reduce the anger, but Professor Robert Hall has pointed out in personal correspondence with me,

> You seem to buy the notion that in the aftermath of Martin Luther King's assassination there were no riots in Boston. You are not alone. Many of the people interviewed by the filmmaker David Leaf for his film on James Brown's concert in Boston bought into the notion so strongly that, in the end, Leaf entitled the film, "The Night James Brown Saved Boston." There was rioting in Roxbury up and down Blue Hill Avenue but from the point of view of the downtowners and the city fathers, it was AS IF Roxbury was not a part of Boston. What Mayor Kevin White and businessmen in the area of the Boston Garden really feared was that Brown's audience would go on a rampage downtown. As long as Negroes were rioting in Roxbury, they could [not] have cared less. Also, I do not think it is accurate to credit Kevin White with the idea of letting the concert go on as scheduled. White wanted to cancel the concert out of fear that the violence that had erupted in Roxbury would spread or spill over into the Garden area with the audience. An elected black politician to whom you give short shrift, Thomas I. Atkins, was actually the one to persuade White not to follow through with his original inclination to cancel the concert.[12]

Additionally, the next day, five thousand people protested Dr. King's assassination at White Stadium, located in the Playstead section of Franklin Park. There was anger, uncertainty, and frustration. The city had lost one of its former student residents, an advocate for nonviolent civil rights protest, and a role model for Black youth. Boston and the nation would never be the same. The nation would later remember King with a holiday, street names, and a statute in the nation's capital.

Throughout the turmoil, Vietnam War protests also continued, and President Lyndon Johnson decided not to run for reelection. The 1968 Democratic Party National Convention was held in Chicago, and Democrats were met with a small riot. Robert Kennedy, who grew up in Massachusetts, had been elected to the U.S. Senate from New York and was also assassinated during his 1968 campaign for the presidential nomination. It is not an overstatement to say the nation was at a violent crossroads and city leaders were on alert for more breakouts of racial violence. The decade of the 1960s left a lot of political questions about whether cities were safe places to live.

The Mel King Phenomenon

In 1973, Mel King was elected state representative and held the job until 1982. In 1983, he ran for mayor of Boston, and John O'Bryant, a BSC member, ran King's campaign. King would be the first Black candidate to run for mayor. The campaign was supposed to be the culmination of a nascent coalition of white liberals and Black progressive activists. The media noted that King had replaced the dashikis he had previously worn with business suits and bowties. King's issues were Black aspirational ones: jobs, better public housing, and assistance from downtown developers to help the city's distressed neighborhoods. Mayor White had a reputation for ignoring such neighborhoods during his sixteen years as mayor and concentrating on downtown development, and that was the reputation he achieved nationally.[13]

The 1983 mayoral race was a critical time for the Black community. White decided to not seek reelection, and King announced his campaign to be mayor. In 1983, Philadelphia and Chicago had elected their first African American mayors. While losing the race against Ray Flynn, King noted that he had received a higher percentage of the white vote than the two successful candidates in Chicago and Philadelphia. His Rainbow Coalition had registered several thousand new voters. King noted, "In 1983, I won the highest percentage of white voters of any person of color running in the country. People's image of Boston is that of a highly racist city. My experience is that when it comes down to voting, people aren't much different across the country. White people vote for white people and people of color vote for people of color.... We talked access and we reached out to women and the gay and lesbian community."[14] King hoped to be the Harold Washington of Boston. And a visit from and endorsement by Washington certainly contributed to this hope.

There was also a concern about Black voter turnout. In fact, because Black voters constituted only 20 percent of the electorate in Boston, even a minority turnout on the order of Chicago's would not have been enough; King would have had to get an unprecedented 35 percent or more of the city's white vote to win.[15] There were eight well-known candidates in the race. King carried the Black neighborhoods of Roxbury and Mattapan.

The voting results showed that King's coalition of racial minorities and white liberals pushed him to the front of an eight-candidate field. By one semiofficial tally, he ended up with 98 votes more than runner-up Ray Flynn and with about 29 percent of the total—including 10 to 15 percent of the city's white vote. Extraordinary public interest in the race was underscored by the 63 percent voter turnout, but King's supporters were disappointed that the turnout among Black voters was only 60 percent, compared with the 80 percent turnout among Blacks for the election of Chicago mayor Harold Washington earlier that year.[16]

The failed mayoral candidacy of Mel King that year and Bruce Bolling in 1993 reminded minority leaders that they needed more than liberal white support to win in the primary and general elections. Research literature suggested that the election of Black mayors did not necessarily mean higher minority voter turnouts. In addition, engaging the white working class continued to be difficult.[17]

Low voter turnout remained a major problem for Black politicians. Many white scholars are attracted by the so-called indirect theory, which suggests that a low rate of turnout can be explained by nonracial factors, that is, low participation rates are byproducts of class position. Since the majority of Black people are disproportionally represented in the lower socioeconomic strata of society, they are less likely to be educated, active, and involved in politics. Poor people, in general, tend to be less informed, less educated, and propertyless.[18]

A competing explanation for the low participation among Blacks is the so-called isolation theory. Low participation is explained as a byproduct of social isolation. As a result, Blacks become more alienated than whites. In Boston, the majority of Black residents live in all-Black neighborhoods. Due to the absence of something like the ward-level organization of the old Chicago machine, high turnout is unlikely.[19]

The low participation of Black citizens was matched by that of Latino residents. Aside from Puerto Ricans, some of these newcomers were not citizens. They also seemed to have less faith in politics. This attitude changed with the development of a strong nascent and ambitious middle class. For second-generation immigrants, there was also a strong assimilationist ethos in their politics.

Finally, another explanation for apolitical behavior is incomplete socialization. Robert K. Merton, the famed sociologist, attributed unconventional civic behavior to incomplete socialization. Simply put, minority children were not

New Faces, New Issues

encouraged to participate in politics and that followed them into adulthood. Their parents might have been nonvoters and apathetic.[20] As Bolling and King discovered, mobilizing such residents was extremely difficult. Simply raising the right issues that affected the lives of these residents of color was not enough. They needed to get more people registered to vote and get them to the polls.

New Faces, New Issues

Even within Boston City Council, political dynamics were changing. In 1986, Bruce Bolling became the first Black president of the City Council. This election was interpreted as a symbol of political incorporation, that is, evidence of inclusion and respect, but this conclusion was premature. As we saw in an earlier chapter, election to the council presidency was part of the internal dynamics of the council chambers itself, not an office that indicated group ascendency. Remember that in the 1980s, the nation was in the throes of a conservative era with Ronald Reagan as president. Civil rights enlargement was not high on his agenda. Furthermore, many Blacks thought the civil rights era was over.

In a specific neighborhood located in the city of Boston, a few Black leaders felt especially disenfranchised and alienated from the city government. Between 1986 and 1988, some residents of Roxbury supported a plan to separate from Boston and form a new independent city, called Mandela. This strategy was a variant of the Black separatist movement, which asserted a self-help ideology with a vision of a self-sustaining Black community. Advocates like state senator Royal Bolling Sr. and his wife, Joyce Ferriabough-Bolling, were at the forefront of the movement. They thought that the next phase of Black development was to gain control over the economic clout of the community. If the movement were successful, the Black community might have been able to rebuild its retail shops. These shops and establishments were having a difficult time, in part because of the decline of the Boston central business district, the invasion of fast-food franchises, and the parking perks of suburban shopping. In the new city of Mandela, Blacks could do business with minority vendors, builders, and banks.

This strategy was highly controversial, in part because it supported the notion that economic separation would create capital accumulation. Once enough capital was accumulated, it would then be used to rejoin the economic games. In retrospect, there was a certain romanticism attached to this proposal. The critics of this proposal argued that white businesspeople would not cooperate with any attempts to displace them in the economy. Blacks would have found it difficult to accumulate enough resources to compete in the mainstream economy.

The critics of the Mandela movement believed that a more rational strategy was to cooperate with the city of Boston. Hence, some key Black leaders opposed the Mandela movement. For example, Reverend Charles Stith, a prominent leader, opposed it and called for "one Boston."[21] Two nonbinding referendums (in 1986 and 1988) that advocated secession from Boston and the establishment of an independent city to be called Mandela were defeated.[22] Again, the city received national attention for its race problem.[23]

Entering Boston Politics

Four years later, Thomas Menino was elected and became the first Italian American mayor of Boston in its 178-year-old history. After being elected to office it must have been clear to him that racial change was happening. Menino had witnessed this tumultuous 1960s era but his education in the 1970s was quite different. He continued his apprenticeship and watched the rise and success of local Black politicians. One of the byproducts of the 1960s was the mobilization of northern African Americans. Consequently, the 1990s saw many racial breakthroughs in race relations nationally and in the city of Boston. When Menino assumed the office of mayor, Boston's minorities were 40.2 percent of the city population. In 2010, the minority population increased by 55.1 percent. For Menino, a new and more inclusive relationship with the minority community was required.

What would a new mayor do to achieve openness and inclusiveness in race relations? Boston's apartheid-like neighborhoods, memories of the 1970s busing conflict, and a failed Black secession movement and mayoral candidacy got national attention. It was time to change directions. In 1990, so-called regular white and Black Bostonians did not know each other and there were few platforms to bring them together. Passing council resolutions and making speeches was not enough to close the racial gap. City agencies needed to be integrated, neighborhoods needed to accept minorities, and the new mayor needed to visit every part of the city.

Within minority groups, there were still complaints about jobs and housing. Menino understood that changing these policies required diversifying municipal boards. This was one of the reasons he appointed Peter Chin, an activist Asian developer in Chinatown, to the powerful Zoning Board of Appeals. This board decides on variances in zoning to make building conversions and gets to know the people who live there.

During the 1993 election, Menino campaigned on a theme of inclusion. Inclusion meant creating equal opportunities for all ethnic and racial groups in all aspects of city life. The nation had come a long way since the 1960s, and the Boston of the 1990s was quite different from the city of Menino's predecessors. Becoming an advocate for inclusion was not difficult for a young man from Hyde Park because in his youth he had felt the sting of "otherness" or exclusion. In his book *A Mayor for a New America*, Menino was asked which issues were personal for him. He stated,

> Racism. I will not tolerate it. . . . That's the interesting thing about my life. I was in the first grade—I will always remember this. It's only a little thing, but I will always remember it. . . . My name is spelled M-E-N-I-N-O, unlike the "Manino" that's on the mushroom jar. . . . And the first-grade teacher told me that my parents didn't know how to spell my name—that the Italians couldn't spell. So, she changes the spelling. And I went through the first grade with my name spelled wrong. . . . That's a little thing. But it's always stayed with me. . . . And I will never tolerate people being discriminated against.[24]

Apparently, Menino felt that his childhood socialization and the treatment he experienced as an Italian American enabled him to empathize with the plight of minorities. Obviously, he had endured ethnic slurs and been touched by anti–Italian American stereotypes. This seemingly led him to embrace liberal views on race that were alien to the people Menino grew up with. His strong religious views may have contributed to his enlightened views but as a pragmatic politician, he foresaw the changing racial attitudes and their meanings for local politics. In his 1993 contest for City Council president, he asserted, "What's a progressive? I'm more liberal than most of the progressives."[25]

Being a progressive does not always mean that an individual is a liberal on race relations. Race relations are a complex set of ideas and actions. However, some white liberals and Black activists believed that personal dialogue among the races would open communication and help solve some of the race problems. Some white liberals had Black personal friends and that for them proved the point to them.

Cultural critic Benjamin DeMott's *The Trouble with Friendship* asserted that whites often conflate personal friendships with Blacks as evidence of a strategy to improve race relations.[26] If only Blacks and whites could be friends, then they could get along and racism would disappear. It is not uncommon for politicians to cite personal friendships with minorities as a liberal credential. In an interview with Tomas Gonzalez, Ray Flynn "reminisced about having played basketball throughout the city of Boston, and through that process has built a sense of camaraderie with some of his teammates, many of whom happened to be Black. He even boasted of having once played on a semiprofessional basketball team, where his teammate was none other than a young Mel King."[27]

DeMott does not deny the importance of interracial friendships, but he asserts that these friendships alone will not eliminate the structural barriers to Black political and economic incorporation into the mainstream. Change involves seriously restructuring social barriers as well as more proactive leadership.

Some of the narratives about inclusion might have seemed abstract to Black people in the street. Mistreatment by law enforcement was a more significant barrier for him. Other barriers include segregated housing, schools, and low-wage jobs. In other words, Boston needed to change its image. For some Black immigrants from the South, Boston was "Up South."

Boston as Up South

"Up South" is a term used by some southern Black migrants to describe their experiences on the streets of Boston that reminded them of the pre–civil rights South. Most lived with Black neighbors and sent their kids to predominately minority public schools and worshiped at predominately minority churches. At night white police officers were considered dangerous and minority males were told it was not safe to travel in white neighborhoods. In the 1990s, academics were still arguing that the lack of Black progress was related to the legacy of poverty and job discrimination. Blacks were poor because of social isolation, racial discrimination, and economic inequality.[28]

Many minority families came to Boston to escape discrimination, get better jobs, and improve their life chances. Boston became a magnet city for Black and Brown immigrant families, including Cape Verdeans, Africans, West Indians, Haitians, Cubans, Mexicans, Dominicans, and South Asians. Neighborhood retail establishments reflected this new diversity.[29] Asian immigrants included Vietnamese, Cambodians, Chinese, and Koreans. Immigrants may not have come to Boston with a political agenda, but some were drafted into the ongoing social activism of the city.

Latinos were not far behind their Black counterparts in terms of rates of poverty and the difficulties of finding affordable housing. They shared the bottom of the economic rung with Blacks. More importantly, Latinos were gaining on Blacks as a larger percentage of the population during the 1990s. Living in proximity to each other, the two groups faced challenges in education and job discrimination. The need for a minority coalition should have been obvious, but building such cooperation was difficult. The relations between these immigrant groups were often characterized by mindless social competition, ethnic chauvinism, and political apathy. Yet the number kept increasing as the city was diversifying in some neighborhoods.

Five years after the 2010 federal census, Marilyn Johnson, a researcher, declared Boston a "minority-majority city."[30] The politics generated from being a minority-majority city should be different from a predominately white one. Sociologist Jorge Capetillo-Ponce found that the "New Majority" was a top-down movement that attempted to create a coalition of people of color.[31] Boston's minority politicians adopted a particular rhetorical style that emphasized homeownership, racial pride, and uplift. However, there were no citywide political organizations, subleaders, or effective communication procedures to consolidate a coalition. Some community organizations remained dormant between crises and elections. The structure was more of an ad-hoc committee rather than a coherent and permanent organization. Apparently, Menino diagnosed this yearning for inclusion as he encountered and understood the multiple messages from minority activists.

Understanding Minority Activist Rhetoric

The reactions of white residents to violent incidents between Blacks and whites, and Black leaders' responses, are critical variables in understanding the state of Boston's racial situation. It was critical for a white liberal mayor like Menino to understand the political rhetoric of minority leaders. Although Black politicians' and community activists' oratory embraced a liberal mantra and working-class aspirations, and sometimes the more radical and confrontational rhetoric of Boston's white progressives, it was designed to appeal to their own audience and make them act. There was also a moral subtext in the rhetoric of Black politicians. This could be traced to the legacy of clergy-led citizen demonstrations. For these leaders, Blacks were on a consecrated journey to equality. Politics was seen as a continuation of the civil rights crusade. The speechmaking sought inclusion, reparation, redistribution, and sometimes retribution.

In a city like Boston, the great recurrent issues were poverty, racism, and unemployment. The minority community looked to their leaders to assess white city leaders. In 1999, the *Bay State Banner*, a Black newspaper, asked Black leaders to assess Menino after six years in office. Former state senator Dianne Wilkerson, who supported James Brett in the previous mayor's election, had a history of antagonistic relations with Menino. Yet she said, "I'd say there's been a tremendous amount of growth. I think he's expanded the whole horizon of whom he talks to." State Representative Byron Rushing praised the mayor for his accessibility. Mel King, a community activist, was less kind: "He has the benefit of having a nice, easygoing image. There's no question that he's a likable person. But you can't confuse that with policies, practices, and programs. We now have a situation where we have absolutely no voice in dealing with the schools."[32] This latter assessment changed as Menino became committed to reaching out to all communities. *Boston Globe* reporter Brian McGrory described Menino as "being "wildly' everywhere. He was there all the time. His driving premise was you had to be there. He was out there all the time."[33]

The Rewards of Reaching Out

In Boston politics, racial conflict seems to be an underlined theme that will not go away. Menino never claimed to understand race problems in academic terms but he was a pragmatist who kept the city together. He strived to be a "let's do what we can to get things done" type of mayor. Race relations were an ongoing problem, and they competed with the fiscal crises of cities, crumbling infrastructure, and debates about the plight of the urban poor and seniors. Boston mayors before Menino tried to solve the racial image problem but years of effort failed to ferret out pockets of discrimination. Since the 1970s busing controversy, relations between the races was analogous to the pressure that built under the earth's tectonic plates. Racial tension could explode at any time. A single incident involving a white and Black person could trigger days of disturbances. An example of this occurred in a 1995 incident involving Assistant Massachusetts district attorney Paul R. McLaughlin, who was gunned down at a commuter rail stop. At first, police speculated that the act was gang-related. Reverend Eugene Rivers described how Black clergy acted quickly to avert a conflict. He stated, "We extended our condolences to the families. We met at the spot of the shooting. We had a press conference and stated that we wanted to bring justice to violent criminals. We stated that the Black community must step up. This will not be an open season on all Black males." Rivers also stated that "preachers were standing with Menino and Evans [police commissioners] and that kept calm in the city of Boston. No one was able to politicize a terrible tragedy."[34] Reverend Ray Hammond of Bethel AME Church in Dorchester stated, "We ask the city as a whole to step back and not allow their conscious or unconscious fears to drive what happens.... This is a time for the city of Boston to come together and to make it clear that we will not be held hostage by either perpetrator of violence or by those who would exploit the fear of violence to promote more racial division."[35]

Menino's working together with the Black clergy helped defuse such crises. He acted in a empathic manner, allowing Black ministers to be seen, speak, and act. This worked for him, in part because of his professed race-neutral attitudes and his personality. This became a part of his crisis management strategy. The politics generated from nascent majority-minority cities with a white liberal mayor was conciliatory and reform-oriented. The rhetoric of white liberal politicians like Menino also reflected optimism that reinforced the ties of the white liberal/Black coalition. According to Zebulon Miletsky and Tomas Gonzalez, this coalition predated Menino's tenure and could be primarily traced back to Mel King:

> A multiracial coalition and trailblazing experiment in minority politics were realized in 1983 when King, who had been elected to the state's legislature in 1973, mounted a serious bid in the Boston mayoral campaign against City Councilor Raymond Flynn and five other White candidates. King was first elected as a state representative from the South End and served in the Legislature until 1982. King mobilized a "rainbow coalition" through a voter registration campaign aimed at Blacks and Latinos. With endorsements from national Black leadership at the time, such as Chicago mayor Harold Washington and Democratic presidential contender Jesse Jackson, King's registration drive swelled the rolls by 25 percent in the months before the election. Although he ultimately lost to Flynn in the final election, King amassed a coalition that was an exercise in the effectiveness of minorities banding together—and attracting White allies—to further their political agenda.[36]

Black politicians and activists such as Mel King often played the role of intermediaries in crises and acted as buffers/mediators/liaisons between the elite and the wider population. Black politicians who assumed these roles often created credibility problems with their fellow minorities. These individuals had personal access to white leadership, but they could not use it to change the objective conditions of their communities. The ascendency of individuals such as King, Dianne Wilkerson, and Bruce Bolling did not signal any distribution of power nor did it anoint them as gatekeepers. Because community activists often advocated massive redistribution schemes, the economic elite increasingly formed temporary alliances with minority politicians to offset such proposals. These individuals were also very dependent on their electoral coalitions. In cities like Boston, for this type of Black leadership the great issues remained political incorporation, coalition maintenance, and outreach to Hispanics and Asians. Menino was the mayor for a long time, and that meant that he had to deal with a series of emerging leaders.

Menino, Black Politicians, and Generational Succession

Menino worked with several different generations of Black leaders, with new leaders emerging each decade.[37] Every generation of Black leaders used different words than their predecessors, but the rhetoric fell close to the traditional racial uplift message. Since World War II, the Boston Black leadership had been a dual leadership class of clergy and community leaders. The 1970s introduced Black elected officials as leaders. During Mayor Flynn's era, Black activists like Don Muhammad, Thomas Atkins, Reverend Charles Stith, Reverence Bruce Wall, Charles Yancey, Doris Bunte, Mel King, Bruce Bolling, and William Owens were the leading Black activists and politicians. William (Bill) Owens served in the Massachusetts House in the early 1970s and served in the state senate from 1975 to 1982 and from 1989 to 1992. During those years he was a major player in Boston politics but left office before Menino became mayor.

The 1980s saw a new set of leaders added to those of the previous decade. Joseph Feaster replaced NAACP head Thomas Atkins. Four new Black state representatives and one senator were elected. They formed the Massachusetts Legislative Black Caucus. John D. O'Bryant was elected to the Boston School Committee in 1977 and named president in 1981. He served for fifteen years and would later have an examination public school named after him (The John D. O'Bryant School of Mathematics and Science).

In 1980, *Boston Globe* reporter Robert A. Jordan cited the diversity in Black leaders nationally and found that some people felt Black leadership in Boston was fragmented. He interviewed King and Emory Jackson, executive director of the Urban League. King stated, "The simplest way to put it is that the leadership is as varied as it is in other communities. There are a number of issues people are working on, such as employment, criminal justice, brutality, educational and housing issues, and youth job issues."[38]

Jackson added, "Black leadership hopefully is in the transition from the old Bostonian to a new breed of young blacks, some in management positions, some in organizations such as the NAACP and the Urban League." However, Jackson and others saw segments of the "old guard" refusing to relinquish power to the newcomers. "I think the battle is on. The old ways of informing the community don't work anymore. I think the new guard . . . is consistent with black leadership in other parts of the country."[39]

King and Bolling would both go on to run for mayor. Both sought the mayor's office to maximize benefits for their communities. Election to public office and career development in the city bureaucracies were, in part, an indication of groups' progress. Some of these leaders were still active in the 1990s. After Menino was elected, the Black leaders associated with Ray Flynn lost influence. New names such as Reverend Rivers, Reverend Hammond, and Byron Rushing gained visibility.

Also in the 1990s, Boston had its own version of white ethnic secession. In Boston, Irish Americans had dominated city politics until Tom Menino. Racial unrest and school integration accelerated white flight to suburbs like Newton and Waltham. Many Irish Americans were culturally assimilated.[40] The loss of the white population, combined with a newly politicized Black population, hastened the arrival of Black-elected politicians. Combining the support of white liberals and public employee unions, Black leaders were able to get elected to the Boston City Council, state legislature, and governorship. These victories were the fruits of coalition-making. So was the election of two Black politicians statewide.

Was Deval Patrick Edward Brooke Redux?

The 1966 election of Edward Brooke as a U.S. senator was considered at the time an anomaly. He was a liberal Republican who opposed Richard Nixon's policies. He was the first Black person to be elected statewide as Massachusetts attorney general. He was a war veteran and had married a war bride from Italy. The latter helped him with Italian American voters. He had support across the state and among all groups. Brooke may have been one of the first Massachusetts deracialized politicians.

Deval Patrick's story was a different one. He came from a poor background and with the help of the A Better Chance Program (a scholarship program for inner-city students), he went to the elite Milton Academy. From there he went to Harvard College and Law School. Social scientist Lawrence Johnson claimed that the *Boston Globe* portrayed Patrick as a likable candidate that could handle racial attacks. On the other hand, the *Bay State Banner* was less concerned with likeability but rather whether he could deliver for the Black community.[41] Patrick got a job as assistant attorney general for civil rights for the Clinton administration. When he ran for governor, some claimed that he ran a deracialized campaign. And that he governed in that manner.

Lawrence Johnson disagreed. He found that throughout his study of the Patrick administration, he wrote, the "evidence demonstrates that Governor Patrick is not deracialized; the fact that he is black and that he advocated issues of importance to the black community, such as Criminal Offender Record Information, does make Governor Patrick representative of black politics. Conceptualizing deracialization as a campaign strategy and trying to figure out if black politicians who avoid race would pursue policy initiatives in the interest of the black community was the source of controversy."[42]

Although the elections of Patrick and Brooke occurred in different decades, and they were in two different political parties, the election of Black men in a predominately white state and at such high positions was hailed nationally.[43] Yet Black residents in Boston could not elect a Black mayor. Why? Remember that only 7 percent of Massachusetts' Black population lived in Boston. Part of the answer was related to the quality of the coalitions Black leaders built in the city. The other answer was the failure to develop a candidate who could challenge Menino.

Coalition Politics, Boston Style

To elect a nonwhite candidate or to present grievances, given the power differential between whites and Blacks, the latter group should form a political coalition. Mel King was aware of this as he associated himself with the creation of a Rainbow Coalition. The coalitional strategy involved combining votes and resources to achieve political and economic goals. In the past Blacks were invited to participate in coalitions with progressive groups, labor unions, Jewish organizations, and groups of Latinos. Blacks and Latinos worked together to elect individuals to the City Council and to help Deval Patrick's gubernatorial campaign. Black citizens worked with civil liberties groups to stop illegal searches of Black youths. White liberals also worked with Black groups on issues of common interest such as rent control. In some cases, the alliances were temporary, lasting only until the end of the life of an issue. In other cases, alliances produced more opportunities for cooperation. In a few cases, these groups ended up opposing each other on new issues. Leaders of the coalitions would often develop working relationships and consult each before taking positions.

In 1990, political scientist Toni-Michell Travis characterized Black politics as having an unfinished agenda. She pointed out that John O'Bryant, Mel King, Thomas Atkins, and Bruce Bollings were no longer major players in Boston.[44] During this period, the last Black candidate to win a citywide race had been O'Bryant in 1977.[45] King had run for mayor in 1983, and many considered this race the epitome of Black mobilization in Boston.

In 1991, political scientist Philip Clay concluded that "unlike those in other cities, Boston's black communities have not developed strong political institutions."[46] In 1993, Bruce Bolling entered the mayoral race against Ray Flynn. Bolling had been on the City Council for a dozen years, had been president of the council, and was well known in city politics as a moderate. However, the press attempted to get Bolling to drop out of the race. The press also underplayed Bolling's support in the Black community and overplayed the comments of Black activist ministers Reverend Eugene Rivers and Reverend Ray Hammond, who opposed Bolling's candidacy.[47] Bolling lost in the primary and endorsed Menino.

In 2003, Chuck Turner, Felix Arroyo, and other leaders of color created a coalition called the New Majority. This multiethnic organization was designed to address health, housing, and economic issues. Arroyo credited Mel King, now seventy-five years old, with the idea for the New Majority: "Mel got involved right from the beginning. He is the spiritual base for the New Majority and the historic base."[48]

The Awakening Latino Community

In 1968, Jorge Rivera started Sociedad Latina in South Boston. This nonprofit organization provided youth services and social and cultural activities and is still operating. Latino Americans are the city's second largest minority group. Between 1970 and 1990, the Latino population in Roxbury doubled from 4,622 to 11,194, and to 59,600 overall in Boston. Latinos have a higher birth rate than African Americans.[49] *Boston Globe* reporter Richard Chacon attributed their immigration to Boston to "good prices for food [and] to the availability of affordable housing in the historically Black enclave of Roxbury."[50] The increase in the Latino population in Boston reflected what was happening nationally. By 2010, Latinos represented 16.7 percent of the U.S. population and had pulled ahead of Blacks as the largest minority group nationally.

Although Latinos are often lumped together, there are many cultural and political differences within these communities. Education researchers Donna M. Harris and Judy Marquez Kiyama have suggested that Latino students are often invisible in schools. They state, "For Latina/o students in the U.S. who have complex cultural, linguistic, and geographical identities, the essence of who they are may be contested in schools."[51] Although they may speak Spanish, they come from different cultures. Puerto Ricans are American citizens and have a different set of problems than documented and undocumented migrants from Mexico and Central America.

Among academics, there was a debate about the future of Latino politics. Peter Skerry's *Mexican Americans: The Ambivalent Minority* suggested that they had a choice of following a traditional immigrant ethnic politics route or a racial minority politics one.[52] Ignacio García's *Chicanismo* promoted the politics of self-identity and a more militant ethos.[53] In Boston, Mexican Americans were not the dominant Latino group. Instead, there was a mix of people from Puerto Rico, Cuba, Central America, and the Dominican Republic. These residents, or their parents, came from different cultures, but they were able to form a Black/Brown coalition with African Americans at the local level.

Because of American civil rights history, African Americans have had strong ties recently to the Democratic Party. Republican politicians have not found Black voters and politicians persuadable. By contrast, Latino voters have been recruited and flattered nationally by both parties. Mitt Romney's Massachusetts gubernatorial campaign was an exception. As a candidate, Romney came out against bilingual education and opted for promotion of English immersion. Although Blacks and Latinos lived in the same communities, there was not the same political competition that existed between Boston Irish and Italian Americans. As Latinos entered the mainstream of municipal life their leaders had to work more closely with other minority politicians. In an interview with city councilor Chuck Turner, Jorge Capetillo-Ponce explained why the councilor was so optimistic about the stability of a coalition of Black and Latino people:

Turner's optimism is based on his view that "Boston's Black-Latina/o solidarity is quite unique when compared with such other northeastern cities as New York, Atlanta, and Philadelphia." In addition, he argued, solidarity was born, ironically enough, out of the White establishment's "resolute policy of housing segregation, which meant not only that Black and Latino/a leaders lived side by side in the same neighborhoods, but that relationships also crossed class lines, preempting the division of neighborhoods based on class in different sectors of the city, as has happened in other northeastern cities. The small Black, Latina/o, and Asian communities, then, instead of creating sharp racial and residential boundaries among them, became one large tribe of people of color."[54]

In 1981, Felix Arroyo, a former teacher and executive director of the Casa del Sol Educational Program, ran for the BSC. He had the support of several Black politicians. His campaign manager, Carmelo Iglesias, said, "We exchanged lists of workers, dropped off each other's literature, and mentioned each other in campaign oratory. . . . You don't normally see that among contending politicians."[55] Arroyo lost that election but when he ran again for the BSC, he raised over $30,000 and had the endorsements of Senator John Kerry and Governor Michael Dukakis. In the 1983 election, he had the endorsement of the *Boston Globe*, but he failed again. Mayor Flynn then got the state legislature to allow the mayor to appoint members of the BSC. Flynn made Arroyo his education advisor and then appointed him to the BSC. Later Arroyo became president of the BSC. Electorally speaking, appealing to a Latino constituency in ethnic terms can present challenges.[56] As the numbers of Latino politicians grew, they may have experienced some of the same types of schisms found in the Black leadership class. Jorge Capetillo-Ponce's review of Menino's relations with Latinos confirms this possibility.[57]

Since his days as a councilor, Menino had recognized Boston's growing Latino community. When he became mayor, he appointed Ramon Suarez as his first Latino liaison. Jeffrey Sanchez and Blanca Valentine also served in that position. In 2002, Tomas Gonzalez, a campaign aide, became the Hispanic liaison and quickly changed the position title to citywide Latino liaison "to make it right." Gonzalez credited Menino with creating the Puerto Rican Veterans Memorial (2005) and for the establishment of the mayor's Three Kings Celebration. This City Hall ceremony was designed to honor long-serving Latino municipal employees.[58]

In 2004, Arroyo was elected to the Boston City Council. John Barros, who was the executive director of the Dudley Street Neighborhood Initiative (a community development corporation), asserted that it was a new day in Boston. "When Felix won it was like, 'Whoa.' That's why [Andrea] Cabral became a tester, that we can do this. Linda [Dorcena Forry]'s winning is further confirmation of what's going to happen, of candidates forming new alliances."[59] Dorcena Forry won a seat in the state legislature, and Cabral was elected the first Black women sheriff.

Coalition-making and bloc voting had worked for Latinos and African Americans. The everyday life of Latinos and other newcomers, their hopes and aspirations, and views of Boston often went unnoticed. It was understandable that they would seek coalition partners, but some were perplexed by ongoing schisms within the Black leadership class. Indeed, these divisions went beyond simple rivalries and ideological orientations.

Schism among Black Politicians

Boston's Black population came from all parts of the Black diaspora—the American South, the African continent, and the West Indies. Sharon Wright Austin in her book *The Caribbeanization of Black Politics* outlined how Blacks with West Indian ancestors have become some of the nation's most famous city politicians.[60] These individuals have played a critical role in Boston. The schism in Boston politics did not occur along ethnic lines but rather among legacy civil rights organization leaders, church ministers, and community activists. The rivalry between the elected Black officials and the so-called traditional Black leadership was a significant yet misunderstood dimension of the politics of race relations.

The relationship between Lenny Atkins and Charles Yancy provided an opportunity to observe the divergence of interest between these two leaders. Atkins was head of the NAACP and Yancy was an elected member of the City Council. They often disagreed. This may be because traditional race leaders believed that they represent the overall interests of the Black community whereas the elected leaders focused their attention on their districts. Elected leaders also had party responsibilities and obligations that restricted their actions.

Church ministers and civil group leaders such as Mel King and Darnell Williams of the Urban League and Henry Owen and Thomas Atkins of the NAACP have always played a role in Boston politics. They proceeded the Black elected officials as brokers for the Black community. These race leaders (self-appointed and those sponsored by the white power structure) acted as brokers and diplomats between their community and elected officials.

In general, the civil rights movement of the 1960s provided a model for these religious leaders to become politicians and social reformers. Accordingly, Blacks were encouraged to register to vote, and many ministers ran for local offices. They had the time and independent power bases to get elected. Although many became politicians, they still saw themselves as race leaders. Nonelected traditional leaders were increasingly seen as rivals. Indeed, the two groups disagreed on several issues. The two leaders often disagree publicly on tactics for resolving racial issues. There also seemed to be incessant personality clashes. Sometimes these clashes captured the attention of the local newspapers, but most rivalries stayed within the community.

When Menino was elected to the mayoralty, the Black community possessed neither the organizational nor the voting strength to demand much from the mayor's office. The NAACP chapter and the Black Political Task Force had become relatively moribund. Perhaps one of the most visible Black ministers, Reverend Charles Stith, head of the Organization for a New Equality, supported the criticisms of Menino's policies and leadership, outlined in a 1995 confidential memo written by State Senator Wilkerson to a group of Black ministers. Stith asked, "Is there a vision emanating from City Hall that translates into the African-American community becoming part of the mainstream of economic life of the city?"[61] This was the critical question of residents from Boston's Black community. Organization for a New Economy, founded by Stith, was more oriented toward the national scene. He became a high-profile leader and was appointed U.S. ambassador to Tanzania. Others remained minor players in city politics.

Arguably the most powerful Black politician in the early 1990s was State Senator Dianne Wilkerson. Her name was always mentioned as a "comer." She supported Brett, Menino's opponent for mayor. In a confidential memo to the Black Ministerial Alliance, later leaked to the press, Wilkerson accused Menino of planning to water down affirmative action programs and attempting to cut minority neighborhoods out of the federal empowerment zone grant funds. She also blamed him for the removal of Boston school superintendent Lois Harrison-Jones. The real thrust of the memo was aimed at the mayor's support of building the megaplex in South Boston, rather than in Lower Roxbury, discussed in chapter 4. She called this action the "straw that broke the camel's back."[62]

Another woman with high visibility was Marie St. Fleur, a Haitian immigrant who served as a state representative (1999–2011) for district 5, which included parts of Dorchester and Roxbury. She supported charter schools at a time when the idea was not supported by the public school cartel. In 2010, she became director of intergovernmental relations in the Menino administration. Like Wilkerson, her career rise was interrupted by tax problems.

Although many children of Black immigrants do well professionally and politically, there can be conflicts between them and the rest of the Black community. The schism between the Cape Verdean community and spokespeople for the TenPoint Coalition was noteworthy. Professors Anthony Braga, David Hureau, and Christopher Winship have stated, "Cape Verdean youth were a notable feature of Boston's surging gang violence problem. Between 1999 and 2004, 14 of the 111 gang-related homicides in the city (12.6%) were attributed to the activity of small gangs of mostly Cape Verdean youth based in the Upham's Corner and Bowdoin/Geneva section of Boston." Braga, Hureau, and Winship blamed the police department for making "overly broad" statements about the Cape Verdean community. The department also engaged the TenPoint Coalition and the Baker House, a center for at-risk youths, to get Cape Verdean Bostonians to join the partnership to prevent youth violence. Eugene Rivers, spokesperson for the TenPoint Coalition also criticized the Cape Verdean community. Braga, Hureau, and Winship concluded that the entire situation was related to a lack of understanding of the Cape Verdean culture and Catholicism. The TenPoint Coalition was led by Protestant ministers who were seen as "culturally inappropriate in the eyes of many Cape Verdean."[63]

Writer Helena Lima Ambrizeth has attempted to explain the cultural divide between Cape Verdean young men and others in the community. She notes that many of them had an "insulation" strategy. They insulated themselves from their environment. Interacting "almost exclusively with other Cape Verdeans was one way they avoided being discriminated against because of their racialized identity. Although the participants had a very strong ethnic identity and did not identify as African Americans, they were subjected to many of the same indignities that their African American counterparts experienced." They distanced themselves from "risks."[64] This strategy also demonstrated the ongoing schisms among communities of color.

Although Menino was not a sociologist, he was aware of the stories told by minority groups and their plight in Boston. He heard those stories, but he never publicly questioned the ethnic divisions among minority groups or attempted to define the nuances of their differences. For many Black Bostonians, being a Haitian American or Cape Verdean Americans mattered. Although they might share a common skin color with African Americans, linking that identity to politics was a conscious process. Political scientist Sharon W. Austin concluded, "Many Cape Verdeans, Haitians, and West Indians have acknowledged having a racial identity with African Americans, but point out the distinctions between their own and African American culture."[65] For some groups, the persistence of ethnic identities is consistent with American political culture and is crucial to psychological identities. According to Ambrizeth, Cape Verdean immigrants say "'Na Buska Bida' which means looking 'of' life i.e., fighting tirelessly looking for ways to survive. This term 'life' in this sense, is all-encompassing, yet evasive; there is a purpose in the words and a measure of uncertainty in implicit action."[66]

There is nothing inherently wrong or antidemocratic with ethnic groups' maintaining their ethnic identities. For some, voluntary identification of ethnic identities has enhanced the American political experience. Most of the immigrant communities attempted to maintain cultural ties with their ancestral countries. This reemergence of ethnicity served to further balkanize Black Boston, however. As more Mexican and Central American immigrants moved to Boston, pluralism might have the same effect on Latinos. These schisms might dissipate as the overall racial climate changes.

Changing Racial Climate

In the late 1970s, sociologist Nicholas L. Danigelis found that Black political participation was determined by the city's political climate. Using data from 1952 to 1972, Danigelis showed that southern white politicians created a climate that discouraged Black political participation. After passage of the 1965 Voting Rights Act, the southern environment changed and there was an increase in Black participation. His data suggested that differences in Black participation could be explained by analyzing the political environment. He admitted that were other areas in the country when the political climate was hostile to Blacks.[67] This was especially true in 1970s Boston. However, the American racial climate had improved radically since the 1970s. Noticeably, the political climate nationally and in Boston by the 1990s was improving.

In cities where Blacks were allowed to participate, they did so with varying degrees of success. Blacks had always enjoyed an active and visible part in

Chicago politics but played a less active role in Boston. In other cities such as Detroit and Atlanta, Blacks were able to elect mayors. Black voters in those cities seemed to have a stronger sense of political efficacy and civic obligation. This was not the case for African Americans in Boston. The failed mayoral candidacies of Mel King (1979 and 1983) and Bruce Bolling (1993) reminded them that they lived in a conservative climate despite Boston's reputation as being a progressive city.

Does being designated a minority serve as a disadvantage for nonwhite politicians? This notion led to a strange move by a leading Black council member. In 2002, Council President Charles Yancey introduced an ordinance to strike the word "minority" from the city's official lexicon. This generated debates within the council and communities of color. Yancey admitted his proposal was symbolic: "Yes, it is a symbolic move. The definition is 'less than,' and that implies not only numerically, but in terms of power, prestige, and significance. If you're called that, you're going to feel less than [others]. The term is demeaning." For him, it was not just a linguistic problem. Reporter Mary Wiltenburg traced the origins of the Yancey proposal to George Steven, San Diego deputy mayor. He objected to the term because it was imposed on African Americans by whites. The San Diego City Council unanimously passed the ordinance. So did the Boston City Council. Menino vetoed it, claiming that it would have caused confusion in election districts and the distribution of services.[68]

Symbolic politics has its place but getting elected to office was seen as a way to improve the Black situation. In 2003, Hubie Jones, a longtime political pundit and former dean of the Boston University School of Social Work, asserted, "I would say the state of black politics is dismal. We have no black congressman; we have no black-at large city councilor. We have no black mayor, [and] we're not in shouting distance of getting one in the near future. During Menino's tenure, the city did elect an at-large councilor, but a congressman was elected after he left office." His comments were seconded by Ted Landsmark, a lawyer attacked with a flagpole during a protest, captured in an infamous 1974 Pulitzer Prize–winning photo entitled "The Soiling of Old Glory." Landsmark also worked in City Hall under Flynn and Menino. In 2003, he concluded, "Black political empowerment has regressed substantially since Mel King ran for mayor 20 years ago."[69]

Many Black and Latino politicians started their careers as critics of municipal government. They have since become elected officials and targets of criticism. Yet getting oneself elected is not the same as governing and managing. Menino discovered that Boston had a high direct service demand in addition to racial situations. Sewerage and water systems, ignored for years, were beginning to show signs of failure. Poor infrastructure, inadequate tax revenues, and a weak economic base exposed Black elected officials to the woes of rising expectations.

In 2012, Menino had the acumen to discern the complaints of small retailers about the possibility of having a Walmart location in Roxbury. Menino opposed the location in the community, the company decided not to build, and local retailers benefited. In 2013, Menino supported the Our Mattapan public awareness campaign and took his anti–gun violence crusade into Mattapan. The mayor said, "Our plan to reduce gun violence across Boston and in Mattapan includes many different approaches. We go after impact players and their illegal guns. We offer job training opportunities. We connect families to city resources and programs. . . . But this work must be paired with a strong public message one that is for residents and by residents to stop the violence and engage everyone in achieving that goal."[70]

The fiscal problems of Boston were compounded by attempts to improve the economic situation of minorities. Menino found himself cast in the role of a grant seeker, continually beseeching the state legislature, private foundations, and federal agencies for assistance. Having promised "real changes" during their campaigns, elected officials like Menino often run the risk of losing their credibility with their minority constituencies when external circumstances hinder their policy initiatives.

Changing Economic Conditions

Even if there was a consensus in the minority community that Menino changed the racial climate in Boston and was a friend and supporter, the needle on the economic meter did not move much. There is a view that place matters and economic segregation is related to racial inequality.[71] Where one lives can affect one's economic mobility. Twenty-first-century minority immigrants to Boston still find job market challenges. A year before Menino took office (1992), the Massachusetts unemployment rate for Blacks rose from 16.4 to 23 percent, and that for Latinos rose from 14.7 to 16.5 percent.[72] When he left office in 2013, the state unemployment rates were 6.3 percent.[73]

Saskia Sassen, a sociologist, claimed globalization had changed the types of jobs available to low-skilled workers.[74] In a city like Boston, there were more spillover jobs—residential building attendants, restaurant workers, preparers of specialty and gourmet foods, dog walkers, errand runners, apartment cleaners, childcare providers, and security workers. These jobs might not be that appealing to minorities. While some of these jobs could be unionized, the bulk would remain low-income. Moreover, automation posed an existential threat.

The rise of self-service cashiers at big-box stores, grocery stores, and convenience stores is eliminating service jobs. The loss of retail clerk jobs was also an existential threat to all low-skilled workers.

Summary

When Tom Menino became mayor, few people knew what to expect. Initially, he appeared not to understand the aspirations of the mobilized Black community that was brewing during the Ray Flynn tenure. In his book *Black Atlantic Politics*, political scientist William E. Nelson termed the situation a "cooptation of black leadership." Flynn hired Blacks in City Hall, integrated public housing, and supported school integration. Nelson stated, "Flynn made a conscious effort to reach out to the Black community. At the considerable cost to his standing in working-class White communities." Nelson admitted that "Black political interests remained marginalized in the executive office of the mayor under Flynn."[75] Upon Menino's retirement, his job approval rates were high. A *Boston Globe* poll found that "an astounding 60 percent say they have met him, and his approval ratings among blacks is a full 9 percentage points higher than even the stratospheric 71 percent among whites."[76] Mayor Menino had also repaired the parks and promoted businesses on thriving Blue Hill Avenue, a four-mile street in Dorchester winding through Dudley Street in Roxbury that ended in Mattapan Square. He had potted plants.

As is the case for most mayors, Menino's performance with racial issues was compared to his predecessor. Sociologist Donald A. Gillis compared Menino to his predecessor Ray Flynn:

> By comparing the approaches to racial conflicts by Mayor Flynn and Menino, it has been demonstrated that there is a need for a strong and consistent focus and public discourse on the issue in order to avoid slippage. While Menino made statements about racial conflict in the city, and it was clear that he had a strong personal opposition to discrimination of any kind, the evidence suggests that he chose a different path than his predecessor. It is understandable that his style and approach differed from that of Flynn, who came to the mayor's office at a time of ongoing racial conflict and had something to prove as a South Boston resident

and an opponent of busing. In contrast, Menino did not face the same constraints as a former city councilor from Hyde Park and someone who inherited the mayor's office at time of relative racial stability in the city,[77]

It was inevitable that Menino would be compared with Flynn. This was not lost on the new mayor. Menino watched Flynn manage the relationship between City Hall and the Black community. Menino was a fast learner and had a more direct style than Flynn. Although Menino learned from watching Flynn's administration, Boston's recurrent politics had undergone a fundamental change. Menino had different political socializations, skills, and ambitions. Nelson, writing in the late 1990s, concluded that "Menino's political instincts are those of a quintessential ward politician."[78] For Nelson, Menino was attempting to coopt the Black leadership agenda and avoid criticisms. However, Nelson made these conclusions too soon. Tom Menino of the late 1990s was a different man than he was later in his tenure.

This early assessment of Menino by Nelson and others occurred during his first two terms. Menino learned these lessons well, evolved, and proved to be a more complicated politician. So did the politics of race in Boston. In predominantly Black neighborhoods like Roxbury (63% Black and 24% Latino) and Mattapan (82.8% Black and 9% Latino), residents viewed themselves as being a neglected minority in the Flynn and Menino administrations. Some Blacks in other minority communities such as Dorchester blamed the white power structure for their situation. One of the mayor's regular critics was the *Bay State Banner*. In 2009, the Black-owned newspaper threatened to shut down. The city of Boston offered Melvin Miller, the paper's owner, a $200,000 bridge loan through the Boston Redevelopment Authority.[79] Again, Menino was able to show he could overcome a reputation of being thin-skinned.

Menino was a student of the dynamics of the different minority communities and sought to establish relations with their leaders. As a cognitive and compassionate empathic mayor, Menino communicated that he intended to treat all groups the same and that they could judge him by what he did. He consulted with minority leaders, and they trusted him. Accordingly, he was able to defuse many situations that could have been defined as racial incidents. His critics saw this reaching out and glad-handing as a way to keep the peace and change the subject. Research suggests that educated white liberal politicians engage Black audiences differently than white conservatives. Social psychologists Cydney Dupree and Susan Fiske claimed that white liberal politicians talk down to minorities—using certain words in their interactions with

Blacks. Liberals downshifted their languages to appeal to Black audiences.[80] Tom Menino was a different type of white liberal politician. The record suggests he was sincere in his relationship with his Black audience. The media accounts and interviewees for this book testified to Menino's authenticity regarding racial issues.

CHAPTER 8

The Failure of Boston Public School Reform

Public school politics are often the bane of low-income families with children and a headache for big-city mayors. This chapter examines attempts at public school reforms, the Boston School Committee, teacher unions, and Mayor Thomas Menino's relationship to those politics. Mayors of Boston have each inherited school policies from their predecessors. They found themselves in policy tunnels with a variety of sunk costs and commitments. Early on, Menino as acting mayor and as a mayoral candidate committed himself to making schools work for all residents of Boston. At first, this seemed uncontroversial and a welcome statement from the mayor. It is important to remember that for centuries, the mayor of Boston had been essentially a bystander in school politics. This changed after the mayor was granted the power to appoint members of the Boston School Committee (BSC), the governing municipal agency, and to hire the superintendent. Professor John M. Cronin did a seventy-six-year history (1930–2006) of the Boston Public Schools (BPS) and concluded "that corporate initiative closed the troublesome gap between the school committee and mayors, ensuring that mayors took the responsibility for school budgets and buildings and that seasoned superintendents from other cities could stay in Boston long enough to provide leadership."[1] As a result the BSC emerged as the center of school politics.

The Boston School Committee

The Boston School Committee, that is, the school board, has had a long and controversial history. Since its inception in 1789, the structure and selection of members were always political. The BSC was one of the city's fastest-growing committees. In 1875, Yankee reformers reduced the number of members from 116 to 24 members. In 1905, the membership was reduced to five members. Reporter Alan Lupo claimed, "The five-member committee, created in 1905 to reform the schools and dilute Irish power, had become little more than a political clubhouse, whose members exacted contributions to political 'times' from school staff, got jobs for friends and supporters and mucked about in the daily business of contracts and curriculum."[2]

It is important to note that before World War II, Boston's Black population was only 3.1 percent. After the war, it increased slightly (5.0%), and Black children were restricted to predominantly Black schools. After the 1954 *Brown v. Board of Education* case, schools formally segregated by race were deemed illegal. The 1960s saw an increase in Black protests over segregated schools. Mel King, a Black community activist, ran for a seat on the BSC three times, in 1961, 1962, and 1965. He lost all three races, and the BSC did not have a Black member until John O'Bryant was elected in 1977.

In the 1970s, membership in the BSC continued its checked history. There was corruption, and committee member Gerald O'Leary was convicted of attempting to extort $650,000 in kickbacks from a school bus company.[3] White members Louise Day Hicks and John L. Kerrigan openly opposed busing as a way to integrate schools. Hicks received nationwide visibility as a result of her resistance to busing. Indeed, Lupo asserted that the beginning of the downfall of the BSC was its refusal to integrate the Boston school system in the 1960s and 1970s, after the federal courts ordered schools desegregated.[4]

Irish American politicians fought the reform of the BSC because they felt their votes would be diluted. In the city charter revision of 1983, the membership of the committee was expanded again to thirteen members with nine members elected by districts and four at large. This new system had its problems because the district lines did not parallel school catchment zones. Meanwhile, local Irish American politicians benefited from the patronage of the BSC. The situation was so blatant that it initiated yet another round of school governance reforms. The BPS had their traditions, patronage, shortsightedness, and scandals. Until the Ray Flynn administration, they operated without much mayoral interference.

Menino's School Policy Inheritance

After Menino took over as mayor, he made several speeches about his administration's being open and inclusive for all individuals and groups. Understandably, he expected the Boston Public Schools—with the superintendent now a member of his cabinet—to follow his lead. Schools were also political institutions. The BSC was more than just a traditional school board as it played a critical role in the evolution of ethnic politics in the city. During Menino's tenure, public schools were among the largest public employers in the city. School teachers were among the most educated workers in city government. As such, teachers and the Boston Teachers Union (BTU) became a critical part of local and state politics. Along with other school activists, BTU has endeavored to address a range of issues from state certification policy to requirements for teacher tenure, pay, pensions, and school construction.

To the casual observer, the BPS seemed to be in a perpetual crisis. In the late 1960, a white Roxbury teacher named Jonathan Kozol wrote *Death at an Early Age*, which indicted the BPS for mistreatment of Black children.[5] In the early 1970s, Boston gained national attention for the resistance to busing. In the 1990s, parents and residents expected their school officials to overcome the BPS's reputation and solve problems ranging from school violence to achievement scores. As Tom Menino assumed the mayoralty, he deliberately took a high-profile position on school issues. But did he understand who ran the schools?

Who Runs the Boston Schools?

In 1994, Menino arrived in the school politics arena after ten years in elected politics, and like most politicians, he took a supportive attitude toward public school policies. Also like most newly elected mayors, he did not have a clear understanding of the numerous players in those politics—teachers, union leaders, parent groups, vendors, and so on. He was not a product of the BPS, but judging from his public statements, he had a respectful impression of the public school community, gained from visiting them as a council member. Menino had to be aware that minority public school students were not performing as well as their white counterparts. The low achievement of minority students was one of the troubling issues of the system. White parents also complained about the achievement and busing of their children to minority neighborhoods.

Aside from student achievement, the BPS faced many challenges including the shrinkage of their enrollments because parents were taking their children out of the system. There were also problems with rising costs, violence in schools, and teacher turnover. In 1990, the system had 145 schools and enrolled 64,000 students. It also employed 4,500 teachers and 127 supervisors and administrators. In 2013, *Boston Magazine* reporter Rob Gurwitt described the BPS as a bureaucracy with multiple functions and responsibilities:

> It is a sprawling operation, responsible for tasks that go far beyond teaching. Each day, BPS must transport 30,000 kids to and from school, and serve about 70,000 breakfasts, lunches, and snacks. Its employees train teachers to work with English-language learners and to meet the needs of special-ed students. They manage the curriculum, run the school-assignment algorithm, and triage requests from the schools: a reading specialist here, a special-ed instructor there. They field daily, if not hourly, calls from principals asking for everything from new furniture to curriculum advice. They run the district's increasingly complex efforts to use student and school data to improve performance, analyze the constant shifts in student population, and design better methods for evaluating teachers. They scramble to find volunteers who can bring arts and music programming into the schools, and strategize new ways of involving parents in BPS's work. They calculate how to respond to the ebb and flow of federal, state, and municipal dollars that keep the system and its myriad programs alive.[6]

Not only was the Boston public schools a sprawling bureaucracy but the historical data on its finances shows that "from 1993 to 2013, the Boston school district had an average of $968,078,571 in revenue and $951,785,810 in expenditures, according to the United States Census Bureau's survey of school system finances. The district had a yearly average of $117,963,286 in outstanding debt. The district retired $14,048,381 of its debt and issued $8,153,619 in new debt each year on average."[7] In other words, public school politics involved serious money and hence attracted serious vendors, policy entrepreneurs, and researchers. Accordingly, internal and external school crises were among the most monitored sector of municipal politics.

In a book entitled *Black Mayors and School Politics*, I suggested that city halls were at a disadvantage when dealing with what they called the public school cartel (PSC).[8] A PSC is defined as a small group of school activists, including the central office staff, parent group leaders, and teacher union leaders, who exercise governing control and make school policy. The use of the term "cartel" was considered controversial because it implied absolute control over school resources, personnel, and outcomes. Absolute control is not possible, but the PSC remains cartel-like since it can defy politicians that challenge it and influence schools' operating routines. In an attempt to control school policies, a mayor can simply be outmaneuvered.

Boston never had a traditional political machine. Like in most big cities, however, chapters of the American Federation of Teachers became one of the most reliable fundraisers for local and state politicians. This allowed the PSC to gain leverage at state and local government levels. Accordingly, school politics can become a highly complicated political thicket that may entrap or at least puncture a mayor's political reputation. This would be the challenge for Tom Menino. The first challenge was to deny the PSC's attempt to strip him of control of the BSC.

The Fight to Turn Back the BSC Clock

The fight to eliminate the appointed board involved the entire BSC and PSC. In 1989, Boston voters approved a nonbinding referendum to create a mayoral-appointed school committee. Ray Flynn had sought a home-rule petition from the state legislature to accomplish this. In 1991, the state approved the petition abolishing the elected school committee, a venerated Boston institution that had evolved into a meddling and bickering body. The public acceptance of the Boston-appointed board was helped by Flynn's inclusive appointments. He expanded the pool for BSC members. He appointed the first Asian board members in the system's 202-year history. The reforms were sold as a cost issue. *Boston Globe* reporter Alan Lupo pointed out that the elected board has a budget of $859,000 and several staff members.[9]

In 1996, the budget of the BSC was $145,000.[10] Boston voted to retain the appointed seven-member board. The decision to retain the appointed board was put on the ballot in a November 1996 referendum. The voters supported the appointed boarded by a three-to-one ratio.[11] Menino's decision to campaign to retain the appointed board put him at odds with former members of the elected committee, assorted community leaders, and city councilors. In an interview with sociologist Donald A. Gillis, Menino discussed his rationale for an appointed board:

Oh, that was a savior. The old-school committee was a swap shop. The custodians' union ran it. The teachers' union ran it. All the unions ran the school committee because the guys running for the school committee had to get campaign funds, and where did they get them, the unions. So they weren't dealing with issues that affect the kids. They were dealing with issues that affect the unions, and that was a wrong thing to do. The appointed school board, these members can never be elected and all they want to do is serve and they've done a decent job. There are some issues also, but they've done a good job. They devoted a lot of time to it, and I think that was a savior of our city.[12]

The establishment of a mayoral-appointed board did not quell the debate about what type of board membership fitted Boston. It became a recurrent theme in public school governance debates. Elected boards are supposed to be more representative. Anyone can run for the board. Through the election, the impacted communities are allowed more direct monitoring of board policies. Members have to answer to the communities they represent. Elected board members are usually closer to the community and supposedly can speak more authentically about issues such as school violence, poverty, and racial discipline disparities.

In addition, an elected board allows rising politicians to achieve citywide visibility and can provide a steppingstone to other elective positions such as City Council and mayor. Jean McGuire, a former BSC member, admitted as much when she said, "When you cut off the school committee, you cut off the training ground. That's the farm team."[13] Menino believed this was just an attempt to control school politics patronage. He asserted, "They want to have an elected board because they maintain control of the patronage. That's wrong!"[14] In addition, Samuel R. Tyler, president of the Boston Municipal Research Bureau, made an accountability argument: "The primary benefit of the appointed committee is that it holds one person accountable for school performance—the mayor. The fundamental flaw of the elected committee was that it did not ensure direct accountability in any one person or board. The mayor was required to raise the funds to support the system, but the School Committee decided how to spend the money. This division of duties contributed to a culture of mistrust and finger-pointing rather than the improved collaboration that exists today."[15]

Professor Steven Taylor analyzed Black and white voting behavior in the 1989 and 1996 referenda and concluded,

> Whereas the votes on the 1989 and 1996 referenda, particularly the latter referendum, reflect a strong difference of opinion between the Black and White communities of Boston, an analysis of the forces behind the vote shows some similarities between the two communities. Voters in both communities responded to the direction provided by the leaders in their respective communities. In 1989, there were White neighborhoods that voted against an appointed BSC, but by 1996, those communities strongly supported an appointed committee. This drastic shift of opinion was a reflection of the change of opinions of the elites in these neighborhoods. Likewise, in Boston's Black community, the voters' position on the BSC was a reflection of the positions of the community leaders. Although the outcome was very different from that of the White community, in both communities, the elites were able to mobilize the masses to vote in a particular direction.[16]

In other words, local politicians made the 1989 vote about differences in public opinion between the two races and not about school governance and management. In 1996, the vote was about the retention of the appointed board. Over time an unlikely coalition of Irish American politicians and rising minority politicians had joined forces with the PSC to control who sat on the BSC. More mayoral involvement was sold to the public as a way to increase efficiency and curtail corruption.

Mayor Menino pointed out that the elected board had lost public confidence. For the 1996 referendum (question 2) campaign, he appointed a citizen's group called the Boston Education Reform Committee. The committee included Reverend Ray Hammond of the TenPoint Coalition; Jean McKeigue, former BSC chair; and Robert Fraser, a lawyer. The opposition called itself the Campaign for an Elected School Committee.

Boston Globe reporter Karen Avenoso's review of the committee began with the claim that although the group had joined together to push for a return to an elected board, they disagreed on almost every other major issue involving education. The committee also had some luminaries, including Councilor Francis M. Roache; Councilor Gareth R. Sanders; Jean Maguire, executive director of Metropolitan Council for Education Opportunity (METCO) and a former committee member; and former BSC member Daniel Burke. Robert Marshall, the local chair of the Million Men March Education Committee, joined them.[17] At first glance, it appears that the PSC seemed united on this issue. A closer look reveals a conflicted and divided PSC. A consensual PSC might have been able to make a stronger defense of the old, elected system.

The most problematic tactic used by the appointed schoolboard supporters was to try to solicit money from school principals. Two weeks before the vote was taken, a fax went out asking principals to lobby for the appointed board. The mayor condemned the fax, asserting, "I've always told them not to allow this kind of politics to get into the school system."[18]

Dr. Lois Harrison-Jones, former Boston school superintendent, publicly supported the elected board.[19] Menino had raised funds for the campaign and had the support of one of Boston's think tanks. Samuel Tyler, president of the Boston Municipal Research Bureau, thought that the pro–elected board group was not an advocate for children. The subtext of his message was that these were people who would bring back the chaos of the past. Elected board proponents were a small group of political activists. As was the case with any grassroots organization, they took longer to organize and were not well funded (they raised only $3,500).[20] Menino had raised $200,000 before the group started. His fundraising in the end totaled almost $600,000. The Boston Coordinating Committee (aka the Vault) made the largest single contribution of $100,000). Yvonne Abraham, a reporter for the *Boston Phoenix*, claimed that one donor did not know what the referendum was about. She called the campaign an electoral dress rehearsal for the mayor's reelection: "[It was] a demonstration of Menino's strength, his ability to marshal the business community to his causes, and his effectiveness at raising cash. All of which served to further deter possible mayoral challenges very early on, and ironically to diminish his need for the hefty campaign contributions he continued to collect."[21]

Menino's fundraising abilities and support from the various communities proved to be too much for the forces trying to return to an elected board. Menino also had the wording of ballot question on his side. A "yes" vote would be a return to the elected committee. A "no" vote would keep the appointed committee. This undoubtedly confused some voters because 20 percent left the obliquely worded referendum question blank.[22] The elected board supporters received only 23 percent of the vote and won in only two wards, Roxbury and Dorchester.[23] The result was a crushing defeat of the opposition and a demonstration of Menino's electoral prowess. Now he could continue to appoint the members of the BSC and superintendents.

The BSC, Superintendents, and the Mayor

In Boston, great care is given to make the selection of school superintendent appear to be a joint decision between the mayor and the BSC. Despite all of the claims of citizen control and parental input, the selection of the superintendent remains the most important administrative responsibility of the BSC. Yet, the confirmation of the mayoral-appointed board represented a fundamental change in Boston politics. It certainly enlarged the mayor's patronage trough. But did it diminish the power of the PSC?

In an essay entitled "Who Is Afraid of a Mayoral Takeover of Detroit Public Schools?" I suggested that the PSC did not fear mayoral control. Mayoral control was simply another layer to its political negotiation.[24] However, making the appointed board a part of municipal government did afford more spotlight and accountability for mayors. Menino understood this, and it accounted for his support of an appointed board throughout his tenure. The mayor screens mayoral appointees and can remove them. Appointed school members are more likely to follow the mayor's lead in the hiring of superintendents and making budget decisions. BSC members are also more likely to be individuals with professional credentials and middle-class social status.

Most of Menino's first months as acting mayor in 1993 were spent developing his image as a "good housekeeper." He formally announced his candidacy for the permanent position a month later. During his first term in office, Menino spent a lot of time visiting public schools and attending school events. Boston political analyst Jon Keller believed that Menino "knew that this [schools] was the one issue in the city. He had to stop middle-class flights from the city. As soon as the children of the middle-class turn grade school age, they left the city or enrolled in parochial schools. This had to stop. Maintaining good neighborhoods meant maintaining good schools."[25] Changing the reputation of the BPS would be difficult because the actors—teachers, parents, and school leaders—had different goals. Teachers wanted more resources and smaller class sizes. Parents wanted higher achievement scores, school safety programs, and schools closer to their neighborhoods. School leaders wanted a larger role in school governance. The local media outlined these expectations and how Menino responded.

The Media and School Politics

In major cities like Boston, reporters are assigned to cover school policy and politics. Once Menino became acting mayor, the spotlight turned toward him. Traditionally the responsibility for reporting on schools lay with the print media. Television and radio only had an episodic interest in schools. If the test scores were falling, the print media usually reported it. Occasionally, the media would try to compare test scores among various cities. Part of the problem with print media coverage was that reporters were not familiar enough with the internal dynamics of school policy to make useful and in-depth analyses. Therefore, reporters ended up "superintendent watching," alerting people to school violence, and, more problematically, "test score reporting." Or on rare occasions, they delved into substantive issues such as reviewing the training and certification processes for teachers or the learning climate in classrooms.

Nevertheless, the media played a critical role in school politics. First, the print media had a basic monopoly on communicating with the public. Traditionally, television and radio spent less time on school issues. Facebook and Twitter were started in 2004 and 2006 respectively, but local school issues were not main topics on those platforms. Put simply, there were no alternative forums that could inform the public. Second, the print media had access to school leaders. This allowed journalists to report news about the activities of schoolboard members and the superintendent. Third, journalists could influence local public attitudes about schools. Policy framing by the print media tended to be fairly consistent in Boston. For the *Boston Globe* and the *Boston Herald*, schools were rarely considered newsworthy unless something terrible happened. Routine school affairs were not seen as audience-catching. There was rarely follow-up on most stories. Occasionally, there was a feature article on a special student or a teacher. Otherwise, the coverage was at best inconsistent. When schools were out for the summer, the coverage usually ended. Finally, this is not to gainsay that the media could not set the agenda by conducting polls, uncovering corruption, and focusing on inner-city versus suburban school disparities. In effect, the media, in this case, the *Boston Globe* and *Boston Herald*, along with some neighborhood weeklies and papers directed to specific ethnic groups, recorded what the mayor and superintendent said, but in the absence of an elected board, newspapers represented the only way the public was alerted to the politics of the school system and its problems.

During Menino's early tenure in the 1990s, the news about big-city public schools across the nation was about the rapid resegregation of schools along racial lines, and about how inner-city schools consistently performed below the math and reading standards of some third-world countries. The media, particularly the newspapers, noted these student achievement problems but tended to be persuaded by the idea that a different superintendent could make a difference. Although the coverage of low-test scores for reading and math was fairly consistent, the public was treated to stories about turnovers of superintendents, rising school budgets, and violence in schools. In other words, coverage of Boston public schools focused on drama rather than on incessant small crises.

Even in the days of small crises, some reporters felt no obligation to make school news interesting. The print media was aware that negative and sensational news drew more readers. Scandals of all types were quickly reported. However, muckraking in public schools was not practiced with the same fervor as regular city politics. Although the editorial pages presented some substantive commentaries, it was not uncommon for a paper to slant or tilt its coverage toward a popular superintendent or mayor.

Professors Kenneth Wong and Pushpam Jain found that the media supported the position of the governing alliance or what the authors called the "unitary actors." They found that the media supported city halls in school disputes. Reports and editorials avoided "unpopular stories critical of the popular City Hall." In their study of the two largest Chicago newspapers, they found that media "were generally supportive of the central administration policy, and discussions of alternatives were rare."[26] Menino assumed a very high profile regarding school issues, and the *Boston Globe* and *Boston Herald* rarely challenged him. There were few if any articles challenging his understanding of what happened in the classroom. He was allowed to get in front of the public-school narrative.

Menino as the Education Mayor

Tom Menino came into office as an acting mayor but soon after winning election for a full term proclaimed himself the "education mayor." As acting mayor Menino stated that education was going to be the cornerstone of his 1994 election. Martha Pierce, his future education policy advisor and a graduate of the University of London and Harvard Graduate School of Education, had worked with Menino since his early days as a staff member in the state legislature. During the campaign, Menino made stops across the city, but it was at the Edwards Middle School in Charlestown that he received a most encouraging response. At that time, Menino was not considered a mayoral frontrunner, but the Edwards eighth graders thought differently. In a straw poll, they overwhelmingly voted for him as Boston's next mayor. He pledged to these young pollsters that if he were victorious, his first visit as mayor would be to the Edwards Middle School. Pierce later recalled, "Tom Menino made good that promise, and by 7:00 a.m. on his first day in office he was at the Edwards School to invite the eighth-grade supporters to his inaugural ball."[27]

After he was elected mayor, he deliberately took a high-profile position on school issues. Pierce stated that "he made it a practice to visit at least one school a week. He liked to go and meet students. But he often gravitated and drew out the kid in the back of the room, the student who was a little mischievous."[28] Although Pierce was his liaison with the schools, the BSC, and his superintendents, Menino was directly involved in policymaking.

The selection of the Boston school superintendent was also a bellwether of the relations between elected officials and the BSC. In some cities, the board simply appointed the mayor's choice. In Boston, great care was given to the selection of school superintendent, and it was made by the mayoral-appointed school committee. The process for selecting the BSC is carefully prescribed by Massachusetts state statute to allow all major stakeholders to have a voice. The thirteen-member nominating panel is composed of parents selected by community groups, representatives from the higher education and business sectors, a teacher, a principal, the state commissioner of education's designee, and four mayoral nominees. It was designed to ensure balanced representation. The nominating panel vetted the candidates and provided the mayor with names of three to five finalists per vacancy. Pierce recalled, "Mayor Menino made it a point of interviewing every finalist, many of whom he had not met before. He wanted the best constituency representation."[29]

During Menino's 1993 campaign, he supported the realignment of school zones to create walkable schools.[30] According to Pierce, "For him [Menino] it was a push and pull in his administration. He wanted to make sure that money saved on transporting students across town went to budget-strapped schools and he wanted to build community buy-in around all schools. At the same time, he knew the importance to ensure that schools in all neighborhoods were desirable."[31] He also wanted to do something about the failing Boston schools. The walk-to-school proposal emerged as a major one for his first term. In 1994, City Councilor Peggy Davis-Mullen joined forces with Black leaders to oppose the city busing plan and the "walk-to-school" concept. The walk-to-school proposal would mean Black children would walk to the school closest to their home, which meant they would be in predominately Black schools. At first glance, it would seem that Black parents would want their children to go to schools near their homes, but a closer look reveals that this could lead to a new form of racially segregated schools.

The school busing controversy and cultural trauma had happened in the 1970s, but it was still referenced as a critical point in the Boston school system.

In a dissertation, Meghan V. Doran, an education researcher, found that different actors acquired different school desegregation memories and narratives. They viewed the past differently and its relations to policy change. Doran stated, "The cultural trauma of school desegregation . . . continues to impact how the city is structured and play a role in its politics regardless of, as well as in relation to, other factors. Thus, while the mayor made it very clear he desired a return to neighborhood schools, he could not simply direct a policy change. A new relation to the past had to be carefully constructed alongside the pro-growth regime politics of public/private relationships that the sociological literature tells us much more about."[32]

Doran concluded, "The past of a city lives not just in its impact at the time; the past also serves a reference point and often inescapable source of meaning that continues to impact how people act in the city in the present."[33] Felix Arroyo, the first Latino member of the BSC, stated, "The idea of walk-to-schools is very attractive to a lot of parents but there's a difference between the theory and the practical aspects of such a plan. I would have to see whether we'd be offering parents in one part of the city the same thing we'd be offering parents in other parts of the city."[34] In the first term, Menino spent a lot of time visiting schools and attending school events.

When Menino took over, the student population was 47.7 percent Black, 23.4 percent Latino, 19.3 percent white, 9.2 percent Asian, and 0.4 Native American.[35] Although the Boston school system was smaller than those for superstar cities like New York, Chicago, and Los Angeles, it had many of the same problems: poorly performing schools, old physical plants, and a disproportionate number of disadvantaged children. But the mayor of Boston had something that fellow mayors could only wish for—complete control of board appointments and budgets. The appointment of the superintendent became a way to assert a new school regime.

Menino and Superintendency Politics

In his first term, Menino insisted that he wanted to be judged by his efforts to improve the BPS. Campaign rhetoric aside, the schools were in trouble and some voters thought that Menino could do something about it. To do so, he thought he needed to put his own people in charge. Menino inherited his predecessor Ray Flynn's superintendent, Dr. Lois Harrison-Jones. Although her contract called for an annual review, she had been in office for over two years without a formal performance review. As is discussed more later, Harrison-Jones was very popular in the Black community and with the PSC. Dismissing her could cause problems for the new mayor. So the mayor had to rely on the media to frame the issues and make the case for a change. Sometimes a school superintendent is asked to stay on until the new mayor can appoint either an interim superintendent or recruit a new one. This is part of the myth that schools are not political and that administrative continuity is in the interest of the students. To understand why the Flynn-appointed superintendency of Harrison-Jones did not end with the Menino election, it is necessary to review the political context of her tenure and the resulting overlap with the Menino administration.

Harrison-Jones Era (1991–1995)

In 1991, Lois Harrison-Jones became the first woman superintendent and second Black superintendent of the BPS following the firing of Dr. Laval Wilson fifteen months earlier. The controversy over the appointed board took place while Harrison-Jones was being wooed for the post. She had been associate superintendent in Dallas and became the first African American woman superintendent of a big-city school system. She was considered a community-oriented superintendent and announced publicly that she had no preference for selecting the board members. The relationship between Harrison-Jones and Mayor Flynn got off to a poor start after a controversy developed around her contract. Flynn felt it was inappropriate for the current BSC, an elected one, to negotiate and offer a multiyear contract. Black elected leaders were incensed. Representative Gloria Fox (D-Roxbury) said, "He's being disrespectful to the entire African-American community by not moving swiftly. The contract is here. There's no reason for him not to have signed it." Flynn's appointed BSC would not take over until January 1992. Flynn eventually signed the contact, and Dr. Harrison-Jones received a four-year deal for $130,000 annually, with a $32,500 benefit package.[36] The Black community leaders made much of this incident. The conflict between Harrison-Jones and the mayor continued when Flynn appointed one of his aides, Robert Consalvo, to be what the media called "a shadow superintendent."[37]

After the first six months, Ed Doherty, head of the BTU, gave Harrison-Jones a ringing endorsement: "Superintendent Harrison-Jones is a coalition builder. She has reached out to the communities, parent groups, political leaders, and to unions. She has enough confidence in herself as a leader to allow everyone to play an active role in school issues."[38] There were no complaints from the central office or school activists. In other words, the PSC had met her and liked her.

She held town meetings in the community and won over many leaders such as Joyce Ferriabough, president of the Black Political Caucus. She was also an advocate for the empowerment of principals. However, near the end of Flynn's tenure, he became dissatisfied with Harrison-Jones. After serving in office for two years as a Flynn appointee, he criticized her for not getting control over the budget and not hiring deputies to help her make changes in the system. Paul Parks, chair of the BSC, told the *New York Times* that Harrison-Jones was trying to nurture the careers of some employees but "she's trying to do it all herself, and that's unfortunate. Sometimes you just don't have the time." This followed the failure of the Consalvo Proposal. Robert Consalvo, the Flynn-appointed executive director of the BSC, wanted to give failing students vouchers so that they could attend a public or private school of their choice. It was a voucher and school choice plan. The BSC did not accept the proposal, and Consalvo resigned. Consalvo had been a critic of Harrison-Jones. He claimed that racial politics forced him to resign.[39]

The new narrative was that the superintendent was too bogged down to make a budget and solve some of the system's administrative issues. In a joint statement by Mayor Flynn and the BSC, they asked her to make thirteen major changes with stated deadlines. Superintendent Harrison-Jones dismissed the call and stated, "Boston schools have had a beating long enough and have succeeded in thwarting any effort to truly change. I'm determined to do it and am willing to take all of this nonsense and all of this posturing and all this politicizing and still go ahead." Ferriabough, one of the superintendent's strongest supporters, agreed and stated, "If I were to make one criticism, I think she might need to get in some new people to move things along."[40] After the conflict over her contract was over, Jones built a community constituency and gained some support from Mayor Flynn. When Flynn resigned on July 12, 1993, Harrison-Jones's political flanks were further compromised.

Acting Mayor Menino's first run-in with school politics came during his first weeks in office. After insisting the BTU negotiate a contract with him, he initially rejected the union's proposed contract offer as being too costly. The BTU had worked for two years with no pay raise or a contract. Members felt that they were due for a raise. Ed Doherty, president of the BTU and a one-time candidate for mayor against Flynn, understood the internal aspects of city politics. In an interview, Doherty claimed he did not try to separate his union from that of politics: "Everything that happens to the people we represent happens in politics."[41] He knew that if his union threatened to strike, it would get a big play in the mayoral campaign.

During the 1993 mayoral campaign, the teacher's union staged a one-day strike. Campaigning on fiscal restraint, Menino rallied the BSC members, appointees whom he inherited and could reappoint, to defeat a controversial $100 million wage contract. This was a contract that did not contain any commitment to school reform. Although there was little public outcry about the contract, Menino apparently sensed an opportunity to fortify his housekeeping image.

Menino's refusal to accede to the negotiated pay raise was a turning point in his mayoralty. Containing the unions became an issue in the mayoral campaign debate between Menino and his opponent, State Representative James T. Brett. Even though they had union endorsements, they both took tough stands against unreasonable contracts with unions.[42]

The *Boston Herald* published a photo of Menino, Harrison-Jones, Doherty, and School Committee Chair Paul Parks smiling and seemingly working together. Mayor Menino rejected the bloated contract proposal that would cost from $50 million to $127 million over three years.[43] A *Boston Globe* headline stated, "Anti-Union Stance Seen Paying Off for Menino."[44]

Peter S. Canellos, a *Globe* reporter, characterized the Menino strategy as a gamble: "Menino is betting again that voters will blame the greedy union and view him as a bulwark against labor run amok." Canellos even made an analogy with Calvin Coolidge, the former Massachusetts governor who took a stand against striking policemen in 1919. His stand received national attention, and Coolidge became president of the United States. The subtext of Canellos's characterization was that Menino was a stand-up guy for the residents of the city. In effect, the public saw the acting mayor as being up to the job.[45]

After Menino won the election, he immediately reopened the negotiations with the BTU. The parties hired Conflict Management Inc., a consultant, to facilitate the talks. It took four days to reach an agreement. The BTU signed a one-year contract for $12 million. After his election for a full term, he managed to negotiate a new contract and avoid a strike.

Following the election, Menino also stated that Harrison-Jones's job was safe and appointed her to his cabinet as director of education and training.

THE FAILURE OF BOSTON PUBLIC SCHOOL REFORM   235

Some top aides complained to the media that Menino did not inform them before he made the decision. The *Boston Herald* reported the appointment as an attempt to improve relations between the schools and city hall.[46] *Boston Globe* reporter Don Aucoin later characterized Menino's approach as nonconfrontational. According to him, the mayor appeared to be cooperative while at the same time he was increasing the pressure for Harrison-Jones to leave.[47]

Harrison-Jones was after all a Flynn appointee. In a June 1994 editorial, the *Boston Globe* stated, "The superintendent has not had an easy time of it since she arrived in Boston in 1991. Mayor Flynn capitalized on every available media opportunity to undermine her. Her own prickly personality became all the more defensive, and relations with city officials and the press have often been strained."[48] The *Globe* wanted her to release her performance review. The appointment to the mayor's cabinet was seen as an attempt to improve communications between the superintendent and the new mayor.

One of the projects Menino and Harrison-Jones worked together on was the updating of the Boston Compact. The first Boston Compact, signed in 1982, was designed to address student dropout rates and employment problems. But it was not stopping dropouts and was out of date. Jennette S. Hargroves, a researcher at the Community Affairs Department of the Federal Reserve Bank of Boston, examined the programs from the years 1982 to 1986 and found that progress had been made but that over three thousand students were still dropping out.[49]

In 1994, Menino was able to get the so-called public school establishment— members of the Boston Compact Steering Committee, the chair of the BSC, the superintendent, the chair of the Vault, the chair of the Higher Educational Partnership Private Industry Council, and the president of the BTU—to update the second Boston Compact. The Wilson Center, a Washington, DC–based research center, did a study for the possible reform of the BPS mission going back to the first and second Boston Compacts (1982, 1989). It concluded,

> Boston Compact III, signed in January 1994, fared better than its 1989 predecessor which fell victim to an economic downswing and governance disputes. Compact III offered a comprehensive agenda for reform. Five major goals were outlined in the agreement: (1) to increase access to employment and higher education for BPS graduates; (2) to expand innovation within the school system, including the extension of school-based management to all schools and the establishment of at least six "pilot" schools (within-district charter schools); (3) to develop new school curricula and assessment standards; (4) to establish a Center for

Leadership Development to strengthen professional development; and (5) to enhance support for parents and families, while expanding early childhood opportunities.[50]

Operationalizing the new compact strategy was the superintendent's job. This would be difficult since public-private programs in schools do not always work. For his 1997 dissertation, Stephan M. Coan examined the implementation of the third Boston Compact. He found management problems and cultural differences between schools and businesses. More importantly, he concluded that Boston appeared to have a disincentive for corporation investment in schools. The initial investment of both participants declined over time. The business community was not an effective advocate for schools.[51]

In effect, Harrison-Jones's tenure could not be saved by the third compact. The media began to focus on her performance and leadership. Although she had considerable support in the Black community and among Black officeholders, there was no way to stop Menino from forcing her out of the office and recruiting a new superintendent. After being told her contract would not be renewed, Harrison-Jones publicly stated that the schools were pawns of the political system. She reacted strongly to a cartoon in the *Boston Globe* showing her performing "voodoo" on Mayor Menino.[52] Two *Boston Herald* reporters described Harrison-Jones as "having a prickly personality, autocratic style and disdain for the media."[53]

Menino noted that his aides needed "no prodding to leak the news that Harrison-Jones has fallen out of favor with Menino." Menino claimed he anticipated that his firing of Harrison-Jones would bring a negative backlash from Black leaders. He did not want to be called a "racist." Mel King took the bait and stated, "We won't allow her to be lynched." During the annual Martin Luther Day Jr. breakfast, Menino braced himself for comparisons with George Wallace. He claimed he was in a "grim mood." He got into a hot exchange with Gareth Saunders, the city councilor from Roxbury: "I don't take accusations of racism well." Harrison-Jones also spoke at the breakfast. She said that she "was a victim of an unreachable standard of perfection. I care too much about children to roll and play dead because someone says I should." Menino interpreted her remarks as a swipe toward him.[54]

Reporter Don Aucoin was correct about Menino's motives. The pressure was on from a variety of sources to replace Harrison-Jones. In 1995, she resigned. Firing a popular and highly visible Black superintendent could have been difficult. She initially made some rumblings about fighting for her job, but she relented and resigned. Political scientist William E. Nelson Jr. concluded that this caused tension in the Black community. He noted, "Harrison-Jones was very popular in the Black community because of her progressive educational ideas and her deep involvement in the work of community organizations. This was in contrast to a former Black superintendent Laval Wilson, who was viewed as estranged from the Black community. Menino's decision to ask her to resign in the middle of her contract set off widespread protests by her supporters in the Black community."[55]

In an interview with *Education Week*, Dr. Harrison-Jones evaluated her tenure. She claimed that she increased instructional spending by 38 percent. She cut 131 positions from the central bureaucracy and overhauled special and bilingual education programs. She also claimed that dropout rates and absenteeism had fallen, and attendance had increased. In partnership with the BTU, she oversaw the expansion of school-based management from 31 schools to 117 and the establishment of 6 "pilot schools" that would be allowed to operate with greater freedom from district and union regulations.[56] These schools could select their own staff, had increased discretion over their budgets, and could set a longer school day. In addition, the pilot school councils could select their own principals. Yet they had to operate within the teacher union's agreement on seniority.

None of these accomplishments mattered. The support from the Black community did not matter. The writing was on the wall. Her tenure was at an end. In an *Education Week* interview, she admitted, "If the Mayor would like to have someone of his own choosing, that's his prerogative."[57] The interview also acknowledged the *Boston Globe* editorial "A Failing Grade for Harrison-Jones" and stated that she had been moving "at [a] snail's pace" on school reform.[58]

In other words, Menino had the leading newspapers on his side. The narrative of Harrison-Jones being a community-oriented minority superintendent and union-supported administrator no longer protected her job. The new narrative was for the new mayor to appoint his own superintendent. The first test of Menino as "the education mayor" came after Harrison-Jones resigned.[59] Would he push for changes and even the reorganization of the BSC staff? Many activists saw the period between superintendents as an opportunity to "clean house" at school headquarters. An ad-hoc group calling itself "Critical Friends" met with the mayor and asked him to remove the "major manager" of the central staff. The mayor refused and stated, "I don't have that authority as mayor. The superintendent in cooperation with the school committee would have to take that step."[60] Aside from removing the superintendent, Menino backed off from a frontal attack on the PSC. The mayor was initially given good marks by the media for his noninterference and for his stewardship of the school system.

Menino's First Superintendent Selection

It is important to remember that superintendents are not necessarily a part of the local PSC. Removing them does not diminish the power of the PSC. Nevertheless, the PSC could not safely ignore the emerging relationship between a powerful mayor and a school superintendent. There is no national consensus model for such relations. In many cities, mayors have allowed themselves to align with superintendents while in other cities they maintain a traditional institutional distance.

Most superintendents are itinerant workers moving from one school system to another.[61] When they get fired, some get another job as a deputy superintendent in a different city or take an academic position. The recruitment of a new superintendent was one of the most important tests for Menino. Firing a popular and visible Black superintendent such Harrison-Jones could have been potentially complicated. Alyce Lee, Menino's former chief of staff, described the situation: "He [Menino] really wanted it to work out. She was well-known in the African American community. It would have been the best of both worlds, [for him] to have a Black woman in the school system. It just didn't work out."[62]

Don Aucoin of the *Boston Globe* heaped praise on the mayor for the way he handled the ouster of Harrison-Jones. After characterizing him as a "plodding tortoise to Ray Flynn's headline-hunting hare," Aucoin stated that Menino's style was more "[Jimmy] Durante than Demosthenes."[63] Aucoin quoted a former council colleague, Michael McCormack, as saying, "He walks away from this whistling like a Charlie Chaplin character. . . . She has been surgically removed without his hand being seen on the knife."[64]

As stated earlier, Menino wisely did not make a frontal attack on the local PSC. Ed Doherty, the former president of the BTU, who remained a powerful figure in the Boston PSC, actually praised Menino. Doherty believed that Menino had been a "strong voice for the public schools and he has used the bully pulpit to say to the citizen that public schools are important."[65] Menino impressed Doherty with his decision to use Jeremiah Burke, a high school that had lost its accreditation, to give his State of the City address. Menino said, "I want to be judged as your mayor by what happens now in the Boston public schools. If I fail to bring about these specific reforms by the year 2001, then judge me harshly."[66]

Vacancies in the superintendency always made for great excitement and anticipation within the PSC, BSC, and City Hall and among parents. Members of the BSC received countless resumes and numerous telephone calls from community leaders. They were expected to interview four or five candidates. These interviews solicited views about anti-dropout strategies, achievement programs in previous jobs, and plans for improving the Boston schools.[67] In addition, the Boston media would get caught up in the drama of the pending search. They framed it as Menino's finally getting a chance to put his stamp on the public school system. In preparation for this new opportunity, Menino met with several university presidents, seeking their advice about the next superintendent. The media allowed that ethnicity should not be the only criterion for the next superintendent. The subtext was that the city had recruited two failed Black superintendents, so now it was time for a white person to try.

During the recruitment for a replacement for Harrison-Jones, only one minority applicant, Dr. Anthony Alvarado, a former school chancellor of New York City, emerged as one of the three finalists. The Alvarado candidacy was compromised by allegations of financial improprieties. Because there were no women and only one flawed minority candidate, many school activists concluded that the search was "wired" or rigged. Many Black leaders thought the charismatic Alvarado was a cover for the mayor's real choice, Dr. Thomas Payzant. Professor Marilyn M. Tallerico suggested that this was not unusual because selection practices worked to the disadvantage of women and minorities. She concluded, "These forces are strengthened by similarity-attraction dynamics at the interpersonal level that increases the likelihood of board members' and consultants' subconscious affinity for candidates demographically like themselves. The broader sociocultural context, characterized by enduring racial bias and gender stereotypes, fortifies these interpersonal and institutional dynamics, as does the current ideological environment—unfriendly as it is to affirmative action in employment."[68]

Although some school activists preferred Alvarado, they accepted Payzant. The two Latino members of the BSC, Felix Arroyo and Edward Melendez, voted in favor of Alvarado. Nonetheless, the next decade of school policy would be led by Menino's selection, Thomas Payzant.

The Payzant Era (1995–2006)

In 1995, Thomas Payzant, an assistant secretary of the U.S. Department of Education, was selected as Boston superintendent. Payzant, a native of Quincy, Massachusetts, had the right credentials (a Harvard doctorate in education) and experience as an urban superintendent in two western cities. Moreover, Menino heavily orchestrated the choice. Three years after winning the mayoral election, he proclaimed himself the "education mayor."[69] Some thought that Payzant's personality matched Menino's low-key style and penchant for avoiding controversies. Jim Vrabel agreed, saying that Menino was "a steady as you-go-person. He did not press for change."[70] Wayne Woodlief of the *Boston Herald* suggested in a headline that the "Mayor's Future Rests with Payzant." He continued, "Make no mistake: Tom Menino's hide is on the line. If Payzant can't reverse the schools' downward spiral, a big reason for the flight of Boston's middle class of both races, Menino is likely to lose in 1997, no matter how popular he is now."[71] In retrospect, Woodlief overstated his case, but there was certainly anticipation with the Payzant appointment. Ed Doherty stated in an interview, "Overall he [Menino] had done OK. He has set up a joint committee on school reform. The union is a partner in school reform. He has worked on portfolio assessments and new curriculum standards. He has put his energy into school without causing conflicts. He replaced six principals in the first year. He hasn't come in as a steamroller."[72]

Menino felt the city schools needed to make "steady progress."[73] Menino's former chief of staff Alyce Lee stated that he felt that turning around the Boston school system was not a quick job and that Payzant was best "over the long term."[74] In other words, although most observers thought the schools needed fundamental change, the mayor opted for incrementalism. However, once Payzant was appointed, most school leaders offered their support. It was supposedly a new era in the management of the BPS.

In 2000, Political scientist John Portz, an expert on the BPS, interviewed a school principal that stated the school committee, superintendent, and administrators were in accord. The principal stated, "All the planets have to be lined up." Finally, after many years of policy disagreements and personal clashes, leadership on the public side of the civic ledger was in place. One of the business leaders Portz interviewed stated, "For the first time we have a mayor, a superintendent, and a school committee singing from the same sheet of music."[75]

Some still had concerns about Payzant's understanding of the challenges of the Boston schools. Hattie McKinnis, executive director of the Citywide Parents Council, stated, "No matter how open and smooth he is, a lot goes on behind closed doors. Things get presented that can't have been decided overnight, but they end up surprising a lot of the people affected." *Boston Globe* reporter Karen Avenoso described the Payzant challenge:

> The problems faced by Boston schools can, at times, seem overwhelming. Half of the city's third graders read below grade level. In 1994, only 5 percent of fourth graders met state grade-level qualifications for math tests. The city's dropout rate has risen from 7.6 percent in 1993 to 9.2 percent last year, while the statewide average fell to 3.6 percent.
>
> Boston students' average combined SAT scores totaled 740 in 1994, compared to the state's average of 901. In addition, Boston schools have to deal with a challenging student population: 11,000 bilingual children—in nine different language programs, from Cape Verdean to Vietnamese—and 12,000 special-education students. Then, there's the fact that the Burke lost its accreditation from a regional agency last year and five more of the city's 15 high schools are on probation.[76]

Generally speaking, the media regarded Payzant's appointment as a solid one, but coverage left some with doubts as to whether Payzant was the right choice. David Brudnoy, a popular conservative talk show host at WBZ, was so impressed with the Payzant appointment that he wrote a glowing editorial for the *Herald*. The editorial called Payzant the most distinguished Menino appointment to date. Brudnoy asserted, "You won't be surprised to know that in my self-assumed task as Boston radio's queller of the bureaucrats I have encountered Thomas Payzant and have found him anything but a wuss. Generous to myself, I'd say that our discussions of education have been polite stand-offs, but more honestly I would have to say that this guy is one tough cookie."[77] In an interview, Ed Doherty was asked if Payzant had done anything to "challenge" school policy and replied, "I would not say challenge."[78] In other words, members of the cartel were satisfied with Payzant. The media was equally satisfied with him. In general, the Black community did not argue with the choice. Alyce Lee recalled, "What would they complain about? I don't remember any issues about him."

Payzant introduced a five-year plan called "Focus on Children," which political scientist John Portz described: "This 5-year plan outlined a series of steps to improve teaching and learning, restructure the school department, provide safe schools, and engage parents and the community in school improvement.

Focus on Children described Boston as a 'community ready for change' with a 'structure for collaboration' that includes the mayor, school committee, superintendent, Boston Teachers' Union, businesses, and general community."[79] It looked like Payzant would have a smooth drive ahead.

Bumps in Payzant's Road

The high public approval for Payzant did not preclude him from receiving criticisms or attracting controversies. Perhaps the most visible political controversy involved the Boston exam schools. The whole controversy erupted as Payzant was coming on board. This admission dispute became one of the contentious issues for the mayor and Payzant. The BSC had created three exam high schools: Boston Latin School (1635), the Boston Latin Academy (1878), and in 1994 the John O'Bryant School of Mathematics and Science (formerly Boston Technical High School). These schools (with students in grades 7–12) were designed to educate gifted students who could not afford to go to private schools. However, some students left private and parochial elementary schools to enroll in the exam schools. To be admitted students had to live in Boston and pass a competitive exam. Over the years, these three schools became very prestigious public schools. Graduating from them almost guaranteed admission to one of the region's most prestigious colleges. The public began to become aware that white students had dominated the admission process. It was difficult for low-income minority students to pass the examination. For many nonwhite students, this seemed inherently unfair since the schools were public and should represent all of the city's demographics. Besides, the BPS student population had become minority-majority, and some low-income schools were not as effective as their private and parochial counterparts.

Expanding the enrollment of the three schools had always been an issue. In 1976, an agreement was made to reserve 35 percent of admissions for Black and Latino students. Was this quota legal? Menino had gone on record as opposing quotas but he favored goals for diversity. He also rejected replacing racial preferences in admission with preferences for low-income students. He stated, "There will be no goals based on income. That's out for me."[80]

In 1996, Julia McLaughlin, a white eighth-grade student, sued the program because she scored higher than over one hundred minority applicants. Judge W. Arthur Garrity Jr., of the famed Boston busing case, ruled in favor of Mc Laughlin. It was a limited ruling since the McLaughlin case was not a class-action suit. For some, this was a mini-*Bakke* suit (i.e., a personal affirmative action suit). Menino told the *Boston Globe* that the judge's ruling raised a "legitimate question" as to whether the judge should also admit the eighty-five other white and Asian applicants who were denied admission along with McLaughlin because 35 percent of Boston Latin School seats were reserved for Blacks and Hispanics. According to Menino, "That's a legitimate question that has to be answered: If [Garrity] wrote the decision ordering admission for one, shouldn't he have to make the decision for all?"[81]

Superintendent Payzant tried to address the situation by increasing the enrollment of minorities. He stated, "At this stage, we should not have to rely on the court to tell us what to do. . . . It's an issue of fairness to those students now that we've agreed to admit Julia and discontinue a 35 percent set-aside."[82] Under the Payzant proposal, 154 current seventh and eighth graders would be eligible for seats at Boston Latin School and another 145 students at Latin Academy. He also stated that students would be invited to enter the schools as ninth graders in 1997 or 1998. If all the students offered seats at the Latin School were accepted, the size of the class would increase by 17 percent to about 500 students. The plan was described as such:

> Under the new plan, blacks, currently 24 percent of the Latin School enrollment, will decrease to about 15 percent, School Department data shows. Hispanics, now at 11 percent, will decrease to about 7 percent. Asians, now at 23 percent, will increase to 24 percent, and whites, now at 43 percent, will increase to 54 percent. . . . Attached to the new admissions policy are several plans intended to better prepare minority students for the exam school entrance test. . . . Advanced classes and accelerated elementary and middle school programs that prepare public school applicants to enter the exam school will be increased to accommodate more students. . . . Summer-school programs to prepare students for the sixth grade exam school test will be expanded.[83]

In addition to the exam school controversy, another challenge for Payzant was to implement Menino's neighborhood schools. This proposal had been proffered initially in Menino's first term. In 1999, he promised to build five new neighborhood schools within the next six years. This was a follow-up on his campaign promise to allow students to walk to neighborhood schools. Three schools were built, but Menino later commented, "What I hear from neighborhoods more often than not is, 'We'd love to go to school near my home,' but the important thing is parents want to have a choice. In 2004, we had many hearings around the city and came to the final analysis and couldn't get public support."[84]

The public continued to hold Superintendent Payzant in high regard despite the fact that the school dropout problem continued under his leadership. In 2005, Boston received $250,000 from the Youth Transition Funder Group to address this crisis. In 1998, the dropout rate had been 8.3 percent, and toward the end of his tenure in 2005 it was 8.4 percent.[85] In other words, there was no improvement. The public became concerned about school leadership and the BSC. A Suffolk University 2005 poll found Menino's approval ratings to be off the charts. The same poll found that the BSC received only a 24 percent "excellent/good" rating, while registering a dismal 47 percent "fair/poor" rating. The director of the poll, David Paleologos, stated, "School's out for the Boston School Committee. These unkind numbers appear to be the seeds for change." Respondents were asked if they would change from an appointed board to an elected one. When asked, "Would you support an elected school committee," 60 percent said "yes," 24 percent responded "no," with 16 percent "undecided."[86] This poll did not impress Menino as he continued to support the appointed BSC.

In 2006, Boston Public Schools won the Broad Prize for Urban Education as the top-performing school system in the nation. This was an honor for the central staff as well as Payzant. However, while such awards are noteworthy, the BPS was similar to most urban public schools in that it had failed to upgrade the classroom performance of minority students.

That same year, Payzant retired. A group of scholars with a grant from the Bill and Melinda Gates Foundation reviewed his ten-year tenure. The group credited Payzant with the changes he made. They also outlined the system's shortcomings. Professor Norm Fruchter stated that 58,000 Boston students did not need a turnaround: "It would be a disaster if a new superintendent decided to redo all of this, and set off on a whole different set of instructional interventions." Some members of the team were not that impressed with Payzant's tenure and his lack of public engagement. One dissenter was former Boston University School of Social professor Work Hubie Jones, who wrote a separate report stating, "I am just sick and tired of this line that been promoted here—that they even have resonating across the country—that this school system is in the midst of serious reform."[87] He noted school reform was needed. He reported that a coalition of community organizations wanted a plan to eliminate achievement gaps in five years. It would be Menino's job along with the BSC to conduct a national search for a new superintendent. In 2006–2007, Michael G. Contompasis served as interim superintendent. The BSC went through the same recruitment process as it had done with Payzant. Menino and the BSC decided that the new superintendent would be Dr. Carolyn Johnson.

The Johnson Era (2007–2012)

In 2007, Dr. Carolyn R. Johnson, a well-known and award-winning administrator, was appointed superintendent of the BPS. She had been superintendent in Memphis and Minneapolis and had received her Ph.D. from the University of Minnesota. She was the third African American to serve in that job. Menino said when she first arrived, "She'll give us the leadership we need in these schools. I think she'll bring us to the next level. We're very fortunate to attract a talent as strong as Carol."[88] Her primary agenda included a reorganization of the school catchment zones to allow students to walk to schools and promotion of the idea of charter schools. In 2008, Menino called for redrawing the bus zones to save $10 million annually. This proposal did not draw the ire of the BTU but a proposal for charter schools would pit Menino against the PSC. Charter schools were now being promoted as a possible solution for failing minority-dominated schools.

In his book, Menino claimed that Johnson favored charter schools but that "I was cool to them." Menino claimed that in 2002 students attending charter schools cost $14 million and a decade later $80 million. Menino's objection to expanding charter schools was "deeper than money." For him, these schools were not inclusive and they drained money from the public schools. Expansion of charter schools would mean fewer students enrolling in the regular BPS. Menino even quoted from a history of Boston schools: "Charter schools are not compatible with the idea of the common school handed down by the Boston town meeting of 1784—'that the Children of all, partaking of equal Advantages and being placed upon an equal Footing, no Distinction might be made among them in the Schools.'.... Notice those big words: 'all' children, 'equal' advantages. Not the few gaining at the expense of the many."[89]

In 2003, Menino went before the state legislature, specifically the Joint Committee on Education, and requested charter schools for level 3 schools., mid- to low-range performing schools needing more assistance, Most Massachusetts charter schools are "Commonwealth Charters," chartered by the state. When a student enrolls in one of them, the city or town where the student lives pays tuition for it and the local public schools lose that money. Nevertheless, the BTU was able to convince the state legislature to create a hybrid charter school model in which such schools could only hire union teachers.

Citing a national poll that found public support for charter schools had increased from 39 to 53 percent, Harvard professor Paul E. Peterson argued that Boston pilot schools were still under the control of the BTU collective bargaining agreement.[90] Professor Matthew Knoester defined pilot schools as sharing "many similar features with charter schools, but there are important distinctions. Unlike charter schools, pilot schools are 'regular' district public schools. They receive the same basic funding, from the same sources, as all Boston Public Schools. Parents must live within the city of Boston, and pilot school teachers are members of the Boston Teachers Union; they receive the same salary and benefits as nonpilot teachers although particular job protections included in the teacher contract do not apply to pilot school teachers."[91] Knoester asserted that the pilots were ineffective and endorsed a BTU proposal for a hybrid model of pilot/nonpilot schools called "discovery schools." Under the proposal, the BTU would allow some curriculum changes and budget flexibility.[92]

The Boston Foundation sponsored a study of students selected by lottery to attend a charter school who performed better than those in regular public schools. Professor Paul Peterson concluded, "To the surprise of the Massachusetts education establishment, the charters won—and the pilots lost the research contest." For Peterson, "Pilots turned out to be no improvement on the status quo whatever." This explains in part why Menino suddenly got "charter school religion."[93]

An alternative explanation may be found in federal largess. Menino claimed that two elections, Barack Obama's 2008 presidential election and his own mayoral election of 2009, persuaded him to change his mind. Menino reversed his longstanding opposition to charter schools after the enactment of the Obama administration's Race to the Top program, which made a $5 billion federal fund available for innovation for underperforming schools. The state's Achievement Gap Act of 2010 raised the cap on charter schools and made other changes to state policy that was intended to (and did) help the state win Race to the Top funds. Menino saw that the idea of charters was catching on, and his two 2009 opponents were gaining traction in the campaign.

Menino told a Boston College Chief Executive Club luncheon, "The status quo won't work. We've got to make a real change." He promised to file for state legislation to bypass union approval to make changes and called for lifting the cap on the independently controlled charter schools. Johnson agreed to the move and stated, "We want to replicate what is working and we need the flexibility to do that."[94] Menino stated that he was for school reforms advocated by Governor Deval Patrick but wanted the charter schools to be in-district. They would not take money from the BPS and would enroll anyone. Patrick agreed to the Menino plan. Johnson supported Menino's call for district-run charter schools as a way to improve low-performing schools. The BTU was not on board as they wanted the teachers under collective bargaining. They persuaded house member to include their demands, but Menino lobbied the state senate to restore the in-district charter bill. Menino reported chastising Democrats over the issue. Menino said in his book what most local politicians knew—that the teachers' union "had paid to elect many state legislators. . . . It was time to remind these Democrats to put kids first."[95] This incident showed the power of the mayor and his allies in the senate.

The debate became an issue in Menino's 2009 mayoral campaign against Michael Flaherty. Another candidate, Kevin McCrea, opposed the plan, but Sam Yoon supported the plan. It got immediate support from the president of the Boston Foundation and Thomas Birmingham, the man who got charter schools into state law in the first place. Charter schools could now be developed for level 4 schools, that is, schools that require district and state intervention.

In February 2010, Menino launched his place-based education policy called "The Circle of Promise" at Jeremiah E. Burke High School. He outlined the geographic area that comprised the failing schools. This was going to be a holistic, community-based organization and a municipal, interagency approach to improving school performance in these high-poverty areas. Sociologists Jeremy R. Levine and William Julius Wilson identified the problems of implementation. They concluded,

> Our critiques of Boston's Circle of Promise similarly point to the problem of institutional entrenchment. With an excessive focus on messaging, broad goals, and assumption-driven data interpretation, institutions are allowed to carry on business as usual. After proposing the Circle of Promise, a few structural changes coincided with the adoption of new rhetoric. That is not to say the City of Boston's policy or motivations were rooted in anything but the best of intentions. Indeed the rhetoric itself signifies a tremendous commitment to equality and a noteworthy acknowledgment of the complexities of urban poverty and the racial achievement gap. But the reality of this policy innovation, once the layers

of messaging are removed, is that institutions continue to operate as they always have. The only change would be "coordination," or in practice, moderate communication. Entrenchment persists under the guise of innovation.[96]

After launching this policy, it is unclear the extent to which Menino directly coordinated the policy with private groups from City Hall. Moreover, operational routine in schools is the enemy of school reform. Outsiders can be safely ignored. This may explain why the Circle of Promise was so disappointing to Levine and Wilson.

The state legislature passed the 2010 Achievement Gap Act. It provided for more expansion of charter schools. By 2013, there were six in-districts charter schools in Boston. Menino endorsed a District-Charter Compact, an agreement between the BPS and the Alliance of Charter Schools. The agreement had to be ratified by the BSC and individual charter schools.

In September 2011, as a part of the Menino public school initiative called Community Learning, the mayor announced a student Boston ONEcard. The program combined the MBTA Charlie Card (a transit pass), a Boston Public Library Card, and a pass to the Boston Centers for Youth and Families. The new card could be used at these facilities and also for school attendance and food service. Menino stated, "In Boston, we are working hard to focus the assets of the whole city on the development of the whole child. This card will help make the assets of our city more accessible and remind each student every day that there are community centers and libraries for them to explore throughout Boston."[97]

Bumps in Johnson's Road

In 2012, the so-called Peterson scandal took place. A local television station, WHBQ-TV, reported that Rodney Peterson, the co-headmaster at the O'Bryant School of Mathematics and Science, had assaulted his wife. It was revealed that Carolyn Johnson knew of the Peterson investigation but had been sworn to secrecy by the police. Peterson was arrested on June 17, 2011. Superintendent Johnson took no disciplinary action and wrote a letter to the judge supporting Peterson. The scandal became public. Mayor Menino said he didn't want to second-guess the superintendent. He said that she made "thousands of decisions every week. In hindsight, things should have been done differently. When I heard about this, I said uh-uh. You've got to deal with it right away. I don't tolerate that stuff." The mayor promised to create "a panel that will investigate any future allegations and decide on punishment so that the superintendent or any other department head cannot exercise personal discretion."[98] Peterson finally admitted to the charges and was given probation and assigned to a battery prevention program. Three days later Mayor Menino stated of Johnson, "She's OK with me; she's done a great job. She did make a mistake, no question about it. But she's done a great job moving the system forward."[99]

The Black community was divided over Johnson's handling of the Peterson situation. One group of residents signed a petition to remove Johnson while other groups rallied to her defense. The Peterson affair allowed Councilor John Connolly to create publicity for himself. He claimed that the failure to remove Peterson had "became a burr in Johnson's saddle, and by extension, in Menino's."[100]

During the Johnson administration, the city was awarded $1.5 million to support the Thrive in Five program. This program was designed to link parents with networks that facilitated the transition of poor kids from home to school. With the United Way, City Hall promoted the notion of school readiness so that when a child reached five years old, they would be able to cope with school achievement. The mayor welcomed the grant and stated, "All of our children deserve the opportunity to thrive, starting at birth. Unfortunately, many of our children arrive at school already facing gaps—in vocabulary, exposure to books, health care access, and experiences interacting with peers and adults. I look forward to working with the Kellogg Foundation to make sure every child enters school prepared, that parents enter as full partners in their children's education, and that we build on that base for sustained success."[101]

Johnson was also tasked with putting into policy a long-term plan for Menino's idea of neighborhood schools. The premise was that students should be able to go to schools that were close to their neighborhoods. BPS's student assignment policy had been race-neutral for years, and the BSC and its External Advisory Committee explicitly said that they were not trying to affect desegregation or diversity. In 2013, the BSC endorsed a plan called the Home-Based Student Assignment Policy. The goal was to get more students into schools closer to home, and it seems to have done that, though there were differences in the quality of schools that kids in different parts of the city got to choose among. The policy was to eliminate bias in the assignment process and base assignments on a neutral statistical formula, not neighborhood enclaves alone. Since Bostonians live in enclaves, it did not generate more school deseg-regation.[102] Professors Kathryn McDermott, Erica Frankenberg, and Sarah Diem concluded,

> In our analysis of the politics of changing race-neutral student-assignment politics, more than a decade later, the enclave school concept continues to be useful. In Boston, Mayor Menino's push for a return to neighborhood schools, or at least to making school choice simpler within smaller geographic areas, can be understood as an attempt to help people in middle-class White neighborhoods make their local schools more like enclaves and less reflective of the city's demographics. Critics of several proposals to return to neighborhood schools pointed out that the changes would limit families in other parts of the city to choosing among undesirable options. As a matter of arithmetic, if some schools in a large system are enclaves, with students who are more-advantaged than the population as a whole, other schools must have student populations that are less advantaged than the city as a whole. Where these schools are also less desirable in terms of their performance or other characteris-tics, we have labeled them "default schools" because they are not schools where families generally seek to enroll their children.[103]

Dr. Johnson had other policy disputes with the BTU over adding time to the school day. During her tenure, she also received intense media criticism. Despite this, Johnson concentrated on improving high school graduation rates and reducing dropout rates. Indeed, the reported dropout rates decreased by 40 percent. It had not been that low since 1977. Johnson was credited with increasing the graduate rates, which went up from 57.9 to 66.7 percent.[104] In 2010, she also partnered with Unlocking Potential, a Boston nonprofit man-agement organization to help improve low-achieving charter middle schools.

Richard Stutman, the new head of the BTU, criticized the move since the union opposed charter schools. He thought that Johnson's strategy was dis-respectful to Boston administrators and teachers. He stated, "It sends a bad message to our hardworking staff. It shows a lack of confidence in our own abilities. It will be taken as a slap in the face."[105]

A Partial Victory over the PSC?

Menino wanted to be the "Education Mayor." He was somewhat successful. Professor Clarence Stone found that all-out civic action by all stakeholders could create school reform.[106] Menino claimed that his electoral coalition stuck with him. He concluded, "Reform took the kids and the teachers and administrators. It took the voters staying the course. It took Payzant and Johnson and me. It took a city."[107] To make real and lasting reforms, there had to be a citywide mobilization of concerned citizens. According to Jim Vrabel, "The continued use of widespread busing and refusal to return to neighborhood schools—even after racial guidelines for assigning students was abandoned in 1999—has meant that parents aren't able to keep watch on the schools. When nobody is looking there is no pressure for change. Menino made slow and incremental changes. He moved the school department headquarters from 26 Court Street to Dudley Square [The Ferdinand Furniture Building]."[108] It is now called the Bruce C. Bolling Municipal Building, named after Bolling, the first African American president of the Boston City Council. It is located in the heart of Roxbury.

The fight for school reform continued. Academics continue to offer suggestions for school reform movements. Professor Clarence Stone has argued school reform is possible if a coalition of business leaders, politicians, parent groups, and education leaders work together to attain a civic capacity.[109] Civic capacity is the ability to develop, mobilize, and sustain a reform movement. Professors Robin Jones, John Portz, and Lana Stein compared Pittsburgh, St. Louis, and Boston and concluded that Boston lacked the civic capacity necessary for school reform. They stated that on the spectrum of civic capacity for change, "Boston occupied a middle position. Although the city's civic capacity was well-developed, public education had not always been seen as a major concern of civic elites." Although the Vault and economic leaders had participated in the third Boston Compact, they did not follow through. Jones, Portz, and Stein also claimed that "a legacy of court intervention and structural separation of the school department from city hall diminished a positional base for authority and contributed to a leadership vacuum."[110] This research was done in 1997, four years after Tom Menino was elected to office. He was not able to appoint a superintendent until 1996. Menino and Payzant tried to fill that vacuum, but the forces of the PSC outmaneuvered them.

Since Menino wanted to be an education mayor he was inclined to listen. Political scientist Clarence Stone and colleagues concluded, "Mayoral leadership is not a quick managerial fix, nor is it necessary a means to impose accountability."[111] When Menino promised to create neighborhood schools it did not happen. John C. Drake characterized Menino's efforts to be an education mayor as one that "continues [to be] bedeviled by opposition to neighborhood—a signature promise that continues to sputter."[112] Yet research by Professor Kathryn A. McDermott and education analyst Anna Fung-Morley found that the algorithm the city used as a way of getting students closer to "neighborhood schools" without having to draw or redraw any attendance zones do not work.[113] It made white enclave schools more white. Moreover, political scientist John Portz concluded, "The mayor's support is not simply rhetorical. He has made public education a funding priority throughout his tenure."[114]

In 2013, Mayor Menino decided not to run for reelection. And after six years in office, Johnson retired. Reporter Yvonne Abraham concluded, "Few, if any, superintendents before Johnson had tried changes as radical as those she has pursued. None has worked in a more fractious environment. Still, she'd be the first to say she's not perfect. She places a high premium on community feedback, but that has sometimes led her to hastily announce initiatives that didn't seem fully thought out. She's famous for her compassion, but had way too much of it for one principal, Rodney Peterson, who was put on probation for domestic assault."[115]

Summary

Menino spent a chapter in his book *A Mayor for a New America* discussing school policy because he wanted the record to reflect his personal commitment. He inserted himself into the superintendent selection process with the hope of finding an individual with whom he could work. Menino framed the school issue as a neighborhood one. He spoke clearly and often, but increases in low-income student achievement defied increments of funding, changes in leadership, and incessant pedagogical innovations.

As previously noted, reporters who covered the Boston schools did not always understand school politics. A few reviewed the academic literature until they found research that supported their argument. For example, in 2005 Derrick Jackson referenced an academic who found that charter-school students were not performing any better than those in regular public schools. For him, charter schools were in "trouble waters."[116] The PSC has made this argument for years. School performance research has become extremely sophisticated. It is sometimes difficult to read and understand. This may explain why local reporters covered mayoral appointments of superintendents and the board as if personalities and credentials mattered.

As I discussed in *Black Mayors and School Politics*, white mayors are given a discount when dealing with predominantly minority schools. It is unlikely that a Black mayor would have been able to dismiss the concerns of the ad-hoc group Critical Friends as easily as Menino did. Nor would a Black mayor have been able to escape the sacking of Harrison-Jones with impunity. Since all Menino wanted to do was reduce controversies, his relationship with the PSC was mutually satisfying. Menino kept the peace with the BTU by first objecting to demands publicly (posturing) and then giving in to what they wanted. Since the mayor of Boston was much more powerful in budget politics than the City Council, it was a game the BTU leaders enjoyed playing. Aside from racial issues, most of the school problems in the 1990s were linked to the poor performance of minority children on standardized tests. The same problems were carried over into the twenty-first century.

Again, the racial and ethnic diversity of the BSC did not insulate Menino from community criticisms. Unfortunately, few local activists knew enough about local school situations to make any substantive suggestions for change. In effect, school board politics was but a mirror of the Menino style. The principal problem for mayoral actions in school policy was that the game rules kept changing in school policy. Aside from having multiple veto points, the PSC could just stall and wait out the mayor. Changing school policy from City Hall was not an easy task.[117] The principal way mayors have tried to intervene in school policy has been through collective bargaining, board appointments, and the budgetary process. However, the Boston PSC was able to remain influential because it adapted to the mayoral control of the BSC. The PSC discovered that they could safely ignore the BSC and take their case to the mayor directly.

John M. Cronin, a historian of the Boston Public Schools, credited the early and continuous intervention of corporate leaders for the attempt to reform the system. He also credited Menino for hiring Payzant. According to Cronin, Menino provided the "political protection that allowed Payzant to transfer or retire principals of the least effective suburbs with a minimum of turbulence." Rather than rely on a civic capacity, Boston relied on a vigorous mayor, Tom Menino, who said, "I want to be judged as your mayor by what happens now in the Boston Public Schools."[118] To some extent, Menino's mayoralty was so evaluated. If he thought that he learned about education, he was in for a rude awakening when he began dealing with the leadership of Boston's higher education complex.

CHAPTER 9

Moguls and Students in Higher Education

Few colleges and universities want to be trapped in perpetuity in their original campuses. Most want and need new facilities to grow and keep current with students' studying and living preferences. Herein lies the challenge. If the city does not have a lot of land for expansion, politics become more difficult. There is also the possibility of resident opposition. It may come from the neighborhoods or community or students being affected, as for example happened with New York's Columbia University and Morning Side Park in 1968. Some universities buy land with a real estate agency and then announce ownership. Taking and acquiring more land in their host city could mean that a city may have less to use to attract companies and families. Still, few big-city mayors want to go on the record as opposing higher education institutions' land purchases and expansions.

When the city is approached by leaders of higher education institutions, seeking to expand universities and college facilities, the question becomes how to fit this into the overall city plan. The land-use policy of a city is the mayor's biggest bargaining tool. Granted, some of these institutions have been historical and economic assets to the city, but land is a limited commodity. Moreover, these institutions are often most willing to accept surrounding land or parcels regardless of the reputation and the condition of contiguous neighborhoods. Proximity may trump other factors. The problem arises with how much land and its location. In addition, what will be the impact on existing neighborhood dynamics?

Mayors as leaders of the city are the epicenter of controversial expansion proposals for these institutions. On the one hand, it is essential for superstar cities like Boston, with ambitions to attract the creative class and their post-industrial companies, to be regarded as university-friendly. On the other hand, creating resentment among voters is not wise. Unlike some cities, Boston was not endowed with unlimited land space, so making land decisions is daunting.

Expansion is just one aspect of town-gown relations. History suggests that policies related to these relations have become increasingly important. Economics, politics, land use, and city planning play a role in mayoral strategy. Accordingly, strong mayors in big cities faced with such challenges can be divided into three types. Mayors in big cities have adopted one of the approaches discussed below.

The first type is a *promoting* mayor. Such mayors see university expansion as an opportunity for neighbor development. Former mayor Richard J. Daley in Chicago was instrumental in expanding the University of Illinois Medical School's westside campus into a larger University of Illinois at Chicago. This was done by arguing for advancing the interests of Chicagoans against those of people in Urbana, Illinois, where the flagship university is located. City Hall's agenda was to transform the small University of Illinois Navy Pier campus into a full university. The university now enrolls over 30,000 students.[1]

The second type of leadership style may be called a *hidden-hand* mayor. Such mayors let others take more visible roles in the expansion. Some small-towns mayors fall into this category. However big-city mayors are not exempt. The expansion of the University of Chicago in Hype Park–Kenwood is an example. The university was trapped in terms of land space and surrounded by low-income communities in Kenwood. The university was contemplating a move to the suburbs when Mayor Richard M. Daley appointed Julian Levi, brother of the university president Edward H. Levi chair of the city's planning commission. He conducted an urban renewal of the area, the Hype Park area was transformed, and the university was able to expand.

Finally, there is the mayor as the *negotiator*. These mayors deliberately try to reevaluate and negotiate expansion claims offered by universities and colleges. The strength of such mayors depends on their support in the state house and city council and among the business elite. Those groups can make it difficult, if not impossible, for colleges and universities to expand. These types of mayors are quite common in cities with less land to develop. In the early days of a city, universities, and colleges simply bought land surrounding them and built dorms and other facilities. In modern times such mayors have other entities vying for space. Which entities will be effective economically? Mayor Menino, like many of his predecessors, was a negotiator.

On Being Mayor of the Athens of America

Metro Boston Metro has been called the Athens of America, and institutions in the entire metro region sometimes market themselves as such. In ancient Greece, Athens was the largest city-state and was the center of learning and home of Greek philosophers. Like ancient Athens, modern metro Boston is a global city with multiple centers of post-industrial economics and financial transactions. Generally, higher education is a multibillion-dollar money-making and money-consuming enterprise. For example, the combined 2013 endowments of Harvard University and MIT alone were worth more than $42 billion.[2] Their campuses contain some of the most historical and expensive buildings in the region. Also, these behemoths are under relentless pressure to expand.

These expansion needs require higher education institutions to engage with city politicians and citizen groups. Yet there is a dearth of academic literature linking the future of Boston and its elected leadership (especially the mayoralty) to these institutions. Being responsible for infrastructure maintenance, the city of Boston plays a critical role in the upkeep of these institutions as well as the nation's economy. The entire Boston metro area's future is, in part, linked to a highly competitive post-industrial global economy, which is based on research and technological developments. With its two major universities, Harvard and MIT, the region is an inadvertent collaborator in the national government's push for supremacy in the post-industrial world.[3] The post-industrial economy focuses on research and development. The search for new knowledge includes work on topics ranging from biomedical pharmaceuticals to artificial intelligence. Unless the United States strives to be number one in knowledge production and research, its leadership and its rising generations' work careers may be truncated or at least put at risk.

Accordingly, the nascent knowledge economy is not a neologism. As early as 1974, Professor Daniel Bell predicted the coming of the post-industrial society.[4] It defines a new way of organizing work, producing goods, and allocating capital. The new economy has created a business leadership class with different social predispositions than its industrial manufacturing predecessors. These workers are connected to the information age.[5] These new groups seem to be more globally oriented than their manufacturing predecessors. The new knowledge search has created multiple centers of production.

Metro Boston was in the headwinds of this fast-changing economic system. Being a nest for so many researchers, theoreticians, start-up entrepreneurs, educators, and financial investors, Boston attracted a more cerebral and global workforce. The presence of these workers has created a challenge for the extant political class and other interest groups. Many of these workers found themselves in the social orbit of these higher education institutions.

This chapter examines the role of metro higher education institutions in the politics of Boston. For this chapter, the central questions are, How did Menino relate to the leaders of these institutions and students? What were the limits of mayoral authority? If some of these institutions' aspects were outside of City Hall's jurisdiction, what were the overlaps with city policies? What did Menino learn from interacting with these kingpins of academia? In effect, did these institutions have quasi-preemptive powers in their relationship with City Hall? Could their growth imperatives offset mayoral preferences? What was the impact of "studentification" on local community politics and housing? What were the mechanisms of cooperation between these institutions and the mayor's office? Finally, what were the civic engagement obligations of these temporary denizens (students) of metro Boston?

Mayors can make decisions about students without making public statements. Some mayors perceive students as just retail customers. Someone once joked that students in Boston are considered cash cows. They graze off the Boston landscape, acquire their credentials for the job market, and then leave. Simply put, the city makes money off them. However, it isn't that uncomplicated. The town-gown tensions are significant for the entire region.

Town-Gown Tensions

In Boston, with such a concentration of institutions of higher education, town-gown tensions should be expected to be extensive. Granting sanctuary status to learning centers can be traced back to ancient Greece. Since these institutions can devour public resources, the city of Boston has to relate to these institutions. Accordingly, the relationship between higher educational institutions and City Hall ranges from Payments in Lieu of Taxes (PILOT fees) to student safety. In effect, there is an implicit symbiotic relationship.

The city of Boston has grown in part because of these institutions, and these institutions have thrived because of their location in the city. Although these nonprofit institutions own property and receive city services, they do not pay property taxes. Higher education researcher Dale H. Allen's 2012 dissertation studying institutions of higher education, citing a variety of sources, found that

> in Boston, Massachusetts 52% of the non-residential property is owned by nonprofit entities; and 24% of the total land in Boston is owned by nonprofit entities. Boston hosts 36 IHEs, only thirteen of which make a payment in lieu of taxes that amounted to a total of $6.7 million in the fiscal year 2005. If this property were taxable, it would generate an estimated $100 million in annual tax revenue for the City of Boston. Despite their tax-exempt status, these property-intensive IHEs play an important role in shaping local land policy and in influencing market values and neighborhood character.[6]

Boston is an old city, and some tax exempted campuses have buildings (e.g., Harvard College) that predated the installation of the Boston mayoralty and the overall built environment of the metro region. Moreover, Boston emerged as the commercial center of off-campus life for most educational institutions within a twenty-five-mile radius. College students, many of whom are still adolescents, often view the city of Boston with its many campuses as an entertainment center.

This characterization of the city as an entertainment center has been a mixed blessing. Some young students in their late teens and early twenties believe that the college years are a time to test the limits of the adult world and see what happens. It is normal for young people to feel that they are invincible and have no political obligations. For them, they are engaging in a higher calling, which is getting a college education and preparing for their futures. For a variety of reasons, students are encouraged by their colleges and universities to limit their off-campus activities. Yet they are temporary residents of the city. The first challenge for Menino was the expansion needs of higher education institutions.

The Expanding Role of the Colleges and Universities

American higher education institutions are among the elites in the world, and there are few rivals in terms of scientific research and academic talent. They are essential vanguards if the nation expects to stay competitive in the new economy. Accordingly, metro Boston higher educational institutions are fortunate to have some of the best-financed research centers in the nation. The prestige and resources of these centers attract some of the best and brightest. To stay competitive these institutions are under pressure to expand, grow their endowments, and attract national government and foundation funding. Because cities like Boston need to facilitate this expansion to stay in the race for human capital, jobs, and businesses, higher education institutions have leverage. The unspoken bargain is that Boston will provide services, land space, amenities, and so on, and in turn colleges and universities will buy goods and services.

Political scientist Carolyn Adams agrees:

> City officials see the meds' and eds' main impacts largely in terms of investments in their campuses that generate spillover effects on surrounding neighborhoods. When institutional improvements drive neighboring land values upward, the increased revenues to the city help compensate for the property tax exemptions that the institutions enjoy. When the spillovers are negative, city officials often find themselves mediating relationships between campuses and their neighbors. The tendency of city officials to see the institutions primarily as land developers explains why their main policy approach has been to use municipal authority to help assemble land parcels for institutional expansion.[7]

Yet Boston and these entities have different sociopolitical goals. The priority of elected leaders of the city is to serve the interest of the voters and residents. Linda Kowalcky, Menino's liaison to higher education, defined Menino's position: "While Mayor Menino valued all community benefits from higher education, I'd argue that his top priority was increasing educational opportunities for Boston's children. That meant higher ed partnerships with the Boston Public Schools as well as college scholarships for BPS graduates. The majority of our colleges, and universities are expensive, private schools—scholarships open their doors to Boston kids who otherwise could never afford a private college."[8]

In other words, local politicians like Menino wanted to address broader educational policy agendas. The priority of higher education institutions is to raise resources (money); accommodate the interests of faculty (offices, lab space, and benefits), students (classrooms, dorms, and recreation facilities), and staff (offices and responsibilities); and develop on-campus facilities. These goals are by definition limited. The city has the responsibility of elections, economic development, public schools, environment protection, water and sewage, streets, parks and recreation, and public safety. It is the last that generates occasional exchanges between the host city and higher educational institutions.

Higher educational institutional facilities also represent tax burdens, challenges to planning, and traffic problems. As these institutions grow, the older buildings, campus landscapes, and walkways need upgrading, and the demand for quality student housing also increases. Although colleges and universities own and control their properties, they have a stake in the surrounding neighborhoods. When the surrounding community begins to deteriorate, it can have an effect on these institutions' abilities to sell themselves to prospective students and their parents. Ergo, the city has a role in creating a safe environment.

Granted, city amenities and reputations for safety do not enhance the academic standing of colleges and universities but they are consequential. The upkeep of city amenities enhances the outside environment of these institutions The physical plants of universities and colleges are a part of the urban built environment. The buildings provide additional architectural character to their host communities. Since the 1960s, these institutions have been expanding their student populations and upgrading their physical plants to serve these new enrollments. Accordingly, they have to interact with their host communities because they need building permits, zoning exceptions, and fire protection.

To manage these external relationships and demands, the leadership (presidents) of the institutions designate an office to interact and network with city officials. The presidential offices of most colleges and universities have special aides whose responsibility is to make the necessary contacts with city agencies like the Boston Redevelopment Authority (BRA), building inspections, and emergency management. Besides, there are occasions when college presidents will make direct contact with City Hall and the mayor.

The personalities and backgrounds of the mayor and presidents of the institutions matter. Political ideology also matters. Political scientists Thomas Rabovsky and Amanda Rutherford's research found that liberal and conservative presidents view their external duties differently. They argued, "Conservative presidents are more willing to engage those in community and business organizations than their liberal colleagues, perhaps because they are more likely to view these actors as legitimate participants in goal selection and resource allocation. Thus, the ideological views of managers can fundamentally influence both the way they interact with political principals and their perceptions of nonofficial actors."[9] This is a critical point since many college presidents consider themselves liberals. Some liberal academics have elitist attitudes and may be prone to talk down to nonacademics. In any case, sizing up the political environment of the host city, key actors, and interest groups are a part of the president's job description.

Several presidents of institutions of higher education served during the two decades of the Menino administration. Among them were one from Harvard, the Massachusetts Institute of Technology (MIT), Boston University (BU), and Northeastern University. They had to size him up and vice versa. A few had outside visibility like BU's John Silber, who ran for political office; Northeastern University's Richard Freedland; and Harvard's Larry Summers because of his public statements. The other ten presidents had lower profiles, but they had to interact with Menino too. Indeed, BU's Robert A. Brown allegedly developed a good working relationship with Menino. All these presidents decided it was important to meet and interact with the mayor for reasons we will discuss later.

These presidents received coverage in the newspapers, but their audience was rarely working-class Bostonians. It was unlikely that young Tom Menino, growing up in Hyde Park, was aware of the ruminations of university leaders. His family apparently did not know people at these institutions and perhaps neither he nor they were initially impressed with them. This is not unusual for someone from his working-class background. His childhood heroes were probably self-made and family men. It is doubtful that as a young man Menino spent his weekends in Cambridge or hanging around the iconic Harvard Yard. He did not receive a trophy degree from its law school. No one would have predicted that one day he would be mayor of America's Athens. Interacting with academics would become an "acquired taste" for the man from Hyde Park.

Menino Meets the Gowns

What does it mean to be mayor of America's Athens? One is not expected to wear academic garb and make philosophical speeches but one must know how to manage the inevitable town-gown conflicts. The town-gown relationship is a multidimensional affair for both sides. Each has its own realm of influence and is averse to encroachment. Education professor Stephen M. Gavazzi's typology of relationships is useful in understanding the challenge of the town-gown communities.

> The *harmonious relationship*—composed of higher comfort and higher effort levels—is the most desirable form of town gown association (and marriage, for that matter), one where campus and community partners are involved in a significant number of activities that are of shared benefit to all parties involved. The *traditional relationship*—a combination of higher comfort and lower effort levels—is thought to be the default state of affairs for most campuses and communities and the one where higher education and municipal leaders typically ignore each other in the pursuit of separate goals. The *conflicted relationship*—composed of

lower comfort and higher effort levels—consists of less-than-optimal interactions that involve continual friction, but at least the partners are still engaged in a process of trying to work things out. *The devitalized relationship*—a combination of low comfort and low effort levels—is characterized by disappointment and loss owing to the fact that this damaged relationship was at some point more vibrant and satisfying.[10]

In the past, presidents who considered themselves campus insiders may have opted for the traditional relationship, but in modern times, all must gaze at City Hall. Generally speaking, relationships between town and gown require attention and diplomacy. What is the nature of these diplomatic relationships? Given that Menino only had a bachelor's degree in community planning from University of Massachusetts Boston, one might assume that he was not prepared to go one on one with leaders of large and prestigious institutions. Interestingly, UMass Boston happened to be a relatively new institution, so the question for some was how he would interact with leaders of some of the nation's leading and oldest higher education institutions. In a city like Boston, one's college attendance often defined one's social status. Menino did not have an academic pedigree. But he did have a growing political pedigree. And Menino was able to hold his own with these presidents and earn their respect. This was in part because Menino was a perceptive/empathic mayor. He was a discerning individual who was willing to work with any person or institution that wanted to work with him and improve the quality of life in Boston. So, it is not surprising that Menino would try to establish and maintain a harmonious relationship with local higher educational institutions.

As mayor of Boston, there was much to be negotiated with these institutions—housing, zoning, access streets, traffic, parking, and the safety of students, faculty, and staff. As discussed earlier, Menino said that he was not a "fancy speaker." Would Menino be awkward when speaking to their leaders and students? Would he be intimidated and avoid issues that put institutions against the city's interest and his beloved neighborhood protectionist policies? What were the economic impacts of these tax-exempt institutions? Even before Menino became mayor, he had gone on record as being in favor of these institutions' contributing more to the city in lieu of taxes. For him, services and personnel cost money, and cities have incessant budgetary shortfalls. More importantly, cities share a growth imperative similar to higher educational institutions.

The Growth Imperative

In modern times, universities and colleges seem to have adopted a growth imperative, that is, expand or fossilize. Even universities like Suffolk, Northeastern, and UMass Boston, designed to be commuter institutions, succumbed to the trend of building residential dorms. Dorms take space and land. They also need water and sewage connections. Understandably, these expansion decisions will reach a mayor's desk. This is especially true in Boston because of its land impoverishment.

How would Menino handle the land space and the building demands of these institutions? What type of mayoral style would he employ? Remember that parcels in Boston are increasingly valuable and scarce, and the boundaries of the city are fixed. Land use is in some ways a zero-sum game. Higher education administrators are good at the game, but the stakes can get complex. Yesim Sungu-Eryilmaz, a Boston University professor of urban planning, concluded, "The competing interests of the university, the neighborhood, and the city have three implications. First, even in the era of the engaged university, land use and development processes at the campus edge will repeatedly put town-gown relations to the test. Second, nearly all real estate activities of universities and colleges are multifaceted and have multiple stakeholders, including residents, businesses, and local governments. Third, land uses at the campus edge have become a crucial element in both the physical and socioeconomic character of cities and neighborhoods."[11]

When academics speak about the relationship between their institutions and the host city, they use the word "engaged" incessantly. Colleges and universities that want to get something from their host cities must be "engaged" in the narrative about the vision for the city. They must also assist the city when they can. For mayors sharing land space with colleges and universities, this is an extremely delicate matter. Granting more land space to these institutions can be a zero-sum game. To make granting land space work, university expansion projects must be sold as a two-person game in which both sides can claim victory. Educational institutions are immobile however, students are usually only temporary residents, and most of them will leave the city after college.

A mayoral relationship with out-of-state college students is interesting. Students may feel that the Boston mayor has little to do with their lives. They may take public safety and mass transit and sanitation for granted. In effect, students are an audience rather than a quasi-constituency. A mayor cannot lead a city for a student class. Moreover, these lessons were not taught in a "mayoral school" and have to be learned on the job. As mayor, Menino was obligated to put his constituency first or risk electoral revenge.

The so-called student piece is a difficult fit into a governing equation. Colleges and universities bring people from all over the commonwealth of Massachusetts and the nation to Boston. They may come with a sense of entitlement and expectations. Students need housing at a time when the city is short on affordable housing for permanent residents. Accordingly, a mayor is forced to balance the needs of residents with those of students. Granted, the two groups may want different types of housing. Students are less likely to want to live in single-family bungalows and at great distances from their colleges. They expect modern apartments with amenities.

Herein lies the potential for conflicts. Social scientist Darren P. Smith calls the process the "politics of studentification" since it can instigate gentrification.[12] Social scientists Joanna Sage, Darren Smith, and Phil Hubbard define the concept of studentification: "Conceptually, the term is ubiquitously employed to describe the impacts of relatively high numbers of university students migrating into established residential neighborhoods—a process that triggers a gamut of distinct social, economic, cultural, and physical transformations."[13] Any higher education institutional office of student affairs will attest to the problems of mixing students with so-called regular neighborhood residents. Students and local residents use the street differently and they expect others to respect public behavior codes. Until 2004, the city did not have a census of students by neighborhood. The city then passed the University Accountability Ordinance, which required colleges and universities to report student residences by zip code. Commuting state colleges and community colleges were exempt because they did not have residential facilities. In a 2006 report, a BRA study stated,

> The City of Boston continues to partner with residents and universities to minimize any adverse impact from students' presence in residential neighborhoods. Each September, for example, Mayor Menino leads a successful Student Turnover Campaign that brings together a team of city agencies to inspect apartments, remove trash, and ensure the smooth flow of traffic during the busy move-in season. And to welcome new student neighbors, the Mayor joins residents and university representatives

in walking the neighborhoods and sharing information with them as well as his expectations about what it means to be a good neighbor in Boston.[14]

Most students who study in the metro Boston area were not born and raised in Boston. Most would never visit some of its venerated neighborhoods, such as Mission Hill and Brighton, of which Menino was so proud. These are young people in search of knowledge and fun, not urban history. The city is an entertainment center, and this fun-seeking can become a minor management problem for the city. Even the places and time for fun have to be negotiated, just as there are more issues of facilities expansion.

The Negotiation Norm

Most of the negotiations between these institutions and the city are conducted with a low profile. Some of the facility expansion negotiations between the city and institutions are done by the BRA and with its planning unit. The institution has to draw up a plan, and the plan must be approved by the BRA. However, the mayor is a key figure since they approve the BRA proposal and have to recommend and promote the proposal to the City Council and the public.

City agencies are also affected. Zoning issues are created by the City Council and the zoning board. Public safety departments such as police and fire have ongoing relations with campus police and security offices. In other words, there are many disparate jurisdictions involved. Nevertheless, the intersection of City Hall and these institutions was and still is critical to the future of Boston. Obviously, City Hall and these institutions cannot safely ignore each other. Again, there will be normal town-gown tensions, but concessions have to be made on each side. Otherwise, there would be endless conflicts. In the 1960s, planning professor Kermit Parson believed that the terms of this relationship were a truce:

> In recent years many urban universities have decided that life in the city is one of the assets of civilization. Some of them are developing new attitudes toward the potential of their city sites, toward their neighborhood environments, and toward local urban-renewal policies. It would be incorrect to claim that a permanent peace has ended warfare between universities and cities; the current state of affairs is more like a truce. The war has never been very fierce, and neither party has

gained many worth-while objectives. The strategy of the universities has been characterized either by retreat before the advance of the city or by voluntary isolation from it. The tactics of the universities and their scholars have been limited to occasional sallies from their ivory towers to throw fine intellectual dust, verbal pebbles, and occasionally a useful critical rock at the follies of cities. For their part, city officials and most citizens hardly knew that the universities were there. They did little or nothing to preserve and advance educational institutions when they were threatened by physical and social change in the city.[15]

In Boston, some universities have thrown more fine intellectual dust and verbal pebbles than others. Given Mayor Menino's personality, he might not have felt affronted on such occasions but when those occasions did occur, he opted to find a way to get things done. In other words, Menino approached the challenge as he did others: be ready to negotiate. Keeping the truce and avoiding open warfare was in both parties' interest.

Menino faced more of these challenges because he was a long-serving mayor. Put simply, Boston mayors must get along with higher education institutions because they have to, and vice versa. Again, these institutions are immobile organizations. They cannot relocate. Granted, they perform an income-generating function. They have inherent leverage, but so does City Hall. Planning professor Eugenie Birch did a study of the role of northeast megaregion anchor institutions and their relationship to economic development and land use. She concludes, "Boston provides one example with its requirement for Institutional Master Plans as a prerequisite for land use permissions. While time-consuming and expensive in the short run, this device, a city-wide requirement applying to all institutions, allows for transparency and negotiation in a relatively neutral environment. And, in many cases, it provides direction for agency work. For example, for Harvard's project in Allston, the Boston Redevelopment Authority undertook the broad planning work necessary to contextualize upcoming institutional efforts."[16]

Consider the conflict over the 1989 secret purchase of land by Harvard University in Boston. With the Harvard Allston Campus Planning and Institutional Master Plan, the university quietly bought fifty-two acres in Allston over a nine-year period for $88 million. The surreptitious purchase was made by Beal Companies, a Boston developer. This increased the university's holdings in the city by a third. With this purchase, the university owns almost as much land in Boston as in Cambridge (192 and 220 acres respectively).[17] The university wanted to expand the Harvard Business School and build student facilities in another part of the property. If Harvard builds on the land, it will take the property off the tax rolls (estimated to be worth $1.5 billion). Journalist Sara Rimer described Allston "as a blue-collar neighborhood of three-decker homes, auto shops and Vietnamese, Brazilian, Greek, and Italian restaurants that reflect its ethnic diversity."[18] As soon as Menino found out about it, he attacked the university in a letter to President Neil Rudenstine as being "arrogant—the highest level of arrogance seen in our city in many years. You have to be upfront with the people, upfront with the city."[19] Joan Nolan, president of the Brighton Allston Improvement Association, said, "It's very disappointing when you realize someone with a $9 billion endowment will stoop to these levels."[20] The *Boston Globe* called it a "Stealthy Land Grab."[21] This scheme was done to deter neighborhood outcry of Harvard imperialism.

In 2012, Harvard submitted an Institutional Master Plan Notification Form (IMPNF) which outlined seven new constructions, including building a replacement for the Business School, athletic facilities, and a hotel/conference center. It also entailed the renovation of a business school building and Soldiers Field Park Housing. The IMPNF noted the 2006 Menino's seventeen members Harvard Allston Task Force helped plan the development. It noted that Harvard had 151.1 acres of land and planned to add 27 acres of land.[22]

Making the Land Snatchers Pay

During Mayor Menino's tenure, the city of Boston remained under fiscal stress. Dwindling taxes and escalating costs were dual threats to his economic development and the pursuit of resources for the disadvantaged. Boston had to pay its bills and meet the rising inflation costs. Hence it needed all institutions utilizing municipal services to help out. Payments in lieu of taxes (PILOT) were a revenue mechanism. In Menino's last year in office, "the City received $23.2 million in PILOT contributions in the fiscal year 2013, a 53.1 percent increase over what was previously paid under the prior PILOT program in the fiscal year 2011. This amount represents 82.3 percent of the $28.2 million requested PILOT amount."[23] Table 4 shows exempted properties including higher education institutions.

Table 4. Types of Exempt Property Owners

OWNERSHIP	ACRES	PERCENT OF TOTAL EXEMPT LAND	PERCENT OF TOTAL CITY LAND
STATE PROPERTY	7,519	51.2%	25.8%
Massport	2,580	17.6%	8.8%
Metropolitan District Commission	1,652	11.2%	5.7%
Massachusetts Bay Transportation	702	4.8%	2.4%
Authority Turnpike	207	1.4%	0.7%
Other MA	2,377	16.2%	8.1%
CITY PROPERTY	4,211	28.7%	14.4%
PARKS AND PLAYGROUNDS	2,023	13.8%	6.9%
Boston Redevelopment Authority and Economic Development Industrial Corporation	406	2.8%	1.4%
Boston Housing Authority	375	2.6%	1.3%
Other City	1,407	9.6%	4.8%
HIGHER EDUCATION AND MEDICAL INSTITUTIONS	661	4.5%	2.3%
Colleges and Universities	445	3.0%	1.5%
Medical/Scientific	216	1.5%	0.7%
OTHER EXEMPT INSTITUTIONS	2,295	15.6%	7.9%
CEMETERIES	768	5.2%	2.6%
Cultural Organizations, Museums, Private Elementary Schools	410	2.8%	1.4%
Religious Organizations	285	1.9%	1.0%
Benevolent Organizations	86	0.6%	0.3%
Other	747	5.1%	2.6%
TOTAL	14,689	100%	50%

Source: Tax Exempt Property in Boston, Analysis of Types, Uses, and Issues, City of Boston, Boston Redevelopment Authority, FY2000, 4, https://www.bostonplans.org. The numbers presented are as in the original and reflect tallying errors there.

Aside from asking educational institutions to compensate the city with student scholarships in return for the land, Menino negotiated deals with universities. In 1999, he reached a deal in which Harvard would increase its voluntary PILOT by over $40 million over the next twenty years. This was $12 million more than previous PILOTs. At that time, the school had a plan to build 288 apartments elsewhere in Allston. *New York Times* reporter Carey Goldberg quoted Menino as saying it was "a new day" for Harvard-Boston cooperation. Harvard president Neil Rudenstine praised the mayor "for his leadership and the quality of his team." Goldberg quoted Paul Grogan, a Harvard vice president, as saying, "There was consternation several years ago about the acquisition of property in the Allston neighborhood, so part of this is all about getting the relationship firmly on the right track. And you do that by building respect and trust and having a positive and open discussion that leads to a good result."[24]

In 2009, Harvard planned to build a new $1 billion science complex in Allston.[25] The Harvard Business School and Harvard Stadium were already located in Allston.[26] Simply put, the university needed more space to accommodate its growth. The plan included a new building for the Harvard Business School, new classrooms, new athletic fields, and more student housing. Interestingly, the entire process was not that controversial because Menino and the BRA worked with the university. After twelve years of negotiations between the city and the university, people in the neighborhood were surprised at Harvard's plan. The Harvard University endowment of $36.9 billion had lost 22 percent, or $8 billion, during the Great Recession, prompting the university to delay construction. Millions had already been spent buying properties. Menino called the delay "a grave disappointment." In a letter to Harvard president Drew Gilpin Faust, Menino wrote, "Our decision must be made together. The university may not make unilateral decisions."[27] *New York Times* reporter Abby Goodnough asserted, "The rats are out in spades this spring in North Allston, a gritty neighborhood wedged between the Charles River and the Massachusetts Turnpike, and residents are blaming Harvard." Goodnough quoted Harry Mattison, who served as an advisor to the Harvard Allston Task Force: "We feel like we've been betrayed and taken advantage of. Instead of Harvard bringing in jobs and excitement and vibrancy, we are sliding backward."[28] The suspended project left a gaping hole and rats, potentially discouraging people from opening retail shops in the area.

Harvard had to admit that it had violated the community's trust. In a statement, Harvard agreed to continue to work with City Hall. In 2013, the city of Boston approved a nine-building, 1.4-million-square-foot set of construction projects. For the *Harvard Crimson*, a university newspaper, the project had the potential of creating a "new Allston similar to the Kendall Square rise in the '80s and '90s and the more recent dramatic growth of the South Boston Innovation District."[29] Students and nonstudents would have to make street adjustments. According to sociologist Elijah Anderson, people from different classes and races have to become "streetwise" and learn to interact without conflict with each other in the same social space.[30] Would the residents of the academic sanctuaries interact with so-called townies? Would they meet under what Anderson calls a "cosmopolitan canopy"?[31]

The Norm of Mutual Recognition

Metro Boston's institutions have been at the forefront of shepherding in the new knowledge basis systems required for the post-industrial society. Knowledge-producing organizations such as universities, research startups, development firms, think tanks, and financial management firms often live in silos in the post-industrial society, but their needs are essentially the same. Cities, industries, and universities are a part of what has been called the Triple Helix. Professor Henry Etzkowitz stated, "The Triple Helix thesis postulates that the interaction in university-industry-government is key to improving the conditions of innovation in a knowledge-based society. The industry operates in the Triple Helix as the locus of the production; government as the source of contractual relations that guarantee stable interactions and exchange; the university as a source of new knowledge and technology, the generative principle of knowledge-based economics."[32]

Increasingly, metro Boston, because of its history of great universities and colleges, found itself at the nexus of the future economy and American cities. No Boston mayor has campaigned against higher education institutions, and few institutional presidents have launched a fight with City Hall. Instead, they look for opportunities to praise each other. It is not a one-way relationship but is quasi-symbiotic. *Boston Globe* reporter Joan Vennochi acknowledged the clout of these institutions when Tom Menino decided to deliver his second State of the City Address at Emerson College. Menino was showcasing Emerson because of its commitment to downtown development. Menino observed, "Why are the universities important? They give us the brain power, and they help feed the businesses of Boston. You are always able to call upon the universities to find an expert to help you think through an issue. You can't do it alone."[33] The audience for this speech included presidents from local colleges and universities. Presidents knew that being there mattered as it allowed them to network with city officials. For most of the attendees, it was a growth planning affair. And they did not expect the mayor to indicate a preference for a particular type of town-gown relationship.

Marketing itself as the Athens of America, Boston has attracted many generations of leading academics to its metro region. In many ways, the reputation of some of these institutions is a natural magnet for students. These institutions can legitimately claim to educate the children of the business elites, political leaders, and scientists of the nation and the world. Boston is known as an academic agglomeration, when students and scholars congregate geographically.

These institutions range from those with the largest enrollment, like Boston University, to the most prestigious, like Harvard University, the nation's oldest higher educational institution. MIT is specialized institution focusing on science. Each school adds to the city's economy and academic diversity.

Boston, Education, and Economics

At the beginning of the fall and spring semesters, students enroll in these local institutions. They arrive with U-Hauls, with boxes and suitcases, and often with their parents. Every year there is a new wave of fresh faces. Some have never visited the city except for a campus visit. The arrival of new students is a windfall for local retailers. Students buy everything from food to emblazoned clothing. Obviously, the financial impact of student spending is significant, but the long-term development of human capital development is more important for the city. Professor Annette Steinacker points out, "Universities can be valuable contributors to a city's economy. They are immobile institutions fairly resistant to business cycle fluctuations, making them a steady presence in the community. They tend to attract revenue from outside the immediate area through tuition, endowment income or state tax allocations and to attract significant human capital—students and employees from a national market—that can contribute to the area's economic growth."[34]

According to planning professors Meagan M. Ehlenz and Sarah Mawhorter, universities are ingrained in city-region identities.[35] Higher educational institutions are considered gold mines for cities, though the assigned value for them depends on who is making the evaluation. Overall, the value of attending college seems to have increased with changes in the economy.

In a post-industrial economy with its knowledge-based ethos, the value of a college education has increased exponentially. Having such an education can improve one's career and life chances. In its inception, Harvard was valued for its training for divinity careers, and it taught the classics. Modern-day Harvard is a multidimensional educational operation with a variety of academic disciplines. Northeastern University, once a city or commuting school, is now a more regional and national institution. In each case, the value of the institutions has increased because these institutions have influenced the nation's economic future. Many more Americans want professional careers and are willing to spend money to make that happen. Accordingly, small downtown retailers in Boston are figuratively miners expecting to strike it rich. They expect to sell to students everything ranging from cellphones to fast food. Students are walking spenders. Each institution has a retail impact on its surrounding community. The largest enrollment, the bigger the economic impact. Table 5 shows the enrollment of selected colleges and universities in the metro Boston area.

Table 5. Enrollment at Selected List of Higher Education Institutions, 2019

INSTITUTION	TYPE	ENROLLMENT
Berklee College of Music	Private, nonprofit	4,255
Boston College	Private, nonprofit	14,605
Boston University	Private, nonprofit	32,603
Brandeis University	Private, nonprofit	5,808
Emerson College	Private, nonprofit	4,431
Harvard University	Private, nonprofit	28,149
Lesley University	Private, nonprofit	5,944
MIT	Private, nonprofit	11,189
Northeastern University	Private, nonprofit	20,053
Tuft University	Private, nonprofit	10,872
UMass Boston	Public	16,277

Source: Reported enrollments by colleges and universities, taken from their websites, 2019

The table shows that most of the universities and colleges in the metro Boston region are nonprofit and tax-exempt, though they do still make a direct financial contribution to the city. Obviously, this table does not show all of the institutions of higher education in the area. The student population is actually much higher.

Managing a city with a multibillion-dollar budget necessitates a more dependable source of revenue than street spending. Retail tax is an important source of income, but it can never be a sustaining source of revenue. The largest source of revenue for the city is its property taxes. Businesses and homeowners pay these taxes. Conversely, cities like Boston also exist in an environment where federal and state buildings are exempt from city taxes. The city cannot even expect in-kind payments. Tax-exempted state and federal facilities located in the city are also not taxable. The city has less jurisdiction over the latter. However, these institutions use police, fire, and sewage services.

In the case of higher education, there has been a history of schemes to get them to pay a service fee, a flat charge for municipal services delivered. In 1984, the Massachusetts Supreme Judicial Court ruled in *Emerson College v. City of Boston* that charging fees for these services was unconstitutional.[36] Since these institutions have large workforces, the city benefits from taxing payrolls. These institutions also purchase a lot of goods and services in the local marketplace.

One of the rarely spoken narratives is the fact that higher education institutions have also made large sums of money from sources besides tuition and fees. At one point in its history, Harvard University's endowment allegedly exceeded $40 billion. The university had to create staff positions to manage its investments. Over the years this type of money-making has become more apparent. Sometimes these universities used some of this money to support local projects. It is not uncommon for alumni at schools like Harvard and MIT to donate several million dollars. These contributions are heavily covered by the media. But an explanation is not always given as to how the money is used. This may explain why some politicians became dissatisfied with the financial arrangements the city had with these institutions. This frustration grew out of the fact that tax-exempt universities and hospitals were clearly in an operating aggrandizement mode, that is, seeking to improve their rankings among other similar institutions.

In 1993, Boston mayor Ray Flynn made the argument that these institutions should pay more. As a councilor and as chair of the Ways and Means Committee on the City Council, Menino joined the chorus demanding that universities pay more. He stated, "The days of not paying their fair share are over. They've had it too good for too long. If they're bringing in money, they should pay their fair share." Yet, Clare Cotton of the Association of Independent Colleges and Universities in Massachusetts told *Boston Globe* reporter Peter S. Canellos, "The mayor can't have it both ways. He can't tax these institutions so that they become uncompetitive and then say they're a vital part of the city's economic future."[37] Obviously, there is a difference between taxing directly and panhandling. Once Menino became mayor he proved that he was not intimidated by these institutions. Menino did ask Harvard for money and received it. For instance, Harvard contributed to Menino's 2003 affordable housing initiative. The inclination to expect more from higher education institutions may be related to the fact they want more of their host city's land.[38]

The Soft Practice of Land Grabs

As stated earlier, Boston is not overly endowed with land space. Any grant of land to any entity means there is less of it to allocate elsewhere. Universities and colleges increasingly occupy larger tracts of land and therefore require more and more city services. There are the necessary zoning decisions, building permits, and traffic decisions. Universities are less likely to build skyscrapers unless they are forced to do. They prefer building facilities close to a central campus.

When institutions want to expand further, it takes away space and sometimes taxable properties from the city. Obviously, Boston needs these institutions, and they need City Hall. To make this relationship work, there need to be negotiations. The city cannot do this alone as state and community leaders often want to participate in these negotiations.

This was the case when Northeastern University wanted to change its profile from a commuter and local school to a regional research university. It wanted to develop the Northeastern University–Davenport Commons. This project was designed for 879 students with commercial space and 60 affordable housing units. In 1996, Northeastern University hired the Madison Davenport Partners to develop the project. One of the partners was the Lower Roxbury Community Corporation. According to planning professor Jonathan G. Cooper and colleagues, this turned out to be a good strategy because it deflected anticipated community criticisms away from the university.[39]

The project became a success because it combined the university's interest with the community's need for affordable housing. In 2003, the project won the Maxwell Award for excellence and innovation in the creation of affordable home-ownership opportunities. Cooper and colleagues found the 50/50 split of land was symbolic for the Roxbury community:

> Davenport Commons represented a different vision. Instead of being a university enclave in the city, Davenport Commons incorporated the wishes and needs of community members. The university presence was

reduced to 610 beds in 125 units, all 60 of the residences were owner-occupied, and retail space had been increased to 2,100 square feet. The original development layout had been altered to separate the student from non-student households. Students were now housed in taller structures on the north side of the parcel, and moderate-income owner-ship units along the southern side. . . . Additionally, the decision to focus exclusively on home ownership responded to the neighborhood's belief that ownership would provide residential stability in the area. The community's interest in reclamation and ownership stemmed from events that had taken place decades earlier, but were recalled with frustration and bitterness by longtime residents.[40]

In 1997, Menino had his first encounter with this trend. The BRA approved an 880-room Northeastern University student dormitory in Lower Roxbury. Black leaders opposed the project, but they were initially ignored. Then the *Bay State Banner* ran an editorial headlined, "Blacks Don't Count."[41] How could the mayor defend this project without possibly alienating Black citizens when they represented 27 percent of the voting population? Through 1998, the university, community leaders, and the BRA continued to negotiate. After more protests, a group of Black leaders met with Menino. Menino called the meeting "amicable" but one of the leaders of the meeting, Sadiki Kambon, a community activist, called the mayor "very stubborn."[42] The BRA approved a preliminary deal in 2000, and the university began planning for its dorm rooms.[43] Obviously, there was a fear of student spillover and what Darren Smith has called "studentification." In 2004, the *Bay State Banner* reported that 55 percent of the 14,000 students at Northeastern University lived on campus. It pointed out that this number "leaves more than 6,000 often rowdy students competing for apartments in the low-income neighborhoods that surround the school."[44]

The management of this project can be a lesson for other universities. Planning should be alert to house-searching by other residents in the community. Just working with the BRA to coordinate and plan was not enough. Using a third party was best to facilitate a project. In 2002, the BRA supported a Boston University proposal to build a new 1,500-bed dormitory and arena. It allowed BU to offer on-campus housing to 100 percent of its undergraduate students. The project included a 6,100-seat arena with 1,000 parking spaces. The new project, located in Allston, would replace the historic Commonwealth Armory Headhouse. The next year BRA approved BU's Master Plan.[45] Interestingly, these projects were planned to minimize neighborhood encroachment by these institutions.

In 2004, Northeastern University again wanted more dorms. It claimed that roughly half of its students lived on campus. Boston councilor Michael Row, whose district included Northeastern, advocated for the university to increase its dorms to house 75 percent of its students. He stated, "I think they need to build more on campus. . . . Because it's becoming less of a commuter school and more of a destination school, they need to bring those folks onto their campus because Boston can't accommodate the influx of students."[46]

Obviously, building dorms and other facilities brings City Hall and these institutions together. They are obligated to negotiate and make deals. This is the essence of transactional politics. During these encounters, City Hall staff only met with higher education institutions' presidents and vice presidents for intergovernmental affairs. Otherwise, their work domains are kept at a social distance.

Nurtured Isolation of Institutions

It is often said that universities know more about the outside than the outside community knows about them. History professor Margaret P. O'Mara observes, "The elite American research university has to a great degree physically and psychically separated its campus from the city. The feeling has tended to be mutual."[47] This is not to imply that Boston professors and administrators from different campuses routinely interact with each other.

There is little interaction among members of the colleges and universities in metro Boston. The various higher education institutions recruit students from different demographics. Harvard and MIT recruit from a national pool of high school students, whereas UMass Boston and Suffolk University recruit from the metro areas. There is also a tiered status structure in some disciplines for faculties and staff at different institutions. Faculties at high-status universities rarely collaborate on academic projects with those at low-status institutions. Universities and college professors are among the most status-conscious workers in America. Institutions within the metro Boston communities seek to carve out images and reputations for themselves. In 1970, Professor Leonard E. Goodall stated, "The point is not to beat Harvard at its own game, but to create new games that may be more clearly related to the problems of the community served by the urban university."[48] This quest has continued into the twenty-first century.

Harvard University and MIT recruit students from all over the nation and the world. Boston University also has a large foreign student population. Few institutions are so clearly aware of their global reach as Harvard and MIT. Their institutional neighbors are Boston College, Northeastern University, and Suffolk University. The last of these is considered more regionally oriented, and that is reflected in its students.

Presidents of these institutions may know each other's names but there is little need or incentive to visit or consult with each other. The boards of trustees do not evaluate them in a comparative sense. Since most are nonprofit institutions and not taxable, they are also not evaluated by profit margins. Simply put, these institutions are reviewed in terms of balanced budgets, student enrollments, graduation rates, and faculty production. As a part of their annual reports, some universities report to their boards of trustees that they have done impact studies to support their claims of creating services and jobs over generating tax revenues. They claim to have a multiplier effect on surrounding retail shops.

Economic professors John Siegfried, Allen R. Sanderson, and Peter McHenry caution us about the reliability of these studies. According to them, "The purpose of many of these economic impact studies is to articulate the value of an institution of higher education, including spillover effects, often to help the institution compete for state funding (or resist cutbacks), maintain tax-exempt status, obtain a subvention, fend off criticism, or bolster fundraising."[49] Professor Margaret O'Mara reaches a similar conclusion:

> University-driven economic development efforts are products of their times, operate upon multiple dimensions, and are reflective of the broader social and political debates and biases of a given era. The way that universities and their advocates have talked about economic development has not always corresponded with the actions they have taken, partly because of circumstance and partly because of organizational capacity. They have reflected less on a broader philosophy of public service and more on the universities' political and fiscal circumstances at that historical moment. As a consequence, discussions of university public service have often revolved around the degree to which universities' receipt of federal and state appropriations obligate it to respond to social problems, and actions around economic development have depended on what kinds of public funds were available to tackle a given economic or social problem.[50]

Implicit in those impact studies is the idea that it is the institution's job to herd the cash cows (students) to pump the retail sector. And in turn that local politicians and city officials will stay of out of their affairs. Outreach does happen but it is usually in terms of mutual interest.

Urban Outreach and Research

This relationship between the region and its schools has its unspoken but implicit understanding. Of course, these institutions must be seen as good and supportive citizens. This has been done through an interesting prism. Universities create knowledge to improve society. They make reports that are useful for policymakers. This means that the host city may become the target of urban and public school research. Universities are happy to assist in planning, report writing, and research because such projects help their graduate student learning and research programs. This phenomenon results in more than public relations for administrators, faculty, and students.

Universities and colleges have a history of attempting to provide services for their host states and cities. Land-grant university extension services are examples of university researchers aiding state farmers and ranchers. Some urban universities have established urban extension offices for their host cities. In the 1960s, Professor John E. Bebout suggested university urban extension services provide what is learned from social science research and apply it to urban change. He observed, "In spite of the apparent simplicity of the general idea of the urban extension service, it is, according to the testimony of virtually everyone charged with developing it, very difficult to conceptualize in terms of its probable ultimate form, dimensions, and consequences. Nevertheless, the role is vital and manageable and universities can come to terms with it." Moreover, he continued,

> The university should not hope through agents of its own to become the principal retailer of all kinds of knowledge needed to enable men to control urban destiny. It should rather devote its energies to what might be described as the frontier of urban extension, exploring and testing new ways of relating its intellectual resources to the need of the community for urban knowledge. As it moves into new frontiers it should seek to leave along the way trained persons, institutional arrangements, and habits of mind—especially among urban decision-makers at all levels— that will so function as to enable it in good conscience to disengage its resources from established or repetitive operations and re-invest them in exploration.[51]

Tom Menino might not have known this relationship in Bebout's terms, but enlightened higher education leaders should have. Professor John Cronin acknowledged that universities have attempted to help the Boston school system. Aside from training teachers and research, Boston University's John

Silber offered to take over the management of the BPS three times. Harvard University's partnership with Roxbury High School did not work but it did establish a Principals' Center. MIT also had a partnership with the East Boston Umana School, but it did not survive. Cronin stated, "Dr. Payzant found too many isolated interventions . . . did not raise student achievement scores."[52] He asked them to work on his Whole School Improvement project.

When Richard M. Freeland assumed the presidency at Northeastern University, he pledged to work with Boston public schools and on issues of healthcare. He stated, "My goal will be to help Northeastern define clearly and sustain a particular role within higher education, and not try to be another variation on Harvard. . . . Our role has everything to do with education-oriented toward preparing people for the workplace."[53] He stated that Boston school superintendent Thomas Payzant had asked the university for help with the so-called cluster four programs (i.e., schools with student achievement problems). The schools included Farragut, Hale, Tobin, and Young Achievers Elementary Schools; Timilty and Lewis Middle Schools; and Madison Park and O'Bryant High Schools. These projects earned the university good neighborhood credit. In an article in the *Chronicle of Higher Education*, Freeland stated,

> At Northeastern, where urban engagement is central to our institutional character, we are participating in two efforts to take the idea of university-community partnership to a new level. We are working with the Boston Redevelopment Authority and a city-appointed, community-based task force to review the development needs of both the university and the surrounding areas, with the goal of crafting a physical master plan for the university that also advances the interests of our neighbors. Simultaneously, we are part of a coalition of local colleges and universities and representatives of key nonacademic constituencies, working under the auspices of the Boston Foundation to improve our region while also promoting Boston's all-important academic sector.[54]

Offering to help the city with its mission also gets these institutions good local and sometimes national publicity. Professors Lee Benson and Ira Harkavy go so far as to say, "We think it axiomatic that universities (particularly elite research universities with selective arts and sciences colleges) function as the primary shaper of the overall American schooling system."[55] Indeed, asking universities to assist with public schools is nothing new for large cities. Most universities have schools of education where they train teachers and do research. There is a direct pipeline between teacher training institutions and Boston's school system. Yet there are problems associated with the system that hires the new teachers and their former training institutions. There are recurring issues with the applicant's pedagogic training, licensing, and commitment.[56]

However, attempting to implement interorganizational relations between the Boston School Committee and education schools is difficult. Sociology professor Herman Turk believed the size and diversity of cities was critical to interorganizational relations. Although his references were to hospital councils, his analysis is useful in understanding the problems higher education institutions and cities like Boston face with trying to interact with each other and city leaders. Turk observed,

> This means that the more densely populated a city is with organizations and the more they interact with one another, the more the city resembles a market or an arena of conflict, the looser and less permanent its coalitions, and the less centralized its means of concerted action. Such a multiorganizational city may be called a "fluid community."
> Under these conditions the capacity of the city for linking some of its organizations into temporary or permanent networks rests partly on the ability that the same or different organizations have to operate in a partly conflictual, competitive, and rapidly changing environment.[57]

Boston's higher education community is by definition a fluid one. Therefore, there is little benefit for institutions in staying in a permanent coalitional relationship. Because Boston is so invested in higher education, it has to tolerate a permanent fluid community and has to work with institutions separately. Accordingly, it is difficult for a mayor to establish an overall plan for dealing with these institutions. Mayors may seek to gain allies within the institutional leadership, but these leaders want to create distance from city politics and to fend off encroachment.

Fear of Encroachment

When considering these issues, the mayor and his staff usually asked the following questions: What are exclusive campus jurisdictions—buildings, classrooms, dormitories, campus quads, cross streets? What is the basis for concurrent city/institution jurisdictions—access streets, student violence, and authorized off-campus organizations? In cases of state institutions, what are the legitimate functions of state departments of education—appointment of institutional leadership, budget oversights, and regulations of institutional foundations? In other words, the commonwealth of Massachusetts has some oversight responsibility for secondary state institutions. These institutions get an appropriation from Massachusetts. In claiming to speak for higher education in Massachusetts, state agencies do not have day-to-day control over state institutions. This is not to say that these institutions are free to violate state laws and regulations.

Colleges and universities see themselves as preparing students for later life and for researching for the general society. Yet they often regard evaluative comments from elected leaders of the host community as a public relations challenge to their mission. The problem occurs when there are overlapping activities in which the campus and local authority claim exclusive ownership. For example, violent crime on campus can engage campus police and Boston's police department. In some instances, the city and these institutions are not prepared to acknowledge the other's claims. This occurs if there is a violent protest demonstration or a felony crime on campus. City officials may regard such incidents as within its jurisdiction but some Boston police interactions with student protests are considered encroachment by the university. For university and college leaders, organizational autonomy is either truly at stake or is perceived to be. Each campus handles police calls differently. This is why there are rarely joint crime statements by university presidents and city officials.

University leaders know that possibility of encroachment can occur at any time. In 1997, an MIT student, Scott Krueger, died from alcohol overconsumption. Menino reacted by proposing a city ordinance mandating that local colleges register any party hosting fifty or more people with his Consumer Affairs and Licensing office. He also wanted to file two home-rule petitions that would have made it a crime for students to manufacture or distribute fake identification cards to buy liquor. Mayor Menino observed that off-campus parties were common among colleges and universities. He noted, "A keg contains 198 glasses of 10-ounce beer. Clearly, such purchases are not for public consumption. College is meant to be fun and educational, but it should also be safe." At first glance, this action seemed innocuous, but some universities regarded it as a light form of encroachment. The key is the relationship between the campus police and the Boston Police Department. The *Boston Herald* reporter Jack Meyers quoted a couple of reactions from university officials:

> Kevin Duffy, a top Boston College official, testified yesterday, "I think you have a full-court press in this area." He said BC has its own patrols to police student parties and works closely with the Boston Police to shut down parties where illegal drinking takes place. Tom Keady, Northeastern University's director of government relations, said the school last year expelled 65 students for violating the university's code

of conduct. He noted that Northeastern officials have worked with local liquor stores to restrict alcohol deliveries in the neighborhood but not all merchants are cooperating.[58]

In other words, the universities were managing this situation and more city regulatory efforts were not necessary. For them, Menino's proposals would not work and represented an encroachment on student life and a violation of their sanctuary status. In 2002, Menino created Operation Student Shield. This was a partnership between the Boston Police Department and campus police. It was designed to designate inappropriate off-campus behavior in the student codes of conduct (e.g., off-campus drinking). This policy eased some of the relations between the police and students, but the latter were not above invoking their so-called sanctuary immunity, that is, shelter from regular Boston police officers' surveillance.

In general, encroachment occurs when one institution invades the exclusive policy domain of another institution. Encroachment also implies that at a previous time, one organization had exclusive control over a specified domain and now that was being challenged. Accordingly, encroachment is different from organizational interactions or exchanges. Sociology professors Sol Levine and Paul White defined organizational exchange as "any voluntary activity between two organizations which has consequences, actual and anticipated, for the realization of their respective goals or objective."[59] The keyword is "voluntary," and Menino continued voluntary exchanges with higher education institutions.

Voluntary is a charged word for the leaders of higher education. They are aware of the need to move out of their original campus spaces. To remain competitive, they needed more public space, upgrades for existing facilities, and better access to streets. Student dorms and apartments must be continually upgraded to attract students and parents. Students may want to be identified with an old famous dorm but they expect it to be modernized.

For these institutions, what are the possible exchanges or bargaining opportunities? Negotiations become the currency used to engage with city officials. Like any negotiation, higher education usually starts by suggesting a large project and then lures the city into accepting a small one.

Even universities designed to be commuter institutions (Suffolk University, UMass Boston) have had to build residence halls to be competitive with other local institutions. Residential facilities allow institutions to recruit statewide and regionally. For state schools, out-of-state students pay higher tuition. More students mean more residential facilities, which attract more students.

Building a new building or rehabilitating an old one often involved taking space from the surrounding neighborhoods. Consequently, it can require intense negotiations with City Hall. This was the case when Boston University wanted to build a School of Management. Despite a legal battle, the university succeeded in building a $100 million, nine-story building with a view of the Charles River. As with many extremely tall or oversized buildings, this one changed the skyline of Boston.[60]

Suffolk University was once a primary commuter institution until its profile changed. Students wanted to live near their classrooms. Residential facilities represented the fact that the university needed to recruit beyond the city of Boston. In 2006, the university wanted a thirty-one-floor tower with eight hundred student beds. The Beacon Hill Civic Association, near where Suffolk is located, opposed this proposal. The discussion lasted for two years. In 2008, Menino supported a 274-bed residence hall at Suffolk. Indeed, Menino spoke out for the smaller facilities. He declared, "I'm delighted to see Suffolk University joining the Downtown Crossing Community. Suffolk students will greatly add to the vitality of this area and ensure that it remains vibrant at all hours of the day."[61]

Students without Civic Responsibility

What are the civic obligations, if any, for students living and studying in metro Boston? In America, students over eighteen years of age can vote but few become active in local political affairs and campaigns. Many do not vote in local elections. Students often consider themselves what political scientist Peter Eisinger called a visitor class.[62] They may have some general knowledge about urban social problems but are less likely to be aware of Boston's recurrent politics and even less about the City Council and mayoral election candidates.

Since students who study in the metro area benefit from living in such a high-profile educational environment, should they have some obligations to the city? At first glance, there seems to be little if any quid pro quo relationship between students and the city. A closer look reveals that students are both a visitor class and a source of revenue. However, unlike hotels, the city cannot charge them a user fee. Accordingly, interacting with students is a difficult process because there is little if any recreational coordination between the city and Boston's higher education institutions. Students and city officials are aware of each other but try to stay out of each other's way. These institutions are aware of these economic impacts on the city.[63]

Boston built amenities to attract students, but do these students feel a reciprocal obligation for the hospitality? Students are not annually surveyed so we have no research on this issue. Generally speaking, college students are not very interested in Boston politics and for many, it is like being a guest in someone's house. Most know how to behave themselves. Behaving is sometimes defined as only acting and complaining about what is being done on campus. How a student defines the campus varies. Some Harvard students might think that going to Central Square is leaving campus even though MIT is located on the other side of the square. Boston University students' campus is totally integrated with the surrounding Fenway-Kenmore-Allston community.

If political issues affect students, protests usually happen on the college campus. Some would consider this a type of campus activism, not actual civic engagement. Civic engagement refers to actions taken by individuals to *change* the welfare of others. Students may just want to improve the living environment on campus for fellow students. The word "change" is used instead of "improving" because some social actions are motivated by a desire to keep in place existing policies and practices.

Political scientists James Q. Wilson and Edward C. Banfield in the 1960s made a distinction between civic actions that are "private and public regarding." They considered any individual actions taken for self-interest as "private regarding." If a student only goes to class, studies, and stays in the dormitory, this would be considered private regarding. "Public regarding" was defined as an individual who takes actions in the public interest. Accordingly, "public regardingness" is a key to understanding individual motives for public action to make changes for the general interest.[64] The latter is considered change-oriented civic engagement. Such action can include volunteering or protesting public policies that affect others. A few students volunteer to do community outreach such as tutoring high school students, working at homeless shelters, and otherwise participating in charity events.

Although the psychological dimensions of change-oriented civic engagement are debatable, it is clear that some people are less motivated than others to take public action on the issues discussed in previous chapters. The type of action an individual student takes may be traced to their political socialization. People who were raised by parents who were engaged in civic engagement may be more likely to become activists and vice versa. For example, some people were stimulated to act by a political trauma such as the 9/11 catastrophe. Although every nation has its share of activists and free riders, a democracy needs more citizen involvement to work properly. Given the fact prestigious colleges and universities supposedly attract the best and brightest, their lack of public regarding is noteworthy.

Living in but Not a Part of Boston

Although America's higher education institutions are world leaders in many ways, the majority of its members—staff, professors, and students—do not consider themselves political activists. Indeed, there is no widespread alarm at the ongoing political standoffs in these organizations. American universities and colleges discourage outside political activity. Although it is never stated publicly, off-campus activities are frowned upon. In turn, city politicians may not read the *Harvard Crimson*, the *Daily Free Press* of Boston University, or the *Huntington News* of Northeastern University to monitor campus life.

As noted in previous chapters, public officials make all types of controversial decisions with very few public reactions. Obviously, a city like Boston can have a sustainable civic life without large numbers of its educated citizens being civically engaged. Survey research suggests that political apathy explains some of the variances but there is also evidence that suggests many Americans are politically alert, thoughtful, and follow their government actions. It follows, then, that a student could be characterized as being a good citizen or student without doing anything that might be defined as political. The U.S. Constitution protects the citizen's right to engage in rational political abstinence. All civic engagement must be considered as a part of the overall sociopolitical context.

The Context of Student Civic Engagement

Menino followed an ongoing narrative about students and the way they reside in the metro area. Like his predecessors, he left the town-gown dichotomy essentially intact. Menino came to the office near the end of an over twenty-year decline in student interest in anti-government protests. He came to office well after the Vietnam War.

Because of the draft, the Vietnam War disrupted the student management routine of universities. One of the 1968 issues that Richard Nixon campaigned on was his promise to end the draft. At the time, the nation was in the midst of the Vietnam War and college campuses were the leading protesters against the war. In 1973, Congress eliminated the draft, and that law changed the nature of student protest in American universities and colleges. Nixon's voluntary military removed the campus as a hotbed for protest against the military and war. In 1970, Harvard suspended its ROTC program but later restored it in 2011. Other issues such as the environment, income inequality, and race relations were not as compelling issues as the draft for students to take to the streets of their host cities.

If context dictates what is appropriate for civic engagement, then what are the situations in which student involvement is unsuitable? Should students disregard homeless people sleeping near campus? Or police conflicts with minorities. What then are the political obligations of ordinary students to their fellow citizens? Do individual students as members of a visitor class have an equal opportunity to become politically active? Do American students in Boston have more opportunities for civic engagement?

Journalist Jenna Russell noted that most student protests took place on campus and involved institutional issues such as student fees, LGBTQ rights, and other campus injustices. She quoted a student who said, "It's easier to organize 1 square mile than the entire country." Russell further noted, "Not every recent student action has been tied to one campus. About 300 students from 14 Boston area colleges and high schools attended an antiwar rally and march on Boston Common in December, organized by the new umbrella group Boston Student Mobilization to End the War. The event featured angry speeches, chanting, and a minor skirmish between students and police [that had] all the hallmarks of 1960s student protests against the Vietnam War."[65]

Cities like Boston must be prepared for a potential protest spillover from college campuses. However, political scientist Eric J. Oliver's research found that Americans in larger cities are much less likely to contact officials, attend community or organizational meetings, or vote in local elections. They were generally less interested in local affairs.[66] One would think that life in a campus town in a rural community would afford more opportunities to become civically engaged. This is not always the case. In 2001, political scientist William A. Galston found that college students knew as much about politics as 1950 high school students.[67] Youth involvement with the internet is beginning to show positive signs of civic engagement.[68] These findings have implications for cities trying to get more feedback from their temporary residents.

Municipal governments cannot function well in a listless civil society. Presumably, students are aware of citizens of other nations on social media incessantly complaining about government policies, marching in the street with signs, and demanding government action. Yet most of the time Boston students are not in the street protesting anything. Occupy Wall Street was clearly an exception.

Occupy Wall Street in Boston

Although the movement had no defined leaders, Occupy Wall Street raised some interesting questions about the nature of American capitalism. Occupy Boston was the city version of this anticapitalistic movement. On September 30, 2011, a few young people took to a street near Dewey Square in the Financial District in front of the Federal Reserve Bank of Boston, erected tent cities, and accused the government of disadvantaging the 99 percent of Americans to reward the rich 1 percent. Over one hundred people were arrested. Most of the cases were dismissed by the Suffolk County District Attorney's office. Yet for Boston, the incident represented mild political trauma. In a study of 191 colleges and universities that had Occupy Wall Street events on campus, Professors Victor Asal, Alexander Testa, and Joseph Young found that expensive colleges in the Far West and New England with higher-paid faculty were candidates for Occupy Wall Street.

> Colleges with higher-paid faculty, more students, higher costs, and more staff are the most likely to be involved in the Occupy movement. Regional differences were also evident, but their effects were less substantive than factors that increased resources for protest. Our model, informed by these factors, can accurately predict where these events were likely to occur both in and out of the sample. However, while resources are found to be important factors, grievances matter as well in the equation. In particular, we found the percentage change in the cost of attendance in the year leading up to the Occupy movement to be a significant factor associated with the occurrence of an Occupy event.[69]

This may explain why some Harvard students started a movement called Occupy Harvard Yard. This happened thirteen days after the more famous Occupy Wall Street standoff in New York City. The reaction of city officials was critical to protesters. They had to keep one eye on City Hall. Ryan Cahill, a protester, stated, "I think Menino's rhetoric has changed depending on who he's talking to. At least he's giving us leeway. He's come out in support of us, but he has an entire city to look out for, not just the Occupy movement. Don't think the Boston Police Department wants a violent crackdown."[70]

On October 11, the city detained 141 demonstrators on trespassing charges. They had tied up traffic on the North Washington Street Bridge and set up a campground on the Rose Fitzgerald Kennedy Greenway. Menino expressed sympathy for the movement's goals but stated, "Civil disobedience will not be tolerated. I understand they have freedom of speech and freedom of expression, but we have a city to manage."[71]

Finally, on December 7, 2011, Boston judge Frances McIntyre issued a restraining order. Menino ordered the removal of the protesters from Dewey Square. Early in the morning, the police raided the camp and arrested forty-six people. Menino stated, "In the interest of public safety, we had to act."[72]

Mayors and Civic Engagement

Boston's mayors generally have a direct and indirect role to play in the level of civic engagement in the city. As Menino said in his first State of the City Address, inclusion and group organizations were a part of his aspirations for all residents.[73] Although many students are temporary residents, they are expected to act as citizens. Everyone was promised an opportunity to participate. Besides, modern technology makes certain types of participation easier. As new mayors enter City Hall, they will find a highly politicized environment competing with the changing technological world. In Boston, word-of-mouth information travels fast. Menino understood that this was not enough and established a citizen hotline that would allow them to reach City Hall. The mayor and his aides introduced technology into his civic engagement strategy. Mitchell Weiss, one of Menino's staff members, was credited with this new vision for citizen engagement and constituency services. Another staff member, Bill Oates, allowed the civic engagement team to launch the project and build partnerships. Finally, Chris Osgood another staff member, was able to implement it in the city agencies. Professors Susan P. Crawford and Dana Walters interviewed the participants and summarized their findings:

> We found a traditional technology story—selection and integration of CRM software, initial performance management using that software, development of ancillary channels of communication, and initial patterns of adoption and use—that reflects the commitment of Mayor Menino to personalized constituent service. We also found that that commitment, his long tenure, and the particular personalities of the people on the New Urban Mechanics team make this both a cultural story as well as a technology story. . . . Even without budgetary authority or staff, the innovation office within the Mayor's suite (the Office of New Urban Mechanics) has been able to nudge, encourage, and facilitate

collaborations inside City Hall and across academic institutions, technologists, and other city governments that have been productive.[74]

This quotation captures Menino's attempt to reach out to all people who lived in the city. He, like most mature politicians, had noticed that young people were becoming addicted to apps and social media. Social media had the potential of changing how politicians related to constituencies. Young people might not go to a political meeting or call the local mayor but they could be reached. This was also true for most Bostonians who were seeking ways to know about what happened at City Hall. This may be why the mayor entitled his book *A Mayor for a New America*.

Cyberspace has become a public space for many Americans. Technology has made Americans more self-sufficient and less reliant on others. We live in a seductive digitized world. Students are often more skilled at this type of technology than regular residents. This is why Mayor Menino's Office of New Urban Mechanics created Citizen Connect, a smartphone app that allowed people to report potholes by taking a picture of them.

However, journalist Stacy Teicher Khadaroo cites research by Professor Joseph Kahne that suggests "participation in online communities increases civic engagement—but just socializing on Facebook doesn't."[75] Obviously, in twenty-first-century America, students are more interested in what their cellphones can do than what local leaders have to say about the world or taking pictures of potholes. They get their news and entertainment from the internet and do not need to relate to other people living in Boston.

Students and their neighbors are using the same technology. Such information does not require a response or reply. There is no reciprocity involved. This might explain why students are often reluctant to sign petitions, participate in demonstrations, join local government reform groups, and join neighborhood associations. In addition, there is the possibility that public engagement will bring more scrutiny from the media and government. This alone will keep some people out of the public arena. Some analysts would argue that American democracy has not suffered because of this lack of civic engagement. Other commentators believe that this type of civil society is a problem for a healthy democracy.

Finally, most Americans indicated their preferences and disagreements at the polls. Voters are mobilized by issues of the cost of government and the need for revenue enhancements such as taxes. Since the 2008 Great Recession, some American students have stepped up their interest and involvement in the debate about the role and cost of government. Students that show up at town meetings and legislative hearings are complaining about the cost of college. This current debate about student involvement is more than just the latest cycle of a student revolt; it is more likely a discourse about loans and stress.

Mayors of large cities blessed with large higher education institutions have to be alert to the possibility of a spillover of events such as Occupy Wall Street–type demonstrations, controversial campus speakers, and racial flare-ups. This is a delicate process since the purpose is not to discourage civic engagement.

Summary

Mayor Menino understood the impact of higher education institutions and their students in the city proper. Students bring new faces and energy to the city. Their presence in metro Boston affects the city's bottom line for retailers and creates an overall economic multiplier effect. Moreover, Menino understood that how downtown campuses helped the vitality of that central business area was critical for the city's image. More residential students, especially downtown students, help pedestrian traffic.

Menino also accepted the role of universities as knowledge-producing entities. He said as much in his second State of the City Address. As a perceptive and empathic mayor, he developed an understanding of why these institutions wanted to expand their share of the city's land. He was willing to meet the leaders of these institutions and listen to their suggestions. He was aware that the city had a space problem, but he accepted their offers of cooperation.

At the same time, he did not interfere with the internal cultures of these institutions. He supported urban extension programs and efforts by several institutions designed to assist Boston public schools. He agreed with Northeastern University President Richard Freeland when he said, "The negative patterns of town-gown relations are no longer viable. The old impulses toward separation on one hand, or coercion on the other, must be set aside. Once, perhaps, universities could flourish by setting themselves apart from their communities. Over the last four decades, however, it has become evident that city-based universities ignore at their peril the well-being of their communities."[76] Professor Eugenie Birch suggests that improving communication with elected officials and university leadership facilitates maximizing good planning and land use.[77] This was a post-industrial lesson Menino learned.

After studying California universities and host cities, Professors Karen Baker-Minkel, Jason Kieser, and Walter Kieser found that these higher education institutions did receive benefits and that their presence imposed a negative fiscal impact on municipal budgets. The authors suggested that universities make direct in-lieu-of-tax payments; charge on-campus students a fee, similar to property taxes; and investigate cost-sharing alternatives like contributions to the capital or program expenditures of city departments.[78] Menino rejected this lesson.

Finally, promoting civic engagement for students in higher education institutions is difficult. Students are temporary residents and are generally not inclined to get involved in city politics. Boston colleges and university could survey their out-of-town students about their host city, but it is not clear how the data would help students adjust to Boston. If the class of 1990 had a higher evaluation of Boston than the class of 2000, what exactly does that mean? Being an apolitical sanctuary may be the goal for some campuses. Yet it is worth groping for the right amount of civic engagement for participatory temporary residents in Boston.

CONCLUSION

Drawing Lessons from the Menino Tenure

On March 28, 2013, Thomas Michael Menino, the fifty-third mayor of the city of Boston, announced at Faneuil Hall that he would not run for another term. He said, "I am here with the people I love, to tell the city I love, that I will leave the job that I love."[1] He was having growing health issues, and this announcement ended a fascinating era in Boston's political history. Hyde Park's own Tom Menino was retiring. Gone was the third-floor office with a great view and aides. But now he could sleep late and not rush to quell a neighborhood conflict. But sitting it out and taking an easy chair was not for Tom Menino as he took a position at Boston University's Institute on Cities. He and Dr. Graham K. Wilson became co-directors of the institute. Additionally, other universities in the metro Boston area including Harvard University reached out and invited the former mayor to spend time on their campuses. But Boston University persuaded him to join them more permanently. Menino had become an unexpected ally of local higher education institutions.

Menino's choice of Boston University was based on his special relationship with its president, Robert Brown. Menino joked, "My passport is not valid for Cambridge." The co-directorship at the institute was not a sinecure for the mayor. He saw it as a challenge and an opportunity. His co-director, Dr. Wilson, stated, "He [Menino] arrived in January and said, 'What is going to get us known is research.' I did not expect that. He came to work firing on all four cylinders until the end."[2] One of the products of that research was the establishment of the *Menino Survey of Mayors* magazine. Obviously, coming to an office at 919 Beacon Street was very different from arriving at City Hall.

Rather than being surrounded by politicians, Menino was now among graduate students and staff.

Menino's Leadership and the Fate of Boston

The length of tenure at City Hall matters because it allowed the mayor an opportunity to establish and maintain urban policy consistency. No Boston mayor has served as long as Milwaukee's Henry W. Maier's twenty-eight years; Menino was eight years short. Being the mayor of Boston was not easy, and it became more complex as the city changed. The office of the mayoralty had changed since its first mayor, John Phillip (1822–1823), and the first one to have a four-year term, John F. Fitzgerald (1910–1914). Simply put, there was more to do, and more time was needed. Also acting in Boston politics was not as easy as it seemed. Some political solutions or actions never occurred to a mayor. Other times, a mayor was constrained by additional factors of which his aides, critics, and journalists were not aware. Menino was fortunate because he had time to learn what needed to be learned, how it could be done, and to watch things change. He had the acumen to discern that the post-industrial city was inevitable, and that it had positive and negative consequences. He probably never bothered to read Herman L. Boschken's article about how global cities like Boston advantage the upper middle class and disadvantage the poor.[3] Menino had a city to lead and poor Bostonians to help. He was an eternal optimist and would have seconded the arguments in Thomas Sigler's *Triumph of the City* that cities made us richer, smarter, healthier, and happier.[4]

The lessons he drew and acted on helped to facilitate his tenure. His political style drew criticisms from both progressive and conservative analysts. During his tenure, Boston changed in ways that Menino wanted it to and then in ways he did not expect. As has been suggested, political time and contextuality matter.

The Menino mayoralty worked for Boston primarily because he was an amenable personality and a true blend of cognitive and compassionate empathy. He never expressed any higher political ambitions than being mayor. In his book *A Mayor for a New America*, he made clear that the new America he envisioned was an inclusive, post-industrial one. All races and genders would be able to regard City Hall as a rallying point for economic development and social change. He lived that inviting political life and allowed all groups to make their case; he understood his effect on individuals and groups who felt left out and unappreciated. He endorsed several progressive measures while mayor from building bike lanes to calling for climate change actions in 2007. He had no problem marching in a gay pride parade or attending a backyard barbecue in the Black community. He told people involved in the Occupy Wall Street movement that he agreed with their objectives but not their tactics. He interacted with Black ministers and made them feel that they knew what was in his heart. He has no problem attending their meetings, praying with them, and soliciting their advice.

Aside from the right instincts, Menino also had high a level of relatedness. Relatedness is defined as the ability to easily relate to others. Such individuals can make strangers and opponents feel comfortable and understood. They make others feel that they share their values and understand their circum-stances. It was not just that Menino was a people person. Granted, he exempli-fied bonhomie and high levels of sociability. This type of avuncular individual is also willing to defer to people they consider experts. Menino was not afraid to ask for help from blue ribbon groups, individuals with Ph.Ds., and people with national reputations. This openness apparently flattered individuals who considered themselves experts. Menino was willing to talk with all stakehold-ers and constituency groups. Such a high level of relatedness was valued in city politics. People liked him because he listened. Few people expected him to fully solve their problems. His lack of a Boston Braham locution endeared him to his constituencies. Even in a city where glibness is an art form, his not being an eloquent public communicator was discounted. Indeed, Menino was an effective and proficient communicator while uttering a few quotable sentences that will survive in Boston history. Moreover, Menino had a plain and con-sistent long-term vision for the city, albeit one not articulated in academic or theoretical terms. Bostonians kept electing him because he had great political skills. The voters felt like they knew him. His audience thought they under-stood him. As someone said when I began the research for this book, "Menino is not difficult to figure out. He is just who he is." And in some ways, this was true and in other ways it was false. At his funeral, many famous people came to pay their respect. These included Cardinal Sean O'Malley, Governor Deval Patrick, former President Bill Clinton, and Vice President Joseph Biden, along with sports stars Bill Russell, David Ortiz, and Pedro Martinez. Most people who knew Menino understood that Boston politics would never be the same.

Leaving Office Changes Many Things

The end of Menino's tenure entailed the disassembling of several politicians' careers and a span of influence. Politicians at every level had to consider their new political reality. This is what happens when a mayor serves a long time: everyone gets used to that person and how to deal with them. Journalist Peter Gelzinis has remarked, "Pols will feel shocked after a historical shift."[5] Matthew Weinstein reviewed the Menino legacy and Boston's future. He credited Menino with reinventing Boston, repositioning its economy, improving race relations, and making neighborhoods safer. For him, Menino left "big shoes to fill." In sum, Weinstein stated, "Menino leaves the city in a position few would have imagined 20 years ago. Boston reinvented itself under Menino and his legacy will permeate Boston's culture for decades to come."[6]

This is precisely why Menino's tenure was so critical to Boston's history and serves as a lesson for future American mayors. Because mayors are seen and heard frequently because of rapid modern communications, they are thought to be close to their constituencies and more visible to their audiences. The growing market for inside information concerning sitting mayors and their decisions is fueled by public curiosity. America is a celebrity-watching society. Menino became an unexpected celebrity. Indeed, the glow from his tenure was so resonant that the mayor's staff members became local celebrities in their own rights. They represented the mayor in local community forums and on television and were supporting actors in this fascinating drama. More importantly, they were expected to implement Menino's policy decisions in intergovernmental relations, economic development, public safety, education, and housing.

The drama started when Tom Menino the Unlikely was elected mayor. When a new mayor assumes office, journalists ask them what they hope to accomplish and how they want to be remembered. In 1995, *Boston Globe* reporter Adrian Walker interviewed Menino (then only three years in office) and asked him those questions. Menino told Walker that he wanted Boston to be a city that works. He was bold to say, "When I leave Boston, my hope is that any young family can live in the neighborhoods of our city, to educate their kids in the Boston public schools, to go to the playgrounds and be safe from violence and that the father and mother can work in Boston because of enough created jobs. That's what I want Boston to be when I leave [office]. Is that achievable? I think that is."[7] When he was elected president of the U.S. Conference of Mayors, a high honor, Menino said,

When asked how I want to be remembered, I've always said that I want my legacy to be about people, not skylines. That's why I have made education, housing, health care, and neighborhood revitalization my top priorities; that's what matters most to working families. As someone who always wants a return on his investment, I have found that investing in people yields the greatest results.

Strong cities make a strong nation. It's important for mayors to be able to meet to share ideas and experiences and to plan for the future. And, in order to protect the future of working families, we need to create and maintain housing that's affordable. Cities can't do it alone. Everyone needs to do their part to bring relief to families who are being priced out.[8]

In retrospect, Menino's goals were laudable and delimiting. There were problems that looked resolvable but weren't. Menino's answer to the reporter's questions acknowledged an Overton Window, that is, what is possible in a given situation, defined by the boundaries of acceptability of government policies. A mayor can only act within these acceptable parameters. And there are limits to government actions and traditional guardrails that City Hall actions must hold. This is an important lesson all mayors must learn.

For this book, individuals who identified themselves as progressives openly criticized former mayors White, Flynn, and Menino. They wanted these mayors to build more affordable housing, enact a permanent rent-control policy, fund more youth programs to undermine children's inclinations to join gangs, make racial equality a reality, force public schools to work for all students, make all Boston streets equally safe, create more jobs, and seek more community benefits from higher education institutions. Although progressives gave the mayors different grades, many were genuinely disappointed. This response may be called the "inevitable urban dissatisfaction syndrome." Put simply, mayors do not have absolute agency in policymaking. For a mayor, progressives are a relatively small segment of a larger constituency and audience. There are more voices to hear, more bureaucratic inertia to overcome, and ever-changing political dynamics to engage. Mayors who do not learn these lessons will have problems governing.

Lawyer Alexander Kasner believes mayors live in a bit of a political paradox. He states, "They are clothed in the aspirations of their friends, neighbors, and peers, nominated from within their ranks to fix the problems that matter most in day-to-day life. Yet their place at the dais is more prison than a pedestal. Many modern mayors are equipped with only weak, ceremonial powers and saddled with high expectations and mounting challenges. These mayors are nothing if not primed to disappoint."[9]

Some of Menino's vision for Boston was limited by what the state legislature allowed him to accomplish. Yet, he knew how to use the post to express the aspirational goals of various neighborhoods and residential groups. Some changes were amenable to City Hall, but others were not. Obviously, some people were disappointed with City Hall and with him. He presented himself as a fighter and voters appreciated his efforts. When they voted, they knew what they were getting.

Menino also understood who he was and did not try to remake himself. He did not have the academic pedigree of a Mayor White (Williams College, Boston College Law, and Harvard Kennedy School) befitting the mayor of the Athens of America, but Menino was able to address the expansion demands of local higher education institutions. He also guided Boston through a critical transition necessary for an ever-evolving post-industrial city. Again, Menino was a true blend of a cognitive and compassionate mayor, opening his office to all sectors of Boston while not trying to grow his own political tree.

More importantly, Menino demonstrated that someone from his background could be elected to Boston's highest office and become one of its beloved politicians. Some Bostonians may have preferred someone who would be able to hold his own with the university and college leadership, but these leaders engaged with Menino because of his authenticity. Amazingly, the city was never bored with Menino's image as an inarticulate housekeeping mayor. In fact, he used his inarticulateness to his advantage. He would repeatedly say, "I am not a fancy talker." To some voters, this was reassuring because sometimes fancy talkers get less done.

In retrospect, this may be the most reasonable explanation of why Menino kept winning elections. His opponents simply could not make a compelling case for removing him and changing the direction of the city. Granted, incumbency mattered, and long service mattered. Fascinatingly, the complexity of the man and his long tenure created varied memories of him.

Moving on from the past is what we expect elected leaders to do. Moving away from the old ways of doing things was a mantra for Menino. Although he never said so, his policy solution efforts were analogous to Pareto Optimality, that is, to make changes in the distribution of resources to allow a group to be better off without making other groups worse off. As discussed, this position represented one of the ways Menino framed policy proposals and related to politicians at every level of government.

Menino, Other Politicians, and Policies

Just as recurrent politics is one obligatory aspect of the job of Boston's mayor, networking with other politicians helped Menino and was achieved throughout his administration. The State House on Beacon Hill and the White House in Washington, DC, became a part of Tom Menino's political life. The record shows that he was able to hold his own with all types of politicians. Most agreed that Menino handled the recurrent politics part of the job with a flair.

Menino should be given some credit for facilitating the continuing rise of the high-tech industry in the city's metro area (e.g., Innovation Districts). This task was and still is facilitated by having some of the nation's highest prestigious educational institutions. Places like Harvard and MIT generate hundreds of graduates with the skills required for this industry. Accordingly, there are few leaders in the industry without connections or branches in Boston and Cambridge. Boston remains a major center for the creative class.

Unfortunately, no buffer exists between cities like Boston and the volatility of the nation's economy. A central challenge of Boston proper is its lack of geographical space. This affects the city's ability to bargain with certain types of industries. Limited-space cities like Boston and San Francisco are heavily exposed. Being at the forefront of rapidly changing economic arrangements may be too much for many of them. Unfortunately, cities have been neither self-corrective nor self-sufficient. Boston prospered and grew because the nation did well economically and financially.

Many city leaders such as Menino bought into this pro-growth agenda because they believed these actions would create jobs and keep the city relevant. As many scholars argued, this strategy had its downsides, and some cities have not been able to attract the requisite manufacturing jobs or to make the leap from a manufacturing town to a high-tech haven.[10] What will the economic future of Boston be in the post-Menino era?

This book attempts to capture the career of Mayor Menino and the politics of Boston in the early twenty-first century, including how he presided over the economic options available to Boston and how his successors' future choices have been defined. The general assumption was that manufacturing or labor-intensive jobs would not return to Boston in their previous forms.[11] It was also assumed that Boston could not sustain certain types of residents without a viable job base beyond city government and services. It assumed that poor people would give up living in Boston if there were few ways to make a living. This does not mean that cities do not engender loyalties. Individuals and groups do have attachments to cities. First-generation Bostonians and immigrants can become attached to the city. But events have a way of overwhelming these attachments. Keeping the city safe was critical for that attachment and for attracting new jobs and residents.

Lessons Drawn from Menino's Mayoralty

There are several noticeable as well as less apparent lessons from Menino's twenty-year term. First, the rumpus of Boston ethnic politics had a purpose. It allowed members of such groups to feel someone cared about their situation. Menino acted to make sure that residents of South Boston knew he cared and that his rise to power was not an Italian American takeover. He also reached out to minority communities and incorporated them as best he knew how. Second, he endorsed the shift in the city economy with the Innovation District project. Third, he discovered that housing policy was a kitchen with too many cooks—federal, state, nonprofit organizations, and city politicians. Housing can be described as an enigma within a puzzle. Rent control does not work, affordable housing runs into NIMBY forces, and affluent residents buy houses in ethnic enclaves and build mansions. Street crime is a national problem with a variety of causes and is perhaps not amenable to direct mayoral action without encountering constitutional problems. Fourth, public school workers (teachers and administrators) are among the most powerful interest groups in the city, and persuasion and concessions may not trigger lasting reforms. Fifth, the Boston higher education complex is one of the strongest real estate interest groups in the city.

There were also some less apparent but related warnings. A mayor should ride the tide of ethnic politics (that is, stay clear of the rough waters of internal disagreements among ethnic group leaders) but get into the water when such politics evolve into conflicts among other city groups. The nascent struggle over residential space will be between the creative class and ethnic enclaves. No community is exempt, including South Boston. Second, mayors who survive economic transitions are those who attempt to understand and signal emerging new leaders. Third, mayors can and should complain about schools, but part of the problem of schools is their relatively powerless clientele. Inner-city schools are best at sorting out talent, not overcoming learning deficiencies caused by low-income families. It is a frustration for all mayors. Fourth, in a free society, mayors cannot violate the Constitution to control criminals. Changing the leadership of the police department can have a temporarily unsettling impact on the membership of the department but it is like a rubber band, it returns to its original shape after stretching it. Fifth, higher education leaders appreciate Teddy Roosevelt's adage, "Speak softly but carry a big stick." They have large endowments and can buy property under assumed names. Lastly, Menino understood that voters were often more interested in the character of the mayor than fancy rhetoric or plans. They wanted their mayor to be caring and relatable but also tough when that was required.

Thomas Menino's background prepared him to be sympathetic to the aspirations of immigrants and minorities. Accordingly, he was able to relate to them and gain their trust. Trust and authenticity are perhaps the most crucial elements of a mayoralty. When Menino campaigned, he was able to reassure his constituencies that the welfare of Boston was uppermost in his mind. Ethnic shibboleths and overpromising may get a politician elected, but voters will catch on to such politicians. Menino was not that kind of politician. His background and mentorships taught him how to understand the context of Boston politics. Voters bought into his authenticity, trusted him, and kept reelecting him. His authenticity also helped him to deal with the recurrent politics of Boston. For all politicians, recurrent politics present an ego minefield—one mistake can blow up a career. Menino was quite deft in managing his fellow politicians, regardless of status. This skill was also apparent in his relationship with one of the city's largest agencies, the police department.

Keeping a Safe Boston

Keeping the city safe was a high priority for Mayor Menino. It was one of his prime directives for his staff. He understood that if the city hoped to keep its residents and attract others, crime had to be kept under control. Unfortunately, the nature of street violence and domestic violence are not amenable to police control. Police usually get involved after the crime has been committed. They are also there to reassure the public this type of crime will not happen again.

Menino linked his reputation as a crime fighter to community policing. Menino's first commissioner, Paul Evans, had a community policing reputation and was credited for facilitating the "Boston Miracle." Evans also led the department during the infamous mistaken-identity incident that ended in the murder of Accelyne Williams by the police, a subject that Menino felt so strongly about that he addressed it again in his book. The Kathleen O'Toole appointment as commissioner was considered trailblazing except she was not a supporter of community policing. The third commissioner, Edward Davis, returned to community policing and his tenure lasted twelve years. The point is that appointment of a commissioner may be a signal to beat officers about what is expected, but personalities and approaches may not affect the crime rate or prevent unanticipated horrible events.

The local newspapers and television stations continue to cover crime and the politics of the city. Local television coverage is often attracted to sensational crimes. The Boston Marathon Bombing made national news. The capture of these two individuals did not take place in Boston but it brought an end to a crime in the city that was as sensational as the 1950 Brink robbery. Regular criminal activity and the criminal justice system rarely get much coverage. Yet the apprehension of so-called atrocious criminals is a common feature of the local evening television news. Although Boston was not called a zombie city, the media unintentionally helped perpetuate this image that a criminal element awakens at night and will move in and out of neighborhoods and homes.

Housing before and after Menino

The housing literature is a cornucopia of policy failures, ideas, and proffered solutions. Boston's housing problem was truly a Gordian Knot. Despite Menino's laudable efforts at rent control and promotion of affordable housing, the city has by no means solved its housing problem. Gentrification remains a threat to neighborhood enclaves like South Boston from upscale and professional workers. Professor Richard Florida was correct about the growing inequities exemplified by the housing crisis: "One thing is certain: if we do nothing, today's urban crisis will only worsen and deepen. The gap between the winners of the winner-take-all urbanism and the rest will widen. Our superstar cities and tech hubs will become so expensive that they will turn into gilded and gated communities, their innovative and creative sparks will eventually fade, and they will price out the essential service workers needed to keep their economies running."[12]

If a zip code apartheid, that is, separating people based on where they live, can be avoided, it could make Boston a truly unwalled city. Housing matters because of location and place. For some individuals, it determines everything from the quality of healthcare to safety protection and schools. Housing policy overlaps with school policy, including policy for higher education. There are lessons to be drawn from Menino's efforts.

Menino, the Education Mayor

Boston's school politics is among the most fascinating to watch in the nation. This book was not meant to be an exhaustive history or analysis. But Boston is the host community for some of the nation's most prestigious graduate education training and research schools in the world. It follows that the Boston School Committee could hire some of the best minds in public education. However, Boston neighborhood changes are a part of school policies. The Boston Public Schools are now a minority-majority system. A lot of water has run under the bridge since the 1970s busing controversy. What is clear is that public schools in Boston continue to have problems. As the schools enroll predominately minority and low-income students, there is a glaring problem regarding student achievement. Yet Boston school politics look similar to those of other large American cities.

In an earlier work, *Black Mayors and School Politics*, I wrote that the group that governs the school system are cartel-like, in the economic sense. In school politics, policies are controlled by a small group of actors—central office personnel, union leaders, and parent advocate groups. *Boston Globe* reporters Brian C. Mooney and Muriel Cohen admitted as much. They called central staff "a groaning, mazelike bureaucracy that clings to power." They referred to a "ticket of red tape," something found in most big-city school headquarters.[13] The policy is tightly controlled, and dissent is ignored, not punished. The superintendent is not a part of the cartel. As we suggest, the cartel could safely ignore the reforms of Superintendents Harrison-Jones, Payzant, and Johnson. Superintendents come and go.

Menino wanted to be an education mayor and publicly asked to be judged "harshly" for his performance. Menino suggested that the problem with education was a "finger-pointing deal no one wants to be responsible. Now, more mayors are not afraid to take more responsibility for their schools." While president of the National League of Cities, Menino established the Institute for Youth, Education, and Families. *Education Week* credited him as "leading the mayoral education charge."[14] When the mayor made those comments, he had been elected three times and had appointed Tom Payzant as superintendent. Nevertheless, neither Menino nor Payzant proved to be a match for the Boston public school cartel.

While mayor, Menino did proffer a ten-year education plan for public schools. Few people criticized the plan because it was not operational. The plan was never fully implemented, and school achievement scores continued to flatline. Such plans never make a real difference because some parents continue to believe that only teacher-student efforts matter. For them, teacher pedagogical skills and student receptiveness is the key to learning. Parents also believe that they need only send their children to "good" schools and make sure that homework is done. Some parents believed intuitively that if all parents would follow these simple steps, students would be more successful. In other words, parents can be persuaded to blame other parents, not the school system. This is a simple characterization, but it captures the relationship between the public schools and their clients. This assessment of parent shortcomings yields an advantage to the school cartel, and the PSC promoted this type of thinking.

In 2006, the Boston Public Schools won the Broad Prize for the most improved schools. Mayor Menino said, "This award today could not have been accomplished without the hard work of the staff in schools and of the students and their families who make the Boston Public Schools an exciting place to be and a great place to learn. We are also tremendously grateful for the almost 11 years of leadership provided by retired Superintendent Thomas Payzant, who helped design and implement the reform plan that guides the BPS today."[15] Despite the praise and support for winning the prize, which included $100 million from foundations, residents who lived in Boston and sent their children to those schools knew better. Menino also knew better. In an interview with Donald Gillis, Menino admitted his shortcomings with regard to schools: "I could have done much better on schools. No question about that. Schools have come a long [way] but still are not perfect. Schools are still an issue for us."[16]

David Passafaro, a Menino staff member, suggested that

> the failure of school reform was Menino's biggest disappointment. (He said so in the Second State of the City Address delivered at the Burke School, which had just lost its accreditation. I wrote it.) We had a lot of victories, setbacks, and losses. He recruited Dr. Thomas Payzant. The mayor was convinced that changes needed to start in the lower grades. [They should be] made in preschool and kindergarten and then

in the elementary schools and then moved on into middle schools, but he [Menino] didn't have enough time or funding to make significant changes in the high schools and that was as a source of great frustration to him, [to] not make changes in the high schools. They [his staff] were never quite able to turn the tide big enough to suit him.[17]

Finally, no single City Hall occupant can change the flow of policies and politics. Boston interest groups like those in other cities are skilled at resisting policy change. To use a metaphor, an entrenched Goliath will not be stopped by one stone from a determined David. Tom Menino made a gallant effort, and some lessons can be drawn from his efforts. The overall lesson is that city, federal, and state political leaders should stop this mindless competition for political credit for solving urban problems. They must openly acknowledge the downsides of the post-industrial economy and globalization on cities. They should admit that housing is more than a living space. In American life, where one resides is so life-defining. If poor residents continue to struggle in a superstar city like Boston, blessed with so many higher education resources, what is the fate of cities with fewer resources? To answer this question will take more than the political skill and vision of the man from the Readville neighborhood of Boston.

When a big-city mayor like Thomas Menino leaves office, it represents a major political transition. The entire political equilibrium of Boston was disrupted. The political dislocation was dispersed. Moreover, the new mayors' legacies began. Menino's first successor, Marty Walsh, faced some of the same problems as Menino, but he had a different style than Menino. Kim Janey was the first African American woman to be acting mayor of the city, but she lost in a primary to Michelle Wu, the first Asian American woman to be elected mayor of Boston. None of them should be expected to be another Menino. They governed at different political times, with some of the same challenges but also new ones. Nevertheless, new mayors are not free agents; old lessons need to be learned and new ones should be heeded and cataloged. Clearly, Menino's successors will have to deal more directly with these new socioeconomic issues, and they may not have the same political leeway and long tenure as Tom Menino.

Notes

Preface

1. George Guida, "The Conflicts of Ethnicity: The (Un) Making of Americans in Italian American Narrative" (Ph.D. diss., City University of New York, 1998), v; emphasis added.
2. Joe Sciacca, "A New Millennium—The Same Menino," *Boston Herald*, January 10, 2000, 19.

Introduction: Contextuality and Boston Uniqueness

1. See John P. Kotter and Paul Lawrence, *Mayors in Action: Five Approaches to Urban Governance* (New York: Wiley, 1974).
2. See Wilbur C. Rich, *Coleman Young and Detroit Politics: From Activist to Power Broker* (Detroit: Wayne State University Press, 1989).
3. See Wilbur C. Rich, review of William H. Hudnut III, *The Hudnut Years in Indianapolis, 1976–1991*, in *Political Science Quarterly* 111, no. 2 (Summer 1996): 372.
4. See Chris McNickle, *Bloomberg: A Billionaire's Ambition* (New York: Skyhorse, 2017).
5. See Wilbur C. Rich, *David Dinkins and New York Politics: Race, Images, and the Media* (Albany, NY: SUNY Press, 2006).
6. See Charles E. Lindblom, "The Science of 'Muddling Through,'" *Public Administration Review* 19, no. 2 (Spring 1959): 78–88.
7. See Wilbur C. Rich, *Transformative City: Charlotte's Takeoffs and Landing* (Athens: University of Georgia Press, 2020).
8. See Floyd Hunter, *Community Power Structure: A Study of Decision Makers* (Chapel Hill: University of North Carolina Press, 1953).
9. Richard Rose, *Lesson-Drawing in Public Policy* (Chatham, NJ: Chatham House, 1993), 27.

10. Three years after Menino left office political scientists Katherine Levine Einstein, David M. Glick, and Maxwell Palmer published a survey of mayors and found that this practice was commonplace. See Einstein, Glick, and Maxwell, "City Learning: Evidence of Policy Information Diffusion from a Survey of U.S. Mayors," *Political Research Quarterly* 72, no. 1 (March 2019): 243–58.

11. Rose, *Lesson-Drawing*, 30.

12. See U.S. Department of Urban Department, *The State of the Cities* (Washington, DC: U.S. Department of Housing and Urban Development, 1998), 1–46.

13. Alison Bass, "Specialists Seek to Explain Slaying," *Boston Globe*, April 18, 1993, 29.

14. Martin F. Nolan, "Boston's Horizon Has Static Skyline," *Boston Globe*, June 4, 1993, 27.

15. See Richard Florida, *The New Urban Crisis* (New York: Basic Books, 2017), 16.

16. See Richard Florida, *The Rise of the Creative Class* (New York: Basic Book, 2002).

17. Octavio Nuiry, "Boston Building Boom Lifts Housing," *Mortgage Banking, Suppl. MBA 103rd Annual Convention and Expo: Washington, D.C.* 16–18 (2016): 21.

18. See Florida, *The New Urban Crisis*.

19. Research by Cynthia Negrey and Mary Beth Zickel confirmed this view. See Negrey and Zickel, "Industrial Shifts and Uneven Development: Patterns of Growth and Development and Decline in U. S. Metropolitan Areas," *Urban Affairs Quarterly* 30, no. 1 (September 1994): 27–47.

20. Richard Schragger, *City Power* (New York: Oxford University Press, 2016), 38.

21. City of Boston, *Payments in Lieu Taxes (PILOT) Program FY 2013 Results* (Boston, 2014), 6.

22. Joseph D. Cutrufo, "Boston We Hardly Knew You," *Planning* 77, no. 1 (January 2011): 10.

23. Henry Etzkowitz, "Innovation in Innovation: Triple Helix of University-Industry-Government Relations," *Social Science Information* 42, no. 3 (1967): 295.

24. Enrico Moretti, *The New Geography of Jobs* (Boston: Houghton Mifflin Hardcourt, 2012), 1.

25. Cynthia Hogan, "Organizing the New Boston: Growth Policy, Governing Coalitions and Tax Reform," *Polity* 22 no. 3 (Spring 1990): 494.

26. Ibid., 510.

27. See David Warsh, "Some Miracles Never Cease," *Boston Sunday Globe Magazine*, August 8, 1989, 20.

28. David Gibbs and Rob Krueger, "Fractures in Meta-Narrative of Development: An Interpretive Institutionalist Account of Land Use Development in the Boston City-Region," *International Journal of Urban and Regional Research* 36, no. 2 (March 2012): 377.

29. Nolan, "Boston's Horizon Has Static Skyline."

30. Katherine Bowers, "Aftershocks in Boston from Filene Closure," *WWD Women's Wear Daily* 190, no. 83 (October 18, 2005): 18.

31. Kieth R. Ihlanfeldt, "The Importance of the Central City to the Regional and National Economy: A Review of the Arguments and Empirical Evidence," *Cityscape* 1, no. 2 (June 1995): 139.

32. Florida, *The New Urban Crisis*, 107.

33. Cited in Akilah Johnson, "Boston. Racism. Image. Reality," *Boston Globe*, December 10, 2017, 1A.
34. See Marilyn Johnson, *The New Bostonians: How Immigrants Transformed the Metro Area since the 1960s* (Amherst: University of Massachusetts Press, 2015), 75.
35. See Marion Orr, *Black Social Capital: The Politics of School Reform in Baltimore, 1968–1998* (Lawrence: University Press of Kansas, 1999). Also see his edited *Transforming the City: Community Organizing and the Challenge of Political Change* (Lawrence: University Press of Kansas, 2007).
36. See Robert Dahl, *Governs? Democracy and Power in American City* (New Haven, CT: Yale University Press, 1961)
37. Adrian Walker, "Menino Stresses Politics of Inclusion," *Boston Globe*, January 9, 1994, 15.

Chapter 1: On Becoming a Boston Politician

1. Dominic L. Candeloro, "What Luigi Basco Taught America about Italian Americans" in *Anti-Italianism: Essays on a Prejudice*, ed. William J. Connell and Fred Gardaphe (Houndmills, UK: Palgrave Macmillan, 2010), 78.
2. Thomas M. Menino with Jack Beatty, *A Mayor for a New America* (Boston: Houghton Mifflin Harcourt, 2014), 11.
3. Dot Joyce, interview, October 26, 2019.
4. Menino, *Mayor for a New America*, 22.
5. Adrian Walker, "Menino's Backers Celebrate the Spoils," *Boston Globe*, November 3, 1993, 25.
6. See Murray B. Levin, *The Alienated Voter: Politics in Boston* (New York: Holt, Rinehart, Winston, 1960).
7. Joyce interview.
8. Menino, *Mayor for a New America*, 25.
9. Peter Canellos, "Menino Recalls Middle-Age Political Education," *Boston Globe*, November 3, 1993, 25.
10. David Nyhan, "The Master Mechanic Politician," *Boston Globe*, July 20, 1993, 15.
11 See "Sketches of Persons Named in the Report," *Boston Globe*, April 23, 1965, 22.
12. See Richard J. Connolly, "Mass. Crime Commission Probes Self," *Washington Post*, April 11, 1965, 7L.
13 Joe Fitzgerald, "Kinnaly Like Dad to Mayor," *Boston Herald*, April 9, 2011, 11.
14. Ibid.
15. This PSA for CLEP featuring Abe Lincoln (College Entrance Examination Board commercial), circa late 1970s or early 1980s, has been preserved by YouTube.
16. Menino, *Mayor for a New America*, 27–28.
17. Bryan Marquard and Jim O'Sullivan, "Thomas Menino, Boston's Transformative Mayor, Dies," *Boston Globe*, October 31, 2014, 1A.
18. Joe Fitzgerald, "The Woman behind the Mayor," *Boston Herald*, January 12, 2011, 2.
19. Joyce interview.
20. Mount Ida College closed in 2018.

NOTES TO PAGES 32–44

21. Brian McGrory, "Menino's Council Work Helped Him Earn Degree," *Boston Globe,* October 8, 1993, 33.

22. Ibid.

23. Ibid.

24. See Lawrence J. Luppi, "Unprofitable Servants: The Italian American Experience in Boston" (M.A. thesis, Tufts University, 2007).

25. Mark S. Granovetter, "The Strength of Weak Ties," *American Journal of Sociology* 78, no. 6 (May 1973): 1360–80.

26. Ibid., 1378.

27. See Herbert J. Gans, *The Urban Villagers: Group and Class in the Life of Italian Americans* (1963; reprint New York: Free Press, 1982).

28. See Steve P. Erie, *Rainbow's End: Irish-Americans and the Dilemmas of Urban Machine Politics, 1840–1985* (Berkeley: University of California Press, 1988).

29. See *Thomas C. Stretch Another v. Walter H. Timilty,* 34 N.E.2d 674 (Mass. 1941).

30. Mayor Tom Menino, interview, May 23, 2000.

31. Matthew Brelis and Brian McGrory, "Timilty, Long the Would-Be-Mayor, Guilty in Fraud," *Boston Globe,* May 27, 1993, 1.

32. Marquard and O'Sullivan, "Thomas Menino, Boston's Transformative Mayor, Dies."

33. Menino, *Mayor for a New America,* 32–35.

34. McGrory, "Menino's Council Work Helped Him Earn Degree."

3. Menino, *Mayor for a New America,* 32.

36. See Jeanne F. Theoharis, "We Saved the City: The Black Struggle for Education Equality in Boston, 1960–1976," *Radical History Review* 2001, no. 81 (Fall 2001): 61–93.

37. See *Morgan v. Hennigan,* 379 F. Supp. 410 (D. Mass. 1974).

38. See James Q. Wilson, "The Mayors vs. the Cities," *Public Interest* 16 (Summer 1969): 27.

39. McGrory, "Menino's Council Work Helped Him Earn Degree."

40. Charles Kenney, "In District 5: Serious Politics," *Boston Globe,* November 9, 1983, 1.

41. Charles Claffey et al., "New Look in Boston: The Nine District Contests; District 1; East Boston, Charlestown, North End," *Boston Globe,* November 16, 1983, 1.

42. Nyhan, "The Master Mechanic Politician," 15.

43. Ibid.

44. Ed Cafasso, "Menino's Days on Council Produced Little," *Boston Herald,* October 24, 1993, 10.

45. Peter Dreier, interview, May 11, 2020.

46. Alan Lupo, "Menino Makes Politics Work," *Boston Globe,* August 2, 1992, 31.

47. Menino, *Mayor for a New America,* 42.

48. Menino interview.

49. Joe Sciacca, "Menino Captures Council Presidency; Veteran Wins on First Ballot," *Boston Herard,* January 5, 1993, 11.

50. See John Aloysius Farrell and James L. Franklin, "Flynn Eyed as Envoy to Vatican," *Boston Globe,* March 13, 1993, 1.

51. Dreier interview.

52. Menino, *Mayor for a New America,* 44.

53. Gloria Negri, "Italian Eyes Are Smiling," *Boston Globe,* November 4, 1993, 37.

54. See Peter Eisinger, *The Politics of Displacement* (New York: Academic Press, 1980).

NOTES TO PAGES 45–57   *309*

55. Menino interview.

56. This writer also thought that Menino was a caretaker. I presented a 1995 paper to that effect entitled "Tom Menino and Boston Politics" at the Northeastern Political Science Association meeting in Newark, New Jersey.

57. David Nyhan, "For Menino, Little Things Means a Lot," *Boston Globe*, November 7, 1993, 5A.

58. Patrick Fitzgibbons, "Boston New Mayor Wipes the Slate Clean for Underwriting Slots," *Bond Buyer*, July 16, 1993, 1.

59. Menino, *Mayor for a New America*, 29.

60. Herbert J. Gans, *People, Plans and Policies: Essays on Poverty, Racism, and Other National Urban Problems* (New York: Columbia University Press, 1991), 94.

61. Jim Vrabel, interview, May 26, 2020.

62. Adrian Walker, "Data: The Honeymoon Continues for Menino," *Boston Globe*, October 30, 1994, 36.

63. Joyce interview.

64. Abraham Lincoln, "Quotes," GoodReads, https://www.goodreads.com.

65. Elizabeth Lusk, interview, October 3, 2019.

Chapter 2: Winning Every Four Years

1. See Angus Campbell et al., *The American Voter* (New York: John Wiley, 1960).

2. Howard D. Hamilton, "The Municipal Voter: Voting and Nonvoting in City Elections," *American Political Science Review* 65, no. 4. (December 1971): 1135–40.

3. Brian McGrory, "Menino, 'A Neighborhood Guy' Now at Center Stage," *Boston Globe*, July 13, 1993, 12.

4. Ibid.

5. Marjorie Howard, "Mayor's Mumbling May Get Embarrassing; Mayor's Mangling of Language Speaks for Itself," *Boston Herald*, November 5, 1993, 1A.

6. Editorial Board, "Can Bratte Street Vote? Tongue-Tied Tom a Winning Personality Separated at Birth in the Bay State," *Boston Herald*, July 8, 1993, 25.

7. Monica Collins, "Menino Sees Nuts and Bolts, Not Visions," *Boston Herald*, October 31, 1993, 29.

8. Brian McGrory, "Rufo Draws Line at Roache," *Boston Globe*, June 24, 1993, 34.

9. Ed Cafasso, "Salerno Raps Real Estate Ties; Blames Acting Mayor for the Crisis," *Boston Herald*, September 3, 1993, 7.

10. Wayne Woodlief, "Menino and Salerno Lead Down the Homestretch," *Boston Herald*, September 18, 1993, 1.

11. Arnold Fleischmann and Lana Stein, "Campaign Contributions in Local Elections," *Political Research Quarterly* 51, no. 3 (September 1998): 673–89.

12. Chris Black, "It's Menino and Brett in Mayoral Showdown; Rufro Edged for 2nd Spot," *Boston Globe*, September 22, 1993, 1.

13. Alan Lupo, "Salerno's Sour Grapes Make a Bad Wine," *Boston Globe*, October 3, 1993, 2.

14. Editorial Board, "Menino for Mayor," *Boston Globe*, October 26, 1993, 14.

15. Brian McGrory, "Mayoral Hopefuls Take to Streets; Brett Says Menino Shares Flynn's Faults," *Boston Globe*, October 31, 1993, 12.

16. Brian McGrory, "Poll Shows Menino Holds Sizeable Lead," *Boston Globe*, October 24, 1993, 1.

17. Tomas Gonzalez, interview, June 2, 2020.

18. Tom Menino, interview, May 22, 2000.

19. Paul Applebome, "Races for Mayors Focusing on Crime," *New York Times*, October 18, 1993, 1A.

20. Adrian Walker, "Salerno Backs Menino for Mayor, Calling Him Closer to Her Agenda," *Boston Globe*, October 3, 1993, 44.

21. Chris Black and Brian McGrory, "It's for Real—Mayor Menino," *Boston Globe*, November 3, 1993, 1.

22. Ibid.

23. See Robert A. Dahl, *Who Governs?* (New Haven, CT: Yale University Press, 1961).

24. Peter Canellos, "Menino Recalls Middle-Age Political Education," *Boston Globe*, November 3, 1993, 25.

25. In 1984, *Esquire* magazine called Schaefer the "American best mayor"; cited in Rob Cassie, "He Did It Now," *Baltimore Magazine*, November 11, 2018, https://www.baltimoremagazine.com.

26. Patricia Smith, "That Our Mayor," *Boston Globe*, December 30, 1996, 1B.

27. "Q&A with Rev. Eugene Rivers, Paster of Azusa Christian Community," *Boston Globe*, February 4, 1996, 2.

28. Yvonne Abraham, "The Un-Campaign," *Boston Phoenix*, October 3, 1997, 16.

29. Joe Sciacca, "Hub's Not-Frills Mayor Stays True to His 'Vision'," *Boston Herald*, November 24, 1997, 6.

30. David R. Guarino, "Mr. Popular; Poll Finds Mayor Menino Almost Unbeatable," *Boston Herald*, March 8, 2001, 1.

31. Stephanie Ebbert, "Menino's Rival to Target Have-Nots; Davis-Mullen Campaign Will Target Have-Nots," *Boston Globe*, April 3, 2001, 1B.

32. David R. Guarino, "David-Mullen Says She's Ready to Take on Menino," *Boston Herald*, April 3, 2001, 8.

33. Jon Keller, "Running on Empty," *Boston Magazine*, May 15, 2006, https://www.bostonmagazine.com.

34. David R. Guarino, "Menino Challenger Comes Out Swinging," *Boston Herald*, April 18, 2001, 1.

35. "9/11: Menino Leading Boston through Chao," WBUR, September 7, 2011, https://www.wbur.org.

36. Editorial Board, "Menino for Mayor," *Boston Globe*, October 30, 2001, 18A.

37. Election Results, Department of Elections, City of Boston, 2001.

38. Andres Estes, "Poll Suggest a Solid Lead for Menino, but the Mayor Gets Low Marks on Services, Safety," *Boston Globe*, October 23, 2005, 1A.

39. Editorial Board, "Vote for Menino for Mayor," *Bay State Banner* (Dorchester, MA), October 27, 2005, 4.

40. Kevin Rothstein, "Campaign 2005; Clinton Phones It in for Menino," *Boston Herald*, November 7, 2005, 4.

41. "Suffolk University Poll Shows Mayor Menino Set for a Landslide Win," *US Fed News Service* (Washington, DC), November 4, 2005.

42. Chan Sewell, "52 Mayors Unite in Washington to Curb Illegal Firearms," *New York Times*, January 24, 2007, 6B.

NOTES TO PAGES 67–74   311

43. See Les Christie, "Home-Price Comparison, State by State," CNNMoney, September 28, 2006, https://money.cnn.com/. The index provides apples-to-apples comparisons of 342 U.S. markets, looking at the cost of a four-bedroom, two-and-a-half bath, 2,200-square-foot house with a two-car garage in a nice, middle-class neighborhood.

44. See Michael Jonas, "Flaherty/Yoon Team-Up Throws the Mayor-for-Life a Curve," *CommonWealth*, September 29, 2009, https://commonwealthmagazine.org.

45. E. S. Jones, "Boston Email-Gate Investigation Expands; Questions Continue on Why Mayor Menino Didn't Use Email Archiving," Business Wire, September 16, 2009, http://www.metalogix.net.

46. Richard Weir, "AG Clears Kineavy in Email Flap—Menino Critics See Possible Political Role in the Decision," *Boston Herald*, July 30, 2010, 2.

47. Ibid.

48. Analyzing Tom Menino's performance over all his elections and how he performed in these wards over time would be interesting. However, the Boston Election Department does not keep data by precincts and wards, only aggregate totals, nor do they analyze the data. A table showing comparative data over time would have explained how he kept getting elected.

49. Rob Gurwitt, "Governing Public Officials of the Year 2001—Thomas M. Menino: Main Street Maestro," *Governing Magazine*, November 1, 2001, 24.

50. Black and McGrory, "It's for Real—Mayor Menino."

51. Mike Barnicle, "Tom Menino, Urban Mechanic," *Boston Sunday Globe*, November 3, 1993, 9.

52. John Power, "Boston's Urban Mechanic," *Boston Globe Magazine*, December 4, 1995, 18.

53. Donald Gillis, interview, July 14, 2020.

54. Ric Kahn, "Police Raid Nets Weapons, Ammunition," *Boston Globe*, July 20, 1995, 24.

55. Richard Chacon, "Boston Expand Its Work Force, Menino Adds 1,102 Jobs in Two Years," *Boston Globe*, March 1, 1996, 17.

56. "It's Time for Winning Strategies," *Boston Banner*, August 9, 2012, 4.

57. Lupo, "Salerno's Sour Grapes Make a Bad Wine."

58. See Jennifer Peter, "Move Over, Irish; Italians Now Rule Boston," Associated Press, October 5, 2004.

59. See Zoltan L. Hajnal and Paul G. Lewis, "Municipal Institutions and Voter Turnout in Local Elections," *Urban Affairs Review* 38, no. 5 (May 2003): 645–68.

60. Peter Ciurczak and Luo Schuster, "A Decade of Boston Elections, in 11 Graphs," Boston Indicators, October 27, 2017, www.bostonindicators.org.

61. Tomas Gonzalez, interview, June 20, 2020.

62. See Curtis Wood, "Voter Turnout in City Elections," *Urban Affairs Reviews* 38, no. 2 (November 2002): 209–31.

63. See Daniel J. Hopkins and Lindsay M. Pettingill, "Retrospective Voting in Big-City US Mayoral Elections," *Political Science Research and Methods* 6, no.4 (October 2018): 697–714.

64. See Alicia Adsera, Boix Carles, and Mark Payne, "Are You Being Served? Political Accountability and Quality of Government," *Journal of Law, Economics and Organization* 19, no. 2 (2003): 445–90.

65. Jim Vrabel, interview, May 26, 2020.

66. Barbara Ferman, *Challenging the Growth Machine: Neighborhood Politics in Chicago and Pittsburgh* (Lawrence: University Press of Kansas, 1996), 208.

67. John C. Drake, "Promises Unmet: The Mayor Has Failed to Deliver, in Whole or in Part, on Nearly Half of His 41 Most Clearly Stated Commitments to the City," *Boston Globe*, April 27, 2008, 1B.

Chapter 3: Menino, City Councilors, Policies, and the Media

1. See Sidney Verba, *Small Groups and Political Behavior* (Princeton, NJ: Princeton University Press, 2015).

2. Joe Sciacca, personal communication, January 21, 2003.

3. Peter Dreier, "How the Media Compound Urban Problems," *Journal of Urban Affairs* 27, no. 2 (2005): 193.

4. Tom Keane, "Burdens for Bicyclists: Fear-Mongering, Tougher Rules (and Winter) Push Riders Back into Cars," *Boston Globe*, October 14, 2012, 10K. Also see Katie Zezima, "Bicycle System Makeover Has Boston Shifting Gears, *South Florida Sun-Sentinel*, August 9, 2009, 20A.

5. Joe Sciacca, personal communication, January 20, 2003.

6. Jon Keller, interview, April 9, 2020.

7. Howard Leibowitz, interview, July 16, 2002.

8. Chris Black, "Menino Plans Cabinet System; New Structure Set to Manage City," *Boston Globe*, January 20, 1994, 21.

9. Howard Leibowitz, interview, July 16, 2002.

10. Conny Doty, interview, May 21, 2020.

11. Tomas Gonzalez, interview, June 2, 2020.

12. See Margery Egan, "Mayor Tom's Not So Terrific with Councilwomen," *Boston Herald*, February 13, 1997, 14.

13. Adrian Walker, "Menino Reaches Out to New Black Leaders," *Boston Globe*, March 26, 1994, 1, 7.

14. Malo Andre Hutson, "Power, Politics, and Community Development," *Community Development* 44, no. 1 (February 1, 2013): 112.

15. Ibid., 119.

16. See Robert A. Dahl, *Who Governs? Democracy and Power in an American City* (New Haven, CT: Yale University Press, 1961).

17. See Wallace S. Sayre and Herbert Kaufman, *Governing New York City: Politics in the Metropolis* (New York: Russell Sage, 1960).

18. See Bryan D. Jones and Lynn W. Bachelor, *The Sustaining Hand: Community Leadership and Corporate Power* (Lawrence: University Press of Kansas, 1986).

19. See Wilbur C. Rich, *Coleman Young and Detroit Politics* (Detroit: Wayne State University, 1989); *David Dinkins and New York Politics* (Albany, NY: SUNY Press, 2006); and *The Transformative City: Charlotte's Takeoffs and Landings* (Athens: University of Georgia Press, 2020).

20. Richard Schragger, *City Power: Urban Governance in a Global Age* (New York: Oxford University Press, 2016), 38.

21. Mayor's Office, City of Boston, *Boston Works: Partnerships for Sustainable Community* (Boston: City of Boston Empowerment Zone Strategic Plan, June 1994), 20–21.

22. See Scott Herbert, "Interim Assessment of the Empowerment Zones and Enterprise Communities (EZ/EC) Program: A Progress Report," U.S. Department of Housing and Urban Development, Washington, DC, November 2001, https://www.huduser.gov.

23. Bob Hohler, "25 Federal Grants Set for Boston Revitalization," *Boston Globe*, December 21, 1994, 65.

24. James Jennings, "The Empowerment Zone in Boston Massachusetts, 2000–2009: Lessons Learned for Neighborhood Revitalization," *Review of Black Political Economy* 38, no. 1 (March 2011): 74.

25. Ibid.

26. Julia A. Payson, "Cities in the Statehouse: How Local Governments Use Lobbyists to Secure State Funding," *Journal of Politics* 82, no. 2 (2020): 415.

27. Margaret Pantridge, "Power Failure," *Boston Magazine*, October 1991, 60.

28. Katharine Bradbury and Peggy Gilligan, "The New England Recovery," *Journal of Commercial Lending* 76, no. 2 (August 1994): 36.

29. Mayor's Office, City of Boston, *Boston Works*, 26.

30. Margo Howard, "Kevin White," *Boston Magazine*, February 1993, 117.

31. Zebulon Milesfshy and Tomas Gonzalez, "Separatist City: The Mandela, Massachusetts (Roxbury) Movement and the Politics of Incorporation, Self-Determination, and Community Control, 1986–1988," *Trotter Review* 23, no. 1 (2016): 29.

32. William I. Robinson, "Saskia Sassen and the Sociology of Globalization: A Critical Appraisal," *Sociological Analysis* 3, no. 1 (Spring 2009): 16. See also Saskia Sassen, *The Global City: New York, London, Tokyo* (Princeton, NJ: Princeton University Press, 2001).

33. Doty interview.

34. Ibid.

35. Ibid.

36. See Phillip Clay, "Boston: The Incomplete Transformation," in *Big City Politics in Transition*, ed. H. V. Savitch and John Clayton Thomas (Newbury Park, CA: Sage, 1991), 14–28.

37. See "Gale International and Vornado Realty Trust Joint Venture Complete $100 Million Acquisition of Boston Filene's Property," *PR Newswire* (New York), January 30, 2007.

38. Christine S. N. Lewis, "Mayor Battle Vornado," *Wall Street Journal*, April 14, 2010, 1B.

39. Ibid.

40. Joe Sciacca, "Hub's No-Frills Mayor Stays True to His 'Vision,'" *Boston Herald*, November 24, 1997, 6.

41. Lisa M. Hemmerle, "Boston's Back Streets," *Economic Development Journal* 12, no. 3 (Summer 2013): 18.

42. Joseph D. Cutrufo, "Boston We Hardly Knew You," *Planning* 77, no. 1 (January 2011): 5.

43. Michael Chmura, "Babson College Coming to Boston's Innovation District," *Targeted News Service* (Washington, DC), June 3, 2011, 1.

44. Anonymous, "Innovation District Officially Welcomes Babson College to Boston," *PR Newswire*, September 16, 2011, 1.
45. Thomas M. Menino with Jack Beatty, *A Mayor for a New America* (Boston: Houghton Mifflin Harcourt, 2014), 206.
46. See Todd Swanstrom, *The Crisis of Growth Politics* (Philadelphia: Temple University Press, 1985).
47. Pantridge, "Power Failure," 61.
48. "Popular Science Magazine Names Boston Third Greenest City in Nation," *US Fed News Service* (Washington, DC), February 13, 2008, 1.
49. "The Greening of Beantown," *McClatchy-Tribune Business News* (Washington, DC), April 17, 2007, 1.
50. "Mayor Menino's Solar Permitting Guidelines Approved," *US Fed News Service*, December 15, 2010, 1.
51. See Nora Goldstein, "Boston Bold on Climate Change," *Emmaus* 52, no. 12 (December 2011): 38–44.
52. See Sandy Beauregard et al., "Is Boston Building Better? An Analysis of the LEED Certifiable Standard in the Boston Zoning Code," *Journal of Green Building* 9, no. 23 (2014): 146.
53. S. K. Clinebell, "The Effect of Advance Notice of Plant Closing on Firm Value," *Journal of Management* 20, no. 3 (Fall 1994): 553–64.
54. J. T. Metzer, "Planned Abandonment: The Neighborhood Life-Cycle Theory and National Urban Policy," *Housing Policy Debate* 11, no. 1 (2000): 31.

Chapter 4: Boston's Day-to-Day and Recurrent Politics

1. See Thomas K. Ogorzalek, *The City on the Hill: How Urban Institutions Transformed National Politics* (New York: Oxford University Press, 2018).
2. See Patricia A. Kirkland, "Representation in American Cities: Who Runs for Mayor and Who Wins?" *Urban Affairs Review* 58, no. 3 (October 2021): 635–78.
3. See Edwin O'Connor, *The Last Hurrah* (Boston: Little, Brown, 1956).
4. See Steve Erie, *Rainbow's End: Irish Americans and the Dilemmas of Urban Machine Politics, 1840–1985* (Berkeley: University of California Press, 1988).
5. Jim Vrabel, *A People's History of the New Boston* (Amherst: University of Massachusetts Press, 2014), 227.
6. Thomas M. Menino with Jack Beatty, *A Mayor for a New America* (Boston: Houghton Mifflin Harcourt, 2014), 222.
7. "Mayor Menino Endorses Warren for Senate," WBUR, September 21, 2012.
8. Katherine Levine Einstein and David M. Glick conclude that "a significant segment of mayors are actively promoting initiatives in a salient policy arena previously thought to be outside their purview." See Einstein and Glick, "Mayors, Partisanship, and Redistribution: Evidence Directly from U.S. Mayors," *Urban Affairs Review* 54, no. 1 (January 2018): 98.
9. David Passafaro, interview, June 2, 2020.
10. Conny Doty, interview, May 21, 2020.

NOTES TO PAGES 106–115   315

11. See Roger House, "Mandela Referendum: Blacks in Boston Seek to Secede," *The Nation*, November 1988, 452.

12. Douglas T. Yates Jr., *The Ungovernable City* (Cambridge, MA: MIT Press, 1977), 34.

13. Elizabeth Ross, "Boston Mayor Outlines His Vision for the City," *Christian Science Monitor*, January 24, 1994, 10.

14. David Passafaro, interview, June 19, 2020.

15. Loretta McLaughlin, "Is the Council Setting Up a Catch-22 in the Hospital Merger?" *Boston Globe*, June 26, 1996, 15.

16. Passafaro interview, June 19, 2020.

17. McLaughlin, "Is the Council Setting Up a Catch-22."

18. Passafaro interview, June 2, 2020.

19. Adrian Walker and Richard A. Knox, "Menino Makes Plea for Council Approval of Hospital Merger," *Boston Globe*, June 13, 1995, 73.

20. Clark W. Bell, "Boston Deal Puts Top Exec to Test," *Modern Heath Care* 26, no. 48 (November 25, 1996): 31.

21. See James Q. Wilson, "The Mayors vs. the Cities," *Public Interest* 16 (Summer 1969): 25–37.

22. Martha Wagner Weinberg, "Boston's Kevin White: A Mayor Who Survives," *Political Science Quarterly* 96, no. 1 (Spring 1981): 91.

23. Wilson, "The Mayors vs. the Cities," 30.

24. See Pablo Eisenberg, "Why Foundation Grants Shouldn't Mix with Politics," *Chronicle of Philanthropy* 15, no. 8 (February 6, 2003): 32.

25. Ross, "Boston Mayor Outlines His Vision for the City."

26. Lew Finfer, personal communication, May 29, 2020.

27. See David Stoesz, *Small Change: Domestic Policy under the Clinton Presidency* (White Plain, NY: Longman, 1996).

28. Passafaro interview, June 2, 2020.

29. Menino, *Mayor for a New America*, 151.

30. Joe Sciacca, "Don't Be Fooled by Mr. Mayor's Simple Demeanor," *Boston Herald*, November 18, 2002, 1.

31. Patrick Fitzgibbons, "Maybe Red Sox Could Use the Megaplex, Boston Mayor Says," *Bond Buyer*, March 3, 1994, 3.

32. Ibid.

33. Passafaro interview, June 2, 2020.

34. David Passafaro, interview, June 23, 2020.

35. See Meg Vaillancourt and Richard Kindleberger, "Megaplex Panel Cites Progress in Finding Funds," *Boston Globe*, May 28, 1995, 32.

36. Meg Vaillancourt and Adrian Walker, "Menino Urges Stadium Be Axed from Megaplex," *Boston Globe*, August 13, 1995, 1.

37. Don Aucoin and Scot Lehigh, "Stadium Dispute Puts Menino in the Hot Seat," *Boston Globe*, January 14, 1997, 1A.

38. Wilbur C. Rich, "Who Lost the Boston Megaplex and Almost the New England Patriots," in *The Economics and Politics of Sports Facilities*, ed. Wilbur C. Rich (Westport, CT: Quorum, 2000), 203–21.

39. Menino, *Mayor for a New America*, 182–83.

316 NOTES TO PAGES 116–128

40. Alan DiGaetano, "Urban Governing Alignments and Realignment in Comparative Perspective: Developmental Politics in Boston, Massachusetts, and Bristol, England, 1980–1996," *Urban Affairs Review* 32, no. 2 (July 1997): 860.

41. Richard M. Perlmutter, "Boston: From Blueprints to Brick," *Urban Lawyer* 34, no. 2 (Spring 2002): 339.

42. Stacey Higginbotham, "Despite New Plan, Fenway Park Project Still Faces Hurdles," *Bond Buyer*, July 27, 2000, 3.

43. See Clarence Stone, *Regime Politics: Governing Atlanta, 1946–1988* (Lawrence, KS: University Press of America, 1988).

44. See David Nyhan, "Assessing the Mayor," *Boston Globe*, May 7, 1991.

45. Martin Nolan, "Menino Offers Pledge: The Ambition Stops Here," *Boston Globe*, November 4, 1993, 37.

46. Jon Keller, *Keller at Large*, WHDH, interview, August 5, 1995, https://whdh.com.

47. Jason Schwartz and Rachel Slade, "A Mayor in Full—Farewell to the Petty Thin-Skinned Ruthless S.O.B. Who Just May Be the Best Mayor We've Had," *Boston Magazine*, October 1, 2013, 1A.

48. Passafaro interview, June 2, 2020.

Chapter 5: Who Gets Housing, When, and Where?

1. David P. Varady and Jeffrey A. Raffel, *Selling Cities: Attracting Homebuyers through Schools and Housing Programs* (Albany, NY: SUNY Press, 1995), 3.

2. Tilo Schabert, *Boston Politics: The Creativity of Power* (New York: Walter De Gruyter, 1989), 274–75.

3. See Michael Hankinson, "When Do Renters Behave Like Homeowners? High Rent, Price Anxiety NIMBYism," *American Political Science Review* 12 (August 2018): 473–93.

4. Cynthia Zaitzevsky, "Housing Boston's Poor. The Philanthropic Experiments," *Journal of the Society of Architectural Historians* 42, no. 2 (May 1983): 157–58.

5. *The Report of the Boston Committee on the Expediency of Providing Better Tenements for the Poor* (Boston: Eastburn Press, 1846), 36, reviewed in *North American Review* 64, no. 134 (January 1847): 266–68.

6. Amy Johnson, "Model Housing for the Poor: Turn of the Century Tenement Reform and the Boston Cooperative Building Company" (Ph.D. diss., University of Delaware, 2004).

7. Robert Treat Paine, "The Housing Condition in Boston," *Annals of the American Academy of Political and Social Science* 20 (July 1902): 136.

8. See Catherine Bauer, *Modern Housing* (New York: Arno Press, 1934).

9. See Kenneth T. Jackson, *Crabgrass Frontier: The Suburbanization of the United States* (New York: Oxford University Press, 1985), 219.

10. See Ira Katznelson, *When Affirmative Action Was White* (New York: Norton, 2005).

11. Editorial Board, "$215-Million Cut in Model Cities Is Ordered by the Administration," *New York Times*, October 2, 1969, 28.

12. David Donnison, "The Politics of Housing," *Australian Quarterly* 48, no. 2 (June 1976): 18.
13. See Wilbur C. Rich, "Political Power and the Role of the Housing Authority," in *Housing Form and Public Policy in the United States*, ed. Richard Plunz (New York: Praeger, 1980), 51–60.
14. See J. R. Gist, "Fiscal Austerity, Grant Structure and Local Expenditure Responses," *Policy Studies Journal* 16 (1988): 687–712.
15. David Warsh, "That Was Then, This Is Now," *Boston Globe*, October 30, 1990, 41.
16. Thomas M. Menino with Jack Beatty, *A Mayor for a New America* (Boston: Houghton Mifflin Harcourt, 2014), 208–9.
17. Joseph D. Cutrufo, "Boston We Hardly Knew You," *Planning* 77, no. 1 (January 2011): 2.
18. Michael Grunwald, "Further Cuts Feared in Housing for the Poor Menino Says the City Needs a Game Plan," *Boston Globe*, January 5, 1995, 1.
19. Richard Chacon, "Mayor Ushers in Housing Week, $8M Initiative," *Boston Globe*, March 23, 1997, 1B.
20. Thomas Grillo, "Leading the Way," *Boston Globe*, November 25, 2001, 1J.
21. Sarah Barmak, "How Boston Made It Work," *Toronto Star*, March 15, 2008, 4.
22. Editorial Board, "Menino's Housing Success," *Boston Globe*, June 27, 2003, 20A.
23. Kevin Joy, "City Build on Housing Plan, Aims for More Units," *Boston Globe*, May 13, 2004, 3B.
24. Chris White, "Two Cities, Mayors and Housing Plans," *Planning: Chicago* 80, no. 5 (May 2014): 8.
25. Casey Ross, "Menino Offers a Formula for More Housing: Puts Emphasis on Fast Action, Affordability," *Boston Globe*, September 9, 2013, 1A.
26. Donald Gillis, interview, July 14, 2020.
27. Lawrence J. Vale, "Public Housing and the American Dream: Residents' Views on Buying into the Projects," *Housing Policy Debate* 9, no. 2 (1998): 293.
28. See Claudine Gay, "Moving to Opportunity: The Political Effects of a Housing Mobility Experiment," *Urban Affairs Review* 48, no. 2 (March 2011): 147–79.
29. See Blair Jenkins, "Rent Control: Do Economists Agree?" *Econ Journal Watch* 6, no. 1 (January 2009): 73–112.
30. Donald A. Gillis, "The Sociology of a City in Transition, 1960–2000" (Ph.D. diss., Boston University, 2015), 246.
31. See Jonathan Witten, "Adult Supervision Required: The Commonwealth of Massachusetts's Reckless Adventures with Housing and the Anti-Snob Zoning Act," *Boston College Environmental Affairs Law Review* 34, no. 2 (2008): 217–58. Also see Lisa Prevost, *Snob Zone: Fear, Prejudice and Real Estate* (Boston: Beacon Press, 2013).
32. U.S. Census, 1940, 1990.
33. See Katznelson, *When Affirmative Action Was White*.
34. Robert Schafer, "Racial Discrimination in the Boston Housing Market," *Journal of Urban Economics* 6, no. 2 (April 1979): 191.
35. See John Yinger, "Measuring Racial Discrimination with Fair Housing Audits: Caught in the Act," *American Economic Review* 76, no. 5 (December 1986): 881–93.
36. See Cullen Geonner, "Discrimination and Mortgage Lending in Boston: The Effect

of Model Uncertainty," *Journal of Real Estate Finance Economics*, 40, no. 3 (April 2010): 260–85.

37. Judith D. Feins and Rachel G. Bratt, "Barred in Boston: Racial Discrimination in Housing," *Journal of the American Planning Association* 49, no. 3 (November 2007): 354.

38. Mark Abrahamson, *Urban Enclaves* (New York: Worth, 2006), 8, 12.

39. See Richard Florida, *The New Urban Crisis* (New York: Basic Books, 2017).

40. See Beate Klingenberg and Roger J. Brown, "Rent Control Revisited: Effects on Property Management," *Property Management* 26, no. 1 (2008): 55–65. Also see Rebecca Diamond, Time McQuade, and Franklin Qian, "The Effects of Rent Control Expansion on Tenants, Landlords, and Inequality: Evidence from San Francisco," *American Economic Review* 109 (September 2019): 3365–94.

41. See Don Aucoin, "Rent control Pits Home Rule vs. Referendum," *Boston Globe*, November 22, 1994, 1.

42. Derrick Z. Jackson, "Time to Revive Rent Control—Boston's Poor in Housing Squeeze," *Providence Journal-Bulletin*, October 22, 1999, B6.

43. Ibid.

44. Adrian Walker, "No Home for Rent Control," *Boston Globe*, November 21, 2002, 1B.

45. Scott S. Greenberger, "Menino Is Rebuffed on Rent Curbs; City Council Rejects Plan as Ineffectual," *Boston Globe*, November 21, 2002, 1A.

46. Geeta O'Donnell Anand, "Boston Plans an Initiative for Housing," *Wall Street Journal*, November 11, 1998, 1.

47. "Ballot Question Results," *Boston Herald*, November 9, 2000, 34.

48. Henri Lefebvre, "The Right to the City," in *Writing on Cities*, ed. Eleonore Kofman and Elizabeth Lebas (Oxford: Blackwell, 1996), 63–181.

49. "Census Finds Soaring Homeless Rate," *Cape Cod Times*, January 5, 2011, www.capecodtimes.com.

50. See Peter H. Rossi, *Down and Out in America: The Origins of Homelessness* (Chicago: University of Chicago Press, 1989).

51. See Brendan O'Flaherty, *Making Room: The Economics of Homelessness* (Cambridge, MA: Harvard University Press, 1996).

52. Michael Kenney, "In City, More Are Homeless Boston Finds 10% Rise Over Its 1993 Tally," *Boston Globe*, December 28, 1994, 17.

53. See Jeff R. Crump, "The End of Public Housing as We Know It: The Public Housing Policy, Labor Regulation and the US City," *International Journal of Urban and Regional Research* 27, no. 1 (March 2003): 179–89.

54. See Martha R. Burt, *Over the Edge: The Growth of Homelessness in 1980* (New York: Russell Sage Foundation, 1992).

55. "Mayor Menino Launches Boston Homelessness Prevention Clearinghouse," *US Fed News Service* (Washington, DC), June 9, 2006.

56. "Homelessness in Boston Reduced 30 Percent after Menino Initiative," *Daily Free Press* (Boston), January 29, 2011, 1.

57. See Lawrence J. Vale, *From the Puritans to the Projects: Public Housing and Public Neighbors* (Cambridge, MA: Harvard University Press, 2000).

58. See Meghan E. Irons, "Blacks Appreciate Menino, Yearn for More: Diverse Legacy," *Boston Globe*, March 29, 2013, 7A.

NOTES TO PAGES 151–163 319

59. See Katherine Levine Einstein, David M. Glick, and Maxwell Palmer, *Neighborhood Defenders: Participatory Politics and American Housing Crisis* (New York: Cam.bridge University Press, 2019).

60. Thomas O'Connor, *Building a New Boston: Politics and Urban Renewal, 1950–1970* (Boston: Northeastern University Press, 1993), 294–95.

Chapter 6: Crime in the Streets and Elsewhere

1. Andrew Martin, "Gangs May Be Too Diverse for Single Remedy," *Chicago Tribune*, April 13, 1997, 1.

2. See Norton E. Long, *The Unwalled City: Reconstituting the Urban Community* (New York: Basic Books, 1972).

3. See Herman Lelieveldt, "Helping Citizens Help Themselves: Neighborhood Improvement Programs and Networks, Trust, and Norms of Neighborhood-Oriented Forms of Participation," *Urban Affairs Review* 39, no. 5 (May 2004): 532–51.

4. Adrian Walker, "Menino's s Basic Vision Is of a City That Works," *Boston Globe*, July 2, 1995, 1.

5. See Richard C. Larson, "What Happened to Patrol Operations in Kansas City? A Review of the Kansas City Preventive Patrol Experiment," *Journal of Criminal Justice* 2, no. 3 (Winter 1975): 267–97. Also see Barbara J. Risman, "The Kansas City Preventive Patrol Experiment: A Continuing Debate," *Evaluation Review* 4, no. 6 (December 1980): 802–808.

6. Adrian Walker, "Boston Police Report Drop in Crime for a Fifth Straight Year," *Boston Globe*, March 3, 1995, 87.

7. Scott S. Greenberger, "Majority in Survey Feels City Less Safe," *Boston Globe*, August 23, 2004, 1.

8. Judy Rakowsky, "Bratton Touts Community Policing Ideas," *Boston Globe*, May 16, 1993, 27.

9. See John Ellement, "Minority Officer Group Endorses Bratton's Community Police Plan," *Boston Globe*, August 9, 1993, 24.

10. See Harrell R. Rodgers and George Taylor, "The Policeman as an Agent of Regime Legitimation," *Midwest Journal of Political Science* 15, no. 1 (February 1971): 77–86.

11. Ibid.

12. Richard L. Block, "Fear of Crime and Fear of the Police," *Social Problems* 19, no. 1 (Summer 1971): 100.

13. See David Easton and Jack Dennis, *Children in the Political System* (New York: McGraw Hill, 1969).

14. See James Q. Wilson, *Variety of Police Behavior: The Management of Law and Order in Eight Communities* (Cambridge, MA: Harvard University Press, 1978).

15. See Al Baker, "City Minorities More Likely to Be Frisked," *New York Times*, May 13, 2010, 1A.

16. See Tony Locy, "Poor Police Work Hamper Investigations," *Boston Globe*, April 7, 1991.

17. Ed Cafasso, "Broadway Bill a Tough Act to Follow: There Are No Front Runners," *Boston Herald*, December 3, 1993, 1.

18. Robert Connolly, "Gripped by Violence . . . as Gov Does About-Face on Guns," *Boston Herald*, September 30, 1993, 1.
19. Cafasso, "Broadway Bill a Tough Act to Follow."
20. Joe Sciacca, "Both Bratton and Menino Have Work to Do; Mayor Facing the First Test of His Term," *Boston Herald*, December 3, 1993, 7.
21. Thomas Duffy, "The Commish," *Boston Magazine*, March 1995, 39.
22. Ibid., 44.
23. Ibid.
24. "United States: First Safety, Then Civility," *Economist*, May 1, 1999, 26.
25. Ibid.
26. Larry Mayes, interview, June 9, 2020.
27. "Text of Mayor Giuliani's Farewell Address," *New York Times*, December 27, 2001, https://www.nytimes.com.
28. Maggie Mulvihill and Joseph Mallia, "Boston Police, Sorry for the Mistake," *Boston Herald*, March 27, 1994, 1.
29. Mayor Tom Menino, interview, May 23, 2000.
30. Joseph Mallia and Maggie Mulvihill, "Minister Dies as Cops Raid Wrong Apartment," *Boston Herald*, March 26, 1994, 1.
31. See Maggie Mulvilhill, "Supervisor Blames Lt. for Botched Drug Raid," *Boston Herald*, August 19, 1994, 14.
32. Donald A. Gillis, "The Sociology of a City in Transition, 1960–2000" (Ph.D. diss., Boston University, 2015), 189.
33. Jon Keller interview, April 9, 2020.
34. For a discussion of the disagreements, see Leonard Greene, "Boston's Black Leaders Commit Crime of Silence," *Boston Herald*, April 1, 1994, 6.
35. Maggie Mulvihill and Joseph Mallia, "Stunned Neighbors Demand Answers to the Question, Why?" *Boston Herald*, March 28, 1994, 18.
36. Ann Donlan, "Evans Rips Reversal of Cop Suspension," *Boston Herald*, December 31, 1996, 22.
37. Leonard Greene, "Apologies Don't Excuse Pattern of Recklessness," *Boston Herald*, April 11, 1994, 4.
38. Menino interview.
39. "Boston Mayor Hopes Healing Has Begun," *Worcester Telegram and Gazette*, March 28, 1994, 2.
40. Alyce Lee, interview, July 5, 2000.
41. Leonard Greene, "Protests Come Too Late to Avenge Minister's Death," *Boston Herald*, March 27, 1995, 4.
42. Greene, "Apologies Don't Excuse Pattern of Recklessness."
43. Derrick Jackson, "Mayor Scrooge," *Boston Globe*, April 7, 1995, 22.
44. See Kevin Cullen and Indira A. R. Lakshmanan, "City to Pay Widow \$1M in Death of Minister," *Boston Globe*, April 24, 1996, 1. See also Ralph Ranalli, "Widow Gets \$1M for Cop Blunder; City Settles Lawsuit over Raid That Killed Minister, *Boston Herald*, April 24, 1996, 1.
45. Gerald O'Neil, Dick Lehr, and Mitchel Zuckoff, "Boston Police Turn on One of Their Own Years after Beating, Officer Has Seen No Help from Colleagues," *Boston Globe*, December 8, 1997, 1A.

46. Brian McGrory, "Cox Case Gets More Shameful," *Boston Globe*, February 2, 1999, 1B.
47. Christopher Winship and Jenny Berrien, "Boston Cops and Black Churches," *Public Interest* 99, no. 136 (Summer 1999): 60.
48. Ibid., 58.
49. Oliver Burkeman, "The Guardian Profile: Paul Evans" *Guardian* (London), September 12, 2003, 13.
50. See Anthony Braga, David Hureau, and Christopher Winship, "Losing Faith—Police, Black Churches, and Resurgence of Youth Violence in Boston," *Ohio State Journal of Criminal Law* 6, no. 1 (Fall 2008): 142–72.
51. Kevin Cullen, "The Neighborhood Cop," *Boston Globe Magazine*, January 7, 1996, 33.
52. Ralph H. Saunders, "The Politics and Practice of Community Policing in Boston," *Urban Geography* 20, no. 5 (1999): 478, 480.
53. Mayor Tom Menino, "No Next Time and Project Peace," October 3, 1997, box 247, City of Boston Archives, Boston.
54. Larry Mayes, interview, June 9, 2020.
55. Ibid.
56. Ibid.
57. Ibid.
58. Noel C. Paul, "The Woman Chosen to Lead Boston's Police; Kathleen O'Toole, Who Took Over after Super Bowl Riots, Pushes Ahead with Toughness and a Personal Touch," *Christian Science Monitor*, March 16, 2004, 2.
59. Daniel Brook, "The Cracks in 'Broken Windows,'" *Boston Globe*, February 19, 2006, 1E.
60. "Suffolk University Poll Shows Mayor Menino Set for a Landslide Win," *US Fed News Service* (Washington, DC), November 4, 2005.
61. Donovan Slack, "Menino Says No to State Police Use; Romney Offered Aid for City's Crime Fight," *Boston Globe*, June 23, 2004, 1.
62. See Pam Belluck, "National Briefing New England: Massachusetts: $5.1 Million Death Settlement," *New York Times*, May 3, 2005, 18.
63. Shelley Murphy, "Snelgrove Family Settles Lawsuit; Kin Sought 10M from Gun Maker," *Boston Globe*, July 14, 2006, 1B.
64. See Shelley Murphy and Suzanne Smalley, "Hunt Is on for Other Police Corruption," *Boston Globe*, July 22, 2006, 1A. Also see Yvonne Abraham and Michael Levenson, "Pulido's Club Offered Sex, Drugs, Prosecutor Say," *Boston Globe*, July 22, 2006, 1B.
65. Joan Vennochi, "Backing the Commish," *Boston Globe*, May 18, 2006, 13A.
66. Edward Davis, interview, January 10, 2020.
67. Ibid.
68. Suzanne Smalley, "Amid Turmoil, Davis Take Police Reins," *Boston Globe*, December 5, 2006, 2B.
69. Yawu Miller, "A History of Law Enforcement," in *Boston's Banner Years: 1965–2015*, ed. Melvin B. Miller (Bloomington, IN: Archway, 2018), 119–20.
70. Davis interview.
71. "Commissioner Davis Welcome $11.8 Million in Cops Funding Heading for the City of Boston," *US Fed News Service*, August 3, 2009.
72. Ibid.
73. Davis interview.

322 NOTES TO PAGES 182–196

74. O'Ryan Johnson, "Police Official Say Pride, Ego Fuel Boston Homicides," *TCA Regional New* (Chicago), July 29, 2014, 1.
75. Davis interview.
76. "Commissioner Ed Davis, Boston Police Speaks at Press Conference at Press Conference on Boston Marathon Bombings," Political Transcript Wire, Lanham, April 16, 2013.
77. See Elaine B. Sharp, "Politics, Economic, and Urban Planning: The Postindustrial City Thesis and Rival Explanation of Heightened Order Maintenance Policing," *Urban Affairs Review* 50, no. 3 (May 2014): 340–65.
78. "Bostonians Are Safe, but a High Cost," *Boston Globe*, September 3, 2009, 10A.
79. Ibid.
80. Saunders, "The Politics and Practice of Community Policing in Boston," 479.

Chapter 7: Boston's Racial Diversity Challenge

1. Brian Wright O'Connor and Peter C. Roby, "Political Highlights of the Banner Years" in *Boston's Banner Years: 1965–2015*, ed. Melvin B. Miller (Bloomington, IN: Archway, 2018), 50.
2. James Jennings, "Measuring Neighborhood Distress: A Tool for Place-Based Urban Revitalization Strategies," *Community Development* 43, no. 4 (January 2012): 468.
3. See Peter Dreier, John Mollenkopf, and Todd Swanstrom, *Place Matters: Metropolitics for the Twenty-First Century* (Lawrence: University Press of Kansas, 2014).
4. See Lee Dembart, "Koch, Criticized by Many Blacks, Seeks to Repair Ties with Theme," *New York Times*, February 27, 1979, 1A.
5. Two anonymous interviews.
6. "Say Brother," Open Vault from GBH, https://openbvault.wgbh.org.
7. Devorah Heitner, "Performing Black Power in the 'Cradle of Liberty': *Say Brother* Envisions New Principles of Blackness in Boston," *Television and New Media* 10, no. 5 (September 2009): 412.
8. Oliver Wendell Holmes Sr., "Quotes," Good Reads, https://www.goodreads.com.
9. See Mel King, *Chain of Change: Struggles for Black Community Development* (Boston: South End Press, 1999).
10. See James Jennings and Mel King, *From Access to Power* (Cambridge, MA: Schenkman Books, 1986).
11. Gilbert Caldwell, "The Day Dr. King Visited Boston Won't Be Forgotten," *Bay State Banner* (Boston), January 19, 2012, 1.
12. Dr. Robert Hall, personal correspondence, December 24, 2019.
13. See "Kevin White: 1929–2012: Mayor of Boston during Busing Battles in 1970s," *Chicago Tribune*, January 30, 2012, 5.
14. Martin Nolan, "Prospect Looms for an All-White Group of Citywide Elected Offcials," *Boston Globe*, October 5, 1991, 1.
15. Ibid.
16. David M. Alpern, Sylvester Monroe, and Jerry Buckley, "Boston: King's First Hurrah" *Newsweek*, October 24, 1983, 33.
17. Since the 1980s, political scientists have spent a lot of time on this issue. See William

Collins, "Race as a Salient Factor in Nonpartisan Elections," *Western Political Quarterly* 33 (September 1980): 330–35. Also see Zoltan Hajnal and Jessica Trounstine, "Where Turnout Matters; The Consequences of Uneven Turnout in City Politics," *Journal of Politics* 67, no. 2 (May 2005): 515–35.

18. See Zoltan Hajnal, "White Residents, Black Incumbents and a Declining Racial Divide," *American Political Science Review* 95, no. 3 (September 2001): 603–17.

19. Zoltan Hajnal and Jessica Trounstine, "Where Turnout Matters."

20. See Robert K. Merton, *Social Theory and Social Structure* (New York: Free Press, 1968).

21. See Margot Hornblower, "Boston, a Dream of Independence: Minority Neighborhoods to Vote On," *Washington Post*, October 13, 1986, 3A.

22. See James Jennings, *The Politics of Black Empowerment* (Detroit: Wayne State University Press, 1992).

23. See Nancy Haggard-Gilson, *Boston's Mandela Referendum: Urban Nationalism and Economic Dependence* (New York: Routledge, 1995).

24. Thomas M. Menino with Jack Beatty, *A Mayor for a New America* (Boston: Houghton Mifflin Harcourt, 2014), 59.

25. Menino, *Mayor for a New America*, 42.

26. See Benjamin DeMott, *The Trouble with Friendship: Why Americans Can't Think Straight about Race* (New Haven, CT: Yale University Press, 1998).

27. Zebulon Miletsky and Tomas Gonzalez, "Separatist City: The Mandela, Massachusetts (Roxbury) Movement and the Politics of Incorporation, Self-Determination, and Community Control, 1986–1988," *Trotter Review* 23, no. 1 (2016): 13.

28. For an analysis of social isolation thesis, see William J. Wilson, *The Truly Disadvantaged* (Chicago: University of Chicago Press, 1987). Also see a more recent validating survey of Los Angeles conducted by Lauren J. Krivo et al., "Social Isolation of Disadvantage and Advantage: The Reproduction of Inequality in Urban Space," *Social Forces* 92, no. 1 (September 2013): 141–64.

29. For an analysis of this phenomenon, see Rachel Meltzer and Jenny Schuetz's "Bodegas or Bagel Shops? Neighborhood Differences in Retail and Household Services," *Economic Development Quarterly* 26, no. 1 (February 2012): 73–94.

30. Marilyn Johnson, *The New Bostonians: How Immigrants Transformed the Metro Area since the 1960s* (Amherst: University of Massachusetts Press, 2015), 88.

31. Jorge Capetillo-Ponce, "Black-Latino/a Relations in Boston: Two Trends of Collective Identification," *Latino Studies* 8, no. 2 (Summer 2010): 244–70.

32. Yawu Miller, "After Icy Impasse, Officials See Progress with Menino," *Bay State Banner*, March 11, 1999, 7.

33. Brian McGrory, interview, October 4, 2019.

34. Rev. Eugene Rivers, interview, October 3, 2019.

35. Jenny Berrien and Christopher Winship, "Lesson Learned from Boston Police Community Collaboration," *Federal Probation* 36 (December 1999): 1–13, 30 (quotation).

36. Miletsky and Gonzalez, "Separatist City," 26.

37. See Wilbur C. Rich, "Civic Engagement Generations Make: Race, Options, and Actions," *Phylon* 52, no. 2 (Winter 2015): 24–42.

38. Robert A. Jordan, "America's Black Leadership Now Speak in Many Voices:

Diversified Group of Leaders Have Evolved to Address the Issues of the 80s," *Boston Globe*, June 8, 1980, 1.

39. Ibid.

40. See Noel Ignatiev, *How the Irish Became White* (New York: Routledge, 1995).

41. Lawrence Johnson, "The Permanence of Race: Governor Deval Patrick and the Deracialization Concept" (Ph.D. diss., Virginia Polytechnic Institute and State University, 2012), 204.

42. Ibid., 202.

43. For an analysis of how the two men each related to the Black leadership class, see O'Connor and Roby, "Political Highlights of the Banner Years," 60–64.

44. Toni-Michell Travis, "Boston: The Unfinished Agenda," in *Racial Politics in American Cities*, ed. Rufus P. Browning, Dale R. Marshall, and David Tabb (New York: Longman, 1990), 108–21.

45. Thomas O'Connor, *Building a New Boston: Politics and Urban Renewal, 1950–1970* (Boston: Northeastern University Press, 1993), 288.

46. Phillip Clay, "Boston: The Incomplete Transformation," in *Big City Politics in Transition*, ed. H. V. Savitch and John Clayton Thomas (Newbury Park, CA: Sage, 1991), 27.

47. See Victoria Benning, "Community Group Backs Bolling with Endorsement in Mayor Race," *Boston Globe*, May 19, 1993, 15.

48. E. Jeanne Harnois, "A Conversation with Mel King; At 75, He's Still Fighting the Fight," *Boston Globe*, August 2004, 6.

49. See Jeffrey S. Passel, Gretchen Livingston, and D'Vera Cohn, "White Births: Explaining Why Minority Births Now Outnumber White Births," Pew Research Center, May 18, 2012, i.

50. Richard Chacon, "More Hispanics Are Taking Root in Roxbury," *Boston Globe*, September 9, 1996, 1A.

51. Donna M. Harris and Judy Marquez Kiyama, *The Plight of Invisibility: A Community-Based Approach to Understanding the Educational Experiences of Urban Latina/os* (New York: Peter Lang, 2015), 43.

52. See Peter Skerry's *Mexican Americans: The Ambivalent Minority* (Cambridge, MA: Harvard University Press, 1995).

53. See Ignacio García, *Chicanismo: Forging of a Militant Ethos Among Mexican Americans* (Tucson: University of Arizona Press, 1997).

54. Capetillo-Ponce, "Black-Latino/a Relations in Boston," 251.

55. Maggie Rivas, "Blacks in Changing America: The Hispanic Role: Rival or Ally," *Boston Globe*, June 28, 1982, 1.

56. For some suggestions for Latino politicians' trying to appeal to Latino voters, see Manny Fernandez, "No Easy Mode for a Latino Texas Politician," *New York Times*, October 23, 2016, 17A.

57. See Capetillo-Ponce, "Black-Latino/a Relations in Boston."

58. Tomas Gonzalez, interview, June 2, 2020.

59. Sara B. Miller, "Boston Develops Melting-Pot Politics," *Christian Science Monitor*, April 13, 2005, 2.

60. See Sharon Wright Austin, *The Caribbeanization of Black Politics: Race, Group Consciousness, and Political Participation in America* (Albany, NY: SUNY Press, 2018).

61. Adrian Walker, "Memo Assails Menino on Black Issues," *Boston Globe*, July 25, 1995, 15.

62. Ibid.

63. Anthony Braga, David Hureau, and Christopher Winship, "Losing Faith—Police, Black Churches and the Resurgence of Youth Violence in Boston," *Ohio State Journal of Criminal Law* 6, no. 1 (Fall 2008): 162–63, 164.

64. Helena Lima Ambrizeth, *Cape Verdean Immigrants in America: The Socialization of Young Men in an Urban Environment* (El Paso, TX: LFB Scholarly, 2011), 136–37.

65. Austin, *The Caribbeanization of Black Politics*, 157–58.

66. Ambrizeth, *Cape Verdean Immigrants in America*, 168.

67. See Nicholas L. Danigelis, "Black Political Participation in the United States: Some Recent Evidence," *American Sociological Review* 43, no. 5 (October 1978): 756–71. Also see Lawrence Bobo and Franklin D. Gilliam, "Race, Sociopolitical Participation, and Black Empowerment," *American Political Science Review* 84, no. 2 (June 1990): 377–93.

68. Mary Wiltenburg, "Minority—What Does It Really Mean," *Christian Science Monitor*, January 31, 2002, 14.

69. Michael Jonas, "Black Power: Why Are African-Americans Still Struggling to Get ahead in Boston Politics," *CommonWealth Magazine*, Fall 2003, 59, 60.

70. "Mayor Menino Launches Violence Prevention Campaign in Mattapan," *US Fed News Service* (Washington, DC), September 7, 2013.

71. See Dreier, Mollenkopf, and Swanstrom, *Place Matters*.

72. Richard Kindleberger, "Mass. Unemployment Jumps to 8.8% Rate for Blacks in the Highest in Years," *Boston Globe*, July 3, 1992, 57.

73. Bureau of Labor Statistics, U.S. Department of Labor, 2013. Also see Chris Reidy, "Mass. Jobless Rate Higher Than US for First Time since '07," *Boston Globe*, December 19, 2013, www.bostonglobe.com.

74. William I. Robinson, "Saskia Sassen and the Sociology of Globalization: A Critical Appraisal," *Sociological Analysis* 3, no. 1 (Spring 2009): 16.

75. William E. Nelson Jr., *Black Atlantic Politics: Dilemmas of Political Empowerment in Boston and Liverpool* (Albany, NY: SUNY Press, 2000), 73.

76. Meghan E. Irons, "Blacks Appreciate Menino, Yearn for More: Diverse Legacy," *Boston Globe*, March 29, 2013, 7A.

77. Donald A. Gillis, "The Sociology of a City in Transition, 1960–2000" (Ph.D. diss., Boston University, 2015), 191–92.

78. Nelson, *Black Atlantic Politics*, 75–76.

79. "Boston Black Weekly, Returning to Publication," *Editor and Publisher* 31 (July 31, 2009): 1.

80. See Cydney Dupree and Susan Fiske, "Self-Presentation in the Competence Downshift by White Liberals," *Journal of Personality and Social Psychology* 117, no. 3 (September 2019): 579–604.

Chapter 8: The Failure of Boston Public School Reform

1. John M. Cronin, *Reforming Boston Schools, 1930 to 2006 to Present: Overcoming Corruption and Racial Segregation* (New York: Palgrave Macmillan, 2011), 206.

2. Alan Lupo, "School Committee Format: A Debate Renewed Factions in Boston Push Elected vs. Appointed," *Boston Globe*, March 31, 1996, 7.

326 NOTES TO PAGES 220–230

3. See Michael Rezendes, "Boston School Committee: Uneven Past, Uncertain Future: Elected School Often Became a Battleground," *Boston Globe*, June 22, 1991, 1.

4. Lupo, "School Committee Format."

5. See Jonathan Kozol's *Death at an Early Age: The Destruction of the Hearts and Minds of Negro Students in Boston Schools* (Boston: Houghton Mifflin, 1967).

6. Rob Gurwitt, "Boston Public Schools," *Boston Magazine*, March 25, 2013, 74.

7. "U.S. Census Bureau, "Public School System Finances: Historical Data," https://www.census.gov.

8. Wilbur C. Rich, *Black Mayors and Schools Politics: The Failure of Reform in Detroit, Gary, and Newark* (New York: Garland, 1996).

9. Lupo, "School Committee Format."

10. Ibid.

11. "A School Victory without Class," *Boston Globe*, November 7, 1996, 30A.

12. Donald A. Gillis, "The Sociology of a City in Transition, 1960–2000" (Ph.D. diss., Boston University, 2015), 218.

13. Michael Jonas, "Black Power: Why Are African-Americans Still Struggling to Get Ahead in Boston Politics," *Commonwealth*, Fall 2003, 61.

14. Gillis, "The Sociology of a City in Transition," 218.

15. Samuel R. Tyler, "The Case for Sticking with Appointed School Committee Setup for Boston," *Dorchester Reporter*, December 2018, 1.

16. Steven Taylor, "Appointing or Electing the Boston School Committee: The Preferences of the African American Community," *Urban Education* 36, no. 1 (January 1, 2001): 22–23.

17. Karen Avenoso, "Factions Unite in Push for Elected School Committee," *Boston Globe*, September 11, 1996, 1A.

18. Karen Avenoso, "Principals' Support Asked for Appointed School Panel," *Boston Globe*, October 24, 1996, 1A.

19. Patricia Wen, "Harrison-Jones Favors Elected School Panel," *Boston Globe*, October 29, 1996, 2B.

20. Andrea Estes, "Big Business Backs Appointed Board," *Boston Herald*, October 25, 1996, 20.

21. Yvonne Abraham, "The Un-Campaign," *Boston Phoenix*, October 3, 1997, 16.

22. Karen Avenoso, "School Board Stays the Same," *Boston Globe*, November 5, 1996, 1B.

23. "A School Victory without Class."

24. See Wilbur C. Rich, "Who Is Afraid of a Mayoral Takeover of Detroit Public Schools?" in *When Mayors Take Charge*, ed. Joseph Viteritti (Washington: Brooking Institutions, 2009), 148–67.

25. Jon Keller, interview, April 9, 2020.

26. Kenneth Wong and Pushpam Jain, "Newspapers as Policy Actors in Urban School Systems," *Urban Affairs Review* 35, no. 2 (November 1999): 241, 239.

27. Martha Pierce, interview, May 27, 2020.

28. Ibid.

29. Ibid.

30. John C. Drake, "Promises Unmet: The Mayor Has Failed to Deliver, in Whole or in Part, on Nearly Half of His 41 Most Clearly Stated Commitments to the City," *Boston Globe*, April 27, 2008, 1B.

31. Pierce interview.

32. Meghan V. Doran, "Narratives of the Past in Contemporary Urban Politics: The Case of the Boston Desegregation Crisis" (Ph.D. diss., Northeastern University, 2005), 176.

33. Ibid., 185.

34. Michael Rezendes, "City Councilor Faces Fight over Walk-to-Schools," *Boston Globe*, January 10, 1994, 9.

35. Boston High School, Enrollment Data, 1993–1994, School and District Profiles, Department of Elementary and Secondary Education, https://profiles.doe.mass.edu.

36. Michael Rezendes, "Black Officials Protest Flynn Delay in Signing Harrison-Jones Pact," *Boston Globe*, July 19, 1991).

37. Patricia Mangan, "Flynn Hesitant to Accept Resignation of Consalvo," *Boston Herald*, November 17, 1992, 14.

38. Diego Ribadeneria, "In First Six Months, City School Chief Builds a Broad Base," *Boston Globe*, January 30, 1992, 1B.

39. Editorial Board, "Frustration in Boston Over Its Schools," *New York Times*, January 6, 1993, 19A.

40. Ibid.

41. Ed Doherty, interview, October 17, 1997.

42. See Adrian Walker, "Brett, Menino Spar on City Education Policies," *Boston Globe*, September 23, 1993, 28.

43. Connie Paige, "Hub Teacher Settled," *Boston Herald*, November 10, 1993, 1.

44. Peter S. Canellos, "Anti-Union Stance Seen Paying Off for Menino," *Boston Globe*, October 28, 1993, 21.

45. Ibid.

46. Ed Cafasso, "Key Aides Unaware of Menino Cabinet Pick," *Boston Herald*, February 19, 1994, 6.

47. Don Aucoin, "Menino Has a Lesson for Flynn on School Politics," *Boston Globe*, February 19, 1995, 41.

48. Editorial Board, "The Superintendent's Report Card," *Boston Globe*, March 19, 1994, 12.

49. See Jeannette S. Hargroves, "The Boston Compact: A Community Response to School Dropouts," *Urban Review* 18, no. 3 (1986): 207–17.

50. "External Actors and the Boston Public Schools: The Courts, the Business Community, and the Mayor," Wilson Center, 1994, 15, https://www.wilsoncenter.org.

51. Stephan M. Coan, "Uncertain Allies: Public-Private Partnership in the Boston Compact, 1982–1996" (Ph.D. diss., Brandeis University, 1997), 203–4.

52. Ed Hayward, "School's Chief Decries City's Political System," *Boston Herald*, February 18, 1995, 8.

53. David Weber and Andrea Estes, "School Boss Out; Embattled Superintendent to Leave Hub Post in June," *Boston Herald*, February 17, 1995, 1.

54. Thomas M. Menino with Jack Beatty, *A Mayor for a New America* (Boston: Houghton Mifflin Harcourt, 2014), 32, 81

55. William E. Nelson Jr., *Black Atlantic Politics: Dilemmas of Political Empowerment in Boston and Liverpool* (Albany, NY: SUNY Press, 2000), 77.

56. Ann Bradley, "Criticism, Politics Buffet Boston Superintendent," *Education Week* 14, no. 19 (February 1, 1995): 3.

328 NOTES TO PAGES 237–244

57. Ibid.

58. Editorial Board, "A Failing Grade for Harrison-Jones," *Boston Globe*, December 21, 1994, 22.

59. Editorial Board, "The Education Mayor," *Boston Globe*, January 18, 1996, 14.

60. Jordana Hart, "Group Seeks School Reassignment," *Boston Globe*, July 24, 1995, 13.

61. See Rich, *Black Mayors and School Politics*.

62. Alyce Lee, interview, July 5, 2000.

63. This was a joke. Jimmy Durante was a 1950s Italian American comedian with a gravelly voice who mispronounced worlds, created new ones, and mangled the rest. He would tell his staff, "Your job is hanging by a string." Demosthenes was a fourth-century Greek orator and stateman. Locution was not Menino's strongest suit.

64. Aucoin, "Menino Has a Lesson for Flynn on School Politics."

65. Doherty interview.

66. Geeta Anand, "Menino Pledges Better Schools Tells City: 'Judge Me Harshly If I Fail,'" *Boston Globe*, January 18, 1996, 25.

67. Andrea Estes, "Menino Accepts Onus of Schools Improvement," *Boston Herald*, January 18, 1996, 18.

68. Marilyn M. Tallerico, "Gaining Access to the Superintendency: Headhunting, Gender, Color," *Educational Administration Quarterly* 36, no. 1 (February 2000): 38.

69. See Editorial Board "The Education Mayor."

70. Jim Vrabel, interview, May 26, 2020.

71. Wayne Woodlief, "Politics Inside Out: Mayor's Future Rests with Payzant," *Boston Herald*, August 6, 1995, 25.

72. Doherty interview.

73. *Keller at Large*, WHDH, August 5,1995, https:/whdh/.com.

74. Lee interview.

75. John Portz, "Supporting Education Reform: Mayoral and Corporate Paths," *Urban Education* 35, no. 4 (2000): 403.

76. Karen Avenoso, "A Tough Assignment: Can Superintendent Thomas W. Payzant Fix Schools without Alienating the Community," *Boston Globe*, June 9, 1996, 17.

77. David Brudnoy, "Editorial: As You Were Saying: Tom Payzant Is One Tough Cookie," *Boston Herald*, August 26, 1995, 11.

78. Doherty interview.

79. Portz, "Supporting Education Reform," 405.

80. Karen Avenoso, "Payzant: Admit 300 More to Top Schools Say in Wake of Lawsuit, Other Shouldn't Be Denied," *Boston Globe*, December 19, 1996, 1A.

81. Richard Chacon and Walter Robinson, "Menino Backs End to Quotas at Exams Schools," *Boston Globe*, August 25, 1996, 1B.

82. Ibid.

83. Avenoso, "Payzant: Admit 300 More to Top Schools."

84. Drake, "Promises Unmet."

85. "Q and A: Boston Public Schools, 2015–2016: Student Dropout Rate," Boston Public Schools, 1, https://www.bostonpublicschools.org.

86. "Suffolk University Poll Shows Mayor Menino Set for a Landslide Win," *US Fed News Service* (Washington, DC), November 4, 2005.

87. Jeff Archer, "Plenty of Advice Awaits Boston Schools' Next Leader," *Education Week* 25, no. 42 (July 12, 2006): 10.
88. Tracy Jan, "Boston Schools Tap Memphis Official," *Boston Globe*, June 17, 2007, 1.
89. Menino, *Mayor for a New America*, 103, 104, 33.
90. Paul E. Peterson, "Powerful Professors," *Education Next* 9, no. 4 (Fall 2009): 1.
91. Matthew Knoester, "Is the Outcry for More Pilot Schools Warranted? Democracy, Collective Bargaining, Deregulation, and the Politics of School Reform in Boston," *Educational Policy* 23, no. 3 (2011): 389.
92. See R. Stutman, "Charting New Paths in Our Schools," *Boston Globe*, December 23, 2007, 9E.
93. Peterson, "Powerful Professors," 2, 1.
94. Michael Levenson, "Menino Boost Charter Schools," *Boston Globe*, June 10, 2009, 9.
95. Menino, *Mayor for a New America*, 34.
96. Jeremy R. Levine and William Julius Wilson, "Poverty, Politics, and a 'Circle of Promise': Holistic Education Policy in Boston and the Challenge of Institutional Entrenchment," *Journal of Urban Affairs* 35, no. 1 (February 2013): 20.
97. "Mayor Menino Launches BostONEcard Pilot Program," *US Fed News Service*, October 30, 2010.
98. Andrea Estersand and James Vaznis, "Johnson Failed to Act after Headmaster's Arrest: Boston Schools Leader Facing Fire for Backing, Not Suspending, Educator Charged with Assault," *Boston Globe*, July 8, 2012, 1A.
99. Andrew Ryan, Andrea Estersand, and Adam Sege, "Menino Steadfast in His Support," *Boston Globe*, July 1, 2012, 1A.
100. Yvonne Abraham, "Making Most of Missteps," *Boston Globe*, November 3, 2013, 1B.
101. "United Way Announce $1.5 Million School Readiness Grant from W. K. Kellogg Foundation," *US Fed News Service*, August 3, 2009.
102. See Kathryn A. McDermott and Anna Fung-Morley, "'Quality, Close to Home' and Invisible Zero-Sum Politics: Boston's Home-Based Student Assignment Policy," *Peabody Journal of Education* 93, no. 4 (October 16, 2018), 395–410.
103. Kathryn A. McDermott, Erica Frankenberg, and Sarah Diem, "Post-Racial Politics of Race: Changing Student Assignment Policy in Three School Districts," *Educational Policy* 29, no. 3 (2015): 542.
104. Shirley Leung, "Superintendent Is Serious about the Business of Education," *Boston Globe*, September 11, 2015, 1A.
105. James Vaznis, "Johnson to Name Nonprofit as a Partner: Charter Group Will Run One of Boston's Struggling Schools," *Boston Globe*, June 30, 2010, 1B.
106. See Clarence Stone, "Civic Capacity and Urban Education," *Urban Affairs Review* 36, no. 5 (May 2001): 595–616.
107. Menino, *Mayor for a New America*, 34.
108. Vrabel interview.
109. See Stone, "Civic Capacity and Urban Education."
110. Robin Jones, John Portz, and Lana Stein, "The Nature of Civic Involvement and Educational Change in Pittsburgh, Boston and St. Louis," *Urban Affairs Review* 32, no. 6 (July 1997): 874, 889.
111. Clarence N. Stone et al., *Building Civic Capacity* (Lawrence: University Press of Kansas, 2001), 164.

112. Drake, "Promises Unmet."
113. See McDermott and Fung-Morley, "'Quality, Close to Home.'"
114. Portz, "Supporting Education Reform," 405.
115. Yvonne Abraham, "The Price of Public Service," *Boston Globe*, April 28, 2013, 1B.
116. Derrick Jackson, "Charter Schools' Troubled Waters," *Boston Globe*, March 30, 2005, 1A.
117. Richelle L. Stanfield, "Bossing City Schools," *National Journal* 29, no. 6 (February 1997): 272–74.
118. Cronin, *Reforming Boston Schools*, 213.

Chapter 9: Moguls and Students in Higher Education

1. For student enrollment figures, see University of Illinois Chicago, www.uic.edu.
2. "College and University Endowment Funds 2015 Edition," Hugh's Mortgage and Financial Calculators, www.hughcalc.org.
3. See Richard Florida, *The Rise of the Creative Class* (New York: Basic Books, 2012).
4. See Daniel Bell, *The Coming of Post Industrial Society: A Venture in Social Forecasting* (New York: Basic Books, 1993).
5. See James Cortada, *Rise of the Knowledge Worker* (Boston: Butterworth-Heinemann, 1998).
6. Dale H. Allen, "The Economic Relationships between Institutions of Higher Education and Municipalities" (Ph.D. diss., University of Massachusetts, Boston, 2012), 5.
7. Carolyn Adams, "The Meds and Eds in Urban Economic Development," *Journal of Urban Affairs* 25, no. 5 (2003): 578.
8. Linda Kowalcky, interview, May 29, 2020.
9. Thomas Rabovsky and Amanda Rutherford, "The Politics of Higher Education: University President Ideology and External Networking," *Public Administration Review* 76, no. 5 (February 2016): 773.
10. Stephen M. Gavazzi, "Engaged Institutions, Responsiveness and Town-Gown Relationship," *Planning for Higher Education* 43, no. 2 (September 2015): 3.
11. Yesim Sungu-Eryilmaz, *Town-Gown Collaboration in Land Use and Development* (Cambridge, MA: Lincoln Institute of Land Policy, 2009), 6. See also Gavazzi, "Engaged Institutions."
12. See Darren P. Smith, "The Politics of Studentification and '(Un) Balanced' Urban Populations: Lessons for Gentrification and Sustainable Communities," *Urban Studies* 45, no. 12 (November 2008): 2542–64.
13. Joanna Sage, Darren Smith, and Phil Hubbard, "The Rapidity of Studentification and Population Change: There Goes the (Student)hood," *Population, Place and Space* 18 (October 6, 2011): 597.
14. Boston Redevelopment Authority Research Department, "Mayor Menino's Report on Boston—America's College Town," *Insight* 6, no. 2 (2006): 6, http://www.bostonplans.org.
15. Kermit Parson, "University and Cities: The Terms of the Truce between Them," *Journal of Higher Education* 34, no. 4 (April 1963): 205.
16. Eugenie Birch, "Anchor Institutions in the Northeast Megaregion: An Important

NOTES TO PAGES 267–275   *331*

but Fully Realized Resource," in *Revitalizing American Cities*, ed. Susan M. Wachter and Kimberly A. Zeuli (Philadelphia: University of Pennsylvania Press, 2014), 223.

17. Jeffrey Selingo, "Boston Officials Criticize Harvard for Secret Purchases of Land," *Chronicle of Higher Education*, June 20, 1979, 36A.

18. Sara Rimer, "Some Seeing Crimson at Harvard 'Land Grab,'" *New York Times*, June 17, 1997, 16A.

19. Jack Meyers, "Seeing Crimson—Mayor Rips 'Arrogant' Harvard for Shortchanging Hub Kids," *Boston Herald*, June 11, 1997, 1.

20. Rimer, "Some Seeing Crimson at Harvard 'Land Grab.'"

21. Editorial Board, "Harvard's Stealthy Land Grab," *Boston Globe*, June 11, 1997, 1A.

22. See Harvard University, *Institutional Master Plan Notification Form: Harvard University's Campus in Allston* (Cambridge, MA, October 2012), 1–67.

23. City of Boston, Payments in Lieu of Taxes (PILOT) Program, FY 2013, Pilot Recap, 5. See also Editorial Board, "Mayor's Money Grab," *McClatchy-Tribune Business News* (Washington, DC), January 9, 2013.

24. Carey Goldberg, "Harvard Deal with Boston Hints at Era of Harmony," *New York Times*, August 26, 1999, 11A.

25. Jay Fitzgerald, "Faust Must Bargain: Thomas Menino Won't Let Harvard Halt Science Center on Own," *McClatchy-Tribune Business News*, February 28, 2009.

26. See Jane Holtz Kay, "Allston v. Harvard" *Planning* 75, no. 3 (2009): 40.

27. Fitzgerald, "Faust Must Bargain."

28. Abby Goodnough, "Slump Revives Town-Gown Divide across U.S.," *New York Times*, May 9, 2009, 1A.

29. Harry E. Mattison and Christina Marin, "Harvard's Opportunity in Allston," *Harvard Crimson*, November 13, 2013, https://www.thecrimson.com.

30. See Elijah Anderson, *Streetwise: Race, Class, Race, and Change in an Urban Community* (Chicago: University of Chicago Press, 1990).

31. See Elijah Anderson, "The Cosmopolitan Canopy," *Annals of the American Academy of Political and Social Science* 595 (September 2004): 14–31.

32. Henry Etzkowitz, "Innovation in Innovation: Triple Helix of University-Industry-Government Relations," *Social Science Information* 42, no. 3 (September 2003): 295.

33. Joan Vennochi, "Now Who Holds the Clout in Boston?" *Boston Globe*, January 18, 1999, 11A.

34. Annette Steinacker, "The Effect of Urban Colleges on Their Surrounding Communities," *Urban Studies* 42, no. 7 (2005): 1161.

35. Meagan M. Ehlenz and Sarah Mawhorter, "Higher Education Centers and College Towns: A Typology of the US Metropolitan Geography of Higher Education," *Urban Affairs Review* 58, no. 2 (November 2022): 419.

36. See *Emerson College v. City of Boston & Others* 391 (Mass. 1984), 415.

37. Peter S. Canellos, "Bill Seeks a Property Tax on Exempt Institutions," *Boston Globe*, January 23, 1993, 1.

38. See Susannah Patton, "More Dorms Are the Norm," *Boston Herald*, February 23, 2000, 37.

39. Jonathan G. Cooper et al., "University Community Partnerships," *Humanities Magazine*, March 2014, 90.

40. Ibid., 91–92.

NOTES TO PAGES 275–283

41. "Blacks Don't Count," *Bay State Banner* (Boston), February 12, 1998, 4.

42. Yawu Miller, "Menino Meets with Activists," *Bay State Banner*, February 19, 1998, 1.

43. See Eric Convey, "BRA Backs Northeastern Project," *Boston Herald*, June 7, 2000, 35.

44. Yawu Miller, "Northeastern Plans Roxbury Dormitory," *Bay State Banner*, August 12, 2004, 1.

45. See Thomas C. Palmer Jr., "Boston Redevelopment Authority Approves University Master Plan," *Knight Ridder Tribune Business News*, March 2003, 1. Also see Chris Reidy, "Housing Shortage Threatens to Cap Enrollments at Boston Colleges, Universities," *Knight Ridder Tribune Business News*, August 2004, 1.

46. Bill Archambeault, "NU Looks to Add Dorms," *Boston Business Journal* 24, no. 2 (July 16, 2004): 1.

47. Margaret P. O'Mara, "Beyond Town and Gown: University Economic Engagement and the Legacy of the Urban Crisis," *Journal of Technology Transfer* 37, no. 2 (2012): 240.

48. Leonard E. Goodall, "The Urban University: Is There Such a Thing," *Journal of Higher Education* 41, no. 1 (January 1970): 53.

49. John Siegfried, Allen R. Sanderson, and Peter McHenry, "The Impact of Colleges and Universities," *Economics of Education Review* 26, no. 5 (October 2007): 546.

50. O'Mara, "Beyond Town and Gown," 248.

51. John E. Bebout, "Urban Extension," *American Behavioral Scientist* 6, no. 6 (February 1963): 21, 39.

52. John Cronin, "Urban Interventions: When a University Tries to Help a City School," *New England Journal of Higher Education* 35, no. 5 (Spring 2009): 21.

53. Alice Dembner, "New Northeastern President Stress Local School Ties," *Boston Globe*, September 19, 1996, 2B.

54. Richard M. Freeland, "Universities and Cities Needs to Rethink Their Relationships," *Chronicle of Higher Education*, May 13, 2005, 20B.

55. Lee Benson and Ira Harkavy, "Higher Education's Third Revolution: The Emergence of the Democratic Cosmopolitan Civic University," *Cityscape* 5, no. 1 (2000): 49.

56. Edward Liu and Susan Moore Johnson, "New Teachers' Experiences of Hiring: Late, Rushed, and Information-Poor," *Educational Administration Quarterly* 42, no. 3 (August 2006): 324–60. Also see Dale Ballou and Michael Podgursky, "Reforming Teacher Preparation and Licensing: What Is the Evidence?" *Teachers College Record* 102, no. 1 (February 2000): 5–27.

57. Herman Turk, "Comparative Urban Structure from an Interorganizational Perspective," *Administrative Science Quarterly* 18, no. 1 (March 1973): 38.

58. Jack Meyers, "Mayor Spouts New Party Line—City Aims to Crack Down on Off-Campus Bashes," *Boston Herald*, October 10, 1997, 7.

59. Sol Levine and Paul E. White, "Exchange as Conceptual Framework for the Study of Interorganizational Relationships," *Administrative Science Quarterly* 5, no. 4 (March 1961): 588.

60. See Anthony Flint, "BU Making Its Mark on the Skyline," *Boston Globe*, June 11, 1995, 51.

61. "Suffolk University to Open Third Resident Hall," *US Fed News Service* (Washington, DC), January 8, 2008, 1.

NOTES TO PAGES 283–292   333

62. Peter Eisinger, "The Politics of Bread and Circuses: Building the City for the Visitor Class," *Urban Affairs Review* 35, no. 3 (January 2000): 316–33.

63. Eliot Marshall, "Harvard's Expanding Universe," *Science* 302, no. 5646 (October 31, 2003): 761. See also Ted Smalley Bowen, "Harvard's Expansion Will Be a Careful Balancing Act," *Architectural Record* 193, no. 2 (February 2005): 3, and Kay, "Allston v. Harvard," 40.

64. See James Q. Wilson and Edward C. Banfield, "Public-Regardingness as a Value Premise in Voting Behavior," *American Political Science Review* 58, no.4 (December 1964): 876–87.

65. Jenna Russell, "Campuses with a Cause," *Boston Globe*, April 18, 2005, 1B.

66. Eric J. Oliver, "City Size and Civic Involvement in Metropolitan America," *American Political Science Review* 94, no. 2 (June 2000): 361–73.

67. See William A. Galston, "Political Knowledge, Political Engagement, and Civil Education," *Annual Review of Political Science* 4, no. 1 (June 2001): 217–34.

68. For a book published during the final months of the Menino mayoralty, see Shakuntala Banaji and David Buckingham, *The Civic Web: Young People, the Internet and Civic Participation* (Cambridge, MA: MIT Press, 2013).

69. Victor Asal, Alexander Testa, and Joseph Young, "Occupy This: Why Some Colleges Had Occupy Wall Street Protests," *Dynamics of Asymmetric Conflict* 10, nos. 2–3 (September 2017): 95.

70. Schuyler Velasco, "Occupy Movement's Last Big Stand: Boston," *Christian Science Monitor*, December 2, 2011, 18.

71. Peter Schworm, "Protester Arrests Decried, Defended: Demonstrators Resolute after City Detains 141," *Boston Globe*, October 12, 2011, 1A.

72. "Police Evict Occupy Boston Protester, 46 Arrested," *McClatchy-Tribune Business News*, December 10, 2011.

73. See Adrian Walker, "Menino Calls Race Relations the Overriding Issue for City," *Boston Globe*, September 19, 1994, 1.

74. Susan P. Crawford and Dana Walters, "Citizen-Centered Governance: The Mayor's Office of New Urban Mechanics and the Evolution of CRM in Boston," Social Science Research Network, Berkman Center Research Publication No. 17, August 7, 2013, 2, https://ssrn.com.

75. See Stacy Teicher Khadaroo, "Does Facebook Boost Civic Engagement among American Youths, Too?" *Christian Science Monitor*, February 24, 2011, 13.

76. Freeland, "Universities and Cities Needs to Rethink Their Relationships."

77. Birch, "Anchor Institutions in the Northeast Megaregion."

78. Karen Baker-Minkel, Jason Kieser, and Walter Kieser, "Town and Gown," *Economic Development Journal* 3, no. 4 (Fall 2004): 13.

Conclusion: Drawing Lessons from the Menino Tenure

1. Dave Wedge et al., "Mayor Menino: 'I Will Leave the Job That I Love,'" *Knight-Ridder/Tribune Business News*, March 28, 2013, 1.

2. Quoted by Graham K. Wilson, interview, October 3, 2019.

3. See Herman L. Boschken, "Global Cities, Systemic Power, and Upper-Middle-Class Influence," *Urban Affairs Review* 38, no. 6 (July 2003): 808–30.

4. See Thomas Sigler, *Triumph of the City: How Our Greatest Invention Makes Us Richer, Smarter, Healthier, and Happier* (New York: Penguin Press, 2011).

5. See Thomas M. Menino Files at the Howard Gotlieb Archival Research Center at Boston University.

6. Matthew Weinstein, "Tom Menino's Legacy and Boston's Future," *Harvard Political Review* 40, no. 4 (Winter 2013): 2.

7. Adrian Walker, "Menino's Basic Vision Is of a City That Works," *Boston Globe*, July 2, 1995, 1.

8. "Boston Mayor Menino Is New President of U.S. Conference of Mayors; Promotes Agenda for Working Families, Will Lead Nat'l Housing Forum," *US Newswire*, May 8, 2002.

9. Alexander J. Kasner, "Local Government Design, Mayoral Leadership, and Law Enforcement Reform," *Stanford Law Review* 69, no. 2 (February 2017): 553.

10. For example, see Paul Lawless, "Power and Conflict in Pro-Growth Regimes: Tensions in Jersey City and Detroit," *Urban Studies* 39, no. 8 (July 2002): 1329–46.

11. See Mark Trumbull, "Entering the Job Market? Your Education Matters More Than Ever," *Christian Science Monitor*, April 12, 2012, 20. Also see Areil J. Binder and John Bound, "The Declining Labor Marker Prospects of Less Educated Men," *Journal of Economic Perspectives* 33, no. 2 (Spring 2019): 163–90, and Kathryn Edin et al., "The Tenuous Attachment of Working-Class Men," *Journal of Economic Perspectives* 33, no. 3 (Spring 2019): 211–28.

12. Richard Florida, *The New Urban Crisis* (New York: Basic Books, 2017), 215.

13. Brian C. Mooney and Muriel Cohen, "A Groaning, Mazelike Bureaucracy Clings to Power," *Boston Globe*, May 22, 1991, 27.

14. Karla Scoon Reid, "Mayors Stepping Up to Improve Quality of City School," *Education Week* 22, no. 30 (April 9, 2003): 8.

15. "Boston Public Schools Wins Broad Prize for Urban Education," *US Fed News Service* (Washington, DC), September 19, 2006.

16. Donald A. Gillis, "The Sociology of a City in Transition, 1960–2000" (Ph.D. diss., Boston University, 2015), 218–19.

17. David Passafaro, interview, June 2, 2020.

Index

Abraham, Yvonne, 226, 252
Abrahamson, Mark, 141
Adams, Carolyn, 259
Alinsky, Saul, 21
Allen, Dale H., 258
Ambrizeth, Helena Lima, 212
American Recovery and Reinvestment Act (ARRA), 181
Amos 'n' Andy, 25
Anderson, Elijah, 270
Arroyo, Felix, 207, 209, 231, 239
article 37, 97
Asal, Victor, 287
Athens of America, 256
Aucoin, Don, 235, 236, 238
Austin, Sharon W., 210, 213
Avenoso, Karen, 112, 225, 241

Babson College, 95
Bachelor, Lynn W., 86
Bailey, Chadwick Martin, 21
Baker-Minkel, Karen, 291
Banfield, Edward C., 284
Barmak, Sarah, 132
Barnicle, Mike, 69, 80
Basco, Liugi, 25
Bauer, Catherine, 127

Bay State Banner, 66, 80, 109, 202, 275
Beame, Abraham, 69, 70
Beauregard, Sandy, 97
Bebout, John E., 278
Bell, Clark W., 107
Bell, Daniel, 256
Bellotti, Francis, 29
Benson, Lee, 279
Berrien, Jenny, 173
Bicycling Magazine, 81
Birch, Eugenie, 266, 290
Block, Richard L., 161
Bolling, Bruce, 56–59, 170, 196–97, 204, 207, 214
Boschken, Herman L., 293
Boston City Council, 32, 42, 51, 76–78, 97, 116, 143, 169, 197, 205, 209, 214, 251
Boston City Hospital (BCH), 106
Boston Compact III, 235–36
Boston Convention Center, 6, 41, 86, 93–94, 113–14
Boston exam schools, 205, 242–44
Boston Foundation, 109, 131, 246–47, 279
Boston 400 Plan, 74
Boston Globe, 17, 29, 36, 40, 52, 57, 61, 64, 65, 69, 74, 79, 80, 109, 111, 133, 159, 184, 208, 209, 228, 236

336 INDEX

Boston Herald, 30, 40, 53, 64, 79, 80, 81, 109, 111, 163, 168, 228, 229, 248, 234, 235, 236, 240, 281

Boston Housing Authority (BHA), 58, 134, 135, 163

Boston Magazine, 10, 22, 109

Boston Marathon Bombing, 11, 182, 185, 301

Boston megaplex, 69, 113–16

Boston Miracle, 23, 30, 63, 165, 172–74, 301

Boston Municipal Research Bureau, 74, 226

Boston Phoenix, 226

Boston Police Department (BPD), 40, 55, 58, 156, 163, 165, 167, 171–72, 174, 180, 181–84, 281–82, 287

Boston Public Schools (BPS), 239, 244, 246, 253, 259, 279, 290, 295, 302–3

Boston Redevelopment Authority (BRA), 27, 37, 45, 68, 74, 82, 84, 85, 92–95, 97, 115, 145, 119–20, 145, 217, 260, 264–66, 275, 279

Boston Red Sox, 27, 66, 60, 79, 113, 114, 116, 178, 182

Boston School Committee, 38, 62, 64, 74, 193, 204, 209, 219–20, 244, 280, 302

Boston Teachers Union (BTU), 86, 193, 221, 223–24, 232, 233–35, 237–38, 245–47, 250, 253

Bowers, Katherine, 17

Braga, Anthony, 174, 212

Bratt, Rachel G., 139–40

Bratton, William, 160, 162, 163–64

Brelis, Matthew, 36

Brett, James, 56–58, 59, 63, 163, 202, 206

Brooke, Edward, 128, 193, 205

Brown, Jeffrey, 165

Brown, Kathy, 144

Brudnoy, David, 80–81, 241

Buchanan, Barbara, 32

Bulger, William (Bill), 41, 56, 57, 115, 119, 156

Burns, Adam, 10

Burt, Martha R., 174

Bush, George W., 64

Cafasso, Ed, 80

Cahill, Ryan, 287

Campbell, Angus, 50

Candeloro. Dominic L., 26

Canello, Peter, 61, 234, 273

Capetillo-Ponce, Jorge, 201, 208

Cape Verdean, 172–73, 213

Carr, Howie, 80

Carter, Jimmy, 38, 71

Cellucci, Paul, 116, 143

Chacon, Richard, 208

Chicago Tribune, 153

Chick-Fil-A, 71

Christian Science Monitor, 176

Chronicle of Higher Education, 279

Clay, Philip, 93, 95, 207

Clinton, Bill, 43, 44, 66, 111, 118, 153, 294

CNN, 67

Coakley, Martha, 68

Coan, Stephan M., 236

cognitive/compassionate mayor, 22

Cohen, Muriel, 302

Collins, Monica, 53

Conley, Daniel F., 178

Consalvo, Robert, 232

Contompasis, Michael G., 244

Cooper, Jonathan G., 274

Cox, Michael, 171

Crawford, Susan P., 288

creative class, 10, 13, 99

Cronin, John M., 278

Cullen, Kevin, 174

Curley, James Michael, 27, 101–2

Cutrufo, Joseph D., 12, 95, 132

Dahl, Robert, 22, 56, 61, 85

Daley, Richard J., 4, 69, 78, 255

Daley, Richard M., 69, 255

Danigelis, Nicholas L., 213

Davis, Edward F., 180–83

Davis-Mullen, Peggy, 63, 65, 231

de-ethnicized, 19

DeMott, Benjamin, 199–200

Dennis, Jack, 161

deterring mayor, 190

Diem, Sarah, 250

DiGaetano, Alan, 115

Dinkins, David, xxi, 3, 56

District-Charter Compact, 248

INDEX 337

Doherty, Ed, 232–34, 238, 240, 241
Doherty, Gerard, 32, 37, 39
Donnison, David, 129
Doran, Meghan V., 231
Doty, Conny, xiii, 83, 92
Downie, Lynda, 148
Drake, John C., 74, 75, 251–52
Dreier, Peter, 42, 80, 189
Duffy, Thomas, 320n21
Dukakis, Michael, 40, 89, 119, 209
Dupree, Cydney, 217

Easton, David, 161
Ebbert, Stephanie, 310n31
Economist, 164
Education Week, 237, 302
Ehlenz, Meagan M., 271
Einstein, Katherine Levine, 150
Eisinger, Peter, 283
Emerson College, 66, 178, 270, 273
Empowerment Zones (EZ), 88, 99
Erie, Steve, 102
Etzkowitz, Henry, 13, 270
Evans, Paul, 163–65, 167, 169, 170–74, 179, 184, 203, 300–301

Feaster, Joseph D., Jr., 89
Federal Housing Administration (FHA), 127, 128, 138
Feeney, Maureen, 107
Feins, Judith D., 139–40
Ferman, Barbara, 74
Ferriabough-Bolling, Joyce, 197, 233–34
Finfer, Lewis, xiii, 110
Finn, Joe, 148
Finneran, Thomas, 64, 82
Fiske, Susan, 217
Flaherty, Michael, 67–68, 120, 247
Fleischmann, Arnold, 56
Florida, Richard, 9, 10, 13, 14, 20, 40–42, 43, 142, 149, 300
Flynn, Raymond (Ray), 17, 18, 40, 41, 42, 43, 44, 45, 47, 55, 63, 70, 71, 72, 83, 87, 90, 92, 102, 103, 106, 117, 118, 131, 134, 151, 160, 162, 193, 169, 170, 180, 188, 189, 195, 196, 200, 204, 205, 207, 209, 215, 216–17, 220, 223, 231–35, 238, 273, 294

Frankenberg, Erica, 250
Freedland, Richard, 261, 279, 290
Fruchter, Norm, 224
Fung-Morley, Anna, 252

Gallup poll, 159
Galston, William A., 286
Gans, Herbert J., 34, 46
García, Ignacio, 208
Garrity, Arthur, 38
Gavazzi, Stephen M., 261–62
Gay, Claudine, 135
Gelzinis, Peter, 295
Gibbs, David, 16
Gibson, Kenneth, 11
Gillis, Donald, xiv, 70, 134, 137, 168, 216, 223–25, 303
Giuliani, Rudy, 64, 159, 166
Glick, David M., 137
Goldberg, Carey, 269
Gonzalez, Tomas, 58, 72, 83, 90–92, 200, 203, 209
Goodall, Leonard E., 276
Goodnough, Abby, 269
Granovetter, Mark S., 34
Great Recession, 112, 149, 182, 269, 289
Greene, Leonard, 171
Guardian, 173
Guida, George, xxi, 48
Gurwitt, Rob, 69, 222

Hajnal, Zoltan L., 72
Hall, Robert, 194
Hamilton, Howard D., 50
Hammond, Ray, 203, 225
Hargroves, Jennette S., 235
Harkavy, Ira, 279
Harnois, E. Jeanne, 324n48
Harris, Donna M., 208
Harrison-Jones, Lois, 211–12, 226, 231–34, 235–38, 239
Harvard Allston Task Force, 267
Harvard Crimson, 270, 285
Harvard University, 11, 19, 133, 269, 271, 274, 277, 292, 299
Hayes, Michael, 193
Heitner, Devorah, 192

INDEX

Hemmerle, Lisa M., 94
Hennigan, Maura A., 43, 65–67
Hicks, Louise Day, 47, 56, 220
hidden-hand mayor, 255
Higginbotham, Stacey, 116
Hogan, Cynthia, 15
Home-Based Student Assignment Policy, 249
HOPE VI, 131
Hopkins, Daniel J., 73
Hopkins, Merita, 176
Housing and Urban Development (HUD), 9, 36, 43–44, 128, 131, 135, 151
Housing Week, 132
Howard, Marjorie, 52–53
Hubbard, Phil, 264
Hureau, David, 174
Hutson, Malo Andre, 84–85
Hynes, John B., 27
Hype Park's Readville, 25, 26, 27, 35, 39, 41, 57, 304

Iglesias, Carmelo, 209
Ihlanfeldt, Kieth R., 19
impeding mayor, 190
inevitable urban dissatisfaction syndrome, 296
Innovation District, 6, 94–95
Institutional Master Plan Notification Form (IMPNF), 267

Jackson, Derrick Z., 143, 171
Jackson, Emory, 204–5
Jackson, Kenneth T., 128
Jain, Pushpam, 229
Jamaica Plain Neighborhood Development Corporation (JPNDC), 85
Jennings, James, 89, 188–89
Jeremiah Burke High School, 238–39
Johnson, Carolyn R., 245–50, 253
Johnson, Lawrence, 206
Johnson, Lyndon B., 30, 35, 151
Johnson, Marilyn, 21
Johnson, O'Ryan, 182
Jones, Bryan D., 86
Jones, Hubie, 245
Jones, Robin, 251

Jordan, Robert, 204
Joyce, Dot, xii, 47

Kambon, Sadiki, 275
Kasner, Alexander, 296
Katznelson, Ira, 128
Kaufman, Herbert, 86
Keller, Jon, 64, 81–82, 169, 227
Keller at Large, 118
Kelly, John, 80
Kennedy, Edward (Ted), 38, 111
Kennedy, Joe, 119
Kennedy, John F., 28, 119
Kennedy Park Homes v. City of Lackawanna, 136
Kerry, John, 89, 112, 119, 209
Khadaroo, Stacy Teicher, 289
Kieser, Jason, 291
Kieser, Walter, 291
Kineavy, Michael, 68
King, Martin Luther, 35–36, 37, 193–94, 236
King, Mel, 56, 102, 193, 195–97, 214, 220, 236
Kinnaly, John, 30
Kirkland, Patricia A., 101
Kiyama, Judy Marquez, 208
Knoester, Matthew, 246
Kotter, John P., 2
Kowalcky, Linda, 259
Kozol, Jonathan, 221
Kraft, Robert, 113, 115–16, 121
Krueger, Rob, 16

Lago, Marisa, 82–83, 84
Landsmark, Ted, 214
Lawrence, Paul, 2
Lee, Alyce, 82, 238
Lefebvre, Henri, 145
Leibowitz, Howard, 82–83, 105
Levin, Murray B., 27
Levine, Jeremy R., 147
Levine, Sol, 282
Lewis, Paul G., 72
Lincoln, Abraham, 48
Lindblom, Charles E., 3
Long, Norton E., 154, 160, 223

INDEX 339

Longwood Medical and Academic Area
(LMA), 84
Lupo, Alan, 42, 72, 80, 220, 223
Luppi, Lawrence J., 34
Lusk, Elizabeth, xiii

Maier, Henry W., 293
Mandela Separatist Movement, 106
Martin, Andrew, 153–54
Massachusetts Housing and Shelter
Alliance (MHSA), 148
Massachusetts Institution of Technology
(MIT), 10, 11, 19, 20, 32, 33, 135, 183, 256,
261, 271, 273, 274, 276–77, 280–81, 284,
298
Massachusetts Miracle, 15
Mawhorter, Sarah, 271
Mayes, J. Larry, 174–75
Mayors Against Illegal Guns Coalition, 67
mayors as the negotiator, 255
McDermott, Kathryn, 250, 252
McGovern, Patricia, 107
McGrory, Brian, xiv, 36, 52, 80, 171, 202
McGuire, Jean, 224
McHenry, Peter, 277
McKinnis, Hattie, 241
McLaughlin, Julia, 242–43
McLaughlin, Loretta, 106
McLaughlin, Paul, 171–72, 174, 202
McNickle, Chris, 3
Menino, Angela, 31–32
Menino, Carl, 26, 32
Menino, Susan, 26
Merton, Robert K., 196
Metro-Future Project, 16
Metroplex, 113–16
Metzer, J. T., 98–99
Meyers, Jack, 281
Milesfshy, Zebulon, 90, 203
Miller, Melvin, 217
Miller, Yawu, 80
Modern Health Care, 107
Mohammed, Don, 169, 204
Mollenkopf, John, 189
Mooney, Brian C., 392
mumbonics, 47
Murphy, Patrick, 163

Nanos, Jannelle, 119–20
Nee, Thomas, 181
Nelson, William E., 216, 217
New England Patriots, 18, 113–16, 182
New York Times, 58, 79, 166, 233, 269
Nixon, Richard, 37, 128, 285
Nolan, Joan, 267
Nolan, Martin, 17
Northeastern University, 173, 261, 263, 272,
274, 275–77, 279, 281–82, 285, 290
Nyhan, David, 29, 41, 45, 80

O'Bryant, John D., 193, 195, 204, 207
Occupy Wall Street, 287, 294
O'Connor, Brian Wright, 188
O'Connor, Edwin, 102
O'Connor, Thomas, 151
Office of Jobs and Community Service
(JCS), 92
O'Flaherty, Brendan, 146
Ogorzalek, Thomas K., 101, 111
O'Leary, Gerald, 220
Oliver, Eric J., 286
O'Mara, Margaret P., 276, 277
O'Neill, Thomas (Tip), 49
Operation Ceasefire, 172–73
Orr, Marion, xiv
Osgood, Chris, 288
O'Toole, Kathleen, 176–78
Owen, Henry, 210

Paine, Robert Treat, 126
Paleologos, David, 244
Palmer, Maxwell, 150
Pantridge, Margaret, 89, 96
Parks, Paul, 233
Parson, Kermit, 265–66
Passafaro, David, xiii, 114, 104, 107, 112, 121,
303–4
Patrick, Deval, 113, 205–6, 247, 294
Patrone, Charles, 29–30
Paul, Noel C., 321n58
Payment in lieu of Taxes (PILOT), 12,
257, 267
Payson, Julia A., 89
Payzant, Thomas, 239–45, 251, 253, 279,
302–3

Perlmutter, Richard M., 116
Peter, Jennifer, 72
Peterson, Paul, 246
Pettingill, Lindsay M., 73
Pierce, Martha, 230–31
pilot schools, 235, 237, 246
Popular Science, 97
Portz, John, 240, 241, 251
Powers, John E., 27, 70
promoting mayor, 255
Proposition 2½, 130
Providence Journal-Bulletin, 143
Public Interest, 108
public school cartel (PSC), 212, 222–23, 241, 302–3

Rabovsky, Thomas, 260
Race to the Top, 256
Raffel, Jeffrey A., 123
Reagan, Ronald, 38–39
Rendell, Ed, 112
Rimer, Sara, 257
ripresa, xii, 48
Rivas, Maggie, 324
Rivera, Jorge, 207
Rivers, Eugene, 52, 172, 202–13
Roache, Francis M., 55, 57, 63, 160, 163–64
Robinson, William I., 91
Roby, Peter C., 188
Rodgers, Harrell R., 161
Romney, Mitt, 112, 113, 119, 208
Roth, Steven, 94
Rudenstine, Neil, 267, 269
Rufo, Robert, 35, 55
Rushing, Byron, 169–70
Russell, Jenna, 238
Rutherford, Amanda, 260

Sage, Joanna, 254
Salerno, Rosaria, 56–59
Sanderson, Allen R., 277
Sassen, Saskia, 19, 216
Saunders, Ralph H., 174
Say Brother, 192
Sayre, Wallace S., 86
Schabert, Tilo, 123, 129
Schaefer, Donald, 61
Schafer, Robert, 139

Schnare, Ann, 139
Schragger, Richard, 11, 87
Schwart, Alex, 122
Schwartz, Jason, 119
Sciacca, Joe, 79, 80, 81
Scondras, David, 42, 52
Sharp, Elaine B., 184
Shelly v. Kramer, 136
Siegfried, John, 277
Silber, John, 278–79
Skerry, Peter, 298
Smith, Darren P., 264, 275
Smith, Patricia, 61, 80
Snelgrove, Victoria, 66, 177–78
solicitous, compassionate, and empathic mayor, 191
Stein, Lana, 56, 251
Steinacker, Annette, 271
Stith, Charles, 198, 211
Stoesz, David, 315
Stone, Clarence, xiv, 117, 250–51
Stuart, Charles, 40
Stutman, Richard, 250
Suffolk University, 277, 282
Suffolk University Polls, 65
Sungu-Eryilmaz, Yesim, 263
Swanstrom, Todd, 96, 189
Syron, Richard, 9

Tallerico, Marilyn M., 239
Taylor, George, 116
Taylor, Steven, 224–25
TenPoint Coalition, 154, 194, 212
Testa, Alexander, 287
Theoharis, Jeanne F., 37
Timilty, Joseph F., 35–39, 40
Travis, Toni-Michell, 207
Traylor, Tom, 107
Triple Helix, 270
Truman, Harry, 29, 32
Turk, Herman, 280
Turner, Chuck, 207–8
Tyler, Samuel, 226

Ullian, Elaine, 107
University of Massachusetts Boston (UMass Boston), 32, 33, 262–63, 276, 282

urban renewal, 27, 35, 128, 151, 255, 265
U.S. Conference of Mayors, 63, 295
using mayor, 190

Vale, Lawrence J., 135, 150
Varady, David P., 123
Vennochi, Joan, 80, 178, 270
Verba, Sidney, 77
Village of Arlington Heights v. Metropolitan Housing Development Corp, 136
Village of Euclid v. Amber Realty Company, 136
Violent Crime Control and Law Enforcement Act of 1994, 153
Vrabel, Jim, 46, 74, 102

Walker, Adria, 80, 295
Wall, Bruce, 170
Wall Street Journal, 93, 94, 145
Walter, Dana, 288
Warsh, David, 15, 130
WBUR (radio), 54, 65
Weinberg, Martha Wagner, 108
Weinstein, Matthew, 295
Weld, William, 85, 115, 119, 121, 177

Whelton, Daniel A., 44
White, John, 82
White, Kevin, 11, 18, 57, 36, 38, 45, 47, 65, 70, 74, 90, 101, 102, 108, 128, 145, 151, 194
White, Paul, 282
Wilkerson, Dianne, 56, 57, 156, 202, 204, 211, 212
Williams, Accelyne, 167, 169, 174, 301
Wilson, Graham K., 292
Wilson, James Q., 38, 108, 162, 284
Wilson, William Julius, 247
Wiltenburg, Mary, 214
Winship, Christopher, 172, 174, 212
Witten, Jonathan, 137
Wong, Kenneth, 229
Wood, Curtis, 73
Woodlief, Wayne, 80, 240

Yancey, Charles, 169, 210, 214
Yates, Douglas T., Jr., 106
Yinger, John, 139
Young, Joseph, 287

Zaitzevsky, Cynthia, 125–26

WILBUR C. RICH is the William R. Kenan Jr. Professor Emeritus of Political Science at Wellesley College. His primary areas of research are urban politics, public policy, and public school politics. Much of his research efforts have concentrated on the nexus between mayoral politics and the ongoing urban crisis. He has written several books and articles on American mayors, exploring how mayors cope with policy challenges and administrative problems. During his full-time teaching career, he was also very active in the political science profession. He has served as president of the Northeastern Political Science Association and the New England Political Science Association. In 2009, he was awarded the Norton Long Career Achievement Award by the Urban Section of the American Political Science Association.